THE **PAN AM** BUILDING

AND THE
SHATTERING
OF THE
MODERNIST
DREAM

THE MIT PRESS   CAMBRIDGE, MASSACHUSETTS   LONDON, ENGLAND

THE **PAN AM** BUILDING

AND THE
SHATTERING
OF THE
MODERNIST
DREAM

MEREDITH L. CLAUSEN

First MIT Press paperback edition, 2006

This book was set in Univers by Graphic Composition, Inc., and was printed and bound in the United States of America.

MIT Press books may be purchased at special quantity discounts for business or sales promotional use. For information, please e-mail <special_sales@mitpress.mit.edu> or write to Special Sales Department, The MIT Press, 55 Hayward Street, Cambridge, MA 02142.

Library of Congress Cataloging-in-Publication Data

Clausen, Meredith L.
The Pan Am building and the shattering of the modernist dream / Meredith L. Clausen.
      p. cm.
Includes bibliographical references and index.
ISBN 0-262-03324-0 (hc. : alk. paper), 0-262-53283-2 (pb)
    1. MetLife Building (New York, N.Y.) 2. Modern movement (Architecture)—New York (State)—New York. 3. Architecture and society—New York (State)—New York. 4. Gropius, Walter, 1883–1969—Criticism and interpretation. 5. Belluschi, Pietro, 1899—Criticism and interpretation. 6. Roth, Richard, 1904—Criticism and interpretation. 7. MetLife Building (New York, N.Y.)—Public opinion. 8. Skyscrapers—New York (State)—New York. 9. New York (N.Y.)—Buildings, structures, etc. I. Title.

NA6233.N5P363 2005
725'.23'097471—dc22

                                                                        2004045468

10 9 8 7 6 5 4 3 2

Illustration credits are found on page 461.

What sphinx of cement and aluminum bashed open their skulls
and ate up their brains and imagination?
Moloch! Solitude! Filth! Ugliness! Ashcans and unobtainable dollars!
Children screaming under the stairways! Boys sobbing in armies!
Old men weeping in the parks!
Moloch! Moloch! Nightmare of Moloch! Moloch the loveless!
Mental Moloch! Moloch the heavy judger of men! . . .
Moloch whose mind is pure machinery! Moloch whose blood
is running money! . . .
Moloch whose eyes are a thousand blind windows! Moloch whose
skyscrapers stand in the long streets like endless Jehovahs! . . .

Allen Ginsberg, "Howl," 1956

Acknowledgments   xiii

Introduction   xv

1

GRAND CENTRAL CITY   1

Grand Central Redevelopment   2

The Railroad Industry in New York City   4

Grand Central Terminal   10

Robert Young and the New York Central   22

Other Proposals   27

Emery Roth & Sons   35

Erwin S. Wolfson, Builder/Real Estate Developer   42

Zeckendorf In, Wolfson Out   44

The Pei Project   46

"Grand Central City"   49

Gropius and Belluschi   50

Ada Louise Huxtable, the Transformation

of Park Avenue, and "Rothscrapers"   51

Walter Gropius   64

The Architects Collaborative   69

Pietro Belluschi   70

The Gropius/Belluschi/Roth Scheme   77

The Grand Vision   84

2

THE PAN AM BUILDING   85

Wolfson Financing   86

The Challenge   89

James Ruderman, Structural Engineer   90

Steel Framework: The Ruderman Plan   92

Gropius/Belluschi/Roth Collaboration:

    The Design Process   94

Roth Office   112

Construction of the Building   114

Carl A. Morse, Diesel Construction Company,

    and Construction Management   114

Construction Begins   117

Complications   119

Bowling Alleys: Haskell versus the Railroads   120

Pan American Signs On   128

The Art   141

3

THE CLAMOR OF CRITICISM   155

The New School Debate, January 1960   160

Huxtable: "Marvel or Monster?"   163

More Criticism   166

The Defense   188

Heliport Proposal   196

Construction Continued   199

Wolfson Dies   210

Building Nears Completion   210

Pan Am Opens   212

CONTENTS

4

THE BUILDING'S IMPACT   215

Economic Success   216
Continued Criticism   218
Jack Cotton Dies   248
Criticism Elsewhere   248
Haskell and the Demise of *Architectural Forum*   255
Fallout in the National Press   259
Criticism Abroad   263

5

THE ARCHITECTS   273

The Architects' Reputations: Emery Roth & Sons   274
Belluschi   276
Gropius   279

6

AFTERMATH   309

Heliport   310
Historic Preservation   324
The Late 1960s   341
Sale of the Building   346
Lobby Remodeling   351
Demise of Pan American World Airways:
    Flight 103 and Pan Am's Final Descent   357
Pan Am Sign Change   363
Pan Am Building: Landmark Status?   368

7

CONCLUSION   369

Pan Am as Symbol   370
Later Criticism   370
Architectural Criticism, Critics,
    and Popular Perception   384
The Pan Am Building: The Vision of Three Men   385
The Significance of the Building   386

Notes   389
Works Cited   431
Illustration Credits   461
Index   467

ACKNOWLEDGMENTS

A book as long as this in its germination calls upon a great many individuals for help. I am deeply grateful to them all, many of whose assistance dates back years ago. First and foremost, a research grant from the Graham Foundation for Advanced Studies in the Fine Arts provided me with the means to embark upon a project that turned out to be far longer and more complex than I initially envisioned; a second Graham Foundation grant, for which I am especially grateful to Richard Solomon, FAIA, provided help with the images, many of which would have otherwise had to be excised. A quarter at CASVA provided me with generous assistance and access to the wealth of material in the Washington, D.C., area as well as time way from teaching to delve more deeply into the research. A grant from the Center for Western European Studies at the University of Washington enabled me to spend several weeks in New York for interviews, securing photographs, and tracking down resources unavailable elsewhere. A sizable subsidy from Harold Schiff of Diesel Construction Company, project manager for the Pan Am Building, then president of Carl A. Morse, Inc., provided needed assistance in the later stages of the book. A last-minute infusion of funds from Bob Mugerauer, Dean of the College of Architecture and Urban Planning at the University of Washington enabled me to include several critical figures. Archival help from the librarians at Avery Library at Columbia University, the New-York Historical Society, the City Museum of New York, the Landmarks Preservation Commission, and the New York Public Library, all in New York; the Rotch Library and the MIT Museum in Boston; and the Richter Library at the University of Miami, proved invaluable. Finally, leave time granted by Michael Halleran, Divisional Dean of Arts and Sciences and Chris Ozubko, Director of the School of Art, University of Washington, gave me time to write free of normal departmental obligations. Janet Adams Strong of the office of Pei Cobb Freed & Partners was most gracious in providing images of Pei's work. I thank all the institutions and the individuals involved for their support.

I have made every effort to provide proper credits and trace the copyright holders of images and texts I have used; if any were inadvertently overlooked, I would be happy to correct this at the earliest opportunity.

Much of my understanding of the Pan Am Building's construction and operation was based on personal interviews, some quite lengthy. I am grateful to Murray Shapiro and Howard Zweig of the James Ruderman office; Irwin Miller of Carl A. Morse, Inc.; Harold Schiff, formerly of Diesel Construction, then president of Carl A. Morse; Alex

Cvijanovic, Norman Fletcher, and John Harkness of TAC; and Richard Roth, Jr., of Emery Roth & Sons.

Among the many others who helped along the way, a few should be singled out: Anthony Alofsin, who in preliminary reading of the manuscript endorsed the concept and helped clear the mind; Victoria Reed, whose undaunted spirit throughout her difficult time provided a constant source of inner inspiration; John Zukowsky of the Chicago Art Institution, whose endorsement early on and continued interest in the project spurred me on at times when spirits sagged; George Rolf, who helped me untangle the complicated financial issues involved in the conception of the building; Martha Kingsbury, whose thoughtful reading of the manuscript as it neared completion helped tidy things up and sharpen the focus; and Jerome Silbergeld, Patricia Failing, and Susan Henderson for their astute comments at the onset of the project. Jennifer Smith stepped in at a critical time, putting in a good word on my behalf; without her sense of the importance of the project, the text and figures would have had to be severely cut. I would like to thank, too, all those individuals in the libraries, slide rooms, and department offices— especially Mary Ellen Anderson, department secretary at the University of Washington, to whom I owe special thanks—for their patience, assistance, and good will throughout the long process.

My thanks, too, to my research assistants, who I hope learned as much from working with me as I did working for Spiro Kostof in a similar role: Delphine Daniels, Russ Craig, Kathleen Randall, Paul Davis, Tinh Lam, Shuishan Yu, Joy Sage, Laura Sandoval, Anasazi Mendosa, and especially Lenore Hietkamp, for her multiple skills in scanning, Photoshopping, and tapping obscure Internet sources.

My gratitude to friends and family for their forbearance, especially Steve and Teri Swanson, who graciously provided a place to stay during my many sojourns in New York; I'm most appreciative of their warmth and generosity that invariably took the edge off the many obstacles I faced.

For transforming my raw manuscript into a polished book, I want to thank and acknowledge the skills of Lisa Reeve, assistant acquisitions editor; Deborah Cantor-Adams, production editor; Michael Harrup, copy editor; Patrick Ciano, graphic designer; and most especially Roger Conover, of the MIT Press. As acquisitions editor for visual and cultural studies at the MIT Press for the past three decades, Roger has played a major role in shaping the architectural discourse at the end of the twentieth century and beginning of the twenty-first. His mark on the field is indelible, and we in the architectural community owe him a huge debt.

And finally, my thanks to Bob Donnelly, helpmate and steadfast companion.

INTRODUCTION

In 1976 Charles Jencks pinpointed the death of modern architecture to a precise moment in time: July 15, 1972, at 3:32 P.M. (or thereabouts), with the demolition of Minoru Yamasaki's Pruitt-Igoe housing project in St. Louis.[1] The time and date were purely fictitious, but the fabrication stuck and was, as Jencks later pointed out, accepted "by nearly everyone (especially the press) as truth."[2] In later reassessments of the modernist era, one frequently sees references to the first sustained criticism of the modern movement as taking place in the early 1960s, and citations of Jane Jacobs's *Death and Life of Great American Cities* (1961) as well as the demolition of Pruitt-Igoe a decade later as important signs.[3] A far more telling symptom of changing attitudes and the growing dismay that led to the profound disillusionment with modernism's ideals was, however, I contend, the massive Pan Am Building in New York. Both Jacobs's book and the demolition of Yamasaki's housing project were events of note mainly to those in the architecture and planning professions, and most likely only to a small academic fraction of them to boot. The Pan Am Building, begun in 1958 and completed five years later in 1963, at the time the largest corporate office tower in the world, on the other hand, was there, in one's face, directly and profoundly affecting everyone—the general public as well as design professionals and ivory-towered academics. Built in the airspace above the Grand Central Terminal in the midst of one of the most congested areas of Manhattan, it blocked the view down Park Avenue, cast deep shadows onto the surrounding area, and poured up to twenty-five thousand office workers daily onto already densely crowded streets. Denounced well before it even opened, once built it was unavoidable, an inescapable fact of city life. That it was designed by two of the foremost modernist architects of the time, Walter Gropius and Pietro Belluschi, only made matters worse: The building was despised from the moment the plans for the mute, massive, overscaled octagonal slab were announced. Despite the public outcry, despite the outrage from those in the profession, the huge office tower was built, a flagrant example of private interests riding roughshod over public concerns. The building was seized on as emblematic of what had gone wrong with the modernist vision. The fact that Walter Gropius himself had once stood as a symbol of modernism's social idealism made the irony all the more glaring.

The subject is complex. In and of itself, the Pan Am is of minor significance, a decent, albeit big, more or less inoffensive building that functions well enough. What lends it importance is its place, both its physical setting over the covered tracks of the Grand Central Terminal on one of New York City's most densely packed commercial sites, and its moment in time, marking not only the pivotal point between the decline of the railroad industry on whose land it was built and the rise of air travel in the late 1950s and early 1960s, but also, several decades later, the demise of its corporate client and major tenant, the pioneering Pan American World Airways, once one of the largest, most powerful airlines in the world. A comprehensive study of the building and the men who brought it about casts a harsh light on the architectural star system and its pitfalls for the public as well as the profession, as it traces the fame of the two renowned designers—Gropius and Belluschi, the one having just stepped down as chair of the Department of Architecture at Harvard's Graduate School of Design at the time he got involved in the Pan Am project, the other still dean of the College of Architecture and Urban Planning at MIT, both at the peak of their careers—and the subsequent decline in their reputations. It comprises a tale of New York City—its culture and politics, real estate tycoons, economic booms and declines, Park Avenue and its transformation in the postwar era, the "death of the street," changing attitudes toward the city, large-scale urban projects, zoning laws, open space, the birth of the historic-preservation movement, and private versus public interests in the built environment. It touches on still broader issues, such as the restructuring of architectural practice nationwide in the postwar era, the revival of architectural criticism in the American press in the late 1950s and early 1960s after a hiatus of some three or four decades, and the change in architectural values, with the demise of modernism and rise of postmodernism, that coincided with a revived appreciation of Beaux-Arts classicism. It also provides a close look at the practice of architecture in the case of large-scale urban projects such as the Pan Am and how buildings such as the Pan Am are actually brought about, from genesis to completion.[4] It is a story of many men—large-scale real estate developer Erwin Wolfson; James Ruderman, his structural engineer; architects Gropius and Belluschi; Juan Trippe, head of Pan American World Airways; and critics Douglas Haskell, Wolf von Eckardt, and Peter Blake—but also (in those times of changing attitudes toward them as well) a few women: Ada Louise Huxtable, Sibyl Moholy-Nagy, Jane Jacobs.[5] The goal in writing such a study was not simply to provide an account of the building, describing who built what, when, how, and why, but also to record its critical reception, how it was interpreted, what it meant to people, what they wrote about it, and how it affected their thinking, especially after the September 11, 2001, terrorist attack on the World Trade Center. Given the complexity of the subject, I have organized the material in sections arranged in roughly chronological order, so that readers can bypass areas that might be of less interest, such as the structural engineering or financing, to focus on areas of particular concern.

Since I broached the subject over a decade ago, methodological approaches in architectural history have changed radically.[6] New perspectives on what buildings should be studied, whose voices should be heard, and what issues should be raised have altered fundamentally the nature of historiography today. The interest in theoretical conceptualizing that dominated the field for several decades appears now to be waning, with rigorous historical research, once denigrated, now back in favor.[7] "New cultural history," crossing interdisciplinary boundaries and focusing on cultural meanings rather than causal explanation, has gained ground, and "microhistory," involving the close study of specific cases, is also now on the rise; combining traditional narrative and newer structuralist approaches, momentary events *and* their impact on the larger forces of everyday life, progressive historians now aim at synthesizing the two.[8] In drawing on this rich conceptual legacy, my intent as an architectural historian has been to provide a clear, solid historical account of the building itself, the discourse around it (that is, what was thought of and said about it at the time), and its historiography (how the event was written up, or, on the contrary, ignored, in history later). It is thus an account embedded, as inevitably any historical account must be, in an interpretive setting.[9] My aim in writing this book was to situate the Pan Am Building within the context of its time and place—mainly the late 1950s and early 1960s, a tumultuous time when things (cities, buildings, values, and attitudes, architectural as well as political) were changing rapidly—to point out its extraordinary impact on ordinary people's lives at the time. New York City in the postwar era had just emerged as not only the economic but also the cultural capital of the world, surpassing Paris in this regard;[10] in 1958 Mies van der Rohe's Seagram Building, a milestone in the annals of modernism, opened only a few blocks from the site where the Pan Am would soon rise; three years later Jacobs published *Death and Life of Great American Cities;* and Robert Venturi was already at work on the Vanna Venturi House in Chestnut Hill, challenging modernism and its hallowed ideals. The Pan Am, begun in 1958 and finished in 1963, spanned them all, the acme of modernism and its demise. Stepping back from the story—what happened when and the context at the time—I sought, too, to situate the building, a building invariably acknowledged in guidebooks, as its huge presence in the city alone makes it hard to ignore, but ignored nonetheless by architectural historians because of its putative banality, in a critical as well as historiographic context, underscoring its significance—beyond matters of architectural paradigms, aesthetics, and fluctuating artistic taste—to historians today.

At the onset of the Pan Am project, then known as "Grand Central City," Gropius was still revered as the founder of the Bauhaus who, together with Mies and other émigrés, brought European modernism to America in the late 1930s; in 1960, as construction of the Pan Am began, he was still celebrated, the focus of a major conference, "The Great Masters," at Columbia University. By the time the Pan Am Building, named for its major corporate client, which signed on that year, was completed three years later, both he and Belluschi, star architects at the top of the profession, had lost their luster and were widely vilified for their role in the project. The Pan Am Building marked a pivotal moment not only in their careers, but in cultural history, when modernism as a rebellious force was co-opted by capitalism and lost its powers of creative negation.[11] On another level, it marked a pivotal moment in life in New York, when the balance of private interests and social concerns sought in the years of the City Beautiful Movement earlier in the century, at the time of the old Beaux-Arts Grand Central Terminal, was lost.[12] A close study of the Pan Am reveals in a remarkable way the change in attitudes toward modernism in the late 1950s and the early 1960s, suggesting that it was more than simply a mediocre building, but one rich with meaning that mirrored not only that attitudinal change, but the power relations that reigned in New York at the time. It also emphasizes the importance of penetrating architectural criticism, now a lost art, to the life and well-being of the city. Underscoring the point that certain buildings enter into architectural discourse as much by the actions of critics as by those of designers,[13] it demonstrates the importance of the press in affecting attitudes and exposes the powerful role architectural critics, such as Haskell and Blake in *Architectural Forum,* Huxtable in the *New York Times,* von Eckardt in the *New Republic,* and Edgar Kaufmann, Jr., in *Harper's,* played in shaping professional as well as public perceptions.

The Pan Am Building aroused such profound feelings (few buildings in recent times have generated so much hatred and been so staunchly opposed) that it served as a major catalyst in the collapse of modernism and became emblematic of modernism gone awry. It remains today a painful, persistent symbol in the eyes of many of how wrong matters in architecture and urbanism can go. Moreover, it signified a major turning point in attitudes away from modernism, with its unrelenting faith in the future, toward postmodernism, with its new appreciation of the past. As such, the building marked a significant moment in the cultural life of the nation.

THE **PAN AM** BUILDING

AND THE
SHATTERING
OF THE
MODERNIST
DREAM

GRAND CENTRAL CITY

The Pan Am Building was conceived in 1958, several years after Ginsberg's "Howl," and opened five years later. Designed by Walter Gropius and Pietro Belluschi, two of the nation's most highly respected modernist architects, it was the largest corporate office tower in the world at the time. With its finely textured, broadly faceted glass and concrete walls rising fifty-nine stories above the street, spanning the full width of Park Avenue just north of the Grand Central Terminal and cutting off its vista, it was also the most controversial.

GRAND CENTRAL REDEVELOPMENT

The controversy over the building began, in fact, well before Gropius and Belluschi were brought in as designers. As early as 1953, concerns had been raised about the explosive growth of New York City, which after World War II was rapidly becoming the most important metropolis—politically, economically, and culturally—in the world. The expansion was especially apparent on Park Avenue, where a spurt of gleaming new, modern, flush-surfaced glass and steel tall office buildings was rapidly replacing gracious elegant masonry luxury hotels and apartments dating mostly from the 1920s that by the 1950s were deemed old-fashioned and uneconomical. Frederick Woodbridge, a New York architect who was later to become president of the New York chapter of the American Institute of Architects (AIA), in an address to the Association of Architects in Quebec, spoke of these impressive new modernist buildings. Marveling at the progressiveness of their sleek, modern forms, he pointed out the drawback: Visually and functionally they differed radically from the old palazzo-inspired residential buildings they were replacing, and as their numbers grew, they threatened to strangle the street. The Lever House in particular, while laudable in most respects, failed urbanistically, as it did little to provide open, publicly usable space on the street level. The zoning laws in force at the time, dating back to 1916, encouraged light and space but did little to control density. And proposals for revising the laws, while supported by the AIA as well as other civic organizations, were being staunchly opposed by real estate interests and property owners, who argued that further restrictions would prevent owners from enhancing profits by maximizing the size of buildings to whatever extent possible. This was precisely the point. Regulating density, Woodbridge argued, was essential in the interest not only of maintaining an attractive, livable city but also of assuring civic values of greater worth than private profits; moreover, if left uncontrolled, such unrestricted development would eventually choke the city.[1] All the issues Woodbridge touched upon—public open space, traffic, density, and most importantly, the rights of private property owners versus those of the public—were to crop up again the following year in the context of the Grand Central area redevelopment.

A year later, Paul Rudolph, a former student of Gropius's at Harvard, in a keynote speech at the annual national meeting of the AIA in Boston, again focused on the city and the importance of its spaces. Space, he maintained, had less to do with pragmatics such as the amount of square feet than with aesthetics and "the creation of living, breathing, dynamic spaces of infinite variety, capable of helping man forget something of his troubles." Noting that modern architecture was tragically lacking in eloquent spatial concepts, he bemoaned the tendency of planners to focus on getting people around efficiently, rather than on the manner of getting them there.

We need desperately to relearn the art of disposing of buildings to create different kinds of space: the quiet, enclosed, isolated, shaded space; the hustling, bustling space, pungent with vitality; the paved, dignified, vast, sumptuous, even awe-inspiring space; the mysterious space; the transition space which defines, separates and yet joins juxtaposed spaces of contrasting character. We need sequences of space which arouse one's curiosity, give a sense of anticipation, which beckon and impel us to rush forward to find that releasing space which dominates, which climaxes and acts as a magnet, and gives direction. . . . Most important of all, we need those outer spaces which encourage social contact.

Departing radically from his mentor's well-known views that rejected the past and the relevance of architectural history, Rudolph held up as laudable the old turn-of-the-century Grand Central station complex in New York. It was, he said, "perhaps unsurpassed in this country" for its urbanistic scale and contribution to the cityscape; bisecting Park Avenue, it served as a focal point for the long straight avenue and provided a grand processional to one of the major gateways to the city.[2]

Ironically, at exactly the same time, Robert R. Young, newly elected head of the New York Central Railroad, owner of the Grand Central, was meeting with developers with plans to demolish the old Beaux-Arts station, and to build a bigger, more profitable modern office building on the site. The Grand Central Station, as it was called at the time, by then was dilapidated. Dirty and rundown, it was also overworked, its capacity peaking during the war with some six hundred trains carrying 240,000 passengers in and out of midtown Manhattan daily. Since the war, however, as increased prosperity and the new federal highway system had encouraged the use of private cars, passenger rail traffic had waned. At the same time, property values along Park Avenue had soared. To compensate, the owners of the terminal, the New York Central and New York, New Haven and Hartford Railroad companies wanted to demolish the terminal and erect in its place a new "Grand Central City" with a tall office building. To understand the momentousness of these plans calls for some knowledge of history, a sense of the Grand Central's past, and an understanding of why, denigrated though it was by the mid-1950s, it was still so remarkable. Had it not been for the Grand Central, there would have been no Pan Am. Their histories are so intricately intertwined that to understand the latter, one needs to understand the former and its long, convoluted role, historically and socially, in the life and physical fabric of the city. And this in turn involves a brief look at the history of the railroad in New York.

THE RAILROAD INDUSTRY IN NEW YORK CITY

The railroad industry in New York City dates back to 1831 with the founding of the Harlem (then New York and Harlem) Railroad, which ran horse-drawn cars on tracks from the bucolic Dutch village of Harlem at the top of Manhattan Island down what was then Fourth Avenue (later to become Park Avenue) to 23rd Street, still well above what was considered "town" at that time (figures 1.1 and 1.2).[3] The first steam engines were introduced three years later, but as the city was expanding northward, it was clear the public would not tolerate noisy, dirty locomotives on city streets, and by 1859 the city had banned their use south of 42nd Street. Other lines soon opened up providing long-distance service to the Midwest and Great Lakes as well as freight service to New Jersey, which enabled goods to be shipped from throughout the continent to New York Harbor. As a result, by the second half of the century, New York City had become one of the busiest ports in the world and the hub of a vast international shipping network.

A key figure in the development of the railroad system in New York was Cornelius Vanderbilt. Enterprising son of a Staten Island farmer, in 1812 at age eighteen he had purchased a ferryboat to haul farm produce and passengers between the island and Manhattan. Within a few years, he was operating steamboat lines on the Hudson River and in Long Island Sound, and by the end of the 1830s, "Commodore" Vanderbilt had amassed a fortune of half a million dollars and was one of the richest men in the city.[4] In 1863, recognizing changing transportation patterns, Vanderbilt began shifting his operations from steamships to railroad, buying control first of the New York and Harlem,

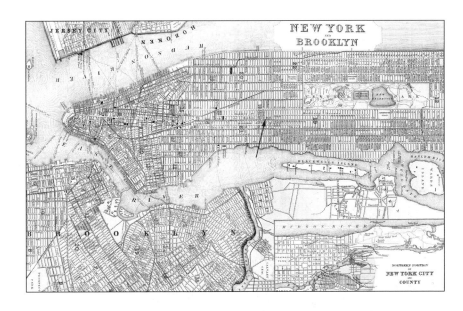

FIGURE 1.1   Map, New York City, 1867

FIGURE 1.2   Harlem

FIGURE 1.3   Grand Central Depot, 1871

then of the Hudson River Railroad. Well aware of Vanderbilt's expansionist vision, the New York Central, a major freight line from Albany to Buffalo with connections to the Midwest, balked at the Commodore's offer to merge with the Vanderbilt railroads, whereupon Vanderbilt, with characteristic ruthlessness, refused to permit his Hudson River boats to handle New York Central freight. The railroad capitulated in short order.[5] Four years later, Vanderbilt took over as president of the New York Central. Astutely recognizing that having separate terminals for each of the three Vanderbilt rail lines he now controlled was inefficient as well as inconvenient for passengers, he consolidated the passenger operations and built a new station on the north side of 42nd Street straddling Fourth Avenue to accommodate all three lines. The Grand Central Depot (figure 1.3) opened in 1871.

As the switching yard of the new station spread out on the city surface north of the terminal, it split the avenue and strewed a steady noxious stream of smoke, soot, and noise throughout adjacent properties. The city, acting on behalf of its citizenry to balance Vanderbilt's private interests with public concerns, demanded the railroad depress the tracks from the head of the station yard at 49th Street up to 96th Street, where they would emerge from the tunnel in Harlem (figures 1.4 and 1.5). As Douglas Haskell, editor of *Architectural Forum* and one of Grand Central Station's initial defenders, was later to point out, the aim of the city was clear: By sinking the tracks below grade, one could stitch up the "great spinal gash" in the city fabric created by the railroad tracks by bridging them over with cross-streets at surface level. This meant the railroad, at its own enormous expense in return for the use of the land, had to tunnel through miles of bedrock, the dense granite of which Manhattan was composed. But it also meant that while other large American cities, such as Chicago or Philadelphia, were being slashed apart by surface-level railroad trackage, great swaths through the fabric of the city that held up traffic with frequent train crossings and reduced large areas of adjacent land to little more than railroad slums, New York was blessed with a rail system down its central spine that allowed surface traffic to move free of interruption and was for all intents and purposes out of sight. In time, a lid was laid over the entire railway yard north of the terminal, and the avenue, hitherto bifurcated by the exposed tracks, reunited to create a single broad avenue then called Park Avenue. In the 1920s, the entire area was developed into an elegant, integrated residential area, with the avenue lined by luxurious masonry hotels and apartment blocks and embellished with a landscaped strip down the center. By the end of the decade, Park Avenue north of the terminal, as a result of

FIGURE 1.4   Grand Central train yard

FIGURE 1.5   Grand Central train yard, with sunken tracks

the railroad's exploitation of the air rights over its subterranean tracks, had become one of the most fashionable neighborhoods in the city (figure 1.6).

The 1871 railroad station, too, by this time had been replaced. Several decades earlier, as the population of the city had exploded and the tide of suburban commuters and long-distance passengers continued to rise, the Commodore's Grand Central Depot was deemed inadequate, and in 1898 it was enlarged, three stories were added to expand its capacity, and its exteriors were remodeled in tune with changing tastes, rejecting the richly plastic mansarded Second Empire forms of the original building in favor of the more restrained, fashionable domed and pedimented classical Italianate (figure 1.7). Its locomotives, however, were still driven by steam. An accident in the winter of 1902 changed that, as a pair of trains colliding in the cold, dark, smoke-filled Park Avenue tunnel killed fifteen commuters and injured scores of others.[6] Pressured by rising public complaints about safety, but even more by heightening competition from the New York Central's chief rival, the Pennsylvania Railroad, which was in the throes of building a magnificent new station designed by prominent architects McKim, Mead & White and fully equipped with electrified trains, in another part of town, William K. Vanderbilt, grandson of the pioneering Commodore Vanderbilt, agreed to switch. In 1903, construction of a new terminus, based on a wholly electrified system, which eliminated the smoke that led to the 1902 collision, was begun.

GRAND CENTRAL TERMINAL

The new terminal was an extraordinary synthesis of a complex, dynamic, futuristic transportation hub, a stately, monumental Beaux-Arts building, and lofty City Beautiful Movement civic ideals.[7] On the one hand, it was a brilliant engineering solution to the growing problem of urban traffic. The below-grade, multitiered transportation center in the heart of bustling New York, with its network of train tracks, bridges, roads, and pedestrian corridors, its sense of speed, movement, and "roar of famished motor-cars," was wholly futuristic in its vision. Concealed by the magnificent, classical Beaux-Arts terminal with its lavishly carved, historicizing stone facades overhead, it was a fantastic structure of multileveled differentiated transportation systems—train tracks, subway and bus lines, pedestrian corridors—all intricately interwoven and coordinated into a flawlessly functioning, highly efficient, finely tuned machine (figure 1.8). Completed in 1913 and recognized immediately as remarkable, the station was published internationally and surely known to the Futurist Antonio Sant'Elia, whose drawings of the Cen-

FIGURE 1.6   Park Avenue, 1922, looking north from below 50th Street

FIGURE 1.7   Grand Central Station, 1898

FIGURE 1.8   Grand Central, section, 1911

tral Station in Milan were done the following year (figure 1.9).[8] The vast, highly complex structure constituting the terminus of the three separate railroad lines had four tracks coming in from the north, which fanned out at 57th Street into two superimposed tiers that looped around at the terminus to avoid having to back out trains, one at twenty feet below street level mainly for intercity travel, the other twenty-four feet below that for suburbanites, accommodating between them some sixty-seven passenger platforms. On top of it all, surmounting the terminal, was to have been a revenue-generating, twenty-story hotel/office building to help defray costs of the enormously expensive endeavor. And to the north, Park Avenue, as it left the station, would form a lid over the below-grade tracks, becoming in effect a three-mile-long bridge, with some fifty side streets crossing it. Coming into the station from the south as it met the terminal at 42nd Street, the avenue would split into two elevated ramps, wrap around the station on either side, and reunite in a single broad avenue above it at 45th, where it would continue north to Harlem. New subways and elevated spurs would connect the new station to the city's mass transit system; below grade in the terminal itself, a maze of underground shop-lined pedestrian passageways was to connect the station to the elevator lobbies of some twenty-one adjacent hotels and office buildings, so one could move from one place to another without venturing out onto the street.

All this was worked out by New York Central Railroad's chief engineer, William J. Wilgus, and his associates. But there was more. In addition to a brilliant circulation solution, with its plan for electrification, enlargement of all the terminal facilities, and addition of the hotel/office structure above, Wilgus envisioned an entire city extending north of the terminal over the tracks—a city within the city, with multistoried apartment buildings, hotels, clubs, churches, tall office buildings and other commercial structures supported on sturdy steel bridgework with foundation footings sunk between the tracks, an enormously costly proposition at the railroad's expense made possible by the railroad's leasing of air rights above the covered tracks. This would transform the railroad's land, on which taxes had to be paid, into revenue-generating property.[9] Wilgus envisioned, thus, more than a simply a building or a railroad station, an entire precinct, establishing a precedent of private concerns collaborating with public interests that later served, as Haskell pointed out, as the prototype for other large-scale, civic-minded urban developments, such as Rockefeller Center.

In striking contrast to and wholly concealing Wilgus's dynamic, futuristic transportation network below grade was the grand, monumental Grand Central Terminal, with its stately but static masonry Beaux-Arts facades rising six stories overhead. This was the

FIGURE 1.9   Antonio Sant'Elia, Central Station, Milan, 1914

work of Whitney Warren. The fascinating story has often been told, but to recapitulate it briefly: Wilgus's plan for the vast transportation network, with its huge cost to be offset by the hotel/office building and other rent-generating buildings in the air space over the tracks, was distributed to a list of the nation's most prominent architects, among whom were Daniel Burnham of Chicago and McKim, Mead & White of New York.[10] Stanford White proposed a colossal sixty-story tower that, had it been built, would have been the tallest in the world; flanking it were to have been shorter, symmetrical buildings, and rising from its summit was to have been a jet of steam shooting three hundred feet still further into the air, transforming the terminal into a landmark visible throughout the city and a beacon to incoming ships (figure 1.10). Despite it and other impressive proposals, the competition was won by the little-known firm Reed and Stem from Minnesota, evidently on the basis of two ingenious ideas. The first called for the use of ramps rather than stairs on the interior to facilitate the circulation of baggage-encumbered travelers throughout the multistoried structure. The second, most likely suggested by Wilgus (who happened to be Reed's brother-in-law), was that instead of running Park Avenue through the center of the new terminal, which was to straddle the avenue like the existing station, it would be bifurcated and raised on elevated roadways one story above street level, so that it encircled the terminal and reconnected on the other side. Reed and Stem's scheme also made provisions for a twenty-story building above the terminal to provide the railroad with administrative spaces, as well as a series of stately buildings above sunken tracks to the east and west to bring in additional revenue (figure 1.11).

Meanwhile, however, Warren, an architect trained at the Ecole des Beaux-Arts, as architects Charles Reed and Allen Stem were not, drew up a competing plan (figure 1.12). As Vanderbilt was well aware of rival Pennsylvania Railroad's impressive new railway station going up across town, he found the plan by Warren (who happened to be his cousin and one of his closest friends) more compelling and suggested that Warren and his partner Charles Wetmore form a partnership with Reed and Stem, the winners of the competition. Working together, the two offices would develop the practical aspects of the Wilgus proposal into the monumental urbanistic scheme Vanderbilt envisioned.[11] Inspired by City Beautiful ideals of monumental city planning catalyzed by the 1893 Chicago World's Fair, Vanderbilt sought an awe-inspiring ensemble of monumental structures on a colossal scale. Influenced by the fair, architects and their clients everywhere were seeking ample sites, grand avenues, spacious greenery, and soaring interior spaces, grand schemes all unified by a comprehensive, harmonious plan, and

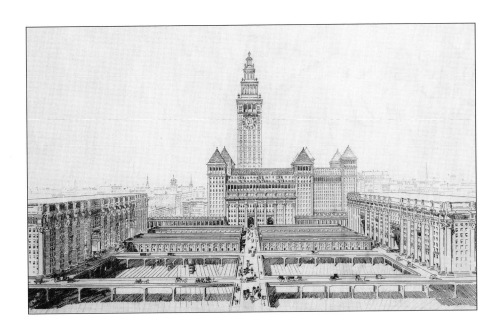

FIGURE 1.10   McKim, Mead & White, Grand Central Terminal perspective drawing

FIGURE 1.11   Reed and Stem, perspective drawing

FIGURE 1.12   Whitney Warren, perspective drawing

well aware that both economy and convenience might have to be subordinated to civic values of more lasting significance. City parks equipped with benches, trees, grass, flowers, and other public amenities were provided typically by private enterprise equipped with the power and means to carry such vast schemes out. Architecturally, time-honored classical forms were adhered to, with expensive materials, uniform color and scale, and a comparatively narrowly defined language of form.[12] Vanderbilt's vision and its complex of buildings—hotels, office buildings, and apartments, with the magnificent new railway terminal as the centerpiece, all governed by a systematic plan—included a grand boulevard with a long vista: Park Avenue. From a mile to the south, where the avenue angled, one would have a clear, unobstructed view of the Grand Central's main facade; from the north, the terminal would be visible from around 68th Street, where the avenue began to descend. Constituting the focal point of these two long vistas was to be the new terminal, a great civic monument and immense railway gateway, on the scale of a Roman bath (figure 1.13).[13] In what Haskell saw as a philanthropic gesture, Vanderbilt deliberately eschewed the profit-generating twenty-story hotel/office building Wilgus had proposed in favor of one that was lower, framed by the Commodore and Biltmore Hotels on either side so that space flowed freely around and above it.[14]

In marked contrast to Wilgus's boisterous below-grade structure, with its multiple levels, crisscrossing corridors, and sloped ramps, the Reed and Stem, Warren and Wetmore terminal itself was to be calm and harmonious. The formally ordered south facade of the building facing the downtown would be opened by three great arches, like ancient triumphal arches with all the associations of a monumental portal; expressive of the daily movement of the public, these great arched windows were time-honored symbolic gestures of welcome long sanctioned by Parisian prototypes and perfectly appropriate for the New York railroad terminal.[15] On the interior, the concourse, a dramatically soaring, barrel-vaulted space at the heart of the station, was to serve as the climax of the whole vast, multilayered scheme (figure 1.14). In accordance with traditional Beaux-Arts planning principles, the circulation was worked out so that no matter where one entered the building, one would follow a clear progression toward the grand concourse with its great vaulted space. Once erected, the building was, as Haskell was to point out, a Beaux-Arts monument par excellence, the focal point of a broad boulevard lined by elegant luxury hotels and apartment houses whose cornices were aligned and facades coordinated by a single governing artistic scheme. The centerpiece of a comprehensive, artistically unified design, it was the kind of planned urban environment

FIGURE 1.13   "Terminal City," circa 1910

FIGURE 1.14   Grand Central concourse

founders of the City Beautiful Movement envisioned, all provided by a private entity, the New York Central Railroad, for public use.[16]

It was this magnificent urban complex combining the engineering brilliance of Wilgus, the Beaux-Arts artistic refinement of Warren, and the noble ideals of *civitas* advanced by the City Beautiful Movement, that after the war had been allowed to deteriorate. The transformation of Park Avenue from a broad, landscaped boulevard lined by elegant masonry, largely Renaissance-inspired, residential palazzi, into a commercial district dominated by towering modern, site-filling, glass and metal skyscrapers was by the mid-1950s well underway. And it was the Grand Central terminal itself at their focal point, now in a poorly maintained and dilapidated state, that the New York Central Railroad was at this point about to redevelop.

By the middle of the twentieth century, the railroad industry in the United States aided by the government's highway expansion program, had declined appreciably. As the use of the private car increased and air travel became increasingly affordable, the accompanying loss in rail passenger revenues led railway companies, owners of some of the most valuable land anywhere—in Chicago, Boston, Philadelphia, and other major cities as well as New York—to turn to exploring the potentials of their real estate holdings. At this point New York Central's Young vowed to turn things around for the company's stockholders and to concentrate on maximizing profits from the New York Central's vast landholdings in New York's midtown.

ROBERT YOUNG AND THE NEW YORK CENTRAL

In the fall of 1954, as the building boom begun in New York City in the postwar years gained momentum, Young, who had taken over the chairmanship of the New York Central Railroad in June, talked of plans to redevelop the Grand Central area and replace the old, outmoded Grand Central Terminal with a new, more profitable high-rise structure.

The New York Central owned about a dozen nearby blocks—some forty-eight acres, bounded roughly by 42nd and 50th Streets and Lexington and Madison Avenues, that included, according to the *New York Times* at the time, the sites of the Waldorf-Astoria, Biltmore, Commodore, and Barclay Hotels, as well as the Yale Club, the Grand Central Palace, ten office buildings, four apartment blocks, and a branch post office (figure 1.15).[17] Young's plans, which included developing the air rights over the property, had been prompted earlier that spring by a letter from Erwin S. Wolfson, a major New York developer with whom Young had worked on other occasions. Wolfson had been eyeing the Grand Central property for some time, and in April, as Young was battling for control of the Central, Wolfson contacted him, pointing out that the railroad's valuable real estate on Park Avenue was ripe for development.[18] Wolfson outlined his thoughts, bringing in a couple of mutual friends, Herbert and Stuart Scheftel, to lend weight to his proposal. According to Wolfson several years later, Young agreed that if he won his battle, he would lease Wolfson the property for development.[19] In June, after winning the fight and becoming head of the Central, Young sent for Wolfson and the Scheftels, as promised, to explore their ideas further. Negotiations, however, broke down, derailed, it was learned later, by another investor, the brash, high-risk-loving New York developer William Zeckendorf. Zeckendorf had also become interested in building on the prime Grand Central site, one of the most coveted and expensive in the city, and had managed to impress Young with a far more grandiose (and eventually unrealizable) proposal. That fall, the *New York Times* announced that the New York Central was considering plans proposed by Zeckendorf, president of the realty firm of Webb & Knapp, with I. M. Pei, architect, to replace the old terminal with an eighty-story skyscraper surmounted by an observation tower that would make it 128 feet higher than the Empire State Building, hence the tallest building in the world.[20]

Haskell, editor of the *Architectural Forum,* then one of the three leading architectural magazines in the country, wanted to publish Pei's project and called him a month after Webb & Knapp's plans for the Grand Central redevelopment were first announced.[21] Pei, however, irritated at the *Forum,* which had recently assumed a new critical approach decidedly different from the promotional role traditionally held by the architectural press, took the opportunity to chide Haskell for casting him as "just a smart operator for big business," contending that the publicity the *Forum* provided "not only did him no good, but did him harm." Acknowledging that Webb & Knapp did not yet have a contract with Young for the development, Pei nonetheless said he felt they were in an excellent position to undertake the huge development, as they understood the

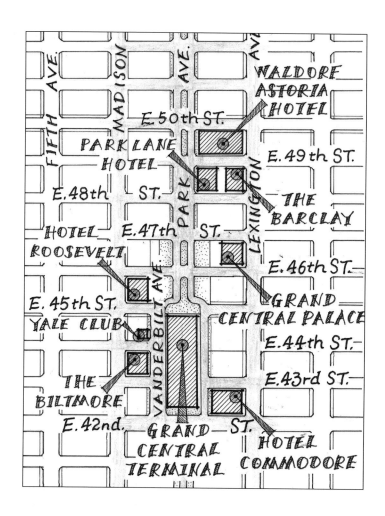

FIGURE 1.15   Site plan, New York Central's Park Avenue real estate holdings, 1955

complexities of the situation and had a broader grasp of the issues than other "free-standing" architectural firms. Questioned specifically about his thoughts on the proposed demolition of monuments such as the Grand Central Terminal, Pei replied that he felt it was justified "if it was done in the service of a monumental idea." By a "monumental idea," according to Haskell's notes on their conversation, Pei meant one "that expressed the potentials of that particular situation as an expression of the public's desires and aspirations." His suggestion that a very tall building be put on the site had nothing to do with breaking records or personal pride, Pei assured Haskell, but rather with his recognition that a tall building would be more appropriate there than anywhere else in the city. His idea was to build an office tower with some six million square feet of rentable space that would include a new concourse whose height, while not the eighty feet of the current concourse, would be at least forty feet.[22]

The railroad company's plans for the demolition of the Grand Central appalled Haskell, who immediately drew up an open letter to Young and Patrick B. McGinnis, of the New York, New Haven and Hartford Railroad, which paid for 30 percent of the terminal's operating costs and claimed a right to the railroad's real estate holdings. Signed by some 235 prominent architects from across the country and published in the November 1954 *Architectural Forum,* together with a photograph of the Grand Central's magnificent vaulted interior, the letter urged Young and McGinnis not to demolish the station. Though built in 1903 and clearly not the most efficient railroad station at the time, the concourse was still one of the finest interior spaces in the country, Haskell argued, and should be saved, as it "stirs something in people, something high and fine, something intangible but real." It was one of America's architectural masterpieces, he asserted, and one of the few whose appeal was universal.[23]

Haskell appealed to the two men's sense of integrity, maintaining that the terminal "belongs in fact to the nation," a point that he was to return to time and again in his campaign to save the station.[24] It was a known and loved masterpiece that he felt had stood the test of time and served as an important link between the living city and its history. His open letter urging the preservation of Grand Central pointed out a number of important questions raised by the railroad's proposal. Was the threat of demolition real? It appeared to be, as the heads of the two railroad companies were expected to exploit the full real estate potential of their holdings for their stockholders. Was the motivation tax savings or income? Both, but chiefly income. Reflecting his interest not just in the aesthetics of buildings but their economics, as well as a concern for fairness to both sides in the case, Haskell laid out the figures, citing the taxes the railroads paid on the terminal: $1.3 million per year, in addition to the $24 million annual operating costs the railroad cited for the terminal. The railroads were riled because their money-losing business was taxed while that of airlines, using publicly owned airports, was not. The main issue was not, however, the operations of the railroad, Haskell contended, but its real estate: The fifteen-acre tract on which the terminal stood, worth an estimated $17 million per acre, was not generating income. An office building of five million square feet renting at $6.50 per square foot would bring in more than $30 million in gross income annually, offsetting operating costs and taxes. In light of these figures, was the concourse worth saving? The consensus of most architects and critics, as evidenced from their support of Haskell's letter, was yes. Was it possible to save the concourse *and* realize adequate income? Both Pei and Alfred Fellheimer, the architect hired by McGinnis to draw up an alternative proposal, thought it was not. Carroll Meeks, a Yale professor of architectural history whom Haskell brought in for comment, sided, in an article in the same *Forum* issue, with those maintaining that the terminal should be saved; Meeks also provided a brief history of the terminal that pointed out the problem planners had faced at the time the terminal was built and the brilliance of their final solution.[25] Haskell concluded his article by proposing an international competion that would open the debate to architects and planners at large.

Haskell's passion regarding the threatened Grand Central was not shared by the *Architectural Record,* the *Forum*'s chief rival, which remained aloof from the controversy and published only a short report on the railroad's proposal.[26] The proposed schemes by Pei and Fellheimer "raised the question whether one should destroy a monument in the name of practicality, even if the owner's tax and revenue problems *and* public convenience argue in favor of it," it noted blandly. Acting in its customary role of advocate of the architectural profession as well as adhering to its policy of promoting modernism, a stance it adopted in the late 1930s, the *Record* differed markedly from the *Forum,* whose editorial aims were deliberately broader and saw itself not as beholden to the architect but as a watchdog for the public, responsible as much to clients, businessmen, and the construction industry as to the architectural profession. The differences between the two major architectural magazines were to grow even sharper over the dispute about the Pan Am.

Haskell's plea to save the concourse *was* endorsed, however, by the *New York Times,* which carried an editorial reiterating the point that "this handsome room belongs to all America." The *Christian Science Monitor* took a similar stand, as did the *New York Herald Tribune,* which quoted Meeks on the history of the concourse. Presumably influenced by the snowballing effect of the *Forum*'s campaign in public as well as professional quarters, the railroad halted the development, and no further progress on the Grand Central was made for several years. Equally responsible for the delay, however, were the weakening economy and the difficulties Young and Zeckendorf were encountering in working out the financing of Pei's huge tower. In the meantime, however, a number of proposals from other architects, including a five-hundred-story tower by Frank Lloyd Wright, were put forward.

OTHER PROPOSALS

Several weeks after Pei's plans were announced, the alternative proposal by Alfred Fellheimer of Fellheimer and Wagner, submitted by McGinnis, was published in the *New York Times* (figure 1.16).[27] Instead of a single gargantuan high-rise tower, which he argued would only exacerbate the already congested traffic, Fellheimer proposed replacing the station (which he called a "Chinese Wall" that blocked circulation) with a roughly fifty-story building aimed less at monumentality than at relieving congestion by increasing mobility in and around the building. Like Pei's, it too would be the largest office building in the world, but it would also involve extensive changes in the existing street pattern to relieve the area's chronic traffic jams and pedestrian crowding. Instead of the existing bifurcated, elevated roadway winding around the building, Park Avenue would be restraightened and allowed to pass through the building, and the city's cross-streets, including 43rd and 44th Streets, which had been closed since 1903 for the Grand Central Terminal, would be reopened. The subterranean tracks would be retained, but the old Beaux-Arts station would be demolished, as in the Pei project, and replaced by a new terminal building comprising three full city blocks—a complex, geometric form marked by a series of setbacks, fifty stories high, with four to six million square feet of rentable office space, a parking garage within the building for 2,400 cars, a rooftop heliport as well as rooftop gardens, plus restaurants and stores providing services for the estimated 30,000 office workers without further congesting pedestrian traffic. Fellheimer previously had worked as a planner in the office of Reed and Stem, architects of the original 1913 building, and his main interest, as noted, was in improving circulation in the heavily trafficked area.[28] In describing their proposal in an article in the *Architectural Record* two months later, Fellheimer assured readers that the firm had "carefully weighed [its] own pride in the present building, and its emotional and aesthetic significance to people all over the world. [The firm's] reluctant but firm conclusion

FIGURE 1.16   Fellheimer and Wagner proposal

is that neither pride nor reverence should be permitted to clot the vitality of a great metropolis. In turn, that very vitality may guarantee that if one expression of human aspiration must be destroyed in the process of growth, it will be replaced by an even greater one."[29] This was a common argument among modernists at the time; ironically, Belluschi was to make the same argument a decade later with the Pan Am Building, maintaining that the architect could not let sentimentality stand in the way of progress. Gropius was to take a similar stand.

THE BRUMOND PROPOSAL AND BROADENING THE "SAVE THE CONCOURSE" CAMPAIGN

Haskell's initial focus was on the terminal's internal vaulted space, which he felt ought to be preserved at all costs. Within several months, however, as other proposals for redeveloping the area surfaced, his thoughts broadened. A proposal put forth by Harry L. Brumond clearly expanded his thinking. Brumond was a member of the Downtown Athletic Club of New York City and an architect connected with Byrne Associates of New York. His proposal, published by the Downtown Athletic Club, a copy of which Haskell retained in his files, called for saving the old 1913 station but adding a new sixteen-hundred-foot-high "modernistic" tower set on a hundred-foot-high base, with masonry exteriors staggered like those of Rockefeller Center directly on top (figure 1.17).[30] Though Brumond's project appears to have gone largely unnoticed, it did catch Haskell's eye. He mentioned it in a memorandum to Walter McQuade, on the staff of the *Forum* at the time, and suggested that the *Forum* staff should be thinking of preserving not just the concourse, but the building itself, including the spaces surrounding it. "If there is ever an object lesson in the way exterior space can be shaped," he maintained, "it is in the Grand Central area."[31]

ROTH PROPOSAL

In February 1955, in the wake of Haskell's mounting campaign to save the terminal, Wolfson stepped up again with a proposal by the architectural firm of Emery Roth & Sons, which, like the Brumond proposal, called for preserving the old Beaux-Arts building (figure 1.18). Widely published in the *New York Times, Wall Street Journal,* and *New York Herald Tribune,* as well as in the *Architectural Forum,* the Roth scheme, development of which had begun in November (and, according to the *Forum,* evidently in response

FIGURE 1.17 Brumond proposal

FIGURE 1.18 Roth proposal

to the *Forum* campaign), consisted of what was described as a new, thoroughly *modern* tower of steel and glass set back from the terminal in the airspace above the sunken tracks.[32] The Wolfson/Roth tower, a speculative office building tentatively called "Grand Central City" and estimated to cost over $100 million, would sit between the old turn-of-the-century terminal and the thirty-five story, intricately crowned New York Central headquarters building, designed by Warren and Wetmore and added to the complex in 1929, to the north. The main lobby floor of the new building would be one story above street level and accessed by escalators; traffic on Park Avenue would continue to be diverted around the building complex on elevated ramps, which would be broadened and extended to continue on through the office building at its lobby level, reconnecting to the north beyond the New York Central headquarters building. The crosstown 45th Street would also be preserved, permitted to continue uninterrupted under the elevated ramps to allow circular traffic around the new office structure. This new scheme, drawn up by Richard Roth of Emery Roth & Sons, and backed by developers Wolfson, the Scheftels, and a fourth investor, Alfred G. Burger, promised not only to preserve the Grand Central but also to set it distinctly apart from the new modern office building by means of a neutral blank wall, a windowless "backdrop" that would serve to frame it. Beyond this would rise a new sixty-five story steel and glass tower with staggered rectangular forms, set on a broad, site-filling sixteen-story base, its height raised still further by a tall, slender broadcasting spire. It was to house three live theaters, a movie theater, restaurants, a private terrace club, several large television studios, five floors of off-street parking facilities, and a roof-top heliport, in addition to four million square feet of rentable office space.

Haskell's article in *Forum* describing the Roth project pointed out its virtue of sparing Grand Central's great vaulted concourse but focused mainly on the urbanistic dimensions of the site that stood to be lost by any such development. The Grand Central Station and the magnificent space around it represented, Haskell wrote, a case study demonstrating how empty space, which most people thought of as nothing but air into which buildings project, could be shaped and used. Haskell, who had majored in fine arts at Oberlin College before going into journalism, stressed the sheer beauty of exterior space, pointing out how a low building like the Grand Central terminal was like a piece of furniture "that lets the tall buildings around it compose themselves as if in a big room," and a tall building like the New York Central Building behind it, with its ornate pyramidal top capped by an elaborately carved cupola, served as a visual terminus, closing an endless vista that was otherwise "much like the unhappiness symbol recognized and used by surrealist painters, [where the] eye has nowhere to stop." He described the Grand Central and its remarkable circulation system of ramps and passageways, sidewalks and elevated lanes, which enabled large masses of people daily to navigate efficiently through and around the building, and how the use of arches and arcades could "shoot holes through the cold walls of city blocks—and open up city neighborhoods for business. A city should be something more than buildings at random," Haskell maintained. "It's high time that planning got up off the map in America and took account of these outdoor rooms we all enjoy." Haskell reminded readers of Rudolph's AIA speech the previous year, in which the young modernist had lauded the Grand Central area for its urbanistic contribution: "the ramps, bridges, tunnels, passageways, elevated roads, connecting arches and organized courtyards in the area" that helped to make it more than a collection of coolly efficient buildings. He included also an admonition from the Manhattan architect Giorgio Cavaglieri, who would continue to play a prominent role in the Grand Central debate, that any new office building would bring increased congestion in the area.[33]

It was a concern Cavaglieri took to the broader public the following month. In a letter to the editor of the *New York Herald Tribune,* he applauded it and other newspapers for their coverage of recent Grand Central proposals but chided them for not making the public more aware of the consequences of any development in the area. The issue, he said, "greatly transcends a purely economic and sentimental problem." Independent of the issue of preserving an architectural monument or the design of a new building, the public needed to be concerned about the problem of space. A new building of four or five million square feet would add, he warned, about 40,000 to the daytime population of the area, over and beyond the some 40,000 people who would be added by the Socony-Mobile Building, then nearing completion, on top of the already existing office populations. And this, he pointed out, was in addition to the pedestrian traffic generated by the terminal itself. If the railroad companies believed they should not be penalized for their ownership of land dedicated to a public interest, he concluded, their air rights should be bought by the city "in order to prevent concentration of people in this area above the already staggering figures."[34] If Cavaglieri's proposed solution fell on deaf ears, his concerns over congestion did not, and they quickly became an oft-repeated refrain. It was one of the first signs of the fierce opposition to the Grand Central development that was about to erupt.

FIGURE 1.19   San Remo Apartments

EMERY ROTH & SONS

Emery Roth & Sons, the architectural firm to which Wolfson had turned for the design of his project, was one he had worked with many times before. It was a well-established Manhattan firm dating back to the early 1900s that had designed hundreds of buildings in the city, most of them ordinary, some of them highly regarded.[35] It was founded in 1903 by Emery Roth, a Hungarian emigrant who had left Budapest in the 1880s seeking professional training abroad and worked for a time as a draftsman in the Burnham and Root office while drawings were being prepared for the 1893 Chicago World's Fair. While there, Roth learned how to design classical buildings but also gained valuable insight into the working relationship of big business and building; he also happened to meet the well-known, highly regarded Richard Morris Hunt, the first American to seek architectural training at the Ecole des Beaux-Arts in Paris and founder of the American Institute of Architects. Securing a letter of introduction from him, Roth left Chicago for New York, where he opened his own architectural office.[36] Focused at least as much on developing efficient planning techniques for residents and commercial buildings as on design, the Roth office flourished, becoming by the 1920s a leading designer of stately Renaissance-inspired upper-class apartments and hotels of stone, brick, and terra cotta, mainly in Central Park West (figures 1.19 and 1.20). His sons Richard and Julian soon joined the firm, becoming partners in 1938.[37] Richard, a graduate of the Massachusetts Institute of Technology (MIT), helped design naval bases in the Pacific in World War II and was the firm's designer; while not a licensed architect, Julian was a construction expert, having spent a number of years in the construction field.[38] After the war, the two sustained the commercial success of their father. Alert as he to changing fashions, as architectural tastes shifted and Beaux-Arts classicism became outmoded, they turned to modernism, which was then gaining momentum in the business community. Hardly design revolutionaries, Richard and Julian Roth followed their clientele, rejecting what by then was considered old-fashioned historicism, which involved extensive hand labor and expensive ornamentation, in favor of a new economical minimalist modernism that also bore a stylish, progressive image. When their father died in 1947, the Roth brothers inherited a legacy of sound business practices and planning techniques and a body of loyal clients, plus a successful, up-and-running organization with a reputation for practicality and efficiency. In the decade that followed, the firm took a lead in the modernized steel and glass "wedding cake" office buildings favored by speculators that filled sites to the maximum allowed by code. The

FIGURE 1.20   Beresford Apartments

FIGURE 1.21   Park Avenue, with Roth buildings

FIGURE 1.22   Roth buildings, New York City

1949   1950   1950   1953

1955   1955   1955   1955

1954

1954

1954

1954

1956

1956

1957

Roths built many of them, especially on Park Avenue (figure 1.21). As the Roths' biographer, Steven Ruttenbaum, put it, they were in business to make money, not to squander it on unessential things such as ornamentation that bore little relation to the building's function.[39] Jane Jacobs described the Roths somewhat differently. In a 1957 *Architectural Forum* article on Manhattan's postwar boom in office space, she wrote that aesthetics were taking a beating and that most of the new buildings, many of them by the Roth firm, were simply dull (figure 1.22).[40]

Highly successful in landing jobs with large-scale Manhattan developers such as Wolfson and the Uris brothers, the Roth office quickly rose to become one of the most prolific postwar architectural firms specializing in high-rise office buildings. A large measure of the firm's success was due, as Richard Roth was later bluntly to explain in his essay, "High-Rise Down to Earth," to their aim "not to create masterpieces" but to provide buildings that worked efficiently and economically for their clients: buildings, that is, that met the programmatic requirements of the client and insured a profit.[41] The Roth brothers' success stemmed from their ability to see the whole picture, their familiarity with the Manhattan real estate market, their sound knowledge of both codes and contractors, and most especially their sheer speed. A client would call Roth to say he had just bought a plot of land and inquire how soon could they have plans ready for a building on the site. Most likely the client had in fact not yet bought the land but wanted a Roth plan to consult in drawing up a bid.[42] Armed with the specifications—plot size, the building's purpose, potential tenants, zoning requirements—the Roths were able to respond with extraordinary alacrity. It was a business based on speed, not a distinctive look or unique design. As Richard Roth (figure 1.23) explained it in 1957 (by which time, the Roth firm had the largest number and volume of office buildings in New York, especially on Park Avenue, where the firm had designed its first postwar office building a decade earlier), the Roths' departure from conventional design was "inspired by . . . pure economics" and the adaptability of the factory-type window module. Since 1946, with their first postwar office building, the Roths had employed "a strip window plan," because it allowed the greatest flexibility in office planning. They arrived at what they considered an optimum module size and other dimensions—for column spacing, floor-to-ceiling heights, and so on—by the same reasoning.[43] And once determined, those dimensions became standard.

Given their priorities of economics over aesthetics, it was clear why the Roths appealed to real estate tycoons such as Wolfson, who was one of their major clients.[44] Moreover, they were old family friends with Wolfson, with a relationship that went back

FIGURE 1.23   Richard Roth

to the 1920s, as Wolfson and the Roths' maternal grandfather had been partners in real estate ventures in Florida. They remained close, with Wolfson and Richard Roth serving together in the war, then becoming neighbors, as both bought property in Purchase, New York.[45] Well before the Grand Central commission came along, then, Roth was Wolfson's architect, responsible for all of his buildings.[46]

ERWIN S. WOLFSON, BUILDER/REAL ESTATE DEVELOPER

Wolfson, owner of the Diesel Construction Company, was one of most highly respected, highly successful real estate investors and developers in Manhattan in the postwar era (figure 1.24).[47] Markedly different from the brash, high-flying Zeckendorf, Wolfson was a quiet, soft-spoken man known for his broad interests and remarkable erudition. Born in Cincinnati, the son of a successful manufacturer of men's clothing, he attended the University of Cincinnati, initially planning a major in engineering before turning to the liberal arts, with a major in philosophy and political science. After graduating in 1924, he went to Florida for a brief vacation, became involved in real estate, and at age twenty-two made a small fortune, then lost it all two years later, when Florida's land boom bubble burst. He moved to New York, where, through an uncle by marriage, he got a job as an assistant timekeeper on a skyscraper project with big-time realtor Abe Adelson of the Abenad Corporation.[48] Smart, personable, and hard-working, he rose in the company, becoming within the next eight years an officer and director; when his uncle died, and presumably left an inheritance, Wolfson bought out the other partners. Then in 1934, together with Saul Lautenberg, a former Adelson associate, he formed the Diesel Electric Corporation, which sold private generators to depression-hit manufacturers, saving them the cost of buying power from a utility company. Acting as general contractors, Diesel Electric took care of all aspects, structural as well as mechanical, involved in the installation of private power plants.[49] In 1937, as mortgage money opened up after the Depression, Wolfson and Lautenberg formed the Diesel Construction Company and began putting up their own buildings. After buying land and erecting on it two apartment buildings, they soon began getting contracts from other firms to do remodeling jobs. During the war, the company stayed alive through government contracts.[50] Then, after the war, as New York City moved into its postwar building boom, Diesel expanded, erecting a building at 24 West 58th Street for themselves, as well as numerous other office structures, movie, radio, and television studios, apartment buildings, laboratories, and other such specialty buildings. When Lautenberg died

FIGURE 1.24   Erwin Wolfson

in 1952, Wolfson bought Lautenberg's interest in Diesel from Lautenberg's estate. Under Wolfson, the company grew over the course of the decade to become one of the city's foremost general contracting firms, noted for its high standards of work, technical competence, and speed of execution.[51] By 1958 Wolfson was reputed to be responsible for more new office space since the end of the war than any other single investor-builder in the city. As part owner and manager of ten office buildings and two apartment houses all built since 1946, as well as general contractor for seven other office buildings, Wolfson had by then helped to build close to $300 million worth of Manhattan's new skyline. An active owner-builder as well as contractor, he was highly thought of by those in the profession, regarded as genuinely likable and a man of integrity who stood by his word.[52]

Respected as much for his business acumen as for his honesty, he was considered shrewd as well as fair. His experience as a builder as well as owner served him well in dealing with potential clients, as he knew what he was talking about rather than deriving it all secondhand. His experience as an owner was a decided plus, especially when Diesel Construction, responsible for all of Wolfson's own buildings, served as the general contractor on other jobs as well. He and Carl Morse, Wolfson's right-hand man to whom Wolfson turned over the presidency of Diesel Construction in 1957, would work over plans together as if they were for his own building; after estimating costs, they would then seek ways the investor could get a better building for the same money, or the same building for less.[53] As head of the Wolfson Management Corporation, the management arm of his investment-building operation, Wolfson also managed his own buildings. Relying on outside agents only for the initial renting process, once the building was rented, he no longer had use for the agents, and his management corporation took over.[54] As real estate investor, owner, builder, and manager, Wolfson was thus able to run a highly controlled, carefully orchestrated one-man show.

ZECKENDORF IN, WOLFSON OUT

In the early months of 1955, as the furor over the Grand Central Terminal continued, the Wolfson/Roth proposal was for all intents and purposes abandoned, as it became clear that Young was going ahead with Zeckendorf. In March, a month after the Roth scheme was published, the *New York Times* announced that the New York Central had named Zeckendorf, together with Roger L. Stevens, real estate developer and former owner of the Empire State Building, as real estate agents to act on its behalf in the development, sale, or lease of all its property in the Grand Central area.[55] This in effect eliminated Wolfson from the scene. No details on the unpublished Zeckendorf/Pei proposal were provided, nor was anything specific said about what the railroad had decided to do with the site of the terminal building. Describing Zeckendorf and Pei's proposal in only general terms as a skyscraper taller than the Empire State Building and consisting of 102 stories, with an 80-story office structure plus tall observation tower, costing, it was estimated, $100 million and housing 60,000 office workers, the *Times* noted the proposal had been criticized on the grounds that it would further congest traffic in the already crowded area. As Zeckendorf was now describing his aims in terms of "urban planning and redevelopment," it was believed he was planning to take a broader approach than that of simply adding a skyscraper. No further information from his office, however, was forthcoming.

One of Young's stated objectives when he had gained control of the railroad the previous June, according to the *Times,* was to use its properties, especially in the Grand Central area, to better financial advantage, and in announcing plans for developing the terminal the following September, Young was only following through on his promise. Under the railroad's franchise, it could not sell the land, which was now covered by scores of buildings in a complicated arrangement of long-term leases and ownership deals covering surface, subsurface, and air rights, but it could develop the air rights above it, which was evidently what Young was planning to do. Progress, however, was evidently being held up by the dispute between the New York Central and New York, New Haven and Hartford Railroads, currently in the state supreme court, over the New York Central's unilateral right to dispose of these properties.[56]

Reading in the *Times* of Young's decision to engage Zeckendorf as his real estate consultant, Haskell sent Pei a letter congratulating him for securing the Grand Central job. He reminded him of the conversation they had had in the fall, then added that though he disagreed with the decision to demolish the concourse, he was sure Pei would do everything possible "to achieve the monumental concept which alone would justify removing a monument," and wished him well.[57]

Galvanized by the *Times* article announcing Zeckendorf's engagement on the project, and noting too that Lewis Mumford had joined the fray with a series of articles in the *New Yorker* on the city's growing traffic problems that had focused on proposals for the Grand Central redevelopment, Haskell at that point proposed an all-out debate.[58] He suggested bringing in Mumford or perhaps the well-known urban planner Clarence Stein "on the matter of openness"; McGinnis, whom Haskell believed was more receptive than Young to aesthetic concerns; Meeks, who could speak to the building's history; and others, including Minoru Yamasaki, Eero Saarinen, and Pei. Although acknowledging that he himself was hardly disinterested, he had boned up on economic issues and felt he had a good sense of what was possible or not, given the financial factors involved. As far as his own stance was concerned, it was also clear: Unless someone was able to come up with "a veritable Taj Mahal of the 20th century," he would fight to have the terminal preserved.[59]

Haskell's editorial in the *Architectural Forum* the following month centered on the Grand Central. The problem, as the *Times* article indicated, was that the future of the Grand Central area was in the hands of the real estate promoters. Noting that it was a key site in the city, comparable to New York to what the Mall was to Washington, he maintained that any redevelopment should open up the area, to provide the city not only with dignity, but also with breathing space. Since the First World War, only a few commercial developments such as Rockefeller Center, he argued, had contributed to the cityscape by introducing light, openness, air, and the easing of traffic. Open space continued to be architecture's greatest luxury, but one the country was running out of. Acknowledging that public funds were not available to help solve the railroad's financial problem and that ultimately the solution had to be made in terms of profits to the railroad company's stockholders, he appealed to the developers to follow Vanderbilt's enlightened leadership and do what they could to preserve open space commensurate with a profit. He noted that the some two hundred architects from around the country had urged that the concourse be preserved but pointed out that other architects felt differently, and they should have a chance to show how a new concourse might be built that combined today's need for efficiency with the expressiveness of the old. "The burden of proof," he concluded, "will lie heavily upon them."[60]

THE PEI PROJECT

For whatever reason, the Pei project, though mentioned or alluded to in numerous articles over the course of several years, was never publicly released.[61] It appears to have been worked out with the help of Eduardo Catalano, a professor of architecture at MIT who was later to write a book on warped surfaces in thin-shell concrete and was considered at the time an expert on hyperbolic paraboloid structures.[62] Drawings from 1956 in the Pei Archives indicate that it was to have been a colossal hyperboloidal tower of 108 stories (heightened, thus, from the 80-story tower originally projected in the fall of 1954), with over three million square feet of space (downsized, thus, from the five million square feet of rentable office space in the earlier proposal), poised on an elevated, landscaped rectangular plaza with Park Avenue running both around and through it (figure 1.25). According to the project description included in the proposal, it was designed to allow the site of the Grand Central Terminal, a prominent city landmark, "to continue to be symbolic of New York's status as a leading city." The tower's hyperbolic design, according to the Pei office, was chosen primarily for aesthetic reasons, as it would draw worldwide publicity and thereby attract progressive, discerning tenants; but it would also result in a more economic building than the norm, as each floor had a different square footage, thereby offering prospective tenants a wide range of choice in the amount of rentable space. Of exposed steel members clad in aluminum, which presented a clear expression of modern building technology, the building was shaped to facilitate wind flow, according to Pei, and on the urban scale it was designed to improve the existing traffic situation, with a large arc around the site for a smoother traffic flow than the existing system of tight right-angled turns.[63]

Whether it was the mounting criticism in both public and professional realms, Zeckendorf's inability to work out the financing, Young's problems with corporate intrigue and the ongoing legal battle between the New York Central and New York, New Haven and Hartford Railroads, or the weakening economy in general, plans for redeveloping the Grand Central Terminal site were put on hold, and no progress was made on them for several years.[64] In the meantime, as traffic in the area continued to grow, the New York Transit Authority began exploring ways of easing congestion, proposing, among other things, seatless shuttle trains to accommodate more passengers and the staggering of employee work hours.[65] Simultaneously, in his capacity as realty consultant to the New York Central, Zeckendorf continued to recommend that it redevelop its Park Avenue holdings by replacing apartment buildings with yet more new high-rise office buildings.

FIGURE 1.25   Pei proposal

After lying fallow for several years, in January 1958, the idea of developing the Grand Central site was revived.[66] Unaware that the project had been abandoned, a large company had approached Stuart Scheftel, one of Wolfson's partners in his original 1954 proposal, wanting to rent space in the new building. As economic circumstances now seemed more favorable for going ahead with the project, Scheftel promptly contacted Young. Young was receptive and sent Scheftel to his real estate agent to begin negotiations. Two days later, ensconced in his Palm Beach mansion, Young shot himself, for reasons that were clouded, though it was clear that the railroad, whose earnings had declined sharply since 1955 and was running in the red, was suffering major financial losses.[67] The idea of reviving plans to develop the site persisted, however, and somehow convinced that Zeckendorf would not be able to derail it again, Scheftel contacted Wolfson. By May, they had come to an agreement with the New York Central to lease the land for eighty years at $1.1 million annually.[68]

"GRAND CENTRAL CITY"

The Roth proposal was revived in short order.[69] Announced on the front page of the *New York Times* in May 1958, the proposed building was for the most part the same as that Wolfson originally put forward in February 1955, and the article was illustrated with the same rendering that had been published three years earlier.[70] It was described as a fifty-story skyscraper (as opposed to the original sixty-five stories) that, when completed in 1961, would have a larger capacity than any commercial office building in existence, with a floor area of more than three million square feet, almost half again as much floor space as the Empire State Building and second only to the Pentagon in volume (though still less than the four to five million square feet envisioned in the original proposal). As before, it would rise over the existing railroad tracks and terminal platforms, replacing the six-story Grand Central Office Building behind the terminal. Its lobby would be at the level of the elevated ramp that currently carried Park Avenue traffic around the terminal, and a parking garage for 2,000 cars on four levels of the building would be included, as well as interior roadways and sidewalks designed to ease car and pedestrian traffic on Vanderbilt Avenue, which formed the western border of the site. Escalators would lead from the main concourse of the terminal to the lobby level of the new structure, forming a pedestrian walkway that would lead through the new building to 45th Street. The plans also called for three theaters and an exhibition area on the third floor, and an open-air restaurant on the roof of the seventh-floor setback on the north side of the building, as well as a heliport on the roof. The building was to be built by Wolfson, together with the Scheftels, and Burger, who had, according to the *Times,* signed an eighty-year lease on the site, with renewal options, which guaranteed the owners of the property, New York State Realty and Terminal Company, a subsidiary of the New York Central Railroad, a return of at least $1 million annually. The new building, designed by Emery Roth & Sons, was to be known as "Grand Central City" and would have simple exteriors of aluminum and glass, intended, according to the architects, to serve as a plain backdrop for the classical architecture of the old terminal.[71]

Several months later, a second *New York Times* article focused on Wolfson's shrewd new approach to leasing space in the new office building. Instead of hiring a rental agent to handle the leasing, which was the norm in Manhattan, Wolfson had retained a realty consulting firm to deal with prospective tenants and their real estate brokers. The firm, James D. Landauer Associates, Inc., was to negotiate directly with brokers and agents acting on behalf of prospective tenants on a fixed-fee basis, thus eliminating the usual brokers' commissions.[72] The building's size, as the biggest office building in Manhattan, as well as Wolfson's rental plan were only the first of a long list of records the building, eventually renamed the Pan Am, would set.

GROPIUS AND BELLUSCHI

At this point Gropius and Belluschi were brought in, with the idea of obtaining a "more aesthetic" design for the building. Why Wolfson thought it important, if indeed the idea came from him, is unclear. According to later accounts, Wolfson was "perhaps appalled" by the Roth proposal,[73] he felt something was lacking,[74] or his refined artistic taste and higher civic aims drove him to seek a higher standard; all of these explanations seem unlikely, however, as he had been perfectly happy with the Roths and their plainly pragmatic approach for his buildings before. Moreover, had he not been pleased with their proposal, it seems unlikely he would have published it, especially the second time around. More plausibly the desire to alter the building's design was due to the heat he was beginning to feel from critics like Haskell to do something more momentous, of clear distinction, on the historically critical site. It may also have been that as critics like Ada Louise Huxtable in the *New York Times* were deliberately focusing on arousing public awareness of what constituted a "quality" building, with examples such as the Lever House or Seagram Building, the Roths' work paled in comparison, raising questions in

Wolfson's mind about whether another Roth building would draw the kind of high-class tenants he was hoping—and financially needed—to attract.

ADA LOUISE HUXTABLE, THE TRANSFORMATION OF PARK AVENUE, AND "ROTHSCRAPERS"

Between the time of the Wolfson/Roth proposal in February 1955 and its revival in May 1958, a series of articles in the *New York Times* and elsewhere had focused attention on what was happening on Park Avenue and its rapid transformation from an old, gracious boulevard lined with elegant masonry hotels and apartment blocks into a commercial street defined by modern glass and metal skyscrapers, a great many of them by the Roth firm. Among the articles were two by Huxtable, the architectural critic of the *New York Times,* that had particular bearing on plans for the Grand Central.

Park Avenue, basically the creation of Commodore Vanderbilt of the New York Central Railroad and his vision of a "Grand Central City" with the terminal at its core, had played a major role in the life, culture, and history of the city ever since the 1920s. Begun as a "street of dreams," it was, by the postwar era, a street of tremendous change.[75] What began as surface-level railroad tracks in the 1830s had, with the sinking of the tracks and the electrification of the trains, then the street's reinvention under influence of City Beautiful ideals, by the 1920s become one of the most exclusive residential quarters in the city, a broad, landscaped boulevard lined by harmonious rows of gracious masonry apartment blocks, below which ran—quietly and smokelessly—the tracks of the New York Central and New York, New Haven and Hartford Railroads. During the Depression, however, rents had dropped, and rent control kept rents frozen at their low rates, even as land values and taxes rose astronomically after the war. Property owners, faced with fixed incomes and rising taxes, began selling. The only buyers available, however, were large-scale Manhattan builders such as the Tishmans, the Urises, and Wolfson, or private corporations such as Seagram or Lever, who had the means to purchase the high-priced land, demolish the rent-controlled structures, and build office buildings in their stead.[76] The first postwar office building to go up on the avenue was 445 Park Avenue, near 57th Street, built by the Tishman Realty and Construction Company with Kahn & Jacobs, architects. This was followed by a twenty-story office building designed by Emery Roth & Sons for the Uris brothers on the northeast corner of 59th Street, then the twenty-five-story Colgate-Palmolive Building, also by Emery Roth & Sons, at 300 Park Avenue between 49th and 50th Streets. The

Colgate-Palmolive, as an example, replaced the Sherry Building, a 1922 building that had consisted of large, eighteen-room apartments renting for $25,000 a year at their peak, but whose rents had dropped to $6,000 and $7,000, as well as six-room apartments whose rents had dropped from a peak of $8,000 to $3,500 or $4,000 per year. Representing an initial investment of land and building of $8.5 million in 1922, the Sherry Building and its land was worth only $3.5 million in 1951, which is what the Uris brothers paid for it. Within the next couple of years, Lever Brothers, Arabian American Oil, and Universal Pictures followed suit with new corporate headquarters buildings. The demand for office space, especially on Park Avenue, continued to grow, as contrary to expectations, existing corporations opted to remain in New York rather than moving to the suburbs, and other corporations moved in. By 1955, demolition was underway on the east side of Park Avenue between 52nd and 53rd Streets for the thirty-eight-story Seagram building; the old Marguery Hotel at 270 Park Avenue across the street was soon razed to make way for the Union Carbide Building.[77]

Continuous media coverage of the rapid transformation, typically illustrated with contrasting photos of old and new, kept the issue at the forefront of the public mind. "The Old-World grandeur of Park Avenue is fast disappearing," one such article began. "In its place has come an array of steel, bronze and glass towers as gleaming in their modernity as their predecessors were subdued in Victorian and Renaissance styles." The article documented the changes, most of which, it pointed out, had occurred within the last decade. Since the war, five massive office structures had been built along the twelve-block stretch of Park Avenue from 47th Street to the north. Two more buildings, for National Biscuit and Seagram, were underway, as were the Union Carbide Building, a building for Pepsi-Cola on the southwest corner of 59th, and the Astor Plaza project, which included a forty-six-story building between 53rd and 54th Streets. Still another was envisioned when the New York Central Railroad announced that 277 Park would be leased for the construction of yet another office skyscraper. The article predicted that with an "endless list of distinguished firms" demanding office space, within five years there would be no residential buildings left except hotels south of 59th Street to the Grand Central.[78]

Other articles pointed out how the city was losing a significant chunk of the city's past to this imposing array of new office skyscrapers.[79] One quoted Charles J. Mylod, president of the Goelet Estate Company, which owned the site on which the twenty-one-story Lever House stood, as saying it was the Lever House that set the pattern of shooting-up land values on the avenue; built in 1951, it was the first of the office buildings on Park to have glass facades and the first to forego use of its street frontage for anything except the building entrance and a small lobby. Since the Lever House, five other office buildings had been completed, with ten more on the way.[80] Still other articles pointed out the increasing number of corporations that were investing in Manhattan real estate by building their own buildings, among them Chase Manhattan, Union Carbide, Seagram, Corning Glass, and the Daily News, and of other new Park Avenue office buildings that were replacing apartment buildings, with land leased from New York Central.[81]

Most of these articles addressed the changes from the perspective of the real estate or business community, and their focus was on the factors, economic or political, that brought them about. Huxtable's concerns were different.

"The Park Avenue School of Architecture," published in December 1957, was Huxtable's first piece of architectural criticism to appear in the *New York Times*.[82] With it she set the tone for the rest of her journalism career, going beyond simply describing what new buildings were going up and what they looked like to point out their impact on the human environment. A New Yorker by birth trained first at Hunter College, then at the Institute of Fine Arts where she majored in art and architecture history, she, like Haskell, who had also been trained in the fine arts, expanded her scope well beyond that of the usual art critic. Like Haskell, she broached her subject broadly, focusing on the aesthetic issues of architecture but relating them always to the social, political, and economic factors at play. She was also acutely aware of her responsibility as well as her power as a critic writing for the general public, establishing as a primary objective educating and arousing public awareness in matters of art. Never hesitant to voice her own opinion, she nonetheless strove to provide a balanced view, typically weighing the multiplicity of factors that figure into the making of a building or place. Her thinking was clear-headed, her writing lucid and incisive. The wife of an industrial designer, Huxtable also had an insider's view of the closed professional architectural community, was thus affiliated with but not loyal to the professional architectural community, and was exceptionally knowledgeable in the ways of professional practice. Moreover, she lived on Park Avenue, in one of those old, gracious apartments then being torn down.

"The Park Avenue School of Architecture" was precisely targeted. Long, penetrating, replete with implication as well as sheer information, it assumed an informed but uncondescending approach comprehensible to the layman combined with a sharply critical tone geared primarily to the profession. It praised the sleek new modern steel and glass corporate towers still foreign to the public that were transforming Park Avenue, the speculative buildings and giant corporations whose names "read like who's who of American Industry: soap, whisky, chemicals." Huxtable explained what modernism was all about, why it was significant, how the curtain wall worked, and why it was so revolutionary; at the same time she called attention to the impact of the spate of new buildings on the urban scene as a whole and to the vast changes on the avenue, not all of them good. She pointed out the factors driving the change and the goals of the architects and developers involved and noted the largely negative public reaction and the need for education to enable the public to appreciate, accept, and distinguish between them what was bad or good. Among the new buildings she singled out were the Lever House, the Union Carbide Building, the Colgate-Palmolive Building, the Seagram Building, and the Pepsi-Cola Building, many of them designed by leading architects, such as Mies van der Rohe, Philip Johnson, and Skidmore, Owings & Merrill (SOM). Though some of the new buildings were elegant, most were not, but were mediocre and unimaginative, relying on a few inadequate commercial formulas. Unsparing in her words, Huxtable placed the responsibility for the uneven quality of their design squarely on the shoulders of their architects. All too often, she noted, architects blamed extrinsic factors such as zoning regulations for their monotony. This was unjustified, she contended. Buildings that were monotonous were so not because of zoning regulations but because of lack of imagination or talent on the part of the architect. Only he (in those days, still on the eve of the modern feminist movement), she said, could save us from monotony.

Addressing its revolutionary role, she pointed out the contribution to and legacy of the new Park Avenue architecture, in the broader, historical perspective, to architectural history, and the significance of the new style that had become a symbol of American business success. A former assistant curator in design and architecture at the Museum of Modern Art (MoMA), Huxtable was a staunch proponent of modernism, which represented, at its best, the path of progress; at the same time, she had a deep respect for the past. The old Park Avenue, she wrote, was "being buried with ruthless efficiency. Today we don't just bury the past, we destroy it. Monuments and memories are demolished with the same cheerful, irrelevant violence."

Another popular excuse among architects for the blandness of their designs was the necessity of cutting costs. Huxtable pointed out that successful buildings could be designed on limited budgets. Zoning, budgets, and the like were easy excuses that skirted around the basic issue: the free, creative choice that every architect must exercise within the specific limitations that vary with the job. By reneging on their design responsibility, she pointed out, architects encouraged ignorance of design standards among the lay public, which led in turn to a lack of judgment and the inability to differentiate between good and bad. This resulted inevitably in the loss of public standards, the lowering of professional standards, and the commissioning of pretentious, inferior buildings.

It was on the basis of the architect's personal, calculated choices of visual relationships, and the integration of aesthetics with structure and function, that these new Park Avenue buildings—and their architects—should be judged, she contended. Unfortunately, too few architects of the day accepted these responsibilities, she noted. Nonetheless, for those interested in the quality of the city's architecture—and architecture *was* the city—the fact remained that a building was usually only as good as its designer, who in turn was dependent on an enlightened or open-minded client.

Because we live in a society in which practical men of affairs distrust art and consider scientific efficiency the ultimate good, Huxtable continued, it had become "a simple, profitable and aesthetically disastrous process to discount the artist-architect and reduce the art of architecture to a commercial operation." The result was a growing series of sizable, superficially impressive, second-rate copies of less-than-first-rate buildings. Most of those could not be called architecture, if one understood that to mean one of the major arts, since their appearance was largely the result of accident, expediency, and economics, rather than aesthetics, and were buildings economically "styled" rather than architecturally designed. Despite the disproportionate number of poor buildings, however, there was much to be said for the new architecture on Park Avenue, Huxtable conceded. Its elegant simplicity was bringing order out of chaos; at the same time, its design drew on and acknowledged sources in contemporary technology. Unprecedented dramatic effects of reflected sun and shadow on flat, vitreous facades were adding a brilliant, if unexpected, beauty to the city scene. New York's new buildings signaled, she concluded presciently, "one of the most important structural and stylistic changes in the history of architectural design."[83]

Huxtable's essay, which followed on the heels of Richard Roth's "High-Rise Down to Earth," published in the *Progressive Architecture* six months earlier and which undoubtedly served as fodder for her essay, was illustrated by photographs of the new buildings on Park Avenue, looking south toward the 1929 New York Central Building (figure 1.26). Focusing on this dramatic vista, Huxtable's article pointed out again the importance of quality buildings and the particular significance of the Grand Central site. What Haskell had done in the professional pages of the *Forum,* Huxtable now did in the *public* arena, challenging the promoters of the Grand Central project and placing the onus for the design of a good building squarely on the architect and his client's shoulders.[84]

It was an article Wolfson could hardly have missed. Focused on the avenue, on his site, and less overtly on his architect, whose lack of imagination and devotion to the bottom line at the expense of aesthetics was well-known, as well as on his own past record of indifference to quality, it underscored how much there was at stake.

The stakes were indeed high. The financial risks were huge. Zeckendorf had already backed out, and to make the project fly at all meant attracting high-end tenants who, as Zeckendorf's success with Pei was proving, were increasingly aware of design issues. In light of this, Huxtable's message would have been hard for Wolfson to ignore.

The following May, just as Wolfson and his associates were drawing up their lease with the New York Central for the site, Huxtable came out in the *New York Times* with another hard-hitting essay. To see the significance of her article calls for some context. The discipline of architectural criticism, which had flourished in the early part of the century, had waned in conjunction with historicism as modernism moved in, undermining traditional classical values without replacing them with anything new, other than perhaps newness itself. As architectural criticism began to revive in the late 1950s, Huxtable played a pivotal role in its resurgence.[85] In "The Art We Cannot Afford to Ignore (but Do)," she pointed out the need for greater public awareness of and press attention to the art of architecture and stressed the need both for astute architectural criticism and for a solid visual training in early education.[86] In the postwar years, she noted, the country had grown more "culturally consciousness," but most of the focus was on paintings and sculpture, with architecture a forgotten art. Buildings continued to be built, but the public had become indifferent to them, which made no sense, as unlike other arts, architecture can't be tuned out. As she put it, there "is nothing optional about our presence at the performance of architecture: the architect has a captive au-

FIGURE 1.26   Park Avenue looking south

dience." She described architecture's subtle psychological effects, generating instinctive emotional reactions and conveying a sense of tranquility or discomfort even to viewers unaware of them. And since substandard rather than superior architecture was becoming the norm, this "under-the-skin perception" was an important factor in generating the twentieth century's notorious tensions. Huxtable was alluding to the increasing awareness among scholars in the social sciences (such as David Riesman's *The Lonely Crowd* [1950] and William Barrett's *Irrational Man* [1958]) of the sense of fragmentation and anxiety beneath the optimism and apparent tranquility of society in the 1950s, an underlying malaise caught by poets such as Ginsberg in "Howl."[87]

The ability of architecture to soothe or distress, and the ability of subtle irritations to affect production and morale, were increasingly recognized, especially by business. Pointing out the undeniable psychological impact of all architecture, mediocre as well as great, Huxtable singled out the speculative builder. Even he knew the value of art. Again, she pointed out that it was the responsibility of the architect to amend this; as practical man, he had to provide shelter, but as an artist, he had to serve a need almost as basic: the desire for beauty. The press too bore a responsibility. While regularly reviewing art, music, theater, and dance, it ignored architecture, and as a standard feature in newspapers, architectural criticism was virtually unknown. Her point was clear: Higher architectural standards were imperative. "To see clearly," she said, "is to become aware; awareness awakens interest; interest creates concern. Concern will inevitably lead to increasing critical evaluation of our environment and to the demand for higher architectural standards. Only then will the $70 billion worth of building predicted for 1958 hold any hope of a brave new world."[88]

Several weeks later, in June 1958, after meeting with Roth, Wolfson was on the line to Walter Gropius.

By the time Wolfson revived the Grand Central City project in the spring of 1958, the Roths' reputation in architectural circles was widespread. Ever since Jacobs had published her article in the *Forum* on the current office boom, citing the number of dull new office buildings going up in Manhattan, the majority of them by the Roth firm, questions about their uninspired, formulaic work had become more frequent.[89] Huxtable's two articles in the *New York Times* drove home the point. Favored by a "virtual club of builders,"[90] the Roths' plain, utilitarian buildings were beginning to dominate the city. As they continued to build "in staggering numbers" their standardized, site-filling, glass and metal high-rise office and apartment buildings all over midtown Manhattan and the downtown financial district, demolishing older structures and replacing them with second-rate Miesian derivatives, Rothscraping and the Roth name became well known, synonymous in the public eye with banal buildings geared solely toward profits.

Given the increasingly *public* awareness of the critical nature of the site, the importance of a reputable architect, and the magnitude of the economic factors at stake, it was a small wonder that Wolfson had second thoughts about going with the Roth firm as initially planned. To blunt further criticism as well as enhance his chances of securing financing for the huge project, Wolfson needed a highly respected design architect, preferably one with a big name, who could provide him with a "prestige" building that would "sell better to the money people."[91] As Richard Roth was a close personal friend as well as long-standing business partner whose professional efficiency and economy Wolfson valued, he proposed their bringing in an "artist-architect" to work with the Roth firm as a design consultant. Understandably reluctant, Roth drew up a list of "leading architects," among whom were Gropius, former head of architecture at Harvard, and Belluschi, dean of architecture and urban planning at MIT, whose titles (if not names) caught Wolfson's eye.[92] Gropius and Belluschi were heavyweights indeed, as not only were they prominent architects, but academics, so their reputations would impress the business community as well as the academic and professional crowd. Wolfson also believed that as academics, they would likely be preoccupied with other affairs, and hence not stay closely involved. The hope was that the two leading modernists would "simply lend their name to the project and then disappear back into the world of academia."[93] That it was their reputations more than their design talent that mattered is suggested by the fact that Wolfson did not ask to see or make a point of visiting any of their prior buildings.

According to notes Gropius made of his initial meeting with Wolfson in June, at which time he was introduced to Roth and shown the Roth model, he was also shown the list of potential design consultants, which included José Luis Sert, who had succeeded him at Harvard, Gordon Bunshaft, Edward Durell Stone, and Belluschi. It was evidently Gropius who at this point suggested bringing in one other consultant and recommended Belluschi, with whom he had previously worked. Wolfson agreed, and Belluschi was asked to join them.[94]

Several days later, on June 25, Gropius and Belluschi drew up a letter to Wolfson specifying their terms.[95] Belluschi had, by this time, acquired years of experience in professional practice, having managed his own highly successful firm in Portland, Oregon, before coming to MIT, and since then, serving as design consultant on a number of commercial projects, many of them large-scale.[96] An astute businessman as well as highly respected design architect, he knew what to expect, what to demand, and what to be wary of, and he made this explicit in their letter. Stating that they would be happy to consider furnishing consulting services for the Grand Central City project, they suggested as compensation that each receive a flat fee to be paid in three installments, a per hour payment, plus monthly compensation for all personnel of the consultants, plus 100 percent overhead. All travel and hotel expenses made necessary by the project were also to be fully reimbursed.

Well aware too, by this time, of the pitfalls as well as potential of the design consultant role working with associate architects typically on their terrain, Belluschi was cognizant of the kinds of problems they were likely to encounter, especially with headstrong firms used to calling their own shots, as well as the Roth reputation for undistinguished buildings. Wary of tarnishing their own reputations by such an association, he was explicit about who was to be in charge of design. Gropius, as head of The Architects Collaborative (TAC) and equipped with an office as Belluschi was not, was to have the final word on design, as in their words (most likely Belluschi's) it had "been proven good business practice to have the design decision made by one person as the coordinator." Knowing that the occasion might arise in which the client or his architect Roth would make a decision compromising the design in their eyes, they reserved the right to request that their names be withdrawn from any credit or any notification of participation in the design of the project and in so doing would waive a portion of their fee.[97]

Two weeks later, they received a letter confirming the agreement.[98] In agreeing to their terms, Wolfson set out his own expectations within a stringent timetable: that the first stage of their work include a complete analysis of the problems involved and a solution to these problems "within the economic scope of the project," so that by the end of the first stage they would have a satisfactory schematic and have determined the bulk and appearance of the project as well as a tentative selection of materials to be used for the exterior. If the project went no further, Wolfson would have no commitment to them other than the first-stage payments. If the job proceeded into the second and third stages, compensation would be as specified by Gropius and Belluschi in their June 25 letter. The first stage, Wolfson's letter stated, was to start immediately and be completed by December 1, 1958.[99] This gave the designers a little over four months to come up with a schematic design, after which it was hoped and expected, at least by the Roth office, that their participation in the project would drop off sharply.[100]

A press release issued several weeks later began with the big names: "Two of the world's most distinguished architects will collaborate in the design of the world's largest commercial office building." In words that later surely came back to haunt them, the press release continued, "Manhattan's world famous skyline will receive the touch of acknowledged masters in the panel of eminent architects who are collaborating." Gropius, "internationally renowned as founder of the modern school of architecture," and Belluschi, Dean of the School of Architecture at MIT, had been commissioned to serve with Richard Roth, partner of Emery Roth & Sons, architect of the new building, on a three-man "advisory panel" to design the new Grand Central City, a fifty-story, 3,000,000-square-foot office structure adjoining the Grand Central Terminal, at a projected cost of $100 million. "With this appointment, Drs. Gropius and Belluschi will, for the first time, lend their genius to the design of a Manhattan skyscraper."[101]

Expanding on the long, illustrious, international backgrounds of the two men, the press release noted that Gropius had first attracted worldwide attention in 1925 when he designed and became director of the Bauhaus in Dessau, the model of "functional architecture" today. It cited his honors, among them the Gold Medal at the 1913 Ghent World Exhibition, the Gold Medal of Honor of the Architectural League of New York, the Royal Gold Medal of the Royal Institute of British Architects (RIBA), the Grand Prix International d'Architecture and the Grand Cross of Merit with Star, presented by the Federal Republic of Germany. It noted that he had been the subject of numerous articles in

magazines and newspapers both in this country and abroad and cited among his designs in the United States the Harvard Graduate Center in Cambridge, Massachusetts.
He was also the founder and senior partner of TAC, Cambridge, Massachusetts.

About Belluschi, the press release was equally effusive, pointing out that Belluschi,
"one of United States' foremost exponents of contemporary design," had been responsible for more than six hundred commercial and residential structures in the previous thirty years, consultant to the secretary of the Air Force on the new Air Force
Academy in Colorado Springs, and a member of the board of consultants for the Lincoln
Center for the Performing Arts in New York City, as well as a member of the seven-man
National Commission of Fine Arts appointed by President Harry S. Truman. In addition
to numerous other awards, it cited his titles: academician of the National Academy of
Design, fellow of the Danish Royal Academy of Fine Arts, trustee of the American Fed-
eration of Arts, allied member of the National Sculpture Society, and life member of the
National Institute of Arts and Letters. Both he and Gropius were Fellows of the AIA and
the American Academy of Arts and Sciences.[102]

Two more illustrious men would have been hard to find at the time. Both were prominent modernist architects whose names were known both within and without the profession, internationally as well as nationally. In looking for a famous, respected
architect, Wolfson got far more than he could ever have hoped for. Ironically, in a
sense—a critical sense—he also got far less.

The press release, accompanied by the resumés and photographs of the two men,
was sent to all the major daily newspapers in the area. It appeared in the *New York
Times* the next day, and in a more expanded version the following Sunday.[103]

The news item as it appeared in the *Architectural Forum* that September was somewhat more penetrating.[104] "To make the world's largest commercial office building 'the
best building in the world,'" it said, New York builder Erwin Wolfson had decided to en-
list the services of "the best architects obtainable" to serve with Richard Roth as architects for the new Grand Central City building. Noting that an earlier announcement in
June had cited only the Roth office as architect, it pointed out that the new building
would "mark the Manhattan debut of both Gropius and Belluschi, as well as Gropius's
first skyscraper," and that while some changes were expected to be made in the preliminary plans initially issued by the Roth office, no change would be made in the building's total size. The previous month, the *Forum* said, all three members "of this unusual
architectural trio" had fended off questions about ultimate design features as prema-
ture, and at a press conference Gropius had told reporters that thus far he and Belluschi

had had only time to look over the site to get an idea on how the building "might fit into the urbanistic whole."

Two months later, the *Forum* published another, fuller account of the new Gropius/Belluschi project.[105] Recalling that earlier that year, in May 1958, Wolfson had announced plans for a fifty-story, $100 million office tower "smack on top" of the train platforms of the Grand Central Terminal, a building that was to house some 25,000 office workers, with restaurants, theaters, and parking space for 2,000 cars, and to provide three million square feet of floor space, easily surpassing Manhattan's two biggest office towers, the RCA and Empire State buildings, all "plunked down on New York's most strategically central site in what would be the biggest commercial office building in the world," the *Forum* reminded readers of earlier schemes for the Grand Central site, including Zeckendorf's proposal to tear down the "magnificent 1913 terminal" in favor of "a glassy blockbuster 80 stories high, complete with sidewalks in the sky and helicopters blithely landing 1,000 feet up," and noted that Wolfson's scheme at least had the virtue of preserving the terminal, siting the tower behind it.

Describing Wolfson, the fifty-six-year-old chairman and principal owner of Diesel Construction Company, reputed to be responsible for more new office space than any other single developer in the city, the *Forum* article said that the Grand Central City project was by far his most ambitious and cited the formidable combination of problems he faced as a builder: finding tenants, then securing mortgage money, then, once committed, carrying the whole huge project out.

Over and beyond the normal real estate problems, which were enormous in this case, Wolfson also faced formidable structural problems in building the tower over the two layers of subterranean tracks without disrupting the arrival and departure of some five hundred trains daily, which could add $4 to $5 million to the cost of foundations. Complicating matters still further, the *Forum* continued, Wolfson sought aesthetic as well as economic success, aiming at "a truly significant piece of civic architecture." Wolfson in the past, like other speculative builders in Manhattan, had produced ordinary structures; this time, however, in bringing in the two academics, he sought "first-rate advice." Why aesthetic factors were suddenly important to Wolfson, who had expressed no interest in them before, was not discussed, but given the growing interest in "quality" buildings and the concern about the rapid growth in the number of mediocre ones, especially by firms such as Emery Roth & Sons, Wolfson must have seen the handwriting on the wall. Although *Forum* implied that in seeking "a truly significant piece of civic architecture," Wolfson was motivated by altruistic concerns, more pragmatic factors likely prevailed, as a prestige building designed by well-known "star architects" would attract the kind of high-toned tenants he needed to secure the funds required to finance the enormous project.[106]

WALTER GROPIUS

Gropius's (figure 1.27) reputation was by this time well established. Known throughout the world as the founder and director of the Bauhaus and respected as one of the leading spokesmen for the Modern Movement, he was considered one of the top men in the architectural profession. His reputation had soared after he moved to the United States in 1937 and became chairman of the department of architecture at Harvard; it remained high throughout his tenure at Harvard until he left in 1953 to open his own office, The Architects Collaborative, with a group of former students in Cambridge. His reputation was as solid in the public eye as in the profession, perceived as he was by the public and profession alike as one the top architects in the field.[107] In May 1957, a year prior to the announcement of his engagement on the Grand Central City project, Gropius was acknowledged in the *New York Times* for having been awarded the prestigious Hanseatic Goethe Prize.[108] He was featured in a *Time* article several months later as a leading figure in modernism known for his steel and glass functionalism who had been appointed by the State Department to design one of its overseas embassies, the new U.S. Embassy building in Athens, designed "to express U.S. democracy."[109] Another article in *Life,* again geared to the general public, described his critical role in the growth of modern architecture and "the continuing vitality of the famous Bauhaus style developed in Germany more than 30 years ago.[110] Attesting to his growing international stature, that same year, the government of Iraq awarded TAC the contract to design the new University of Baghdad, with Gropius in charge of the entire project, from the master plan to the design of individual buildings.[111] For all of his experience, however, Gropius had never designed a tall office building, and ever since his 1922 Chicago Tribune Competition project with Adolf Meyer (figure 1.28), he had coveted the chance to do so.[112]

In May 1958, a month prior to Wolfson's contacting Gropius about the Grand Central project, Haskell had written an editorial in *Architectural Forum* celebrating Gropius, "master architect and master teacher," on his seventy-fifth birthday.[113] Emphasizing the artistic, humanistic side of Gropius in an attempt to counter the entrenched, commonly held view of the modernist as a proponent of machine-driven "functionalism,"

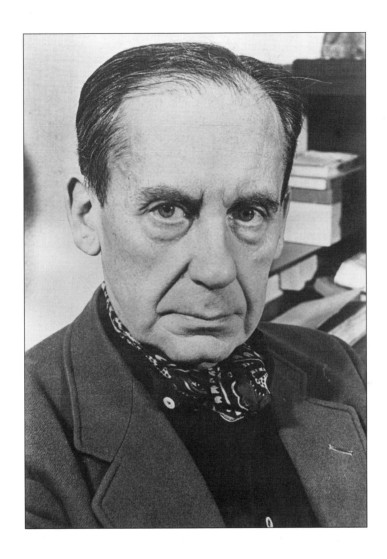

FIGURE 1.27   Walter Gropius

FIGURE 1.28   Gropius, Chicago Tribune Competition entry, 1922

Haskell reminded readers that Gropius had grown up in an age when art and the machine were polarized, and that his role in the 1920s had been revolutionary in uniting the two. As democratic institutions had spread throughout the world, the public had become responsible for decisions hitherto made by an elite, Gropius had said, which created problems for the artist; as untrained as the public was in the visual arts, it was unprepared to make sound aesthetic judgments. In an age governed by mechanization, the public also lacked an understanding of symbolism, of the poetic meaning conveyed in the arts. Providing this understanding, Haskell maintained, was what Gropius saw as the task of "Apollo in the democracy" and the challenge of the artist in the modern world. Drawing upon his intuitive abilities and his independence, it was up to the artist to create an "antidote to overmechanization," and a symbolic expression in terms comprehensible to the public of the experiences of the industrial age. Far from promulgating the doctrine that only machine-like forms were "modern," Haskell pointed out Gropius and his colleagues sought that broad visual training and collective effort that would let all modern artifacts, "from teacup to city," be expressive of the modern age. Coupled with this was his opposition to the notion that art should be confined to a cultured elite, as he believed artistic beauty was an essential part of life in general and should not be the privilege only of the aesthetically initiated. This, Haskell concluded, was still a noble aim.

Gropius's views on the role of art in an industrialized age were brought to still broader public attention when the *Saturday Evening Post* published his essay "The Curse of Conformity, the Problem of Architecture in the Assembly-line Age," that fall. American mastery of technology was the envy of the world, but the American way of life was not, Gropius declared in his typically long-winded, broadly philosophical, discursive style. It lacked culture, an appreciation of aesthetic quality. America's economic abundance and civic freedoms were laudable, but not enough, and the introduction of mechanization had only produced confusion. The failure, he believed, was one of leadership in the arts, and of an educational system that focused on technical and scientific skills at the expense of aesthetics. The general level of visual education in society needed to be raised to the point at which the artist was recognized as the prophet and leader he was and respected for his search for an artistic expression of society's aims and ideals. "By virtue of his ability to give visible symbols to significant order," Gropius said, "the artist may once again become society's seer and mentor, and as custodian of its conscience solve the American paradox."[114] Published in fall of 1958, just months after it had been announced that he had been given the opportunity to create just such a visible symbol, to become an "Apollo in the democracy," and to revive the role of the artist as society's seer and mentor with the biggest commercial building on one of the most prominent sites in the world, Gropius's statement was loaded.

In hiring Gropius to lend his name to the Grand Central City project, Wolfson had no way of knowing what he would be getting for his money. Six months after their involvement was announced and while the two famous design consultants were hammering out their design, the *New York Times* announced that Gropius was to be awarded the 1959 AIA Gold Medal, highest honor the professional organization bestowed.[115] *Time* followed with its feature article on Gropius.[116] Referring to Gropius as the high priest of the famed Bauhaus school in Dessau, "acknowledged shrine of modern architecture," it described its "boxy building with flat roofs and ribbon-glass windows" and "concrete, steel and glass functionalism," which had laid down the line architecture was to follow for the next three decades. An exile from Hitler's Germany, Gropius had introduced his methods as chair of Harvard's department of architecture and revolutionized architecture in the United States. At age 76, *Time* continued, seven years after leaving Harvard, the "old Lawgiver" had had a new burst of creativity and was showing an unexpected flexibility in design. Now working with TAC, a group of younger architects, Gropius had all the commissions he could handle, including Grand Central City, a $100 million structure now described as having fifty-five stories (the exact number tended to change but also depended on how the stories were counted) adjacent to the Grand Central Station. "I've been 'nobody's baby' during just those years of middle life which normally bring a man to the apex of his career," *Time* quoted Gropius as saying at the AIA award ceremony. "My various roles as architectural revolutionary, political persona non grata with Hitler, enemy alien here during the war and—most suspect of all—university egghead, did not help my prospects as a practicing architect much, and so I stand before you as a man who has just begun—after a long teaching interlude—to pick up an architectural career he left behind in Germany 25 years ago." Gropius concluded portentously, "We stand at a moment in history that calls for a bold, imaginative inter-pretation of the democratic idea."[117] Again, Gropius's words served only to focus at-tention on the momentousness of the occasion and the extraordinary opportunity he'd been offered to embrace the challenge that lay ahead.

THE ARCHITECTS COLLABORATIVE

The Architects Collaborative had by this time been in existence for over a decade. Founded in early 1946, it was an association Gropius had formed with a group of seven architects a generation younger, many of whom were former students or associates at Harvard. Based on principles Gropius had formulated and refined over the course of over twenty years, its governing rule was a collaborative approach to design that Gropius had initiated at the Bauhaus, then brought to the Harvard Graduate School of Design in the late 1930s.[118] As members of the office recounted later, TAC saw archi-tecture as a response to broad social forces, not as personal artistic expression, a re-sponse shaped by the most advanced technology available that nonetheless prioritized the human element. Its organization revolved around teamwork, with regular weekly meetings during which various options, plans, drawings, and materials were repre-sented by the person in charge and discussed by the group as a whole; the project leader, in the end, had the final say and was free to accept or reject suggestions by the group, as the belief was that to maintain the integrity of original conception, one person should have the final authority.[119] Rather than ambition or ego driving the individual designer, TAC endorsed service and restraint in the interest of the common good. Rather than focusing on the single building, it saw as its field of action the whole built environment and believed buildings should be an integral part of the context, rather than a novel, artistic statement that stood apart. Prefabrication was essential, but in TAC's eyes this meant relying on an array of standardized interchangeable parts, not uniformity: what Gropius called a wholesome variety within a limited vocabulary. Art was also an important component, one that worked best when the painters and sculp-tors were involved in the early, conceptual stage of design, rather than brought in as an afterthought, in the interest of a unified, organic whole.

Operating as team of designers rather than a partnership of specialists, TAC had no in-house structural or mechanical engineering departments, and consulted with outside firms for this on a job-to-job basis. Salaries and profits were spread equally, as equality was considered to be the basis of TAC teamwork. Even fees for outside work, such as teaching, were generally considered to be income of the firm. Although the use of modern technology was essential, the psychological dimensions of a work, according to Gropius, took priority. Good design was both a science and an art; as a science it analyzed the pertinent facts; as an art, according to Gropius, it "sublimates human activities into a cultural synthesis."[120]

The concept of teamwork was at the core of the organization, a give and take, as Gropius put it, among of a group of equals. The conception of the architect as a self-sufficient operator who, with the help of a good staff and competent engineers, could solve any problem, was isolationist in character, Gropius believed, and ran counter to "Total Architecture."[121] Recognizing, however, that the creative spark always originated with the individual, he believed it could be shaped, be made "more mature," and broadened by the participation of others. Sarah Harkness, one of the two women in TAC (both wives of other TAC members), summed it up succinctly: competition or collaboration. Competition was wasteful, with an overlap of time and energy; the collaborative approach was efficient, with an interaction of collective forces aimed at a single appropriate solution.[122]

PIETRO BELLUSCHI

Belluschi (figure 1.29) was an architect radically different in nature, used to flying solo. A quiet, soft-spoken man, he was in fact fiercely ambitious, and underneath the modest demeanor was a driving ego. Gropius's depiction of the lone architect, the "self-sufficient operator with the help of a good staff and competent engineers," perfectly described Belluschi, who rarely acknowledged the participation of others in his work prior to his closing his office in Portland, Oregon, and moving east. His whole approach to design was hierarchical, his Portland office highly stratified and staffed by skilled architects who worked for him under his supervision, with him firmly in control.[123]

Like Gropius, he too was an émigré. Born in Ancona, Italy, in 1899, a decade later than Gropius, Belluschi came to the United States in 1923 on a grant for a year of architecture study at Cornell. Though highly intelligent, he had been an indifferent student, and facing the draft during World War I, he enlisted, fighting in the war, as did Gropius, on the opposite side. After the war, he enrolled at the University of Rome, from which he received a degree in engineering, and was about to join his father and uncle in their construction business when the opportunity arose to study in the United States. After completing a year of architecture at Cornell, instead of returning to Italy, then in an

FIGURE 1.29   Pietro Belluschi

economic slump and increasingly succumbing to Benito Mussolini's autocratic control, he stayed in the States, ending up in Portland and working in the office of A. E. Doyle, one of the most highly respected, successful offices in the region at the time. A skilled draftsman with a first-hand knowledge of the refined, classical, Italianate buildings for which the Doyle office was famous, he rose quickly in the ranks, and after Doyle died in 1927, took over the office, changing its name to Pietro Belluschi, Architect, in 1943. Unlike most architectural firms at the time, Belluschi's flourished during World War II with a series of war-related government contracts, and when peace was declared, the office was poised and ready to meet the demand for buildings held up first by the Depression, then by the war. By the 1940s, Belluschi had gained a national reputation for his simple, regional but elegant, modern houses and churches, mostly of wood. After the war, his fame as a modernist spread internationally with the completion in 1948 of the sleek, startlingly progressive, glass-and-aluminum-skinned Equitable Building in Portland (figure 1.30). A graceful, eloquent writer as well as speaker, Belluschi was a well-known figure in the architectural profession, and by the late 1940s, one of the most highly respected architects in the field. In 1950, MIT invited him to become dean of the School of Architecture and Urban Planning. He left his office, by this time one of the most lucrative in the Portland area, but not the practice of architecture, and continued to design in the then-pioneering role of design consultant in association with an established, usually local firm. The association freed him from the costs and responsibilities of running an office and allowed him to focus his efforts solely on design as the "design architect." He continued practicing in this capacity throughout the rest of his career.

Thus when Gropius broached the subject of collaborating on the Grand Central City project, Belluschi was well prepared for the job. He was by this time experienced not only in running a firm, but also as a design consultant, and was skilled in dealing with corporate clients as well as designing tall office buildings, as Gropius was not.

Moreover, the two had worked together on the Boston Back Bay Center project, a large-scale commercial complex of office buildings, shopping center, hotel, and convention hall on twenty-eight acres of the by-then obsolete Boston and Albany Railroad yard in the middle of Boston for the New York developer Roger L. Stevens (figure 1.31).[124] The project did not go ahead for financial reasons, but in working together on it, Belluschi and Gropius had developed a comfortable working relationship based on mutual respect, with most of the drafting and designing done in the TAC office and the articulate Belluschi serving as spokesman for the team.

FIGURE 1.30   Belluschi's Equitable Building, 1943–1948

FIGURE 1.31   Boston Back Bay Center project

But they had fundamental differences. Belluschi was used to running a one-man show and calling the shots, especially in matters of design.[125] A man of highly refined tastes, he prided himself on being part of the "cultural elite," above the norm, and respected for his discerning eye and discriminating tastes. Unlike Gropius, who had led a revolution, Belluschi was not a fighter. Used to running things his own way, when things went awry, he tended simply to withdraw and focus his efforts elsewhere.[126] He also tended to yield or adapt, conciliatory rather than confrontational in manner. Endowed with a shrewd, pragmatic business sense, he was wholly uninterested in theory, nor was he, despite his MIT appointment, an educator.

Belluschi was also from the West Coast. Although clearly a modernist, he was not an orthodox, European modernist in the Bauhaus tradition. Known as a regional modernist, he was among that group of architects whom Saarinen described as revering nature and the use of natural materials, open plans, and handcrafted architecture, humanistic in approach—the antithesis of Gropius's more abstract, philosophical, machine-age approach, which celebrated industrial materials and processes.[127]

Unlike Gropius, who was known more as an educator than as a designer, Belluschi was a true designer, with a good eye for color, materials, and detailing, as well as scale, proportion, and the sculpting of three-dimensional space. He could also draw, as Gropius could not,[128] as adept at quick freehand sketches as he was at more exacting measured drawings. Recognized widely as a man of artistic talent, Belluschi understood the art of architecture in the broadest sense.

Like Gropius, by 1958 Belluschi had a long list of honors and honorary degrees. In 1950, on the eve of his departure for MIT, he was awarded an honorary LL.D. degree from Reed College.[129] In 1957, he delivered the keynote address at the AIA centennial convention in Washington, D.C. and was subsequently proposed as a candidate for the presidency of the AIA.[130] In 1958, *Architectural Forum* awarded him, together with Henry R. Shepley and Ralph T. Walker, a special citation for their contribution to the State Department's overseas building program, the first such awards offered by the *Forum* in its sixty-six-year history.[131] Appointed to the National Commission of Fine Arts by President Truman in 1950, an advisor to the State Department on the design of foreign buildings, an associate of the National Academy of Design, a trustee of the American Federation of Arts, past president of the board of trustees of the Portland Art Museum, life member of the National Institute of Arts and Letters, he was, by the late 1950s, one of the foremost architects in the profession.

He was also involved as chief designer or planner in number of projects at the time. In addition to several churches and synagogues in New England, there was the Bennington College Library, the Baltimore Civic Center, and the Lincoln Center, where he was responsible for the Juilliard School design.[132]

Among the many, many speeches Belluschi was asked to deliver as dean at MIT, one of the most significant, in the context of the Pan Am, was the talk he gave at Reed College on the eve of moving to the East Coast. He began with customary modesty, regarding the award he was receiving as recognition less of his own merits than of the ideas for which many architects of his generation had fought: freedom from dogma of the past; the right to interpret the world in its own terms suitable to the times; the belief that architects must use and give meaning to modern methods of construction and materials; and finally, the belief in the right to speak on behalf of contemporary society, "if we can ever hope to be of help in bringing some degree of order out of the confused and ugly environment which is the modern city."[133]

He was glad, he said, to have lived through such a momentous period of change. His early life in Italy had been influenced "and not a little stifled by" the glory that was Rome. As a student, he could hear the wide discontent of the Futurists and their desire for revolution. Led by a few men of genius, the younger generation was aiming "to shake architecture out of its lethargy, slay the 'Beaux-Arts dragon,' and clear the ground for a new era." It was a telling statement, revealing the antipathy he and Gropius, both archmodernists, felt toward historicism and historic preservation, which in their eyes impeded progress, convictions that put them at odds with changing attitudes in the profession in the late 1950s and 1960s.

Summarizing the ideals of the modern architect, Belluschi proclaimed that "he must come to terms with his environment; only then can he hope to become again creative, not in the anemic method of the academy, or as a fashionable hireling of the wealthy, but as a lively interpreter of a new social order and a prophet of his age." Thus far, architects had fallen short, and evidence from cities today suggested "that we have not been the interpreters and the prophets we had wished to be." The architect's vision might be utopian, but the complex events of modern life, which forced fundamental decisions, were accelerating. Wars, obsolescence, traffic, air travel, mass education, inevitably brought new demands for change and from them, new forms. "If we are prepared, and if our vision is clear, we can make each move—however small—an orderly and logical step toward the total plan."

Expressing his faith in students, he hoped they would abandon "styles" and the dogma of the past and instead acquire the discipline of mind that would enable them to do work of integrity. At the same time he urged a respect for symbols, "because people need them and live by them to a greater extent than is realized." Times were dark, and faith in the future was needed more now than ever. He was optimistic, however, believing a "better environment for a happier mankind" was in the making. It was for that reason, he maintained, he was forgoing a busy practice to take part in education and looked "with great misgivings at [his] accomplishments of the past, full as they are of compromises, failing of their goals, yet never doubting that there were ideals to sustain."

It was this lofty idealism, this sense of mission and of architecture's larger civic role, that he and Gropius shared, setting the two of them decidedly apart from Richard Roth, whose stolid, site-filling set-back office buildings and pragmatic aims of maximizing rental space and therefore profits, views made explicit in his 1957 *Progressive Architecture* essay, could not have been more different. Altogether, the team was, as *Architectural Forum* had put it, "unusual."

THE GROPIUS/BELLUSCHI/ROTH SCHEME

The terms of the collaboration among Gropius, Belluschi, and Roth were clear: Emery Roth & Sons, experts in space planning of large office buildings, would be responsible for the interior and working drawings; Gropius and Belluschi, the "design experts," would handle public spaces and the building's skin.

For all their pooled experience, the project was nonetheless a first all around. For Wolfson, it was his most ambitious undertaking ever, presenting the toughest problems, economically and structurally, he had ever faced. For Emery Roth & Sons, it was their first in an associate role, where they as Architect of Record were responsible for the planning and production, but not for design, surely a role they did not relish. For Gropius it was his first and probably last chance to do a skyscraper, an opportunity he had coveted ever since the 1920s with the Chicago Tribune Competition, for which he had submitted an unsuccessful design. And for Belluschi, it was the opportunity to build something truly momentous, on a far larger scale than he had ever done before, on one of the most critical, conspicuous sites in New York City, one of the foremost metropolises in the world.

Their scheme, as Gropius described it in a press statement that December, called for a broad, lozenge-shaped fifty-six-story tower rising from a low, eight-story, site-filling base, but visually set back from the street front to allow it a sculptural presence of its own.[134] Gropius wanted the tower to dominate, so that it would serve not just as a corporate emblem, but as a significant new monument in the city at large. Not only was it to mark the city's major transportation node, rising above the Grand Central with its complex, multileveled, transportation network below grade, but also, in its towering height, it was to symbolize New York and express its new postwar image of cultural hegemony and economic power. The broad sides of the tower, its axis turned east-west to span Park Avenue, would provide "forceful end views," a dramatic visual terminus as one looked down the boulevard, as well as reduce the air-conditioning load, he argued, on the east and west facades; the prismatic form, with its sides angled to catch the light, would give it "a sculptural quality" whose "crystal form is bound to become, by its contrast to the many square and rectangular shapes of other towers in the vicinity, a significant new landmark of New York City," while also accommodating the large bank of sixty-seven elevators at the core; the two horizontal bands across the facade, behind which were mechanical equipment, would divide it into thirds, adding visual relief to an otherwise monotonous wall. The projecting mullions at the crest of the tower were to be uncapped, without a cornice that would visually terminate the building and arrest the soaring, unbroken vertical movement the architects sought at the summit. And finally, it was to be enhanced by a single, unobtrusive spire, set dramatically off on one side.

The Gropius/Belluschi/Roth project was published in the *New York Times* in February 1959 (figure 1.32).[135] Their scheme, prepared by the same renderer in the Roth office who had done the earlier Roth proposal, was described as a fifty-five-story tower octagonal rather than rectangular in form, rising behind the Grand Central Station on the site of the old six-story office building behind the Grand Central, with 2.4 million square feet of office space (reduced, thus, from the 4 to 5 million square feet of the original Roth proposal, but still believed to be the largest capacity of any commercial office building in the world), with a surface of textured masonry rather than flush, smooth steel and glass. According to the *Times,* the "unusual" shape was prompted by aesthetic factors and the desire to offset the bulk of the massive structure, but it was also functional, as it would provide more usable space for elevators, restrooms, and stairwells in the core. Construction was to start late that year.

FIGURE 1.32   Gropius/Belluschi/Roth proposal for Grand Central City, 1958

An article on the Gropius/Belluschi/Roth project in *Progressive Architecture* was less straightforward. It noted somewhat cynically that the designs for what was being described as the world's largest commercial office building in terms of floor space rising on a site between the Grand Central Terminal and the New York Central Building on upper Park Avenue, in one of the world's most densely populated business districts, were announced just days before the New York City Planning Commission revealed new zoning proposals designed to eliminate crowding caused by overbuilding. The 2.4-million-square-foot building, which would surpass the RCA Building, then the world's largest in square footage, was to consist of a forty-nine-story octagonal tower of metal, masonry and glass, on a broad, six-story base that would cover virtually all of the 151,000-square-foot site between the existing elevated Park Avenue ramps. The article was illustrated with a plan and series of photos of the model (figure 1.33).[136]

The write-up of the project in *Architectural Record* (amply illustrated with renderings, views of the model, and photographs of the site with the proposed tower montaged in), by contrast, focused mainly on Belluschi and was unabashedly promotional.[137] For years the major publicist of Belluschi's work on the West Coast, *Architectural Record* began by quoting Walter Gordon, then dean of the School of Architecture and Allied Arts at the University of Oregon (and a former employee and close, long-time friend of Belluschi's, though this was not mentioned), who described Belluschi's vision, which combined functionality with art that appealed to the spirit. It then quoted Belluschi directly: "We architects of the common working variety, who must be frontline men facing frustration and compromise; we, who must understand, absorb and give visual form to so many of the forces which make our world move, must not be ashamed to listen to nor to understand what lives around us, ever mindful that each one of us can give more in a creative way by being part of the great mass of people, sharing their loves and enthusiasms, guiding them in the realization of their obscure ideals—not disdainful, temperamental stars—but men of vision among men." Belluschi's eloquent proclamations were followed by a description of the Grand Central City project. "The finest location in the world deserves the finest building in the world," it quoted Wolfson as saying at the press conference announcing the new scheme. Defending the colossal development in the densely congested area, Wolfson magnanimously pointed out that in fact they had *reduced* its size, and that the new design was some 600,000 square feet smaller than the building originally proposed. "Perhaps this site deserves not to have a skyscraper at all," the editors of *Architectural Record* com-

FIGURE 1.33   Model, Gropius/Belluschi/Roth project

mented, "but that is another story, and now only a fairy story. As it is," the article concluded, "the development of the design for the world's largest commercial office structure by Gropius and Belluschi as consultants with Richard Roth of Emery Roth & Sons constitutes a milestone in the history of commercial office buildings in New York: a signal reaching toward architecture."[138] Accepting the project as a fait accompli despite the controversy it had aroused, *Architectural Record* adhered to its traditional role as uncritical propagandist for the architectural profession.

As the design moved into the development stage, Gropius was asked to provide information that could be used for publicity purposes to draw tenants.[139] A description of the project he had previously sent was mainly factual, according to Ray Colcord, Vice-President of Grand Central Building, Inc., which Wolfson had set up to manage the operation, and he wanted something more "to sell the building to prospective tenants." Gropius had sent him study sketches of the exterior, which Colcord found helpful, but he was still in "quite a fog" about how the building was actually going to look. "Although from all sides I have been told that the building would be 'unique,' different from most all other modern office buildings, I couldn't put my finger on a concept," Colcord wrote in an August 1959 letter to Gropius. Requesting photos of their work as soon as they were available, he added, "As we are in the midst of an intensive effort to rent space to the major industrial firms of this and other countries, we need badly all of the ammunition we can get which will help induce them to come to the building and help convince them that this is in fact going to be the best building in the world." He hoped the architects would be able to inform him and his staff of "the values being designed into the building which will hopefully be recognized and appreciated by the executives heading up the corporations which will be tenants there" and wondered if Gropius could give some thought as to the reasons why a business executive "would find this building (as opposed to a more conventionally designed office building in the same location) a better value for his company. These thoughts should," Colcord said, "center around the outstanding contributions which you and Dean Belluschi have made" and be cast in layman's terms for consumption by businessmen.[140]

Gropius responded several days later, mentioning in passing a panel discussion at the AIA convention the previous June, "The Economic Value of Design," which he thought would be of interest, and drawing Colcord's attention to a speech by the public relations director of Lever Brothers, saying he thought it might "give us some hints for the handling of publicity on the Grand Central Building."[141] "The basic aim of the design of the Grand Central City Building in New York," Gropius began his rather lumbering statement on their design conceptions, "has been to take a radical departure from the usual square or rectangular skyscraper and to erect a new landmark, a characteristic symbol for this unique central location in the heart of the city. The inherent quality of the suggested octagonal tower will be that it creates an image subconsciously in the mind of the passers-by, totally different from the towers within the surrounding area or even within the whole of New York. According to the zoning law," Gropius continued, "a tower of any height may be built on an area of 25% of the site in question. Since this site is unusually large, the building mass of the octagonal tower is enormous and will dominate the whole neighborhood while keeping sufficient distance from adjacent towers."

"As the architect must always anticipate the varying distances from which the beholder may view his work," he continued, "we proceeded in the following manner: From far away the silhouette of the building is simple and significant, so that it can be grasped at a glance like a symbol. When the onlooker approaches nearer he will find protruding and receding building parts which, casting shadows, will offer new interest," Gropius said, pointing out visual nuances he thought Colcord would find useful. "Finally, standing close by, he will be attracted by new surprises of colors, textures and materials of the building's surface." The octagonal shape, he thought, was "a happy conception," giving the tower slenderness and uplift. And for the close-up view, street-level-arcades, with their shadow-generating depth effect mitigating flatness, were important and should be high and powerful to stand up to the large architectural forms of the rest of the building. As an additional attraction for tenants, he hoped (apparently without much thought to the budget) they could incorporate a recreation establishment with relaxing and exercising facilities on or adjacent to the roof of the base building, which he believed would be an asset to the executives and employees working in the building, a suggestion that went nowhere and was not mentioned again.[142] Aesthetic issues aside, Gropius's statement made clear that whatever larger social ideals he or

Belluschi might have at one time held, they were not uppermost here. Their primary objective, it was clear, was to provide an eye-catching, memorable image, a symbol and landmark for the city at large.

THE GRAND VISION

To Gropius, it was the opportunity of a lifetime, the chance to build a skyscraper—emblematic modernist image, celebration of modern technology, ultimate symbol of modern culture—as a brilliant capstone to his long, illustrious career.[143] "Make no little plans, they have no magic to stir men's blood," the famed City Beautiful Movement architect and planner Daniel Burnham had urged, setting the scale for modernist city planning. They were all thinking big: Wolfson, the Roths, Gropius, Belluschi. Their vision of the Grand Central City fit the modernist ideal of the "machine city," a rationalized comprehensive urban design destined for the midst of midtown Manhattan. Gropius and Belluschi's "grand unifying plan" linked via Wilgus's complex multileveled transportation network to the rest of the city, their quest for novelty with a form that differed visually from the norm, their marked indifference to history and its role in the collective consciousness of the city, their pursuit of a large-scale plan by means of a logical, rational process—all represented modernist principles that were to prove out of step with changing times, as values shifted, and other architects began pursuing a very different approach to architecture and urban planning.

A sleek modern tower rising unadorned from a broad multistoried base and surrounded by open space above a vast transportation system, with train tracks, motorways, and pedestrian thoroughfares woven throughout, some below grade, some on ground level, others elevated, all bespeaking a futuristic fascination with speed, movement, mobility, and a faith in modern technology—it was all part of the grand vision. Each—Wolfson, the Roths, Gropius, Belluschi—expected the building to be momentous, a landmark that would outlive them all, marking their contribution to New York and the history of the twentieth century.

2

THE PAN AM BUILDING

WOLFSON FINANCING

The Grand Central City project, which was raising hackles in architectural and planning circles, was making headlines elsewhere as well. In October 1959, the business community was rocked by the news that Wolfson had secured British funds for the controversial project, deemed "New York's most ambitious postwar office building." Announced in the *New York Times,* it was the first major foreign investment in a purely real estate venture in the country.[1]

Securing the funding was a major coup. With $25 million from Jack Cotton, chairman of City Centre Properties, Wolfson and his business partners did not need to secure a mortgage loan from banks or other financial institutions at a time when interest rates had peaked, and they could start construction, scheduled to begin the following spring.

A second *Times* article several days later described in more depth why the deal was so significant. Wolfson's Diesel Construction Company was one of the city's most productive general contracting companies, and Wolfson himself owned or participated in the ownership of several large local office buildings. This was his biggest venture yet, indeed, the biggest known venture yet undertaken in commercial office building anywhere.[2] The building's 2,400,000 square feet of floor space would make it 100,000 square feet larger than the RCA Building and 600,000 square feet larger than the Empire State Building. As this was the first Anglo-American realty venture inside the United States, it raised the question of why other such investments had not been made before. The main reason, according to the *Times,* seemed to be that never before had such an attractive proposition been put to foreign sources of capital. Why was the proposition so attractive? American tax laws, unlike British, provided a depreciation allowance on real estate property before taxes were computed; thus the British sponsors of the project could expect a substantially greater return on their investment than they would get from a domestic venture.

Moreover, assurance that the project would go ahead would make the leasing of space easier than was usually the case with a speculative office building. Prospective tenants of planned office buildings typically waited until they were sure the building would be built before committing themselves to a lease, which made it difficult for the project's sponsors, since they had to have substantial commitments from tenants before they could approach lenders about a construction loan. With British funding, the conundrum was, in the case of the Grand Central project, moot, and the biggest hurdle of the venture was behind them.

A long article in *Business Week* described the deal more fully.[3] Illustrated by a pho-tomontage of Grand Central City (figure 2.1), it told how the pledge of $25 million from the British firm ended questions over financing the huge project, paving the way for construction to begin. The funding process typically was easy, but in this case it was not, because Wolfson, who had announced plans for the project as long ago as May 1958, had held off on securing long-term financing, figuring that the longer he waited, the more tenants he would have, which would improve mortgage terms both in size and interest. In the interim, however, he found attracting tenants difficult, because of the doubt about whether he'd be able to carry off the huge project as planned. The British funding dispelled the uncertainty.

The appeal of the project lay in its good location and strong demand. Since World War II, Wolfson had invested in several new office buildings, and his contracting com-pany, Diesel Construction, had built eight more for others. All that time, Wolfson had been eyeing the Grand Central site. "Here was an area that cried for development," *Business Week* quoted him as saying. "You could see a lush period coming up. You could see buildings on inferior streets coming up. And you knew Park Avenue had to become the best office street in the country."[4]

The *Business Week* article described the history of the project, its origins in 1954, Zeckendorf's intervention, Stuart Scheftel and revival of the idea in January 1958, Young's suicide several days later, and Wolfson and Scheftel's meeting with the railroad that spring. On May 5, 1958, the developers agreed with the New York Central and the New York, New Haven and Hartford to lease the land for eighty years at $1.1 million an-nually. At that point the clock started ticking, and the race was on to get funding, the building built, and tenants moved in so they could begin paying rent.

For the design, the firm of Emery Roth & Sons had been retained, together with Har-vard's Gropius and MIT's Belluschi. Although Wolfson had hoped for a forty-five-story building of 2.5 million square feet, the architects aimed for a taller building with less rentable floor space: as many as fifty-seven stories and 2.4 million square feet. Wolf-son consented, though he was aware that a lower, bulkier building would have been cheaper to build, because of the prestige he hoped the new design would bring. De-spite the building's enormous size, Wolfson was unconcerned about filling it, as he be-lieved there was still a market among large corporations requiring 300,000 to 400,000 square feet. A recent survey by the New York Real Estate Board had shown only a 2.5 percent vacancy rate in rental office space in Manhattan and only 1.8 percent in the Grand Central area, despite the postwar addition of 45 million square feet. Though at

FIGURE 2.1 Photomontage, Grand Central City

this point Wolfson had tenants lined up for only 500,000 square feet of space, he was sure he could get the others he needed, and the sail ahead seemed smooth. Demolition of the existing six-story building on the site was to start in March, and construction of the new one was to be completed by 1962.[5]

Progress was delayed, however, as a result of the long-standing dispute between the New York Central and New York, New Haven and Hartford railroads, which led to an annulment of the lease agreement signed between Wolfson and the New York Central in October. In January 1960, a new agreement was drawn up among all three parties in which Wolfson and his partners agreed to lease the Grand Central City site for $1.1 million a year and to pay the property taxes, amounting to $400,000 a year, on the new building as well as a major portion of the taxes on the land it occupied.[6]

A construction loan for $65 million, believed to be the largest construction loan ever placed on a single commercial property, was granted for what had by then been renamed the Pan Am Building after its major tenant signed on in September 1960.[7] A temporary construction loan of $45 million was to be provided by six New York lending institutions: Bankers Trust Company, Morgan Guaranty Trust Company, Manufacturers Trust Company, Chemical Bank, New York Trust Company, and Empire Trust Company. The balance of the financing, amounting to $20 million, was to come from a group of five British banking institutions: Barclays Bank, Hambros Bank, National Provincial Bank, Schroeder Bank & Herbert Wagg, and Westminster Bank. A permanent mortgage of $66 million was to be provided by an undisclosed pension fund.[8] Their negotiations were held in the board room of the Bankers Trust Company, with over thirty individuals attending, among them banking officials, and legal representatives of the owners, lending institutions, and the New York Central and New York, New Haven and Hartford Railroads, from whom the site was leased. This was a *big* deal. By this time, the building, already more than 60 percent rented, was scheduled for completion in December 1962.

THE CHALLENGE

The financing of the Grand Central City was a major challenge. Another was the structural engineering.[9] It was complicated not only because of the location of the building just north of the Grand Central Terminal—the city's major transportation hub, with its intersection of two railroad and three subway lines, thus one of the densest, most cramped sites in the city—but also its sheer size.

Building an office building over railroad tracks was not in itself new. The concept dated back at least to the turn of the century, with Wilgus's master plan for the development of the Grand Central area with the new terminal at its core. The enormous difficulties and huge expense encountered in sinking the foundation footings of buildings on upper Park Avenue down fifty feet below grade through the New York Central Railroad's steel double-decked track structure to bedrock, then threading the foundation steel and other construction materials for a new building overhead through the two track levels without interrupting train service, had been encountered as early as 1923, with the building of the twenty-story Park-Lexington Building on Park Avenue.[10] Space both for operations and for the storage of materials on the confined Park-Lexington site was severely limited, and workers had to operate from platforms suspended from above, as they could not erect anything from below that might obstruct the operation of trains. To avoid vibrations from trains, all steel for the new building had to be wholly independent of the railroad structure, with columns resting on steel billets supported on independent foundations, cushioned to minimize transmission of movement. The problems encountered in the Park-Lexington Building had been solved so successfully that it served as a model for the subsequent buildings on Park Avenue that mushroomed in its wake.[11] What magnified the problem with Wolfson's proposed building in the late 1950s, however, was both its far greater height than any building in the 1920s and the by that time far denser traffic in the Grand Central area, which not only could not be disrupted by construction but also presented a serious public-safety factor. By this time, the city blocks around the terminal had filled with large office buildings replacing the old 1920s hotel and apartment blocks, new, huge site-filling structures providing working space for thousands of people, plus scores of restaurants and cafés as well as hotels for out-of-town visitors.[12]

It was the biggest engineering challenge Wolfson had ever faced.[13] Knowing that the structural problems would affect the design of the building, he brought in James Ruderman, his structural engineer, at the outset, setting him to the task of exploring the various options the site presented.[14]

JAMES RUDERMAN, STRUCTURAL ENGINEER

Ruderman was an obvious choice for the job, in part because of his long years of experience in working on Park Avenue buildings built over the tracks, but also because of his long-standing relationship with Wolfson. Ruderman also knew New York. He had received degrees in civil engineering from the College of the City of New York, Polytechnic Institute of Brooklyn, and Columbia University; after serving in the army during World War I, he worked as a draftsman, then as an assistant engineer for the city. In 1927, he formed a partnership, Ruderman and Severud, specializing in the structural design of office buildings and other large buildings, such as theaters, factories, churches, and schools. In 1932, he went into business on his own. After serving in World War II as he had in World War I, this time in the navy, joining Richard Roth, whom he had known for some time, he returned to New York and resumed practice, focusing at this point, just as the office building boom in Manhattan began, on large office buildings.[15]

The process of building over the tracks had started with the Uris brothers. According to Murray Shapiro, one of the engineers who joined the Ruderman office in 1950, the Urises had acquired an apartment building at 300 Park Avenue that they were slowly converting to office spaces; facing complaints from tenants, among whom were Mrs. Randolph Hearst, the Myerses of Bristol-Myers, and a number of other influential people, it occurred to them to demolish the old residential building and replace it with an entirely new building devoted solely to office space, which would be free of rent control, and they contacted Ruderman for an estimate of costs. In studying the situation, Ruderman found that a number of the structural columns of the old masonry building threaded down through the railroad structure could be reused, which would substantially reduce the cost of a new building. On the basis of Ruderman's analysis, in 1955 the Uris brothers demolished the prewar apartment building at 300 Park Avenue and built in its stead the glass-and-aluminum-curtain-walled, stepped-back Colgate-Palmolive Building, with Emery Roth & Sons as architect.[16] It was the first building to be built over the tracks and, following SOM's Lever House in 1952, the second Park Avenue office structure to go up after the war. Basking in its success, the Uris brothers immediately bought the air rights to 320 and 350 Park Avenue, whereupon other builders, recognizing the potential, quickly began buying up land and following suit, hiring Ruderman as their structural engineer.[17] Ruderman was thus one of the most experienced structural engineers in the field, responsible for close to a dozen of the buildings on upper Park Avenue, including the American Tobacco Building and the Chemical New York Trust Building.[18] According to Shapiro, Ruderman was responsible for all the buildings on Park Avenue built over the railroad, with the exception of the Union Carbide.

Ruderman also had a long history with Wolfson, who relied on him for the structural engineering of all of his buildings. They were long-standing friends who had known each other since the 1920s when they worked together in construction. They remained in contact, over time establishing a relationship that went well beyond that of the usual developer and his engineer. This was typical of Ruderman. Known as a likable individual with a quick wit, he had attended high school with the Uris brothers, for whom he also continued to do work. He was also a close friend of the Roths and did a lot of work with the Roth firm. During the Depression, as work had slowed in the Roth office, Richard Roth left to find a job elsewhere; unable to find work, he turned to Ruderman, who hired him as a draftsman. During the war, the two men went into the navy together, with Ruderman serving as a commander, Roth as a lieutenant commander. His friendship with the Roths, particularly Richard, thus had deep roots.[19]

The Ruderman office had a wealth of experience in building over the tracks, as well as a solid track record with Wolfson, but the Grand Central City project was different. Designing the steel structural framework of the exceptionally tall building over the subterranean double-decked, fantailed tracks and platforms of the railroad was a big challenge; the wind encountered by a building of such height was another. No buildings over twenty-five stories or so had been built since the seventy-story RCA Building completed in 1940.[20] There were thus few people in construction at the time experienced in building truly tall buildings.

STEEL FRAMEWORK: THE RUDERMAN PLAN

In the initial stages of the project, according to Ruderman, it was thought that the new building would have about three million square feet of floor area and a height of forty or more stories. After analyzing the entire Grand Central site, from 42nd to 45th Street and from Vanderbilt Avenue to what was formerly Depew Place, Ruderman concluded that even though the provisions had been made for a future twenty-six story hotel/office building over the terminal, introducing the structural supports required for a building twice that height would not only have been extremely slow and prohibitively expensive but also disrupted railroad operations, which the railroad had stipulated had to continue to function as efficiently as before. These structural considerations appear, then, to have been the principal factor, rather than any aesthetic or sentimental reason, for the decision not to demolish the old Beaux-Arts monument. On the other hand, pushing the proposed tower back from the terminal with its great vaulted concourse would enable them to use some of the bearing columns of the six-story terminal office building behind it and thereby greatly reduce costs.[21] At this point, upon Ruderman's recommendation, Wolfson asked Roth to draw up a preliminary architectural design, based on the location of the existing columns. Additional columns would have to be threaded between the two layers of railroad tracks and sunk into bedrock over fifty-feet below street surface as needed to support the tower, and as the existence of the railroad tracks precluded a basement, bumper space for the elevator shafts typically located below grade would have to be at ground level, with the elevator lobby of the new building located on the second floor and accessed by escalators.

The design of the steel framework was daunting. Although Ruderman had done other buildings over the Park Avenue tracks, this was the first time he was to build a structure directly over the passenger terminus, with its broad fantail of double-decked tracks and platforms, which greatly complicated construction. As the railroad operations had to remain continuous during the entire construction process, the structural steel columns straddling the two levels of tracks had to go in with a minimum of disruption to commuter traffic. The street-level floor slab of the former office building was to be left intact to provide a platform to work on in the highly constricted site as well as a protective roof for the railroad structure below, and a reinforced deck of steel girders planked over by heavy wood timbers was to be placed on top of the slab as a temporary truck lane for off-street deliveries of steel and other materials. Three derricks would be required to erect the 808-foot-high tower, with four additional derricks for the broad ten-story supporting base section. In setting the new columns, each of which was 60 feet long and weighed between twenty-two and forty tons, the derricks would lower them through small holes cut in the roof of the train room; they would then pass through similar openings cut in each of the train levels, to be anchored to grillages below the tracks. The grillages, a platform of I-beams about 10 feet long surmounted by a foot-thick 5- by 6-foot steel block or billet, were to be capped with a brace of slice plates, with special pads of lead, asbestos, and sheet metal inserted between the grillages and the columns to eliminate vibrations from the trains. It was exacting work: With work space so cramped, steel crews would have to set columns in some places within inches of third rails; elsewhere columns eighteen and a half inches wide encased in two inches of fireproofing concrete had to rise through channels of only twenty-four inches.[22]

Another major challenge Ruderman faced was wind, which again, because of the building's extraordinary height and bulk, plus its location over the railroad tracks, was far more complicated than usual.[23] Providing adequate wind resistance in the structure above grade required little more than an especially rigid frame, with heavier beams incorporated between the columns and the use of special connectors. But below grade, the horizontal force of the wind had to be carried down through the steel structure of the railroad to the foundation, and as beams could not be carried across the tracks, another solution had to be worked out.[24]

Once the project was revived in 1958 and as Gropius and Belluschi began working on the design, Ruderman proceeded to develop the plans for the steel framing. The complicated construction process was begun the following year. It was to take place in two stages, with the base section of the building rising directly from street level and resting on the preexisting columns from the old six-story office structure. While the old building was being razed, but before construction was to start on the base of the building, the new footings and foundations for the tower were to be sunk between the tracks, with the new steel frame dovetailing with, but wholly discrete from, the railroad structure (figure 2.2).[25]

GROPIUS/BELLUSCHI/ROTH COLLABORATION: THE DESIGN PROCESS

By hiring the two "eminent architects," Wolfson apparently hoped that Gropius and Belluschi would "simply lend their names to the project and then disappear back into the world of academia." Things, however, were not so simple. First of all, by the time the Grand Central City project was revived in the spring of 1958 and Gropius and Belluschi were brought in, much of the basic planning had already been done by both Ruderman and Roth. Evidently apprehensive about their joint endeavor, Roth had asked Gropius in their initial meeting with Wolfson in June 1958 for his frank opinion of their original proposal. According to notes Gropius made of the meeting, he told Roth only that though he felt the base of their building appeared "too brutal" against the Grand Central building, the overall silhouette "did not appear bad." He anticipated, however, objections on urbanistic grounds. Evidently relieved at Gropius's response, Roth agreed to the collaboration.[26]

Contrary to expectations, however, Gropius remained closely involved in the entire design process, at first with weekly meetings in the TAC office in Cambridge, then, as the project moved from schematics into design development, with regular meetings in the Roth office in New York (figure 2.3). That he in fact assumed leadership rather than merely an advisory role was evident from the start. Even before their contract was signed, he was making notes on the Grand Central City design, itemizing the issues he felt had to be addressed. The first item was to ascertain the most favorable grid system

FIGURE 2.2   Grand Central City Building under construction, view from north

FIGURE 2.3   The Grand Central City team. From left to right: Belluschi, Gropius, Richard Roth

FIGURE 2.4   Original Gropius/Belluschi proposal

for the columns, given the existing rail lines. The second item was the orientation of the slab or tower, a decision, according to his notes, that would depend on the best arrangement of elevator shafts. Another item was the elevation, and his concern for sufficient depth or plasticity; and another was an architectural expression of the building's mechanics in the elevation, such as mechanical stories, which he thought might be incorporated as a horizontal design feature. A final item was his concern for the treatment of the lower street-level stories, which he thought would be most visible to pedestrians, as well as the transition between the existing station and the new building.[27]

Several days later, on July 18, 1958, he and Belluschi signed the contract with Wolfson formalizing their agreement. Initially, Belluschi too was closely involved, contributing sketches as well as ideas. His participation, however, began to drop off after some months.[28]

In their first joint meeting in New York after signing the contract, Gropius and Belluschi, accompanied by Norman Fletcher of TAC, met with Wolfson and his associates Ruderman and Roth to go over operational requirements and to review the Roth proposal. It was at this time, less than a week after they had signed on, that the Gropius team came up with their initial scheme (figure 2.4). It called for a low, site-filling base like that of the Lever House, surmounted on one side by a tall slab oriented east-west and pulled back from 45th Street to allow a spacious forecourt or plaza; this would also provide ample distance between the new tower and the 1929 New York Central Building just to the north. Well aware of the criticism Roth's formulaic rectangular metal and glass buildings were receiving, they also sought a more sculptural, faceted form for the tower and exteriors of nonreflective materials, rather than a shiny, transparent curtain wall. To enliven the facade, they also suggested a more plastic overall texture, rather than regular horizontal or vertical divisions to break up the form. The discussion then turned to more pragmatic factors such as the ideal square footage for a typical floor, expected occupancy of 25,000 workers, and the use of escalators for the connection between the Grand Central and the new building, as well as developing an identity for major tenants, each of whom was expected to rent 300,000 to 400,000 square feet.[29]

Several weeks later Roth called Gropius with the results of a long talk he had had with Wolfson, who indicated his desire to incorporate a number of other features, including at least 100,000 square feet in the base building for tenant storage; bulk space of 1.2 million square feet for either Metropolitan Life or a post office branch; two live theaters of 1,000 seats each; 40,000 square feet for electrical switchboards, steam, and other mechanical systems; and space for retail stores and perhaps a small department store, plus a parking garage. Roth also passed on news from Ruderman that because of the structural difficulties it would present in the foundations, he had concluded that the tower of sixty-five stories that Gropius's scheme evidently called for was too high.[30]

Early on, Gropius had determined that his team wanted an octagonal tower that would "provide dramatic contrast to the simple square and rectangular forms" of other buildings in the area as well as reduce the effect of its great mass. This meant persuading Wolfson to reduce the size of the tower from three million square feet, which at the time was considered huge, to 2.4 million, which was still very large.[31] There were, however, evidently other reasons beyond aesthetics for cutting the size, as given lingering questions about Manhattan's ability to absorb so much new office space, it was thought that a three-million-square-foot building was simply too big for renting purposes.[32] Whatever his reasons, Wolfson agreed to the reduction, knowing that despite the change, the building would still be the world's biggest commercial office building, and over half a million square feet larger than the Empire State Building.

The building's octagonal slab, with the sides faceted to make it appear more slender and to reduce the effect of bulk, was Belluschi's idea.[33] The form, however, was not new. Gio Ponti's new Pirelli Headquarters Building in Milan (figure 2.5), begun in 1958, was under construction at the time and much in the news.[34] Belluschi, a religious reader of the architectural magazines, of course knew of it and had in fact recommended that Wolfson visit it on a trip to Europe; the well-connected Belluschi also mentioned that he knew the architect of the building personally and would be happy to provide Wolfson with a letter of introduction.[35] The Pirelli building in turn had roots in Corbusian design, in Saint-Dié (1957) and earlier in Algiers, in the 1930s. Even closer to home, Belluschi and Gropius themselves had explored a similar six-sided version in the Boston Back Bay Center project.

Turning the axis east-west so that the tower spanned Park Avenue instead of being aligned with it was Gropius's suggestion. It was a controversial issue in the Roth office, far more so than the change to an octagonal form. Ruderman, in addition to recommending that the height of the building be restricted for structural reasons, maintained that shifting the principal axis to an east-west orientation would mean it would span all of the tracks and platforms between Depew Place and Vanderbilt Avenue, which would increase the cost of the superstructure by $100,000 to $150,000, as well as appreciably affecting the ease and time of construction. "The architectural and tenancy considerations are of prime importance," he wrote Roth, but the cost difference "should be considered in the final decision, and the reaction of the railroad to matters affecting train

FIGURE 2.5   Pirelli Headquarters Building

schedules, certainly had to be."[36] Gropius, however, argued that as long as they were going to put a big building there, it had to be monumental, a visual terminus that would fill the vista entirely, an opinion with which those in the Roth office, so it was later said, only reluctantly agreed.[37] But turning the axis also made sense from a real estate perspective, as the broad building would command panoramic views across the width of Manhattan, from the Hudson to the East Rivers, and provide clear vistas north and south down Park Avenue.[38]

As Belluschi believed that the bold plastic exteriors Gropius proposed would be overbearing on a building of such a huge size, he suggested a more lacy, finely textured facade, not unlike that of the recently completed United Nations Secretariat several blocks away (figure 2.6). Although personally preferring a more muscular exterior like that of his own entry for the 1922 Chicago Tribune Competition, with its pronounced projections and recessions and shadow-generating plasticity, Gropius conceded to this, as well as to Belluschi's suggestions to reduce the size of the windows in the interest of a lighter, more delicate handling of the facade. The fenestration pattern was eventually worked out in the TAC office, with Belluschi's comments and contributions.[39]

On the other hand, the choice of materials, especially the use of textured precast concrete containing a quartz aggregate that would catch light and add sparkle to the facade, was Gropius's.[40] Gropius disliked the glass/metal flush curtain wall, which gave buildings what he felt was an insubstantiality and moreover had become by then a cliché. He much preferred simulated stone, which endowed buildings with more visual interest.[41] Concrete exteriors would necessitate the use of a heavier structural steel to support them but would require less frequent cleaning, as was pointed out in a *New York Times* article on the building, and had better insulating properties than those of metal and glass.[42] But it was primarily the "freshness" of the design that appealed to Gropius, a preference that followed the growing trend in architecture in the late 1950s toward more brutalist forms, as taste shifted from sleek Miesian glass-and-metal slabs to a more Corbusian sculptural massing such as seen in the La Tourette Monastery or buildings of Chandigahr.

There were other compromises. Instead of the low, site-filling base and spacious plaza the Gropius team had wanted, the plaza was abandoned and the base heightened, as a drawing by Belluschi, dated August 10, 1958 indicated, to provide the large expanses of continuous square footage Wolfson thought major tenants would demand (figure 2.7). The tower was also pushed northward to 45th Street and the New York

FIGURE 2.6   United Nations Secretariat

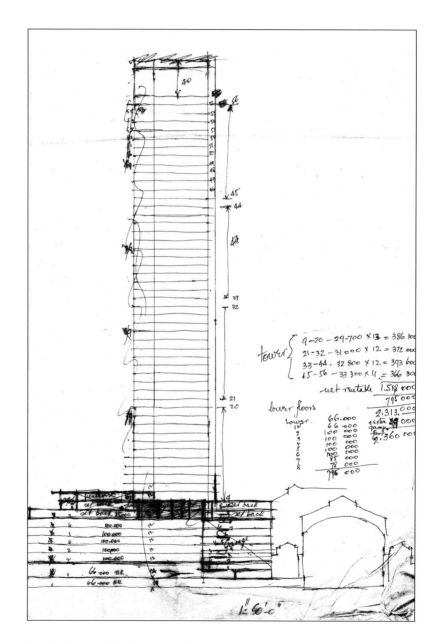

FIGURE 2.7   Belluschi drawing, section, August 10, 1958

Central Building, to allow for individual private entrances off Vanderbilt Avenue, in addition to the main public entrance on 45th Street, for the two or more principal tenants Wolfson hoped to acquire.[43]

Although the basic circulation pattern between the old Grand Central Station and the new Grand Central City building had been established by the Roths in their 1954 scheme, working it out was a major challenge for the whole design team. Their aim was to separate pedestrian, truck, car, and taxi routes completely, with a loop road around the new office building for vehicular traffic, a separate unloading area, passenger platforms, and garage facilities in the linking structure between the two buildings.[44]

By September 4, 1958, two months after they had begun, a number of major design decisions involving Ruderman as well as Roth, Gropius, Belluschi, and Wolfson had been made. The tower was to be octagonal, oriented east-west, approximately fifty-five stories high, with a minimum net rentable space of 2.35 million square feet; the theaters and department store were eliminated, and two or three private entrance lobbies for major tenants were added on the Vanderbilt Avenue side. The main public entrance would remain on 45th Street.[45]

Several months later, by which time the design was for the most part established, Gropius drew up his statement to the press describing their intentions in turning the axis, giving the building its prismatic shape, and selecting the materials they did, and predicted the new building would become "a significant new landmark of New York City."[46] He wrote Roth several days later, telling him how pleased he was with the overall effect, adding that he thought only the base building would "still need some refinement as to scale." He also had other ideas about how to make the entrance on 45th Street more grand and to improve the ramp level. Gropius concluded by enclosing his proposal for the 1922 Chicago Tribune Competition, of which Roth evidently was unaware, presumably to give him an idea of the kind of masonry and texture on the facade he would like.[47] By this time, then, December 1958, the main concept of the building was set.

Most of the work henceforth took place in the Roth office in New York. Gropius and Alex Cvijanovic, another associate from TAC, came down from Cambridge for regular meetings; occasionally Belluschi came, but more to be briefed than to participate. It was clear that for all of their talk of a good collaborative relationship, the team approach did not work as equitably they had hoped. Several months into the design, Belluschi began to pull out, leaving Gropius and others in the TAC office to do the actual work, and thenceforth served largely as a critic.[48] As Belluschi himself was later to put it (an impression others confirmed), faced with the Gropius's headstrong, assertive, domineering personality, he, by nature quieter and more accommodating, simply withdrew.[49] On the other hand, he and Gropius had agreed in signing on with Wolfson that Gropius would be the team leader and have the final say on design issues; Gropius, too, clearly listened to Belluschi, was responsive to his design suggestions, and greatly valued his advice. It seems likely that the real factor in Belluschi's withdrawal was not so much Gropius's domineering personality as Belluschi's own involvement with other affairs. At this point, his work on the Lincoln Center across town was picking up pace, he was responsible for the design of several churches and synagogues up and down the East Coast, among them the Portsmouth Abbey in Portsmouth, Rhode Island, the Church of the Redeemer in Baltimore, and Temple Israel, a synagogue in Swampscott, Massachusetts, as well as a new library for Bennington College in Bennington, Vermont. Gropius, too, had other projects on the boards, such as the master plan for the University of Baghdad, but all of his design work was shared by others in the TAC office, unlike that of Belluschi, who worked alone. Then too as the Grand Central City project evolved, Belluschi had other personal demands, as his wife became increasingly ill, his two boys were experiencing problems in school, and there was grumbling at MIT about the number of outside consulting jobs he was taking on at the expense of his academic obligations. His first wife died in 1962, then not long after the Pan Am Building was completed, he retired from the deanship at MIT, and he remarried. Thus although their collaboration started out on a strong collaborative footing, Gropius and Belluschi's working relationship gradually changed, and Gropius "just sort of took over."[50] By the time the design of the lobby was begun, it was mainly Gropius and TAC alone.

Progress on the design for the building continued throughout the winter and spring of 1959, with Gropius expressing concern that the mullions be carried up approximately a foot and a half beyond the roofline, which at that time was defined by the top of the building's mechanical penthouse, specifying the color of mullions and spandrels, and addressing other architectural details.[51] As work continued that summer, Gropius sent Ray Colcord of the Grand Central Building, Inc., sketches for proposed landscaping and greenery. One of his suggestions was for roof gardens along the two broad sides of the tower, which could be arranged with low plants, flowers, and some shrubs; he also thought it would be good to plant trees alongside 45th Street between the elevated vehicular ramps, assuming railway conditions permitted it.[52]

That September the design team was at work refining the exterior and exploring possible designs for the precast concrete panels, and were moving ahead on the construction of an eight-and-a-half-foot-high Plexiglas model to be exhibited in the concourse of the Grand Central Terminal.[53] The Mo-Sai prefabricated panels were selected to give the building a "freshness of design and freedom of architectural expression" in terms of color, shape, and form," as well as for their economy.[54] Each of the nine thousand panels, of a precast exposed aggregate concrete, was to form the framing for a window four feet wide by eight feet high (figure 2.8). The panels, proportioned to complement the Pan Am Building's octagonal form, were eggshell in color, with a quartz aggregate to give the surface a rough, dense, crystal-like texture and to lend sparkle to the building's facade (figure 2.9), which would be accentuated as sunlight shifted around the perimeter. The plane surfaces of the precast panels were also to be given additional plasticity by mullions projecting thirteen inches beyond the spandrels, imparting the effect of ribs to the facade.

In November 1959, despite a lingering dispute between Gropius and Roth about the entrances on Vanderbilt Avenue, the project was made public. The event was celebrated with an extensive write-up in the *New York Times,* illustrated by a photo of the plexiglas model, which included a cutaway of the terminal, with its two levels of trains below grade, on display in the Grand Central concourse (figure 2.10).[55] Evidently surprised at how well things were turning out with their collaboration with Gropius and his team, people in the Roth office expressed their delight with the way matters were progressing, and apart from a question about the height of the garage, which hinged on a response from the Building Department, told Gropius they thought that they had come up with "a very successful design." Gropius was urged to continue reviewing details and integrating refinements into the overall design, particularly the intersection of the

FIGURE 2.8   Mo-Sai panels, detail, 1991

FIGURE 2.9   Faceted façade, 1986

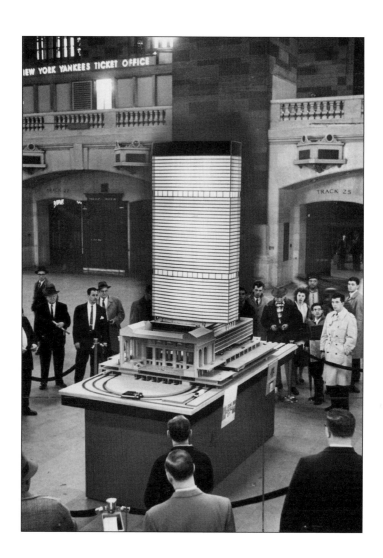

FIGURE 2.10   Model, Grand Central City, in Grand Central concourse, 1959

faceted walls on the north and south elevations and the spacing of the columns at the mechanical levels. The Roth office's communication concluded with a word on timing: Carl Morse, in charge of construction, was in the process of assembling bids on the exterior and would be ready soon to give them a complete analysis of costs.[56]

In another joint meeting in New York that November, exterior materials were discussed.[57] The cost of granite for the base building was estimated to be $1.5 million more than for the Mo-Sai precast concrete panels they were using in the tower: thus it was agreed that concrete panels like those of the tower would be used for it as well. Final dimensions of spandrels, mullions, sills, and so on were to be determined after the design team had studied a sketch model. They also agreed to hold off on the final design for the entrance under the elevated vehicular ramp on Vanderbilt Avenue until more information from Ruderman on the spacing of the ramp columns was available. With regard to the tower, it was agreed that the columns in the "waistlines," or the mechanical (32nd and 44th) floors, be spaced at sixteen feet plus on center, which would entail the introduction of a fake column in the center of each thirty-two-foot span of the two rows, and that their walls be recessed. In a meeting later in Wolfson's office, the designers were told to move ahead on the selection, design, and treatment of the escalators, as they were an important component of the entrance to the building from Grand Central Station.

The budget was clearly a factor in the team's discussions. Regarding the design of the elevator doors and jambs, Harold Schiff, project manager on the Pan Am job, responsible for running the day-to-day operations of construction, pointed out that although the design of these items was an architectural issue, nonetheless cost was a concern. "In transmitting this information [on elevator cabs and their costs]," he wrote the designers tersely, "Mr. Morse requests that I please advise that there once was a budget for this building."[58]

Traffic was another major concern. Pedestrian traffic through the Grand Central Terminal was estimated at 425,000 persons per day, of which 215,000 arrived by subway; car traffic on the elevated Park Avenue ramp amounted to 15,600 cars southbound, 16,300 cars northbound. On Vanderbilt Avenue alone, there were some 9,000 cars daily in both directions.[59] Gropius remained highly involved, in both this and other affairs. In February 1960, he was told that Ruderman, who was waiting for a decision on the location of the escalators between the building and the Grand Central could wait no longer, and needed an answer from the Gropius team on the disposition of the escalator and stair off the Vanderbilt Avenue entrance so the structural engineers could incorporate any changes in the working drawings and proceed with the framing.[60] On the basis of memoranda concerning their meetings, it seems clear that design decisions were being made by, or at least cleared with, Gropius, and that Wolfson was moving ahead rapidly on what later would be known as "fast track," with construction proceeding even as the design was being worked out. Proving to be anything but the absent professor, Gropius was particularly concerned about the problem of traffic, especially pedestrian, in and around the Grand Central, believing that their design would greatly ease the congestion.[61]

Several months later, evidently in response to the criticism of scalelessness being hurled at recent modernist buildings, Gropius expressed his concern about the base of the building, saying his team felt it was necessary "to bring a lot of activities and surprise effects into the street level of the building to avoid dullness and overmonumentalism."[62] It was a point, he said, that he and Belluschi considered "extremely important," and they were tossing around proposals, several of which he enclosed in his correspondence. Instead of pushing the wall along Vanderbilt Avenue out to maximize interior rental space, which Wolfson wanted, Gropius hoped they could push the wall back to incorporate a pedestrian arcade under the Vanderbilt ramp, arguing that the shops in the arcade would contribute rental space, hence income, and at the same time add visual appeal. He held off making specific recommendations about what kind of stores he would like to see there but underscored the importance of creating places "where people can meet," such as bars or a cafeteria. Including several sketches for the Vanderbilt entrance, he added that he had also done some thinking about the artwork, that was intended for the lobby and, after consulting Belluschi, would provide suggestions for it.

Although regular meetings of the entire team—Wolfson, Colcord, Ruderman, Roth, Morse, and Gropius and his colleagues—were held throughout the construction process, as the project got underway, Gropius was evidently consulted on all matters pertaining to design. Minutes of construction meetings in March and April 1960, while principally devoted to air conditioning, storage space, vibration problems, security issues, and other such items, specifically mention preliminary plans for exterior lighting that needed to be reviewed by Gropius and Belluschi, as the lighting constituted an important architectural detail on the exterior of the building.[63] By this time, too, work was moving ahead on the lobbies, for which Gropius was largely responsible. The mezzanine in the Vanderbilt entrance lobby, which Wolfson insisted on, was particularly problematic, as in Gropius's view it hindered a good design solution to both the elevation and the space of the lobby itself.[64] Throughout the process, copies of the exchanges between Ruderman and Roth were regularly sent to both Gropius and Belluschi to keep them abreast of progress.

By May of that year, as the design of the lobbies, entrances, and exterior lighting continued, word came that despite the fact that the demolition of the existing six-story building was being held up until August, when the New York, New Haven, and Hartford Railroad planned to vacate the building, work on the substructure had begun.[65] As it proceeded, the designers continued their work on the 45th Street arcade, entrances, garage traffic, and lobby wall design, a Mo-Sai mock-up, and the Vanderbilt Avenue escalator design.[66]

Meanwhile, renters for the building's substantial space were being lined up.[67] Although progress on this front continued apace, it sped up considerably after Pan American World Airways signed on as the major tenant in September 1960. The agreement between Wolfson and Juan Trippe, head of Pan American, led to a number of significant design changes, not the least of which had to do with the building's signage. Within a month of its signing the rental contract, noted graphic designer Ivan Chermayeff was retained by Pan American as consultant on the signage, which clearly concerned Gropius, who insisted on getting in touch with Chermayeff immediately "to establish details for the various Pan Am signs."[68] Gropius was equally anxious about the floodlighting of the exterior and the preliminary designs of Wolfson's lighting specialist.[69] There were other issues—the choice of ventilation blinds and their color, which Gropius felt were of "utmost importance," the proportions of the elevations, particularly having to do with the fenestration in the arcade on 45th Street, and the Vanderbilt Avenue ramp, which he thought was becoming clumsy.[70] It was clear Gropius took his role as design architect seriously and remained involved in matters of all scale, from traffic problems to detailing.

There were disagreements over other design decisions as well. One involved the granite columns in the main lobby (figure 2.11), which Gropius wanted to be rounded. Morse, however, insisted on square or quirk corners, as they were less expensive. Roth concurred, maintaining that economic factors aside, architecturally and aesthetically square or quirk corners were more in keeping with the design of the building, and the columns were redesigned.[71] Gropius had other demands as well, some minor, others major, such as that the finish of the bronze in the lobby be matte, and that the height of the elevator tower on the top floor of the roof extend no higher than twenty-six feet, lest it "look silly."[72]

ROTH OFFICE

All contact between the architects and the structural engineers on the Grand Central City project was through the Roth office, with whom Ruderman worked closely. Working drawings were prepared by Emery Roth & Sons, who with their "design factory" setup were skilled at producing detailed drawings quickly and efficiently and used to designing buildings as places to work, rather than "monuments to posterity."[73] They also had a good understanding of structure and worked well with Ruderman, with whom they had done a number of jobs, especially on Park Avenue. Ruderman would sketch the possibilities as he saw them, then he and Roth would sit down together, tossing ideas back and forth, to hammer things out. With the Roth office, the Ruderman people had to work fast: As they started out on a project together, within a short period of time, often two weeks or so, the Roth people would want to know what Ruderman wanted and the maximum sizes of everything—the head room on every floor, sizes of the columns, the column arrangements—so they could design it right the first time and not have to go back and redo it. Everything was fast. The Roths would come up with a concept, run it by Ruderman, who would come back with possible options, then they would work it out. Once a decision was made, rarely did the Roths change their minds.[74] Thus,

FIGURE 2.11   Lobby

as work began on the complex Grand Central City project, their working relationship was well oiled and functioning smoothly.

CONSTRUCTION OF THE BUILDING

For the Diesel Construction Company, the challenge of constructing the exceptionally tall, $100 million Grand Central City building over the two levels of the terminal's tracks and platforms with the trains in continuous operation, plus the constant flow of pedestrians within the station and vehicular traffic without, none of which could be interrupted by construction work, rivaled that faced by Ruderman in the design of the structural steel framing. The problems presented by the cramped site were especially serious, as construction, constricted also to a limited time span, had to be meticulously planned. Each step had to be scheduled, the schedule rigorously monitored, and all operations flawlessly executed, as given the enormous costs involved, the ongoing railroad operations, and the city traffic, there was little room for error.[75]

Challenging as it was, the construction of the Grand Central City building was facilitated by the fact that Wolfson, the client and developer, was also the owner of the Diesel Construction Company, the contractor for the construction of the building. It helped that both Ruderman and Roth were also long-standing friends as well as business associates with whom Wolfson had worked on most of his buildings. And there was Morse, Wolfson's right-hand man, who had joined Diesel Construction in 1952 as vice president of the company and succeeded Wolfson as president of the company in 1957, when Wolfson became chairman of the board.[76]

CARL A. MORSE, DIESEL CONSTRUCTION COMPANY, AND CONSTRUCTION MANAGEMENT

Morse ran the Diesel Construction Company. Upon graduating from Yale in 1925 with a degree in civil engineering, he worked for Bing & Bing, a New York real estate and construction company, as assistant superintendent of construction; he remained associated with Bing & Bing for more than twenty-seven years, before joining Diesel Construction in 1952.[77] When Wolfson restructured the company in 1957, he turned over the construction side of his operation to Morse, who he knew was a tough negotiator, to devote himself to real estate.[78]

Like Wolfson, Morse ran a tight ship. He too was an indefatigable worker, someone whose hands-on approach meant he was as likely to be donning a hard hat to inspect a plastering job as a black tie for a ribbon-cutting ceremony. Known for his ability to carry prices and figures on the availability of materials or equipment around in his head, he used this to advantage in dealing with owners, architects, engineers, subcontractors, and suppliers.[79] When an owner came to Diesel with a project, Morse, after examining the architect's initial sketches, could estimate with legendary accuracy what it would cost and how long construction would take, and would work out a budget while the job was still in the formative stage. Checking the feasibility of the plans and doing most of his own contract estimating, he also made a point of keeping in close touch with the architect, as well as a close watch on the construction process. He was known for his exacting construction schedules, setting a timetable and sticking to it closely. On the job early, he stayed late; rigorously disciplined, he was reputed to be neither closed minded nor preprogrammed, remaining open to alternative products and ways of doing things when his original ideas did not pan out.

Morse was also a major innovator in construction after the war and a pioneer in what later became known as "construction management."[80] Traditionally, an owner who wished to put up a building contacted an architect, who drew up the building's design, then brought in an engineer to make sure the materials the architect had chosen and the way he had joined them would stand up to the expected forces; the engineer would then approve the drawings or suggest changes. The revised drawings were subsequently sent out for the lowest bid, with each party working in succession. As contractors typically worked for a percentage of the construction costs, there was little incentive to keep costs down. Morse changed that, working on a professional basis for a fixed fee. This eliminated the usual adversarial relationship between owner and building. It also enabled him to start the job without waiting for the completed architectural drawings, significantly reducing cost. In the case of the Grand Central City project, Morse was there right from the beginning as a key member of the planning team. As all members of the team worked together in the design process, this avoided miscalculations that required the architect to go back to the drawing board to redo plans if their designs had called for something unbuildable; it also sped up the process in other ways, as instead of waiting until a project's architect finished the working drawings for the building, then putting them out to bid, the contractor worked in conjunction with the architect as the design unfolded, at a great savings in cost. With this system one could thus dovetail the various tasks, so that different parts of the project could proceed concurrently in fast track.[81] But it was more than "fast track," as the term later became known, for cost as well as speed was a critical factor. With Morse's system, one could let a contract for the steel for a building even though the plans for the building were not finished, since the steel company knew the engineer, who in turn knew the architect, had a rough idea of what he was going to do, and thus could quote a price. Diesel Construction was one of the first companies that understood the value of knowing not just what it was building, but also how it was going to build it, that is, the *logistics* of the whole process, right from the beginning. With the Grand Central City project, Morse was there on the scene as Ruderman drew up his framing plans and worked with him in pointing out what construction difficulties would be faced as a result of doing something in one way instead of another, or in suggesting ways of saving money by doing something one way rather than another. And although the Grand Central City project was not the first time Morse had employed his new, streamlined system, it was one of the first, and certainly the first ever attempted on such a large scale.[82]

Behind Morse and Ruderman, who worked closely together throughout the process, was of course Wolfson, developer of the building and owner of Diesel Construction. Together with Roth, Wolfson had a tremendous advantage over competitors—men like Zeckendorf, the Tishmans, the Urises—whose approach was far more splintered. An article in *Architectural Forum* several years before work got underway on the Grand Central City project, part of a series on changes in the architectural profession that pointed out how critical the role of the contractor was in the building process, described the traditional approach. It pointed out what had been lost with increasing specialization in the nineteenth century, and the cleavage that had developed between builder and architect as a result of the professionalization of the architect and the founding of the AIA in 1857. As the building industry grew more complex, especially after World War II, with the increasingly complicated materials and labor markets and the wide variation in the clarity of and precision in architects' drawings and specifications, as well as the constantly changing equipment and methods, which precluded doing things in a routine way, the gap between designer and builder had widened, and creative solutions to whatever problems were encountered on the part of either were becoming increasingly difficult for the other to accommodate. An architect might design something that the contractor would later find unbuildable; by the same token, as new mechanical equipment—electrical work, plumbing, air conditioning, acoustical systems—was developed, requiring an increasing number of highly trained specialists for installation, designers were left with little room for improvisation, as their drawings had to be specific to the last detail. On the other hand, there was little incentive on the part of the builder to implement an improvement, as the architect might come in several days later and, failing to see the change specified in the contract documents, insist it be taken out.[83] With his team of Ruderman, Roth, and Morse all working together, Wolfson was able to cut through this fragmented process and streamline it by coordinating the financing, design, and construction of a building from the very beginning.

It was an exceptional team, as they all were highly experienced and esteemed in their respective fields. All had solid track records; they all knew and respected each other and worked well together. What set the team on the Grand Central City job apart from those on Wolfson's other projects was the addition of Gropius and Belluschi, the design experts brought in for prestige.

CONSTRUCTION BEGINS

In May 1959, three months after the Gropius/Belluschi scheme was published, Grand Central Building, Inc., began awarding construction contracts for the job. The first was to American Bridge, a division of the United States Steel Corporation, for forty thousand tons of structural steel, believed to be the largest volume ever for an office building.[84] That September, the Ruderman plan for the building's framework was announced;[85] the Roth office filed plans for the building with the city two months later.[86] The acoustical soundproofing contract was awarded in February of the following year,[87] then a week later, the contract for the building's elevators. Thought to be the largest ever, the $8 million contract called for six of the fastest elevators in the world, to travel at sixteen hundred feet per minute—200 feet per minute faster than the previous record; the elevators were also to be fully automated, allowing them to be operated without operators.[88] Other firsts in terms of office building technology included the building's centralized telephone service, the first of its kind in the country.[89] Serving thirty thousand telephones in the building and nearby offices, as many as were installed in the entire city of Newburgh, New York, the new $11 million system eliminated costly, space-consuming telephone equipment rooms for individual tenant offices. Bell Telephone Labs, which developed the system, was to lease the entire twentieth and twenty-first floors of the building, thirty-five thousand square feet of space, which had to be re designed to handle the heavy, bulky equipment, with floor heights increased to provide thirteen and a half feet of clearance and floor load capacity raised to 150 and 200 pounds per square foot (from the normal floor loading of 50 per square foot).

Demolition of the six-story Grand Central office building behind the terminal began in June 1960, clearing the site for the construction of the new building.[90] The offices and other facilities of the railroad in the old building were moved to other spaces, and with excavation and foundation work set to begin August 1, Grand Central Building, Inc. began holding regular meetings to discuss the construction schedule. The job at this point was running late, delayed apparently by the refusal of the New York, New Haven, and Hartford Railroad to vacate the old office building completely before August,[91] but it was hoped lost time would be picked up by the first of the following year. By the end of July, demolition of the old office building was well underway, and work on the new building's substructure was about to start.[92] At this point, as work on the building was behind schedule, Wolfson began getting anxious. He informed Roth in a letter in late August that he was pushing the steel erection up to begin December 1, rather than January 1, as originally scheduled, and emphasized how critical it was that he, Roth, and Ruderman work out the design on the lower floors so that American Bridge and Fenestra, which was to provide the flooring, could get started.[93] "We know that steel is released on part of the upper floors, but unfortunately, buildings are built from the bottom up," he wrote rather testily. Noting too that the lobby design was still "kicking around," he insisted that they move ahead on it, so a mock-up for prospective tenants could be made. "Code requirements are to be ignored" he added. "I am counting on you to see to it that Grand Central City, architecturally, structurally, mechanically and design-wise, goes full speed ahead and to hell with everyone else," he asserted; he also informed Roth in no uncertain terms that jobs that had come to the Roth office after his were "not to take precedence for manpower over that required for Grand Central City."[94] What was not said in his letter, but may explain his growing anxiety, was that at this point, Wolfson was in the midst of highly secret negotiations with Juan Trippe, president of Pan American World Airways, about signing on as the building's major tenant.

COMPLICATIONS

Construction of the huge Grand Central City building involved more than two hundred engineers and seventy-five hundred craftsmen from seventy-five different trades, whose activities all had to be carefully orchestrated and coordinated by Diesel Construction.[95] In addition to the complicated logistical arrangements to accommodate the train, vehicular, and pedestrian traffic on and around the site, one of the specific problems Morse faced on the job stemmed from the sheer height of the building. As construction proceeded, the time it took to lift a piece of steel from the street to the upper floors increased, and the hoists the builders put in had to be temporary, with high-speed engines designed especially for the job. Any building that rose above six hundred feet posed problems not encountered with lower buildings, as with each floor, additional strength had to be added at the base—a problem exacerbated with the Grand Central City, as "at the base" was below grade, amidst the steel framework of the railroad.[96]

Another problem Morse encountered was with the precast concrete sheathing Gropius had specified for the building's facade. Simply transporting the specially fabricated Mo-Sai panels to the building and hoisting the heavy panels, each of which weighed thirty-five hundred pounds, up into place presented a daunting logistical challenge. Details of the delivery, hoisting, and finishing of the panels had to be worked out with precision to avoid overlap and a loss of time in the limited work space. Separate crews, each with their own foreman, had to be brought in to perform specific duties, with a hoisting crew raising the panels, a setting crew fitting the panels into the building in place, and a lineup crew performing the final alignment before the panels were secured into place and the joints sealed.[97] Complicating the situation still further, the company that manufactured the Mo-Sai panels went bankrupt while the building was under construction, and Diesel Construction was forced to buy out the company to maintain production.[98]

BOWLING ALLEYS: HASKELL VERSUS THE RAILROADS

As construction picked up and the design of the Grand Central City building moved into later stages, another hitch occurred, casting negative light on the new building. The railroads, which in addition to installing a huge Kodak sign, television monitors, and other commercial displays in the once-noble vaulted space of the terminal's concourse, were moving aggressively to exploit their property holdings on Park Avenue in yet other ways. In hopes of offsetting mounting operating costs and declining passenger revenues, they devised a scheme to install bowling alleys in the terminal's waiting room. It called for slicing the 210-foot-long space horizontally by means of three concrete slabs supported on a steel structure that would span the sixty-foot width of the chamber, whose weight would be borne by existing columns on the room's periphery, thus freeing the interior from obstructing supports (figure 2.12).[99] "Just when the airlines are extending themselves and putting their best foot forward by creating superb public waiting spaces at our major airports," a letter in the *New York Times* from New York architect Robert C. Weinberg said, "the railroads 'cut off their nose to spite their face' by chopping up their great terminals, disfiguring them and cluttering them with advertising and other extraneous internal constructions." Weinberg cited the railroads' proposal for bowling alleys in Grand Central Terminal and called for a public hearing before plans for the forty-four lane bowling center went ahead. Pointing out that the station was in a district from which bowling alleys were banned under the current zoning ordinance, he maintained that they would be banned as well under the new zoning law that had been proposed, should it be in effect by the time the matter came up. "If the railroad asks the Planning Commission to change the zoning district, every civic organization, from the Municipal Art Society to the local taxpayers' groups, will be out in force to argue against it; and should it come to the Board of Standards and Appeals for a variance, the same forces will be on hand to answer the owner's plea of 'hardship.' Hardship, indeed! A triple-decker bowling alley literally squeezing the daylights out of Grand Central's crowded waiting room will be a hardship to travelers and to the thousands of others who have to go through the station to and from work."[100]

Rebutting Weinberg's argument was S. T. Keiley, manager of the Grand Central Terminal and spokesman for the railroad. In a carefully worded letter to the *Times,* he spelled out the railroad's reasoning. The terminal was operating at a serious annual deficit, he began, predictably pleading economic woes. In 1959 it had cost the railroad $6.7 million more than the revenues it generated to operate the terminal. Considered only as a railroad facility, the terminal's deficit was over $13.5 million. Keiley found the fact that railroads pay heavy taxes on terminals especially pertinent. To offset this deficit, the railroad was forced to seek revenue from nonoperating sources. He added that the proposed bowling alleys would "in no way disfigure the building nor detract from its architectural grandeur."[101]

Leading the protest against the bowling alleys was Haskell of the *Architectural Forum*. Reminding constituents of their campaign six years earlier to save Grand Central Station, he appealed to them again for support in a form letter sent out to them in August 1960. Although it was unclear whether it had been the *Forum*'s efforts that had led to the railroad's decision to spare the concourse, it appeared so, as newspapers and air outlets all around the country had picked up the *Forum* story in support of the cause. Much had happened to mitigate the victory, however, as obtrusive displays in the terminal's concourse had since then mushroomed, but it was still one of the great spatial experiences in American architecture and should, he argued, be preserved. And whatever one might think about the new tower, Haskell added, voicing reservations about Wolfson's new Grand Central City building then under construction, at least it would leave the monumental concourse intact. In fairness, Haskell acknowledged the plight of the railroads, which had worsened markedly since 1954, when the original campaign to save the station had been conducted, but pointed out that much of their hardship was already compensated for by their large and highly profitable real estate operation, which had the terminal as its focal point.[102]

Haskell fleshed out these concerns more fully in a *Forum* editorial the following month.[103] The railroads' predicament was real: Passenger traffic was no longer profitable, railroads were no longer getting the huge government handouts they once had gotten, and their properties were taxed, whereas airlines had their airports built by municipalities and operated them tax-free. Railroad men were used to being pitied, sometimes with justification. "But when two railroads appeal to pity in justifying the continued downgrading of the once-grand interior of Grand Central Station which they have inherited, and where they now propose to make passengers and others creep to seats in the main waiting room under an 11-foot ceiling height caused by hanging three tiers of bowling alleys down from the high ceiling, the time has come for some hard realism about railroads and real estate." He reminded readers that when proposed development of the Grand Central involved demolishing the concourse in 1954, the New York Central had also pled heavy property taxes. After six years of "progressive cannibalization" of the concourse, filling its once magnificent space with signs, turntables,

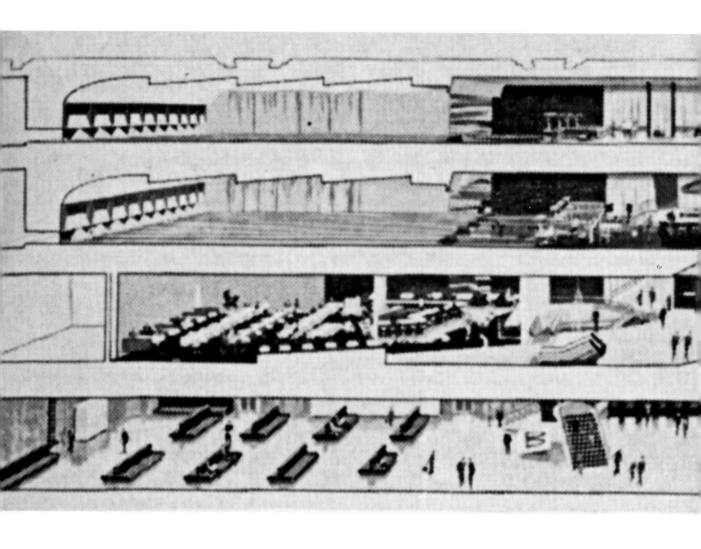

FIGURE 2.12   Bowling alleys proposal, section

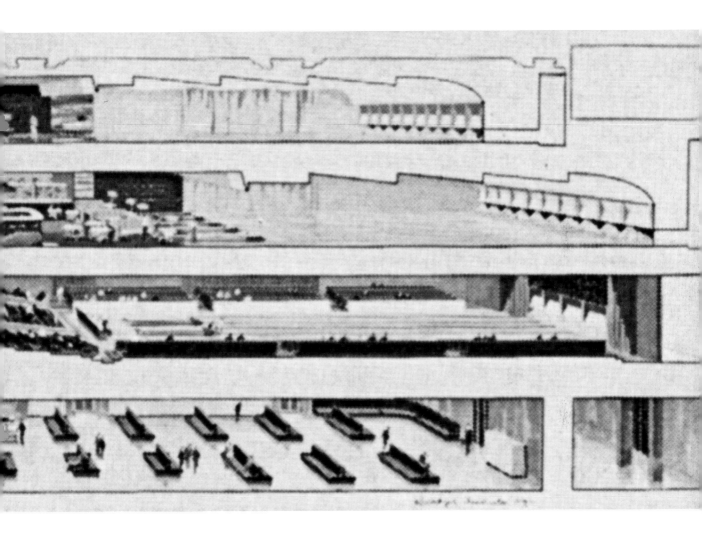

sales booths, oversized clocks, and other gimmicks, all meant to offset declining "railroad" revenue, it was doing it again, as if all its property pertained to railroading. The truth, Haskell said, focusing on his main point, was that Grand Central Station from the beginning was far less of a railroading operation than a real estate operation. Apart from its 70 percent interest in the station (the other 30 percent held by the New York, New Haven, and Hartford), the New York Central held a huge chunk of land on which it and its associates or its subsidiaries owned outright three major hotels and two office buildings and was now "erecting a tower of 2.4 million square feet for perhaps 15,000 occupants as 'Grand Central City,'" which it proclaimed would be the biggest office building in the world. It also held the underground leases of four major hotels, including the Waldorf-Astoria, and of eleven existing office buildings, including the Union Carbide, and two projected office buildings. From the beginning, he said, the terminal was built to be a real estate magnet, the focus or drawing card, so to speak, for all of the highly profitable realty flanking it. To deal with it solely as "railroading money" was, he said, "a laugh." He ended by noting that given the fifteen thousand workers expected to be added by the new Grand Central City tower, the building "will need every inch of breathing space the terminal next door can provide, and if the owners didn't think that way, the city had to."

In another article, this one unpublished, written in the wake of the railroad company's press party in late November announcing that it was going ahead with the bowling alleys, Haskell pointed out that in all their rosy pronouncements the railroad had failed to mention that it had yet to obtain a variance from the Board of Standards and Appeals to permit it to construct the bowling alleys.[104] He then zeroed in on what he saw as the key issue: Those who hesitated to oppose the railroad's bowling alley scheme, on the ground that the station was private property and property owners had the right to do as they wished with property they owned, pitied the poverty-stricken railroads and bemoaned the city's taxing the Grand Central Station while providing the airlines with their airports free. What they overlooked, he said, was that the Grand Central was not chiefly a railroad facility but the lobby, anteroom, and drawing card of a big real estate empire. Again he spelled out the railroad's vast holdings, in addition to the new (by then) Pan Am Building, which its developers promised would draw twenty-five thousand new occupants to the Grand Central but more realistically would draw fifteen thousand, plus all those who do business with them, and the congestion this would bring. "The congestion already being caused by the high density of development is unmistakable—and this before the Pan Am has even started to aggravate it." If anything was needed in the area, he maintained, it was some grand open space.

In his defense of big open spaces "to match the scale, power, and dignity of the community itself," Haskell appealed to Wolfson, whose intelligence and responsiveness he respected, to support the cause of those who opposed the bowling alleys, pointing out how they would demean his new building's interior "forecourt." Wolfson agreed: It was important "to keep Pan Am's 'front yard' clean."[105]

Although Haskell spearheaded the protest against the planned bowling alleys, he was not alone. Others joined the outcry, among them the well-known architect and urban designer Victor Gruen, who in a letter to the *New York Times* said that "as a New Yorker and an architect," he was shocked and alarmed that a beautiful public arena, which served hundreds of thousands of people daily and would have to serve thousands more when the "largest office building in the world," the Pan Am Building, was completed, "should be thus despoiled."[106] A special committee of the New York chapter of the AIA was also organized to oppose the project; John Crosby, critic-at-large of the *Herald Tribune,* joined the crusade, calling public attention to a hearing scheduled by the Board of Standards and Appeals to consider the railroads' request for a variance.[107]

Despite the mounting protest, plans proceeded for the $3 million, forty-four-lane "Grand Central Bowl," which was expected to open in July 1961.[108] An editorial in the *Times* in support of Haskell's campaign stated the issue bluntly: The Grand Central Terminal, one of the great architectural monuments of the country, was about to be disfigured. The railroad's financial plight could not serve "as an excuse for every desecration of a magnificent public monument, even though privately owned."[109] At the heart of the issue was the question of private versus public rights.

Nor was the matter confined to New York. In the December 1960 *Saturday Review,* an editorial on the problem of architecture of American cities used the dispute over the bowling alleys to focus directly on civic values and the question of public versus private interests: "Would the Golden Age of Athens have been entitled to that designation without its architectural wonders? Probably not. However towering its achievements in art, poetry, drama and philosophy, early Greece derived a large part of its historical majesty from its consciousness of design, its awareness of the relationship of form to beauty, and its ability to translate stone into a living and enduring concept." Drawing out the comparison, the editorial's author, Norman Cousins, concluded that New York, at least, had fallen short architecturally. The city's physical beauty, he asserted, was now largely dependent on window washers. Almost all the new buildings were encased in glass, which created striking effects when the glass was clear, but an appalling monotony when it was not. While acknowledging some "powerful items of distinction," such as the United Nations Secretariat, Lever House, the Union Carbide Building, and the Seagram Building, there were dozens of other glass-encased structures that were uninspired and grossly imitative to the point of seeming to have come from a bulk catalog. Cousins then turned his attention to the plans for the bowling alleys in the Grand Central. Next to the railroad terminal in Rome, he said, New York's Grand Central was "probably the most magnificent station in the world" and was now facing desecration. Already it had been converted into something of a bazaar, with its commercial signs and displays. What the legal rights of the public were in this situation, he asked, wasn't clear, but lawyers were exploring it, as well as the possibility of a taxpayers' suit to block it. "The people of New York donated the valuable land on which the railroad trains operate; they are part owners of the terminal, and are entitled to be heard," he concluded.[110]

Still more articles, including another editorial in the *Times,* were published on the mounting efforts by architects and civic groups to abort the railroad's plans, urging the public to attend the hearing scheduled by Board of Standards and Appeals to insist that the board refuse to grant the railroad a zoning variance to go forward with the bowling alleys and start preserving buildings that were landmarks in the city and contributed to its historic and cultural appeal.[111]

James O. Boisi, Vice-President of Real Estate for New York Central Railroad, appeared at the hearing to defend the railroad. Reassuring his audience of the Central's pride in the historic terminal, he called it "the very symbol of our railroad, its rich history and of the relationship between the Central and the City and State," but then went on to point out that the desecration of the terminal was not the issue before the board, but rather the zoning variance. He then pointed out several facts he thought pertinent. "Because of Grand Central's pre-eminence in the heart of Manhattan, it is looked upon by most of the public as 'public property,'" but in fact it was not. It was owned, he noted, by the forty thousand shareholders of the New York Central Railroad, who had invested in the company's stock and had every right to expect a fair return on their money. The railroad's very business, he said, was to provide transportation services at a profit, for the benefit of these investors. The Central faced serious problems as a result of the losses it was incurring in operating and maintaining the terminal, on the one hand, and paying city taxes, on the other. Dropping his deferential demeanor, Boisi then turned to threats: If the deficit of the Grand Central continued, the railroad might be forced to demolish the whole building. The railroad's concession policy was to develop those areas in the terminal that would not interfere with the basic features of the building itself. The need for revenue to operate the Grand Central was great; so was the public's interest in seeing the station maintained as a landmark. But the public could not require the railroad to maintain the station's dignity *and* pay taxes on it, Borsi concluded. It had to decide what it wanted from the railroad: taxes, trains, or terminals.[112]

Borsi's threats notwithstanding, by a vote of four to zero, the Board of Standards and Appeals denied the variance. To Borsi's contention that the question of aesthetics was irrelevant, Max Foley, chair of the board, asserted the contrary, maintaining that the monumental character of the building would indeed be "adversely affected," as its character depended not just on its facade, but on what was inside. In response to Boisi's argument that the railroads were losing money, paying heavy taxes, and not getting the same governmental aid the airlines or shipping companies were receiving, and that the rail lines had to do whatever they needed to do to make a profit for their stockholders, Foley replied simply that "unfortunately it was not the function of the board to provide economic aid."[113]

Acknowledging that denial of the variance might not end the matter, that Central could still petition the City Planning Commission to rezone the terminal, and that in any case the railroad was still free to install other concessions, like stores, showrooms, offices, and restaurants in the waiting room air space, subsequent articles in the *Times* pointed out that the issue at least had put architects "on guard" against further encroachments, and that there was talk of an attempt to convince the City Planning Commission that "a new legal weapon was needed to protect public, quasi-public, and historic buildings" against changes that would detract from their distinction.[114]

The issue was important in the context of the Pan Am, as it aroused public as well as professional awareness of what changes were occurring in the urban environment, the public arena. It also revealed a growing ambivalence about the Pan Am Building, then under construction, and its impact on the surroundings. Pitting the railroads against the public, it declared that the station "belonged" to the public despite its being privately owned. Finally, it marked another stage in Haskell's long campaign to preserve Grand Central Station as a public monument and his growing concern for the protection of public spaces, even if privately owned. His demand for a sense of civic responsibility on the part of large institutions and other powerful bodies was to be heard again in the case of the Pan Am.

PAN AMERICAN SIGNS ON

While the New York Central Railroad was developing its plans to exploit the air space in-side Grand Central Terminal with bowling alleys, Wolfson was busy making plans of his own with one of the nation's leading airlines. Throughout the summer of 1960, he had been holding highly clandestine meetings with Trippe. That September, it was announced that Pan American had, in the largest lease of its kind, signed a lease for fifteen floors in the new skyscraper rising over the Grand Central, becoming the major tenant in the build-ing. As part of the negotiations, the building was to be renamed the Pan Am (figure 2.13).[115]

PAN AMERICAN WORLD AIRWAYS AND THE AIRLINE INDUSTRY

The deal was a sign of the times, marking the nation's turning its back on the rail in-dustry and entry into the jet age. Just as Haskell and others were writing about the plight of the railroads, with their obsolete railway yards and dilapidated stations, still others were writing about the wave of new airports, and the excitement of airport archi-tecture such as that of Idlewild, (later renamed JFK Airport), "America's gateway to the world." "America's greatest aerial gateway, New York's International Airport . . . has outgrown its adolescence," began one such article in May, just months before the Trippe/Wolfson deal, expressing the thrill, speed, and glamour of the new jet age. "Within a dozen years air travel has become *the* leading means of transportation be-tween nations. In 1958, for the first time, more people crossed the Atlantic in planes than on steamships. Now the Jet Age is here, and Idlewild is ready. . . . Now that the Jet Age, with its breathtaking potential, has begun in full force, air-passenger figures are bound to soar. . . ."[116] New York International Airport, a 655-acre landscaped trans-portation hub fifteen miles from midtown Manhattan, described as "a glittering, $150 million showplace for modern architecture, art, and scientific wizardry," included the new Pan American World Airways Terminal, with its four-acre umbrella roof (figures 2.14 and 2.15). To go from New York City to Albany by train, such articles breathlessly exclaimed, took longer than to go from New York to Nassau in the Bahamas by jet; Los Angeles was only a six hour nonstop hop from New York, Paris only seven hours from Idlewild. Since the late 1950s, *Architectural Forum* too had been including articles on new airports, the advent of jet travel, and "the fabulous age it portends," acknowledg-ing airport construction as one of the fastest-growing areas of building activity.[117] Back then air travel was still an adventure.

FIGURE 2.13   Erwin Wolfson (left) and Juan Trippe (right), with model of the Pan Am

FIGURE 2.14   Pan American Boeing jet at Idlewild

FIGURE 2.15 Boarding a Pan American jet

One of the big three transatlantic freight carriers and for more than half a century the most powerful international airline in the country, Pan Am was at the forefront of the aviation industry. Ranked at one point among the world's largest, by 1960 it was the nation's leading international carrier, its planes by that time a symbol of global reach.[118] Its history is that of aviation history in the United States. Founded by Trippe in 1927, the next year Pan American World Airways was one of the first in history to run scheduled international flights between Key West, Florida, and Havana, Cuba (figure 2.16); it ushered in trans-Pacific air travel in the mid-1930s with the sea route planes Trippe dubbed "clippers," after the tall-masted seagoing sailing vessels of the past, and launched the first scheduled trans-Atlantic service in 1939, when international aviation was still a dream (figure 2.17). During the Second World War, when the United States needed to get bombers to the British in West Africa, it called upon Pan American World Airways, which by this time had so much experience in overseas flying that it was said jokingly that the defense effort should be an arm of Pan Am.[119] In 1947, Pan American introduced round-the-world service, then in 1958, it was the first U.S. airline to fly Boeing's 707 commercial jetliner, which doubled the speed and passenger capacity of its propeller-driven predecessor, the Boeing Stratocruiser (figure 2.18). Its first jet christened by First Lady Mamie Eisenhower, in the fall of 1958, Pan American ushered in the jet age (figure 2.19).

Pan Am founder Trippe (figure 2.20) developed his passion for aircraft as an aviator in World War I. The son of an engineer, Trippe spent two years on Wall Street after graduating from Yale, thereby learning much about business and corporate power. He made the most of his Yale connections, among them Henry R. Luce, in his business transactions. Known as a fierce competitor, "a robber baron and buccaneer, albeit a gentleman," polite but devious, even ruthless, obsessed with his airline, he was a shrewd businessman with a one-man, solo management style.[120] Knowing the American fascination with cultural heroes and the power of prominent names, in the late 1920s, Trippe hired Charles Lindbergh, then famous as a result of his record-breaking 1927 flight, as Pan American's "technical advisor" on new routes and equipment, well aware of the public relations value Lindbergh's name alone would have. A man in perpetual quest of power—the political power to secure the routes he wanted as well as powerful aircraft to operate them—Trippe was determined to hold a monopoly on foreign routes as the "sovereign of American skies" and ran head on into President Franklin D. Roosevelt, who favored a more competitive "open skies" policy.[121] At the beginning of World War II, Pan Am was the only airline carrying the American flag abroad; by then Pan Ameri-

FIGURE 2.16   Pan Am's first scheduled passenger flight from Key West to Havana on a ten-passenger Fokker F-7 aircraft, 1928

FIGURE 2.17   Pan Am's China Clipper, mid-1930s

FIGURE 2.18   Pan Am Boeing Stratocruiser, 1950s

FIGURE 2.19   First Lady Mamie Eisenhower christening first Boeing 707 jet, 1958

FIGURE 2.20   Juan Trippe

can World Airways was a symbol of U.S. economic power around the world. In the words of a retired agent of the CIA, in the 1950s "Pan Am *was* the American flag, for all practical purposes an extension of the United States Government. In many places, it was the only symbol of America besides the embassy. Even before there was Coca-Cola in some places, there was Pan Am."[122] Flush with success, in October 1955, the company took one of the largest steps in its expansion by ordering forty-five jet airliners at cost of $269 million. Trippe at that point was president of the International Air Transport Association, an organization of seventy airlines.[123] Three years later, Pan American made headlines again in becoming the first U.S. airline to fly the Boeing 707 commercially.[124]

By the late 1950s, just as Wolfson was preparing plans for his new skyscraper over the Grand Central, Trippe, who had initially rented an office on 42nd Street directly across from the Grand Central Station, then later in the 1930s moved into larger quarters in the Chrysler Building, had again run out of space. At this point, late in the spring of 1960, Wolfson, with Cotton as his financial partner and demolition of the existing six-story office building about to begin, was aggressively looking for a high-profile major tenant for the new building, which he needed to attract other tenants. On learning that Trippe's thirty-year-old lease in the Chrysler Building was soon to expire, Wolfson met with Trippe that July. Insisting on absolute secrecy in their negotiations, Trippe was clearly interested. Besides his need for more space, there were advantages to staying in the Grand Central area, which had become the hub of the closely knit aviation industry.[125] Trippe was also impressed by the fact that the building was partly British owned, which seemed appropriate for an international airline. And he was drawn to the notion of being housed in a big new modern building on Park Avenue, with what promised to be a distinctive form designed by two of the foremost architects of the time, which would bear the name of Pan Am—a factor that, according to a study done while negotiations were taking place, was estimated to be worth between $500,000 and $1 million in publicity.[126]

In September of that year, Wolfson and Trippe signed a twenty-five-year lease believed, according to an article the *New York Times,* to be the biggest ever for commercial office space in Manhattan. The airline would have 613,000 square feet, or about fifteen floors on the top level for home offices, consolidating the Pan American offices, as well as space at the corner of Vanderbilt Avenue and 45th Street for the airline's main ticket office, at a total rental of $115,500,000.[127]

Interest in the deal was widespread. Both the mayor of the city and the governor sent the builders congratulatory notes, expressing their delight that the airline's headquarters would remain in New York. A fuller article in the *Times* several days after the lease was signed pointed out how momentous the deal was, emphasizing the vital role played by leases in building a speculative skyscraper.[128] Pan American World Airways' commitment to lease 613,000 square feet of floor area in the fifty-nine-story building amounted to its occupying more than a quarter of the building's space, with each of the airline's fifteen floors comprising over an acre.

PAN AM NAME

The prominence of the Pan Am name presented a major hurdle in the long, difficult, detailed negotiations to work out the terms of the lease.[129] Trippe insisted on thirty-foot signs bearing the name "Pan Am" on all eight sides of the building, which was by this time seen as certain to become a major landmark in the city. Gropius argued against this, maintaining that it "would appear overdone" to have so many signs and such large ones, and that "the dignity of the building" would suffer. He felt one sign on each of the broad northern and southern facades, which would be visible, he said, "from everywhere," would suffice. In a session of hard bargaining in which Gropius was included, Trippe finally agreed to fifteen-foot signs on four sides of the building only, with "Pan Am" spelled out on two of the broad facades, and a globe, the company's logo, on the two narrow sides.[130]

An article on tenant's having their names on buildings if they rent enough space appeared in the *New York Times* shortly before Wolfson broached his proposal with Trippe and surely spurred Trippe's thinking. According to the article, a tenant who leased one third or more of a building's total floor space could generally determine the name of the building, and the prestige and promotional value of having a building named after oneself was enough to have some companies actually renting more space than they needed. The article also mentioned, again a point that was surely not lost on Trippe, then flush with his company's success, that the search for a structure "impressive enough to mirror the success a company has achieved" was, according to real estate men, highly competitive.[131] Wolfson's offer of what promised to be an attention-drawing building, bigger in terms of bulk than any in the city thus far, on Park Avenue, a distinctive monument that provided a visual terminus to its long, dramatic vista, in a neighborhood within which Trippe wanted to remain, and on top of the Grand Central

Station, the city's main transportation hub, yet, would seem made to order. But it was in fact Wolfson who went to Trippe, and Trippe who, knowing he held the trump card, drove the hard bargain, down to demanding the name of his company on top of Wolfson's building.[132]

The problem of signage had in fact come up even before the Wolfson/Trippe deal was publicly announced. In August 1960, midway through the lengthy, detailed two-month process of negotiating the Pan Am lease, the building's design team was grappling with Pan American representatives Edward Larabee Barnes and Charles Forberg, both noted modernist architect/designers who had been engaged by Pan American as the company's designers, to hammer out a compromise on the type of lettering for the sign on top of the tower as well as its location and size.[133] Months later, they were still haggling over the problem. Gropius's team had wanted the east and west sides left bare and reluctantly agreed to the use of a globe, the Pan Am logo, which the company insisted on, only as long as it was without the Pan Am lettering.[134] This did not resolve the sticky issue in the eyes of Gropius, who called the negotiations deadlocked. In a letter to Wolfson, he acknowledged that Pan Am had the legal right, according to its contract with Wolfson, to put up its sign, but the problem, he said, arose after it was realized "that a proper installation of the sign *off* the façade would encroach on the air rights at the eastern elevation." To overcome this, it had been suggested that the sign be put as a disc flush with the vertical mullions, an arrangement that he, "as your responsible designer," vigorously protested because he thought it would have the effect of a billboard. He offered two solutions: to put the twenty-six-foot-diameter globes directly under the Pan Am signs on the north and south facades, or to leave out the globe on the eastern side altogether, with the one on the western side set off the mullions as originally intended.[135] Though he questioned whether the City of New York would approve the signs at all, they were approved, and the Pan Am logos were installed on both the east and west sides of the building.

PAN AMERICAN TICKET OFFICE

Forberg and Barnes, whom Pan Am had hired in the mid-1950s to develop a new corporate imagery announcing its liftoff into the jet age, were responsible for the design of the main ticket office in the Pan Am Building as well (figure 2.21).[136] The new ticket office, located in the northwest corner of the Pan Am Building, a long (135-foot), low (11-foot) space nestled under a 25-foot overhang off the main lobby, was large, at ten

FIGURE 2.21   Pan Am ticket office

thousand square feet the largest airline ticket office in the world at the time. To counter the long, low space were fluid, sweeping forms evocative of flight favored in recent airport design. Instead of the usual long, straight counters, which would have reinforced the length of the space, tickets were sold at freestanding, circular "islands" that were ultimately to be connected to a worldwide computer reservation system located elsewhere in the building. Behind them were expansive curved, sweeping backwalls with a sculpted white plaster relief map of the world. The curvilinearity of the whole was echoed by the gently flaring mushroom columns and serpentine seating, which coiled around low, circular coffee tables. Clearly inspired more by the sweeping, sculptural, flight-evoking forms of recent airports, particularly Saarinen's Trans World Airlines (TWA) terminal then nearing completion at Idlewild, than Gropius's more rigorously rectilinear orthodox modernism, the ticket counter was in dramatic contrast to, or, depending on your view, at complete odds with, the Pan Am Building itself.

THE ART

Despite Gropius's long-standing conviction, articulated in his 1958 essay "The Curse of Conformity," that along with the engineer and businessman, the artist should be a full-fledged member of the production team and involved in projects from the start, it wasn't until after the lease with Trippe had been negotiated in the fall of 1960 that his thoughts began to turn to the building's art.[137] The trend for incorporating contemporary art in new office buildings was not new and in fact had been gaining momentum since the mid-1950s. In the eyes of later historians, the buying of art for a building's lobby served two purposes: It was a sign of cultural sophistication, and it showed a civic-minded support for the arts.[138] Behind these obvious motivations, however, was often another somewhat less lofty aim: to allay potential criticism of an otherwise mundane building.

Skyscraper builders, "long regarded as arch-conservatives in matters of décor," a *New York Times* article in 1958 observed shortly after Gropius and Belluschi had signed on as design consultants on the Grand Central City project, had become "ardent patrons of modern art in their search for eye-catching appointments for new office buildings." Far beyond the decorative work in buildings built between the wars, the article noted, now many famous artists were being commissioned to devise sculpture and murals for new office buildings, and surprisingly these artists were being given considerable freedom to design.[139]

Huxtable's analysis was more penetrating. In the fall of 1959 she wrote an article on the subject in the *Times,* "Art with Architecture: New Terms of an Old Alliance." In the article, she argued that the charge of inexpressiveness, frequently directed at modern architecture, was hurled at contemporary art as well, and that the two were in fact perfect allies, the boldness, freedom, and explosive color of the one mitigating the cold austerity of the other. Art was coming "out of its ivory tower and into the office building lobby," she said, forming a natural union, she believed, with abstract art extending and enriching contemporary architectural design. Among works she cited were SOM's Manufacturers Trust Company building, with a seventy-foot-long rough golden screen by Harry Bertoia; the Tishman Tower, with artwork by Isamu Noguchi; Josef Albers's "Structural Constellations" in the Corning Glass Building; and works by Juan Miro, Jackson Pollock, and Pablo Picasso at the Seagram Building's Four Seasons restaurant, which also had a twenty-six-foot-square Richard Lippold construction of five thousand slender brass rods suspended over the bar. Not all such alliances of art and architecture were happy, however. Huxtable cited an artwork ostentatiously displayed in a lobby that "dazzled the gullible public" but couldn't redeem the shoddy structure, and another in one of New York's largest new offices in which "an ill-considered mosaic added to a distressingly fussy curtain wall did nothing to define or clarify the building's monumental scale." The fault in such cases, however, was not the artist's, Huxtable contended, but the architect's. "Almost 2,000 years ago, Vitruvius said of the architect, 'It is by his judgment that all the work done by the other arts is put to the test.'" The words, she said, were still pertinent. "The total building is the architect's work of art."[140] These were loaded words, of particular significance for the Pan Am.

Where the initial idea to incorporate art into the Pan Am Building came from is not clear. Trippe had of course hired well-known architects and industrial designers since the mid-1950s as part of the image of glamorous, futuristic air travel he wanted his company to project.[141] Wolfson, on the other hand, had shown little interest in devoting much of a building's budget to art in his buildings prior to the Pan Am, as had the Roths, well known for their aesthetic indifference. It may have been the general expectation by this time that a building of the magnitude and stature of the Pan Am would include art. And it was certainly something Gropius, who by then had incorporated the work of contemporary artists, often his former colleagues at the Bauhaus, in his other buildings, would have endorsed.

Belluschi too had for years been an active proponent of the collaboration of art and architecture. He had been asked to review Eleanor Bittermann's *Art in Modern Archi-*

tecture for *Progressive Architecture,* and was a former member of the board of trustees for the Portland Art Museum and a member of the National Commission of Fine Arts. In June 1960, as work on the Grand Central City project continued, Belluschi had received a letter from Harris K. Prior, director of the American Federation of Arts (AFA), of which Belluschi was also a trustee, regarding art in the new building. Prior thought that there might be some areas in which the AFA could be of service in planning the Grand Central City tower, either in the use of art on a permanent basis in the building or in planning for some kind of exhibition space in the public areas and keeping it supplied with temporary art. Belluschi sent a copy of the letter to Colcord, saying it merited attention, and suggested that he mention it to Wolfson.[142] After some delay, Colcord responded to Belluschi by pointing out they had already been thinking of "decorative panels" in the new building, that Gropius had been in New York the week before, and that Wolfson had authorized him at that time to proceed with preliminary designs.[143] Belluschi was apparently at this point beginning to fall out of the loop, at least as far as daily progress on the building was concerned, and although it is clear that Belluschi was consulted, Gropius alone was responsible for the selection and location of the building's art.

By December 1960, Gropius had firmed up his thinking and in fact moved ahead with some of the Pan Am artwork. He had talked to several artists about preliminary sketches, for which they were to be paid a thousand dollars each—Albers, for the screen above the escalators down to the Grand Central Terminal; Gyorgy Kepes, for the screen in the large lobby on 45th Street: and Lippold, for the screen and globe at the Vanderbilt Avenue entrance—and had met with them to discuss the model of the building and other issues such as materials they would need to proceed. At this point he was hoping that they could meet with Pan Am's representatives to go over the sketches as well as the design of the lettering and emblems that Chermayeff was preparing for the building.[144]

All three artists were well known and had designed pieces for corporate clients in the past. Moreover, they were known to both Gropius and Belluschi, with whom they had worked on previous jobs. Albers was a long-standing colleague of Gropius's dating back to Bauhaus days, who along with Kepes and Lippold had done work in the Harvard Graduate Center. Kepes was also a close friend and colleague of Belluschi's at MIT and had designed the monumental glass in two of Belluschi's East Coast churches, the Church of the Redeemer in Baltimore and the Trinity Episcopal Church in Concord, Massachusetts. Lippold did the sculpture in Belluschi's Portsmouth Abbey in Portsmouth, Rhode Island, and together with Kepes was to do another for Belluschi's St. Mary's

Cathedral in San Francisco, which was commissioned about this same time.[145] It may in fact have been Belluschi who recommended Lippold, whose gossamer-thin wire sculptures had proved to interact highly successfully with the light and space of Belluschi's architectural forms.[146]

The Lippold work, destined for the Vanderbilt Avenue lobby, was clearly the most important of the three. In January 1961, the artist was asked to draw up a statement on the work he was designing. It was to be "a sculptural symbol" for Pan American World Airways, he said in the statement he submitted, its form "derived from the performances and shapes of modern aircraft, except for the sphere of the world in the center." Since one could walk under the work, it would also suggest, he thought, the excitement of passing under the great sweeps of wings and tails during boarding and disembarking.[147]

Lippold's statement was drawn up in preparation for a meeting with Trippe, whose tastes accommodated the forward-looking, clean-swept lines of his modernist industrial designers but stopped short of abstract art. Unfortunately, Trippe's approval was needed for the sculpture for the Vanderbilt Avenue entrance, which opened onto the Pan American Airways lobby. In an effort to garner support for their cause, Gropius asked René d'Harnoncourt, then director of MoMA, to join him for a meeting with Trippe, whose "somewhat commercial realistic approach" needed turning around. Both Belluschi and Lippold, he said, would also be at the meeting.[148]

The meeting, with Trippe, Wolfson, Colcord, Gropius, Belluschi, d'Harnoncourt, and Lippold, plus Cvijanovic, Chermayeff, and Barnes, as well as a host of reporters attending, was considered enough of an event to be written up in the *New Yorker*.[149] "In case you haven't noticed" (as if anyone could miss it), "Talk of the Town" began in its usual jocular, meandering fashion,

> the old six-story Grand Central Terminal office building has been demolished, and in its place, on three and a half acres behind the Terminal, a New York investment builder named Erwin S. Wolfson, in partnership with a London investment builder named Jack Cotton, is putting up a 59-story octagonal building (address: 200 Park Avenue) that will have the world's largest number of enclosed square feet of commercial office space—two million two hundred and seventy thousand. More than a quarter of these square feet—six hundred and thirteen thousand, on sixteen floors—have been rented by Pan American World Airways, and the skyscraper will, as a con-

sequence, be named the Pan Am Building. And because Mr. Wolfson, a thoughtful, modest, athletic, alert, fresh-air-loving man of fifty-nine who majored in philosophy at college and has since plunged into a variety of educational pursuits, has a keenly wistful eye on the arts, he has, while adroitly arranging with his right, or practical, hand for the financing of the building (banks' construction loans of sixty-five million dollars and a mortgage of seventy million dollars, just to give you an idea), with his left hand knowledgeably engaged the celebrated talents — in addition to those of the building's architects, Emery Roth & Sons — of Walter Gropius and Pietro Belluschi, to work on the building as design consultants.

That, said the article, was just the beginning, as Wolfson, now free of the business aspect of the building, was planning "to join his business monument to the arts." To this "heroic end," Wolfson had, the previous week, invited a *New Yorker* reporter to a meeting at Trippe's office in the Chrysler Building, the article continued, on the possible purchase of a Lippold creation expressive of Pan Am for the Vanderbilt Avenue entrance lobby. If things worked out, Lippold's sculpture—thirty feet high and eighty feet across—would be in the center of the large hall. As they all walked over to Trippe's office, according to the *New Yorker*, the architectural members of the delegation

seemed faintly uneasy: Dr. Gropius, founder of the Bauhaus in prewar Germany, former chairman of the Department of Architecture of Harvard's Graduate School of Design, and now member of an architectural firm called the Architects Collaborative, wearing a beret and looking, at seventy-seven, energetic, literally highbrow, noble, suntanned, bow-tied, and as powerfully definite as a face on Mount Rushmore; Dr. Belluschi, born in Ancona and raised in Rome, dean of the School of Architecture and Planning at MIT, devotee of quality and humanism in architecture, and a gray-haired, gray-brush-mustached, gentle-voiced, patient man.

Lippold was pale-faced, but looked confident and ready to fight. They went up via express elevator to Trippe's office. Trippe was there with Willis Lipscomb, a Pan Am vice president who, like Trippe and Wolfson, was neatly dressed in business grays and blues. The "Talk of the Town" columnist then described the scene: Lippold opened with a cavalier slap on the table, which drew a small, reluctant smile from Trippe; Wolfson cleared his throat and politely but briskly got the meeting down to business, turning straightaway to Walter Gropius.

> *All heads turned toward Mount Rushmore. Dr. Gropius took a deep breath and said, "It is a way of making sculpture many of us think is beautiful." He held up a drawing of the planned sculpture — very abstract. "It symbolizes the globe of the world."*
>
> *"Yes," Trippe said, cordially but not batting an eye. "I wish we had some way of seeing how it would look."*

The columnist went on, describing the meeting with one side trying to sell the work, the other side resisting.

> *"I want to tell you," Dr. Gropius said. "All my life I have tried to cooperate with painters and sculptors to create work for buildings that would be at one with the buildings, and this is the first time it has happened. Lippold's sculpture comes to one with our building."*
>
> *"Yes," Trippe said again, cordially, and gave a nod to Vice-President Lipscomb. "We have a twofold problem here," Trippe went on. "I have a board of directors to reckon with, and when I showed them this flat picture they didn't go for it. We have several directors interested in art, but we've got a lot of doubting Thomases who just don't go for it. And then we've got a large number of directors in need of education in modern art. I don't know if I include myself with them or not." He smiled apologetically at Dr. Gropius. "Couldn't we get something better than just this flat picture?"*

Then Lippold took the floor, and told the assembled troops he'd finally gotten his parents to fly for the first time, in a jet from Chicago to New York. When he got them home and showed them the drawing of his proposed sculpture for the Pan Am, they said,

> *"Why, it looks like our flight."*

A parent-loving murmur went around the table, and Lippold took a sheet of paper from an inner coat pocket and read:

"The forms in this work are derived from the performances and shapes of modern aircraft except for a sphere of the world in the center. From this sphere, a seven-pointed star radiates symbolically toward the seven continents (and seven seas), its long conical arms originating in Great Circles of the globe, like the routes followed in intercontinental travel. . . . Surrounding this world-sphere with its radiating elements are silver forms whose general character suggests the direct ascents and descents and flight patterns of jet aircraft, as well as wing and tail sections of modern planes."

Trippe and Lipscomb leaned forward to look at [the drawing Lippold was holding up], as though trying to make out a wing or tail section.

"Two materials are used," Lippold read on: "a high-carat gold over bronze for the globe and star, and stainless steel for the silver-colored elements. These relate to the gray Travertine marble of the interior. The shapes have been chosen and placed with regard to the space of the lobby, in an effort to continue the unity of form of the architecture, and also to echo the unique angularity of the exterior of the building."

Lippold stopped reading.

Dr. Gropius said, "It goes up like a flower," and threw his arms open to indicate a flower.

"Perhaps this is a dumb question," Trippe said, "but where is the light?"

"Inconspicuously built in," Dr. Gropius said.

"One of the beauties of this is that it has size without weight," Dr. Belluschi added.

"Will this symbolic globe be held by wires?" Trippe asked.

"The whole thing is in a state of tension," Lippold said.

"Well, it's hard to tell," Trippe said, and again nodded to Vice-President Lip-scomb, who threw Lippold a friendly smile and said, somewhat apologeti-cally, "We've been doing considerable thinking about this versus a more literal approach. We ran a survey internally on the question to determine which would linger longer in the minds of the people who see it. The major-ity felt that a more literal approach to a globe might capture the interest of the public on a more continuing basis."

"To be expected," Lippold said quickly. "It's people dealing with the unfa-miliar. It's like asking somebody if he likes his own mother better than some-body else's mother."

Another parent-loving murmur . . .

"There are two ways of approaching it," Dr. Gropius said. "One is the real-istic way — to show a great globe. The other is the artistic *way. Art always tries to symbolize the* image *of what is behind the scene. This design will re-ally make a hit with the people."*

Then d'Harnoncourt chimed in.

"We were the first people lucky enough to have one of Lippold's space de-signs in our lobby. I would say that this *one would be one of the most im-portant pieces of indoor sculpture of the twentieth century. If you want the impact of a great symbol, giving the feeling of speed through space, of ex-pansion and lightness, you have it in this sculpture. No one who sees it is ever going to forget it."*

Trippe and Lipscomb looked reflective.

"You feel as though you're in this *sculpture," Dr. Gropius said. "You stand in the lobby and you're right in the sculpture."*

"But are you sure people will remember it?" Vice-President Lipscomb asked.

"Let me ask you," Trippe said. "On modern art, I know the Rockefellers are for it. As a matter of fact, they took me on a tour of their museum when it was finished. But I wonder—about modern art, won't many people be offended by it?"

Trippe then asked where Lippold would put his signature.

"This needs no signature," Lippold said.

"Tremendously interesting," Trippe said. "I've been partly educated. Now I've got to put it up to our doubting Thomases."[150]

The meeting was written up somewhat more dryly in the *New York Times.* Lippold was described as an American "who has won renown in avant-garde circles here and abroad for his shimmering geometrical constructions," and the article noted that his work was on display in several museums, including the Metropolitan and Museum of Modern Art.[151]

In an article the following year in *Art in America,* Lippold elaborated on his ideas for the Pan Am project. Gropius had asked him, he said, to design a work that would serve as a screen concealing the escalators in the lobby opposite the entrance. A screen, he felt, would only accentuate the narrowness of the space "and make no gesture toward the very interesting spatial possibilities in the lobby," which he wanted to explore. The space was extremely wide and fairly shallow, but in the center between the main supporting columns the space formed a square, which he found interesting. Saying nothing about how the form evolved or what inspired the shapes, he added that the work's title, "Flight," had just been chosen. He hoped the work would act physically as a means of "squaring" the rectangle of the lobby and provide visual excitement for all levels of movement in and out of the building, even from the escalators, which were left exposed. Psychologically, it might effect a liaison, he maintained, between the scale of the building and the scale of man, "holding hands with each, so to speak, quite literally touching the floors and the walkways in delicate contact with these surfaces on which men will walk." Its symmetry of form, which seemed natural to him, would also provide "a means for tranquil contemplation in a center of unordered movement, thus being party to the concurrence of law and chance."

FIGURE 2.22   Lippold sculpture, Vanderbilt Avenue lobby

To further this possibility, he had commissioned avant-garde composer John Cage to compose a continuous program of music that would provide different sounds from each of ten loudspeakers in the lobby's ceiling, under the mezzanine, and in the base of the sculpture—as an alternative to the piped-in program of Muzak originally planned for all the building's public areas. Cage devised a system whereby the movement of people going in and out of the lobby would activate photoelectric cells; these in turn would release Muzak (for which the Pan Am had a contract), that had been electronically pulverized and filtered in the process. The result would be "a constantly changing, continuous concert of music in three-dimensional space, becoming in effect, a part of the sculpture."[152]

The piece never materialized. As an article in the *New York Times* on Cage's project for the Pan Am put it, noting that musical projects that aren't realized rarely make news, but that this one was particularly fascinating, "the American businessman and the esthetic do not always see eye to eye."[153] Lippold's sculpture (figure 2.22), initially entitled "The Globe," was installed without music in April 1963. The occasion was marked by front-page coverage in the *Times,* including a photograph of the artist and his sculpture, accompanied by Lippold's long explanatory notes on its meaning.[154]

Another *Times* article later that year addressed the art in the Pan Am building and the lobby's "new look."[155] "The public lobby area in the Pan Am Building is taking on aspects of an art gallery, with the display of an enormous metallic sculpture, a dual architectural form, a large mural, and a heroic-sized bust," it said. The Lippold sculpture, renamed "Flight," was three stories high and forty feet deep and extended eighty feet across the Vanderbilt Avenue lobby. Overlooking the 45th Street lobby on the balcony level was the forty-foot-long mural by Kepes (figure 2.23). The twenty-eight- by fifty-five-foot red, white, and black mural by Albers, of laminated materials and based "on a design of optical mixtures," was displayed above the escalators forming the entrance to the building from the Grand Central terminal (figure 2.24). A bronze bust of Wolfson, who had died the previous year, by the sculptor Robert Berks, was also displayed in the main, 45th Street lobby.[156]

The *Times* articles were mainly descriptive, based on press material prepared by the Grand Central Building, Inc. Of the Lippold work at least, the *Forum* was more critical: Though the lighting by lighting expert Abe Feder put it to good effect, shooting "a myriad of fantastic, dazzling rays of light (taut wires in curving planes) on all sides of a symbolic earth," the Lippold sculpture was "almost crippled" by the space surrounding it.[157] It was not the first time the new building, still under construction, had been openly criticized, and it was hardly to be the last.

FIGURE 2.23   Kepes mural, 45th Street lobby

FIGURE 2.24   Albers mural, entrance from terminal

3

THE CLAMOR OF CRITICISM

Criticism of the Grand Central City project had been growing ever since plans for the re-development of the Grand Central area first surfaced in the fall of 1954. At that time, the focus was on the threatened demolition of the Grand Central Terminal itself, de-railed at least in part, or so it would seem, by Haskell's campaign in *Architectural Forum*. Other articles followed, among them Huxtable's, calling attention to the architectural significance of the area and the critical nature of the site. A long *New York Times* editorial in June 1958, two weeks before Wolfson contacted Gropius about the Grand Central City project, was devoted to the Grand Central Terminal and its significance to the city.[1] It was a place, the editorial observed, used not only by commuters and travelers from afar, but by New Yorkers going about their daily lives in the city: thus any proposed changes in its architectural scheme was, as the *Times'* editors put it, "a matter of concern to a great many people."

The involvement of Gropius and Belluschi in the project was a positive sign. An exchange of letters between Belluschi and Weinberg, who remained keenly involved in the matter, indicated not only how widespread the concern for the proposed development was among members of the profession, but also the profession's high hopes for what Gropius and Belluschi could bring to it. Calling Belluschi's attention to an *Architectural Forum* article, "Can Civic Beauty Be Legislated?" illustrated by a photograph of the Park Avenue vista, Weinberg urged him "to try to get in on the ground floor, so to speak, of the promoters' planning processes and give them the benefit of your experience in respect to the more fundamental question involved on whether the placing of such a building at this location is appropriate at all." Weinberg pointed out that the city's planning commission was officially powerless to take any action in the matter, since it involved private land and private funds, but that those architects who were concerned about the planning of "our home town"—alluding to the fact that Gropius and Belluschi were both outsiders—were "greatly concerned with the effect of so large a bulk of building and consequent people and traffic being dumped into an already overloaded part of town." He hoped that Belluschi and Gropius could persuade Wolfson to build elsewhere.[2]

Belluschi's response was telling. "You have placed a finger on a sore spot in my conscience," he replied, "and like in all sinful deeds I have been busy making up alibis." There were a number of things, such as cars and trucks, that he didn't like about modern civilization, he pointed out, but that did not mean he was going back to walking on foot. He agreed with Weinberg about the problem of adding thousands of more people to the already congested Grand Central area but argued on behalf of the railroads, maintaining that to meet their tax obligations in the face of declining passenger revenues, they had to seek other sources of funds in order to survive. The economics of the competitive system were inescapable, he said. Wolfson had large tenants eager to locate in such a central location; moreover, pedestrian congestion was easier to justify than that of cars. "I will agree with you that this is rationalizing what may well be a central sin, but it seems to be in the nature of the American city," Belluschi concluded, then added that he and Gropius would do their best to see "that the urban form becomes clear and perhaps more responsible than it otherwise would be."[3]

Emboldened by Belluschi's gracious response, Weinberg wrote again, expanding on his concerns and pointing out the importance of the visual impact the proposed tower would have on the urban scene, particularly the base and its relationship to older buildings. Noting that the retention of Belluschi and Gropius had aroused considerable interest among New York architects, he expressed his hope that the pair would be able to influence Wolfson on *basic* design features before the program was so tied up that they were left "with nothing but the trimmings" and ended by suggesting that their studies be the subject of a New York chapter AIA evening discussion meeting. With the chapter's headquarters and the offices of so many of its members there in the Grand Central district, he thought there would be "tremendous enthusiasm" for such a meeting.[4]

The idea of a meeting to discuss the plans for the project was deemed of sufficient interest to expand it to include the regional chapter of the American Institute of Planners.[5] Whether, however, this joint meeting was ever held is unclear. If so, no evidence suggests that either Belluschi or Gropius was there.

The project clearly *was* of major concern to those in the profession. In one of the first overt criticisms of Gropius, voiced even before the Gropius/Belluschi scheme was published, Walter C. Reis, associate professor of architecture at Penn State, pointed out the seeming contradictions between what Gropius had written in his 1954 essay "The Scope of Total Architecture" about "the sickness of our chaotic environments" resulting from "our failure to put basic human needs above economic requirements" and Gropius's participation in a project that seemed destined to add to that chaos and perpetuate the neglect of human needs he seemed to be criticizing. "The key for a successful rebuilding of our environment," Gropius wrote then, was "to let the human element be the dominant factor." Gropius was too great a man to doubt the meaning of his words, Reis said, but wondered what result, what "kind of value or improvement, what new idea, lesson, or experience can we expect from his collaboration in this 'biggest office building in the world,'" and wondered if it was possible "that the eminent and noble strength of a great architect, teacher and humanist" might become "a fatal weakness in the commercial slum of business opportunities."[6]

Once the eagerly awaited Gropius/Belluschi scheme for the building was published, other letters critical in tone began to surface. One in the *New York Times* noted that the announcement of a building of record size on the site of the six-story Grand Central office building had come hot on the heels of a new zoning plan for New York, which according to calculations by the letter's author would allow a building with only a third of the total floor area of the "monstrous" structure. Even if the new zoning regulations were adopted right away, he noted, it would be too late to prevent construction of the overscaled building. To protect the already crowded area "from this combined product of simple greed and architectural irresponsibility," the letter's author recommended sardonically that the architects and builder be forced to take the subway at rush hour daily for a week, at which time, he predicted, "these gentlemen will have acquired enough wisdom to desist from adding 30,000 more human beings to the intolerable crush now existing."[7]

These were mere trickles, however, compared to the flood of criticism that was to follow. The first real sign of the onslaught to come was from Sibyl Moholy-Nagy, the widow of one of Gropius's former colleagues at the Bauhaus, who was then teaching at the Pratt Institute. In a letter published in *Progressive Architecture,* she attacked the journal's editors for their mild "note of concern" over the Grand Central City project, rebuking them for not emitting "a roar of protest and indignation." Calling the new building a triple offense, sociologically, aesthetically, and ideologically, she doubted that any of the gentlemen who were financing and designing "the world's largest office building" ever used the subway or had ever witnessed the "nightmarish moment when the crowds are caught in total paralysis because no one can move," had ever heard women scream with pain as they were punched into subway cars so doors could close or watched older workers "cling frantically to platform columns for fear of being pushed onto the tracks. Those people do not live in New England villas. They live in tenements in the Bronx and Brooklyn." The one bit of aesthetic relief afforded these people, she said, was the silhouette of the old Grand [New York] Central tower, whose play of light and shadow, providing human scale and architectural personality, she predicted would be lost "against the umptiest glass curtain wall." "In the passionate arguments that have gone back and forth about this project, the participation of two of our most renowned educators has stirred the deepest protest," she wrote. Those kind enough to look for apologies, she noted, had pointed out that Roth would have built "the world's largest anyhow—with or without the pedigrees of Gropius and Belluschi. For anyone engaged in the education of young architects, this is a dreary justification. By blurring over the lines of ideal and compromise, our standards go down the drain. This would be true in any case where an architect of fame is willing to sell out to a promoter. In the case of Gropius and Belluschi, it is a profound tragedy." She then quoted at length from Gropius's "Apollo in the Democracy" lecture on the importance of leading by moral initiative, of prioritizing quality over quantity, of pursuing spiritual rather than utilitarian ends, and of staving off the tendency to go with inorganic piecemeal improvements instead of far-reaching concepts of planning.[8]

Gropius agreed with Belluschi that it was best that he not answer Moholy-Nagy directly and instead gave her letter to Natalie Parry, Wolfson's public relations counsel, promising to equip her with information that would clarify the issues. "I personally think the question she raises is not to be taken lightly," Belluschi wrote in his note to Parry. He suggested Parry point out that many of the new building's tenants would most likely be traveling only short distances between buildings and would not add substantially to the subway load; he also thought she might mention the plans afoot to add an additional express station not far from the Grand Central. Arguing in favor of high density in the downtown, an argument he would return to time and again, he said: "It is in the nature of the modern city, particularly in America, to concentrate business populations into high densities to minimize the necessity for surface transportation in the daily contacts between businesses. If the same numbers were scattered over a larger area, there would be need for more autos, taxis, buses, etc. Finally," he added, "as the building of enormously expensive highways had to follow the equally fantastic growth in automobile transport, in the same way means will be found to accommodate the crowds if traffic gets too difficult. The point may be challenged, but it is in the nature of our society where change and adjustment are the laws of life."[9]

Parry's rebuttal appeared in the August *Progressive Architecture*. "Do I detect a note of personal ill-will?" she wrote in defense of the project, without mentioning her connection to Wolfson or her contact with Gropius and Belluschi. "Otherwise Mrs. Moholy-Nagy's sibylline outburst against Dr. Gropius makes almost no sense." What Moholy-Nagy's roar of indignation added up to, Parry wrote, "is that sociologically screaming women escaping from the 9 A.M. subway nightmare supposedly find an aesthetic moment of relief in glimpsing the profile of the Grand Central Tower; but Dr. Gropius, in an alleged ideological switch, is out to worsen their nightmare and deny them their relief." Dismissing Moholy-Nagy's argument, Parry responded by toeing the party line, that the Grand Central Terminal sits on one of the largest and most valuable real estate sites in the world, and that with declining revenues from railway passenger travel, commercial exploitation of the site was inevitable. Noting that the late Robert Young had envisioned liquidating the terminal building completely, replacing it "with a hundred-story office beehive," and that others had toyed with "similar spectaculars" for developing the site, it had finally devolved upon Wolfson to undertake it. It was perfectly obvious, she said, that neither Wolfson nor his architects were responsible for the mere fact that another huge office building was going to rise in the Grand Central area. Wolfson's responsibility, she maintained, was that of an "obstetrician to a pregnant site," contending that given that some building was going to be built there in any case, relevant criticism should be restricted to "how well it is brought to fruition." She went on to point out the proposal's praiseworthy features and the large debt of gratitude subway riders actually *owed* Wolfson. It was he, she said, who saved this "otherwise wasteful monument to our past" otherwise destined for destruction. "All of us who deplore the architectural wastelands of our city, including Mrs. Moholy-Nagy, must certainly appreciate this sensitivity to civic and aesthetic values on the part of Erwin Wolfson who, as a commercial builder, was in no way obligated to offer either his investment group, his prospective tenants, or the city anything more than a well-paying, well-equipped conventional blockbuster design."[10] It is not without significance that rather than including her letter among others to the editor, *Progressive Architecture* featured her letter in "P/A Views." Personal vitriol aside, the issue was clearly hot.

THE NEW SCHOOL DEBATE, JANUARY 1960

Far more significant than the squabbling between the two women was a debate held at the New School for Social Research in January of the following year: "What Is Good Design and Planning in New York?" Catalyzed by the massive new structure then under construction, the discussion was devoted to what was then still known as the Grand Central City Building. Panelists included Gropius, Belluschi, Richard Roth, and Wolfson on one side, Gruen, Thomas H. Creighton (editor of *Progressive Architecture*), Peter Blake (by then editor of *Architectural Forum*), and Paul Zucker (architect and professor of the history of art at the New School) on the other. It was billed in brochures issued by the New School as a forum in which "distinguished" architects, community planners, design critics and "a leading New York investment builder" were meeting to discuss "one of our pressing urban problems." Focusing on the new building, "destined to be the world's largest commercial office structure," the panelists were to probe such questions as, Was New York in danger of overcrowding? Could aesthetics be balanced with economics? How much responsibility should the architect bear for his product? At what point should civic consciousness influence building design?[11]

An article by critic Walter McQuade summarizing the debate, "What Is Good Design," in *The Nation* later that month signaled the widespread interest in the subject. Tickets for the debate were costly, indicating it was not aimed at general public; nonetheless, the room was packed. Observing the uniqueness of the occasion, which was accompanied by cheese, fruit, pastry, coffee, brandy, and liqueurs (compliments, evidently, of Wolfson), McQuade regretted there was no professional planner among the panelists, as it might have invigorated the discussion, which needed "a verbal explosion against the insane commercial exploitation which takes the form of very high-priced real estate proportions in the glittering but already overcrowded central sectors of our large, depressed cities." He and others bemoaned the fact that the discussion was all on money, not city planning, and that the "increasingly desperate subject of New York's decline as a place to live in, commute to, or do business in, was all focused on a discussion of the scheme for Grand Central City, which promised nothing more than to add 2.4 million square feet of space to an already congested place." Addressing Roth's original design, which had conformed to the standard wedding-cake, fill-it-completely pattern of the New York City Building Code, McQuade said that although Roth's original building was not as tall as, by law, it could have been, his proposal had called for three million square feet of floor space and was draped with a commercial curtain wall, with massing resembling a "disorderly stack of crates." McQuade surmised that Wolfson, "perhaps appalled by this picture of what he would be allowed to do by law and custom," engaged Gropius and Belluschi to improve things. They persuaded him to cut back the number of square feet to 2.4 million in order to open up the street level space, to widen sidewalks, and to permit the reshaping of the building into a tall, broad, rather good-looking tower. Nonetheless, even with his "somewhat shrunken scheme" for producing rental revenues, Wolfson seemed remorseful. His professionals seemed on the defensive too. Gruen gently prodded them, describing the two men as "rumored to be aesthetically very conscientious," but in this case "victims of circumstances." Implying (fairly enough, McQuade said) that they were operating on the level of the industrial designer, packing and rewrapping merchandise, Gruen got Gropius to admit that it was "the best they could do under the circumstances."

And those circumstances? Almost everyone on the platform, McQuade observed, was forced to give basically the same answer: "They shouldn't let us do this kind of building, make this kind of money. There should be a law against it. We are strangling our city, victimizing it; but so long as there isn't a law."

The critics seemed depressed, even fatalistic, and had a right to be, McQuade said. As the financial situation of the city, its transportation problems, housing and school situation, became increasingly appalling, the only signs of municipal vitality to seize upon and celebrate were monstrous enormous pieces of finance like the one being debated.

After a break for more brandy, questions resumed, this time from the floor, and these questions were more challenging, more aggressive than those from the guests. But the evening "could not be pulled back from the gently negative morass into which it had sunk." An atmosphere of politeness prevailed, with certain issues skirted "perhaps to minimize professional humiliation." Is New York overbuilding? Yes, but that is the only thing that pays. Can aesthetics be balanced with economics? Probably not, as it all comes down to a calculation of rents and mortgages. What is the future for large urban centers? They can be improved, if drastic methods can be brought to bear, but it may already be too late.

One other question announced on the program was pointedly avoided throughout the evening: How much responsibility should the architect bear for his product? Gropius came close to a response. When asked about a detail of the design, he replied, wearily but with characteristic honesty, "We cannot do otherwise." As the evening wore on, a young woman finally paraphrased the question of architectural involvement, to which a "tensely jocular" Belluschi attempted a reply. Never squarely addressing the question, Belluschi said he wanted "to put in a good word for urban congestion . . . the nature of the city is this. . . . It's an excitement you can find only in New York City. . . . You have decay, yes, but Times Square is a wonderful thing," which he found preferable to Central Park, with the muggings and murders in its large, open, uncongested space. Unconvinced, on this rather dismal note, McQuade joined others in leaving.[12]

The account of the evening in the *Architectural Record* was drier, but nonetheless revealing. The aim of the meeting, it said, was to explain the thinking that would put the world's largest office building on one of the world's busiest commercial sites, and the meeting consisted of a "presentation panel" that was confronted with a "questioning panel." The audience was invited to participate in the discussion, which focused on five rather formidable questions, which, the *Record* acknowledged, were not answered. The gist of the discussion was summarized by Gruen, who noted the modesty of the presenting panel in making its claims, and in turn the kindliness of the questioning panel. "I guess the reason is that we all feel that under the circumstances the developer and architect did a good and workmanlike job, and maybe one could even say that they did the best they could under the circumstances. The question then arises, how about those circumstances? I believe that they are highly unfortunate from the point of view of urban planning. . . . If the developer and architects are, as I believe has been proven, victims of circumstances, who then is the culprit? The villain of the piece is the official attitude towards environmental planning." It was, he concluded, "all of us, we on the panel and you in the audience. As inhabitants of the city, and as citizens of this country, we have the democratic right and possibility, and duty, to ask for action in order that our urban areas may be saved from destruction by chaos."[13] Gruen's formulation of the question, and his response to it, saved face all around.

HUXTABLE: "MARVEL OR MONSTER?"

Huxtable's account of the debate was more pointed. Accompanying her article in the *New York Times,* which appeared the following week, was a figure of a scale model of the "proposed behemoth" superimposed upon a photograph of the area, underscoring its immense bulk (figure 3.1).[14] In her inimitable way, she began by talking of togetherness, which we were told, she said, was the trend of the times. Grand Central City, she continued, is togetherness on a monumental architectural scale. She described the huge building: $100 million, 830 feet high, fifty-four stories [sic] covering a three-and-a-half-acre plot from 43rd to 45th Streets, spanning Park and Vanderbilt Avenues, containing 2.4 million square feet of space, housing twenty-five thousand office workers and four hundred cars, with an expected total of two hundred fifty thousand visitors per day, and scheduled for erection in 1960–61 on the site of the old six-story Grand Central office building. The question raised by "this record-breaking commercial colossus," she said, was: How much togetherness is enough?

By virtue of its size and location, Grand Central City "will inevitably be New York's most important structure," she predicted. She found it commendable that Wolfson had retained "a distinguished pair of architects, Pietro Belluschi, dean of the School of Architecture and Planning at MIT, and Walter Gropius, a revered founding father of the modern movement," to work with his own architect, Richard Roth. There was no doubt, she said, that the four of them, Wolfson, Roth, Gropius, and Belluschi, had designed a major monument. But whether it was a monster or a marvel was being hotly debated in professional circles. The debate, she continued, became public at a special forum at the New School, where it was obvious that the outsized structure posed "an important and prickly problem" for the city. The presentation panel was, as she put it, modest to the point of apology, and she cited Wolfson's stated aims "for a fine artistic

MARVEL OR MONSTER?

Grand Central City Is Mass Architecture

By ADA LOUISE HUXTABLE

TOGETHERNESS, we are told by the family magazines, is the trend of the times. Grand Central City—the world's largest office building, planned for one of New York's busiest commercial sites—will put togetherness on a monumental architectural scale.

This $100,000,000, 830-feet high fifty-four story building, covering a three-and-a-half-acre plot from Forty-third to Forty-fifth street, spanning Park and Vanderbilt Avenues, will contain 2,400,000 square feet of space and house 25,000 people and 400 cars, with an expected total of 250,000 visitors every day. It is scheduled for erection in 1960-61 on the site of the old six-story Grand Central

PROPOSED BEHEMOTH—Scale model of Grand Central City superimposed upon a photograph of area as it exists achievement," Roth's stress on the common architectural bond among the collabora-tors, and Belluschi's brave admission that "some criticism had been heard."

Criticism, she said, had been, in fact, loud and clear from the time the preliminary design was announced. It had focused on three points: that a building of this magnitude would bring more people, cars, and traffic into an area already crowded almost to im-mobility; that this concentration of people would strain to the breaking point surround-ing facilities and an already outdated system of public transportation; and that the overwhelming bulk of such a building would "preclude architectural distinction." The building's sponsors responded by pointing out that the building would provide many of its own services, such as restaurants and shops, so that its inhabitants would not have to rely on neighborhood resources. As for its effect on public transportation, she quoted Belluschi: "When the baby grows out of his shoes, you don't cut off his toes—you buy new shoes," noting that he had added, with resigned pessimism, "Probably the city will die eventually anyway." She then addressed the question dodged by the panelists. Aes-thetic criticism of the project had been answered by the involvement of the two re-spected architectural consultants. But just how effective had they been? She walked readers through the evolution of the design, from Roth's original massive, rectangular tower with its three million square feet of rentable space, then the suggestion to cut the building's bulk to 1.8 million square feet, and the final compromise at the present 2.4 million square feet, which Wolfson maintained was necessary for a reasonable fi-nancial return. She noted other changes Belluschi and Gropius had made, such as their turning the axis of the building east-west instead of north-south and faceting the sur-face for a less bulky look. She pointed out the numerous restrictions on their design flexibility: the preselected site, the existing columns and foundations, the problem of the railroad underneath, the need for the maximum number possible of "premium" floors of large area demanded by corporate tenants, the profitable economic ratio be-tween land and construction costs and rentable square footage. Noting that the archi-tects had been given pathetically little creative scope, she quoted Gruen as saying they were "victims of circumstance," who, given the limitations, could propose only certain aesthetic refinements of the building's inescapable mass. Their efforts, she concluded, were a compromise, "and compromise is rarely art."

But beyond the question of its aesthetic merits (about which she clearly had doubts), the basic question remained as to whether a building of this magnitude should be built at all. Most planners agreed this addition to an already overbuilt New York was "one more rapid step toward the certain strangulation of the city, and its eventual reduction to total paralysis." However, as long as private enterprise controlled city land use, and economics and legislation offered no incentives to improve urban design, such buildings were inevitable, and neither developer nor designer was to blame. The blockbuster building was here to stay, "a singular symptom of one of the most disturbing characteristics of our age: a loss of human scale that seems irrevocably tied to a loss of human values."

The one bright spot in all this, Huxtable concluded, was the serious consideration this major commercial enterprise gave to architectural aesthetics. But "[w]hether the result is monumentality or megalomania, however, is still open to debate."[15]

MORE CRITICISM

The issues raised by the Grand Central City project—economics versus aesthetics, civic responsibility versus personal gain, private versus public interests—were far reaching, affecting the thinking of people well outside planning and architectural circles in New York. The Reverend Theodore P. Ferris, minister of the Trinity Church in Boston, used the proposed development as the subject of a sermon to point out the moral issues involved and their impact on the lives of ordinary people. Standing in line in the Grand Central Terminal amidst all the brightly illuminated ads and commercial demonstrations on a recent trip to the city, he had noticed the huge model of the new Grand Central City, which was to rise above and behind the station, and was reminded of how things had changed since he was there as a boy. Recalling the grandeur and dignity that once was, he was chagrined, then angered by what he saw was about to happen. Then he reflected: "The Grand Central Station was not publicly owned or supported, but privately owned and in fact a business, and he acknowledged that there were changes one might not like but had to accept, and that compromises had to be made between beauty and business, the practical and the ideal. At some point, however, he said, one had to draw a line. At some point, there is a truth that must be fought for, whether it is expedient or not. . . . There comes a time when there is an excellence which must be pursued, whether it pays dividends or not."[16] This was the kind of steadfastness to moral principles and to humanistic values and the kind of idealism that many, even those beyond the profession, had expected of Gropius, apostle of modernism, if not Belluschi. Their involvement in the Pan Am was seen as immoral, a betrayal undermining faith.

Criticism by this time resonated in households throughout the country. The February issue of *Time* included an article on Wolfson and his new building, noting "the heated controversy" over the "biggest building job of its kind ever undertaken in New York City."[17] As the debate spread, other ordinary citizens increasingly voiced their concern. "I am appalled to read that the huge office building to be erected above the Grand Central Terminal is expected to house 25,000 workers and attract 250,000 daily visitors," wrote one individual in a letter to the *New York Times*. "To impose this massive burden upon an area of the city already clogged beyond belief reveals callous indifference on the part of the builders to ordinary human needs."[18]

In May, four months after the New School debate, Edgar Kaufmann, Jr., formerly on the staff of MoMA and a lecturer at New York University's Institute of Fine Arts, published a scathing article in *Harper's* lambasting the Wolfson project.[19] "Into one of the most congested square half-miles in the world a new building of colossal size will bring another 50,000 people each day. Why was it allowed to happen? What will it do to New York?" From now on, entering or leaving Manhattan on any one of the five hundred trains scheduled daily on the tracks of the New York Central or the New York, New Haven, and Hartford Railroads, one would, Kaufmann said, pass inside and under one of the most extraordinary structural enterprises ever undertaken. A lot of resources, ingenuity, and artistic skill had been lavished on the huge venture. "To some people it has seemed one of the great sagas of modern commercial enterprise; to others, it threatens to be the largest and newest patch of metropolitan Hell's pavement," he commented. Kaufmann recited the history of the Grand Central development so readers could make up their own minds, before expressing his own thoughts; about the development, he claimed, no one who had followed the story could remain neutral. He described the station, "New York's most familiar gateway for rail traffic," its crowded neighborhood, the building site, "the biggest undivided parcel of mid-Manhattan real estate not hitherto developed," and Park Avenue, lined with metal-framed glass facades that shimmered back the big lights and shadows of the city, forming "an icy, craggily irregular canyon unlike any city ever built or dreamed of before." Now, he said, a surprising terminus to "this crystal chasm" had been designed by two famous architects, Gropius and Belluschi, "whose massive new building was to span Park Avenue and dwarf the New York Central tower as well as everything in view." From near and afar, the new Grand Central City was destined to be "one of the most conspicuous representatives of New York's mid-century might."

The building itself, unlike other recent skyscrapers, was to be, he said, "a white cliff of rough quartz, sharply patterned by vertical and horizontal shadows," and "the colorful, generally feminine sleekness of the glass canyon to the north will be closed by a great, grainy, masculine slab." From the south the slab would rise "in strange contradiction to the sumptuous academic stone arcades of the station." From all sides, it would appear in conflict with its neighbors.

But what about its inhabitants, the citizens and business visitors: How would the new colossus affect them? He described its size: world's largest office building, bigger than the RCA Building, and destined to house twenty-five thousand workers and to receive at least twenty-five thousand visitors daily. It would be, he pointed out, more than ten times as big in population as thousands of American communities typically thought of as cities.

Bold, even *kolossal,* but grand? Architects, planners, and educators have answered, he said: not only not grand, but uncomfortably out of human scale and downright ugly, an opinion that should be weighed "against that of the men behind the building, all experienced and esteemed in their fields, and one, at least internationally respected as a great idealistic architect, planner, and educator."

He then opened fire. Gropius: founder of the Bauhaus, then head of architecture at Harvard, more recently designer of the U.S. embassy in Athens; Belluschi: dean of the School of Architecture and Planning at MIT and until recently professional consultant to the governmental committee that passed judgment on embassy buildings abroad, "a man recognized as a skillful, active conciliator where the architectural chips are blue." As they had been appointed to serve as design consultants, the professional onus for design, as Kaufmann put it, was on them.

Kaufmann sketched the situation: the leasing, financing, securing of a major tenant, phases in the project's evolution for which Wolfson was responsible, then the history of the concept, which had to be worked out before the architect was brought in. He described Pei's 1954 scheme, which would have "swallowed up the Grand Central Station in an 80-story Gargantua," and Fellheimer and Wagner's scheme, also huge and overscaled, both of which had been abandoned. This was followed by Wolfson's proposal, which left the station untouched, primarily, Kaufmann contended, because the engineers figured that replacing it would be uneconomical. Like Penn Station's in New York and another in Montreal, the site appealed to developers for two obvious reasons: One, such sites were in the heart of the city, with every kind of horizontal transportation already well connected, and two, they were either "open to the skies," or as at Grand Central, only lightly built over.

Summarizing briefly the history of the large office building, Kaufmann cited the Merchandise Mart in Chicago, a four-million-square-foot wholesale center built over railroad tracks, which after the Pentagon was the biggest building in the United States. It, however, was only eighteen stories tall, compared to Grand Central City, which was fifty-nine. This pointed up an important difference between building types. Bulk space, as in the Merchandise Mart, was spread out generously over low, wide floors, whereas strip space was stacked high and narrow around a core of transportation and utility ducts, with each side of a floor no wider than daylight could penetrate. In the high, narrow, strip space, made possible by the passenger elevator, originated the concept of the sky-scraper. With the advent of fluorescent lighting and air conditioning in the 1930s, however, strip space economically became obsolete. The passenger elevator gave the large office building its height; lighting and other technical improvements allowed it its bulk. These were facts well known to Wolfson, Kaufmann said, when he began to develop the Grand Central City concept.

Wolfson claimed he merchandised space according to a classic formula of selling—give 'em what they want, where and when they want it, with just a little extra on top. The extra in the case of Grand Central City, Kaufmann maintained, was its visual embellishment. After securing an option on the site, Wolfson went to his architects, who, with Ruderman, their structural engineer, came up with a proposal for a simple, fifty-story set of cubes aligned north-south "that would have satisfied any hard-headed businessman and might have proved a gold mine." Wolfson was unsatisfied. Something was lacking, though the size of the Roth project in itself, Kaufmann added, might have been somewhat daunting.[20] In any case, Wolfson asked "an understandably unenthusiastic Roth" to suggest names for a committee of experts. Gropius's was on top. Wolfson called Gropius, "the patriarchal functionalist and propagandizer of collective design," who at once suggested limiting the committee of experts to two, himself and Belluschi, who, like Gropius, was in Cambridge. Their initial proposal for a tall tower, centered on 44th Street with its axis turned—"two gestures of self-assertion"—and corners beveled to create an elongated octagon, resulted in a less boxy, more interesting form that also eliminated some six hundred thousand square feet.[21] They also suggested a low, wide block that opened on the north with a rectangular courtyard, providing open space on the street level.

At this point, the revised scheme had shrunk to half the original size. It was again revised, for economic reasons, Kaufmann said, the tower thickened, the courtyard closed in, and the low base block raised to match the cornice level of the adjoining Grand

Central Station. Throughout all of this, Kaufmann was gratified to hear, the design consultants, architects, and engineers worked in friendly cooperation.

But then came the clamor of criticism from all sides. Businessmen thought the tower too thin and too high, for no good purpose. Planners said it was immoral to congest the already choked Grand Central district still further. How could the subways handle it all, or the streets, or the restaurants around, especially those priced for office workers? What was the good of tearing down a well-built structure when so many slums needed replacing? It all looked like a dangerous—but fully legal—disregard for human decencies!

Architects and tastemakers were no less dismayed, he said. A clumsy variant of an elegant octagonal original, the new building lacked even the plaza that had become a passport to postwar skyscraper respectability in New York. The tower bestrode the base mass like Don Quixote on Rosinante. Where was unity? Why those overemphatic horizontal gashes that took all the soaring height out of the tower and turned it into a set of three lumpy building blocks set up by some child giant?

Some of the criticism, Kaufmann acknowledged, was sour grapes on the part of other developers and architects. But primarily it stemmed from a clash of intentions. The design consultants were unwilling to concede to the inevitable compromises that the profit motive had imposed and continued to press for more—simpler street-level detailing, more workable lobby arrangements, smoother design at the juncture between the tall and wide masses. The tower, the most visible part of the project urbanistically, had to have texture, so they proposed sinking each separate window back into the mass, to create a regular pattern of heavy shadows overall; but as this encroached on rentable floor space, the windows were soon pushed out to the wall line again. The designers proposed broad, thirty-six-inch-wide vertical ribs to serve as sun breaks, as well as further articulation by shadow with the verticals breaking at each floor line, leaving a small, deep pocket of space inaccessible to the sun. Two huge horizontal breaks at the mechanical centers on the twenty-second and forty-fifth floors interrupted the vertical fins and constituted the major features of the facades. They were, however, far more emphatic than required for any practical reason and would include columns that held nothing up, introduced purely for effect, like the recesses themselves. The aesthetic desirability of all this, Kaufmann added, was "as dubious as the pseudo-functional appearance."

Kaufmann then voiced his own views. Knowing something of the aims and factors that governed the design of Grand Central City, it was reasonable, he said, to ask why Gropius and Belluschi undertook the task, as such a building could "only worsen the urban disorder that Gropius has talked against long and logically." Was size alone the bait that hooked these men? Kaufmann quoted Belluschi as saying no worthy architect should turn his face away from progress or turn down a client who wants help in building a better structure. And Gropius had dreamed of doing a skyscraper ever since the 1922 Chicago Tribune Competition, where his design was "as textured and as picturesque as the functionalist style of that era could allow." Here at last was a project that seemed likely to be built: Who could resist?

"But what is one to think of Grand Central City?" Kaufmann asked. "Is it grand, is it good, did Wolfson do the public as well as himself a favor when he scaled the architectural Olympus nearly to the top? It was a sincere effort," Kaufmann concluded, "but in the very middle of the ruins of a short-lived grandeur it has failed to grasp the spirit of what is grand. Infinitely larger than any work that stood or stands nearby, its design shows none of the scale of urban greatness that is still exemplified in the station next door. The great architecture of New York at mid-twentieth century, it seems, has yet to be imagined."[22]

Kaufmann's article focused specifically on the building's architecture. Another long feature article in *Fortune* the following December was broader in its coverage, but no less harsh.[23] Accompanied by a cutaway of the Grand Central illustrating its complex structure, the *Fortune* article again focused on the tower, then under construction and by this time known as the Pan Am Building (figure 3.2). The author described the building and its site, the deal with Pan American World Airways, "long held a secret" but finally signed with the largest lease ever written, and pointed out that Wolfson still faced immense engineering problems in building the tower over the two levels of railroad tracks and platforms, but that the lease dispelled any lingering uncertainty that the building would be built. It mentioned the long, drawn-out negotiations with Trippe on the signage, the renaming, for Trippe's airline, of the building, which, *Fortune* said, was certain to become a major landmark in Manhattan. Other buildings were taller, but none would offer as much rentable space. It described the tower in greater detail—its exterior; its materials; the floodlighting at night; its mechanical stories ringed with columns; the four-hundred-car garage; the absence of a basement, which meant the sixty-five elevator pits had to be on street level, with the building's lobby on the second floor; the enormously complicated job facing the contractor; Ruderman's contribution as structural engineer; and the statistical superlatives: The Pan Am Building would require more utility services than any other building in the city, with 2,000 gallons of water per minute, and 20,000 kilowatts of electricity; and the telephone company was treating the Pan Am Building as a city in itself.

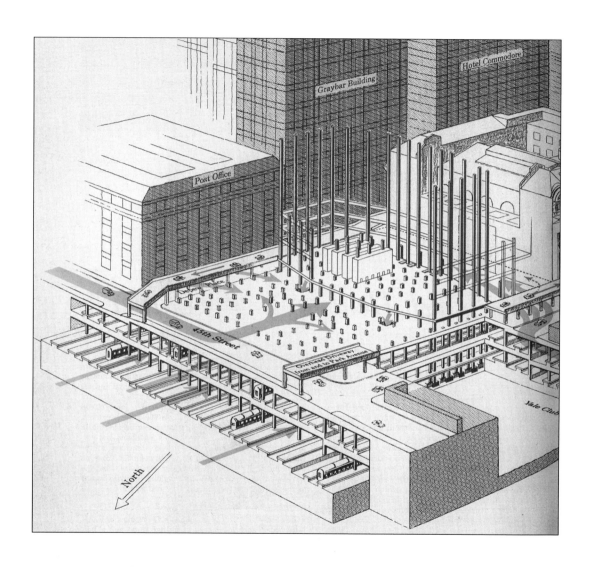

FIGURE 3.2   Structural diagram

Fortune then addressed the "howls of protest" Wolfson's project had drawn from the start. The author quoted Kaufmann as contending the building could "only worsen the urban disorder that Gropius has talked against long and logically." He quoted John Ely Burchard, dean of the School of Humanities and Social Studies at MIT and a colleague of Belluschi's, who described the project as "disastrous . . . a monstrous denial of urbane urbanism," which, Burchard predicted, would "tarnish the reputations of two of our best-known architects." And he quoted Sibyl Moholy-Nagy who said the building "challenged all rational and decent standards." *Fortune* summed up the criticism by saying it fell basically into two categories: aesthetic and sociological. From an aesthetic standpoint, the building, critics said, would plug up north and south views of Park Avenue like a gigantic cork, and hemmed in by other towers around it, it would be visible in fragments only; the attempt by Gropius and Belluschi to break its slablike monotony by ringing two upper stories with columns was seen as "an affront to diehard functionalists who note they serve no purpose." From a sociological perspective, the criticism boiled down to the charge that the addition of so many people to the already heavily congested area would overstrain facilities like restaurants and paralyze pedestrian and vehicular traffic, and that the building's garage would only attract more cars. *Fortune* cited the figures: Railroad trains arrived in the terminal on average once every seven minutes, disgorging a total of sixty-seven thousand passengers per day; roughly 150 entered the subway system; subway trains roared into station once every forty-eight seconds around the clock; a shuttle train that ran between Grand Central and Times Square carried an estimated one hundred twenty-seven thousand persons per day. All told, *Fortune* said, it was estimated that five hundred thousand people walked through the terminal daily. Outside, vehicular and pedestrian traffic often slowed to a crawl, with the river of people turning into a flood at rush hours and lunch. The four restaurants planned in the Pan Am Building were expected to seat only twenty-five hundred at most, leaving twenty-thousand workers to find meals elsewhere.

Wolfson took the criticism good-naturedly, *Fortune* said, and quoted him as saying that had he "only wanted to slap a profitable building on the site without regard to aesthetic or sociological considerations," he could have taken full advantage of the city's building code. Legally he could have constructed a five-million-square-foot building that would have dumped twice as many people into the area, and initially he had his regular architect, Emery Roth & Sons, design a three-million-square-foot, fifty-five story, "ordinary bulk" building similar to those he had built elsewhere. Instead, he had brought in Gropius and Belluschi, who redesigned the building as a slim, octagonal tower set back on a low, two-story base built around a big courtyard on 45th Street, and they had then compromised, thickening the tower, raising the base to ten stories, and substituting massive lobbies for the courtyard. The redesign, even after Belluschi and Gropius's compromises, had magnanimously stripped six hundred thousand square feet of rentable space out of the proposed building, Wolfson pointed out, which was about the same amount of space as was to be rented by Pan American World Airways for $117 million.

But "Does Prestige Equal Money?" *Fortune* bluntly asked. In making the basic economic decision to swap space for elegance and prestige, Wolfson was hopeful that the strategy would pay off in attracting first-rank tenants and higher rents. His experience with the prestigious Pan American World Airways suggested that he had made the right decision.[24] Regarding the impact of the building on the neighborhood, Wolfson defended it by saying that by providing huge lobbies and passageways—the corridor that ran from Grand Central through to 45th Street would be wider than Madison Avenue—he was actually relieving rather than aggravating crowding on the streets. The sidewalks surrounding the building, too, would be wider than they currently were. Amidst all the objections, Wolfson acknowledged finding only one criticism of merit. This had been made by Creighton, who argued that one should not be able to build on the site at all and that it should be left an open plaza. "You have to agree with that," *Fortune* quoted Wolfson as saying. "It would be nice if it were possible."[25]

The *Fortune* article was aimed at a broadly based business community. Meanwhile, criticism from architecture and planning circles continued. The remarks of Chicago architect Bertrand Goldberg, a former Bauhaus student who had later apprenticed in Mies's office in Berlin, to the Chicago Real Estate Board were published in *Architectural Forum* the following February, indicating widespread interest in the Grand Central project and the critical nature of the issues it raised, especially in city planning. Goldberg was dismayed at the lack of sensitivity among New York planners in the reshaping of Park Avenue, as apartment buildings were being torn down and replaced by office towers, representing "the real estate man's answer to need for additional income." In addition to the rebuilding of Park Avenue as an office area, there was a proposal, he said, that was "very actively being developed to rebuild Grand Central Station with a new population of 25,000 office workers." There was obviously enough money in New York to provide the service facilities for this new and highly concentrated daytime population, but there was another factor that ought to figure into the thinking: a twenty-four-hour-a-day, seven-days-a-week population was being replaced by a seven-hour-per-day population for only five days per week.[26] There was pressure to reduce the work week even more, and a thirty-hour week loomed in the future. Thus one had to look at "this expensive machine—Park Avenue—headed by the Grand Central Station, being developed for usage only 30 hours a week. Can our economy stand this kind of specialized development?"[27] Significantly enough, it was the Pan Am Building that raised the issue and was the target of Goldberg's discussion. He made no mention of other buildings—Union Carbide, Socony Vacuum, now Socony-Mobile, Colgate-Palmolive, Seagram—that clearly also contributed to the problem.

Architectural photographer and writer Wayne Andrews weighed in, with a review in the *Reporter,* of Carl Condit's newly published *American Building Art.*[28] Andrews began his article, "Something Less than Chartres," with the Pan Am. "If you believe that mid-Manhattan is already overcrowded and suspect that the new Pan Am Building rising at Forty-fifth Street above the tracks at Grand Central Terminal is something less than the Chartres of our time, you could not possibly spend a more pleasurable weekend than in reading Carl Condit's two-volume history." Andrews noted that Condit, a professor of general studies at Northwestern University who wrote with some authority on such matters, was "just the man to face the perpetrators of the Pan Am Building—if the directors of the New York Central and the architects . . . ever dare meet the critics of what is advertised as the biggest commercial office building in the world." According to Condit, Andrews said, "the Pan Am will transform the corner of Park Avenue and Forty-second Street into 'the first intersection rendered permanently impassable by traffic.'" After briefly summarizing the content of Condit's two-volume book, a textbook on structural forms and techniques in American architecture, Andrews concluded by pointing out that Condit was a modest man, rarely guilty of hyperbole. But buried amongst his discussion of the history of steel frame construction and metropolitan railway terminals in the United States, in describing the new Grand Central City, the largest building of all in the Grand Central air rights development, Condit lost his scholarly detachment: "This monster can serve only to move traffic congestion in the terminal area one step nearer to total impasse." Observing that the development of those air rights might make the difference between solvency and bankruptcy for the New York Central, for that reason the railroad had "vigorously encouraged the present reckless program of rebuilding along Park Avenue, a program which can hardly be said to have improved what was once the most beautiful street in America."[29] Of significance is the fact that Andrews's review of Condit's dry, academic textbook on structural forms in American architecture focused on the Pan Am Building not so much for its structural advances, but for its urbanistic implications, over which Condit evinced uncharacteristic vehemence, and which was a topic Andrews knew would be of interest to the public at large.

That the public followed these issues closely is clear in letters to the editor in the *New York Times.* In response to an editorial proposing staggered transit hours to relieve congestion, one letter writer asked why employers and employees should be expected to cooperate with the staggered hours, why $200,000 should be spent on a survey asking the opinions of people employed in the central area, and why there should be any attempt to stagger working hours when, as he wrote, "the largest office building yet constructed is being erected in the very heart of the most crowded area in Manhattan, with an anticipated daily office load of some 50,000 workers?" Furthermore, the author of the letter continued, when the building was in the planning stage, they had been promised that traffic on the ramp around the Grand Central building would not be disrupted, but in fact it had been. "Again," he wrote, "the citizenry suffers and the big real estate powers prosper."[30]

Tourists, out-of-town visitors, and architectural buffs were also aware of the controversy. Huxtable, in her *Four Walking Tours of Modern Architecture in New York City,* a guide to (and apologia for) "new buildings not always understood or appreciated by the general public," made no effort to conceal her antipathy for the Pan Am or her disenchantment with Gropius. Aimed not only at heightening public awareness of architecture in general but also at sharpening the public's ability to discriminate among good, bad, and merely mediocre buildings, her text began with a description of the growth pattern of the city, the rigid gridiron pattern laid out in 1811, and the ruthless grid of streets that had enforced a certain monotony. "But the breathtaking depth-in-perspective and the sheer cliffs of Fifth Avenue and Park Avenue that seem to march to infinity," she wrote, "have been judged by visitors one of the great visual experiences of the New World." She then turned her attention to the Pan Am Building, still under construction: "The new terminal focus for the long sweeping vista of Park Avenue will be the Pan Am Building, a behemoth-sized office structure astride the Grand

Central Station complex. . . . The erection of such an overwhelming structure—the largest single office building in New York—will radically alter the existing scale of the buildings along Park Avenue. It will also add an extraordinary burden to the existing pedestrian and transportation facilities, and in these aspects its antisocial character directly contradicts the teachings of Walter Gropius, who has collaborated in its design."[31] As an object lesson for newcomers to the city, Huxtable's assessment of the Pan Am was less than glowing.

In the midst of the criticism, much of it focused specifically on him, the *New York Times* mentioned that Gropius had been awarded the $20,000 Kaufmann International Design Award for 1961 in recognition of his revolutionary influence on design education. In a highly significant interview after he received the award, Gropius brought up the "Anti-Uglies" movement in Britain, a group of young students who were protesting "any blotting out of the landscape with grotesque construction," and suggested that a comparable movement was needed in New York City. The irony, of course, was that this "blotting out of the landscape with grotesque construction" was exactly what critics maintained his Pan Am Building was doing. Evidently oblivious to the link between what he was saying and what critics were thinking, Gropius applauded the success of the Anti-Uglies movement in blocking the construction of an office building in Piccadilly Circus, the original design for which was withdrawn and a new design commissioned. (Small wonder Gropius was applauding, as TAC, as the *New York Times* article pointed out, had been awarded the commission for the new design.)[32]

Architectural Forum, picking up on the *New York Times* piece the following month, pointed out the irony and quoted Vincent Scully, a professor of architectural history at Yale, who in a recent symposium had called the building "the death blow to Park Avenue."[33] Scully's remarks were also quoted by Emerson Goble, editor of *Architectural Record,* who was to become one of the few supporters of the Gropius/Belluschi building.[34] Describing Scully's talk, "Death of the Street," at an Architectural League of New York meeting, Goble prefaced his article by saying Park Avenue was becoming "a focus of the confusion that surrounds our cities today." It was fashionable to bemoan the ruin of one of the few splendid avenues in America, he noted. Park Avenue, however, was not a planned architectural wonder like the Rue de Rivoli or Place Vendôme, but an ad hoc lineup of fourteen-story buildings and penthouse apartments, which had a beauty of their own. But now, he said, that was disappearing "under the onslaught of Lever House, the Seagram's Building, Union Carbide, and soon the Pan-Am." The ruin of this handsome street, Goble said, had been the subject of the Architectural League meeting, with Scully as the principal speaker. "So, on Park Avenue," Goble quoted Scully as saying, "the street is going, as each of the new skyscrapers fights the other when they are placed in close proximity, and they fight the Avenue most of all." Park Avenue was indeed undergoing a transformation, Goble acknowledged. He, however, saw it as a positive development. The onslaught of business offices represented the influx of business, as the avenue became the new capital for industry's headquarters offices. He urged having "one more good cry" about what was being lost and moving on to think about what to do in the future, the development of new concepts and "a newer image, for a great business street." He concluded that Park Avenue, like many other American communities, was becoming a place of skyscrapers, a vertical city, and if the population was to double within the life span of a building, they had better start thinking seriously about a vertical city, with the buildings densely packed.

One of the questions dominating the discourse was that of aesthetic responsibility and who was to blame. It was the focus of a one-day "Conference on ugliness," as the *New York Times* dubbed it, sponsored by the AIA in April 1962.[35] Attesting to the conference's importance was a *Times* editorial that described it as a "serious, frequently provocative one-day session on aesthetic responsibility, or why our cities are so ugly, held in New York (ugly) at the Hotel Plaza (beautiful) by the AIA." "Culprits" identified by the group in response to the key question—who is responsible for ugliness?—included Wolfson, one of the panelists and "builder of New York's gargantuan and highly controversial Pan Am Building (ugly); big business, which finesses esthetic judgement by recourse to evasion; and today's society, which wants convenience and conformity first and 'beauty' last, as a kind of optional 'extra,' like sun visors or whitewall tires." What the conference proved, the *Times* editorial maintained, was that ugliness was here to stay, and that the only effective weapon against it was increasing the number of people who were aware of it and cared about stopping it, or at least slowing its progress. The most remarkable thing about the conference "in this age of ugliness," the editorial concluded, was the fact that it took place at all. Humiliating to Gropius and Belluschi, the assessment in the

Times must have been even more painful for Wolfson, who had poured so much into the building, a building he considered his greatest achievement and for which he had gone to such lengths to hire design consultants he thought would assure a "quality" building. He was to die of cancer less than two months later.

A Huxtable article later that month in the *New York Times Magazine* took up the responsibility issue. "Our New Buildings: Hits and Misses" began by describing to her readers her criteria for judgment, lest her grading seem arbitrary or capricious, and provided, in short, a lesson in taste. She noted the extraordinary amount of building in New York City and the transformation of half a dozen avenues since the war, pointing out that it was a building boom greater than any the city had ever experienced, with more than seven million square feet of office space added in Manhattan alone. But what did all this new architecture add up to, architecturally? How many successes, how many failures? It depended on how you measured it, she said. First of all, standards of great building don't change, she maintained, drawing on her own rich training in art and architectural history. Though current construction methods, function, size, appearance, and technology all differed from that of earlier ages, the criteria for greatness remained the same: Vitruvius's utility, strength, and grace. Function was primary. Whether an office building, museum, or railroad station, a building must work. Second, excellence of construction or structure was vital, even as construction costs rose and it became more difficult to achieve. Third, beauty, which was the most elusive and hardest to define, was also key. One could say, however, that a beautiful building had the qualities of any successful work of art: good lines and proportions and a proper relationship of the parts to the whole. The success with which the work was coordinated, the skill with which each detail was designed, the care with which those details were proportioned, and the taste with which the materials, colors, and forms were chosen all added up to either beauty or boredom. Because architecture was three-dimensional, there also had to be a sense of scale, or setting, and (most elusive of all) of controlled and created space.

Measured by these criteria, she said, New York was not faring well. There were exceptions, but in general, New York was producing few buildings that were great, or even good. In spite of their glossy exteriors, most of the big new office buildings set no standards and were in fact no more than copies of better buildings. As with all pirated designs, style, materials, and workmanship suffered, and the overriding concern, she noted, was simply "to produce the greatest amount of rentable space at the least cost for the largest profit."

Park Avenue could have been a street of contemporary commercial palaces to rival the best of the Renaissance, she continued—had there been a "corporate Medici" for every block. Unfortunately, for every Lever House, Seagram Building, Union Carbide Building, or Pepsi-Cola Building, there was a retinue of less distinguished buildings, many of them put up by short-term investment groups. The loser was the tenant, who got a lower standard of living that could not be compensated for by the paintings in the lobby.

Huxtable then reviewed the recent spate of New York buildings, zeroing in on one or two greats, three in between, and two failures, one of which was the Pan Am. It and the Summit Hotel by Morris Lapidus had "the dubious distinction of being the largest most spectacular failures that New York has seen in years." The $100 million, fifty-four-story Pan Am rated low because of its bulk and location, which, she lamented, "continues to cause consternation among those who believe that such an oversized structure will overtax our already burdened midtown facilities." As the building was still incomplete, she refrained from judging it on construction or details but failed it on the grounds that it ignored its context. "There was no pleasanter sight in New York than the open space after demolition of the old Grand Central office building, no more depressing sight than the heavy steel of the Pan Am Building filling it up again," she observed. There were also those who maintained that its gross size precluded beauty. Unwilling as she had been in the past to let the designers off the hook, Huxtable continued: "As its rising mass blacks out sky, light and view, the attempts of its distinguished architectural consultants, Walter Gropius and Pietro Belluschi, to 'smooth up' its overbearing profile seem particularly misguided."

She concluded with the hope that 1961 represented the nadir, and that the record in 1962 would be "less conspicuously downhill from now on." Her optimism stemmed in part, she said, from the new zoning regulation passed in 1960, which would preclude buildings of Pan Am's bulk, as well as the awareness on the part of an increasing number of builders and the city itself of the importance of "quality" design.[36]

The Pan Am Building, marking an all-time high in mediocrity in her thinking, topped out a week later.[37]

The decline of distinctive architecture in New York's recent building boom was also the focus of an *Architectural Forum* article.[38] Summarizing a series of five symposia devoted to the issue sponsored by the Architectural League of New York and MoMA, Blake, who had moderated the symposia, posed the question bluntly: Could one build a civilized city in a free-for-all society: could communal interests (*communitas,* or civil society) be served in a free-enterprise system (individualism)? The conclusion was inconclusive, "the question often garbled, confused, misunderstood and on occasion deliberately obscured." Instead of receiving answers, Blake said, participants in the symposia were given "some astonishing performances." At the top of the list was the Pan Am. "We have had one of the architects of the new Pan American Building tell us, with the utmost frankness, that he deplored that building; we have had the Planning Commissioner of the city of New York tell us, with the same utmost frankness, that he deplored that building too; we have had an impassioned historian, Vincent Scully, tell us that he deplored it, and everybody else has been deploring it. So we now find that everyone—even its builder, I suspect—is really against this huge clod rising in the middle of one of Manhattan's worst bottlenecks—but nobody seems to be able to stop it." The obvious question all of this deploring posed, according to Blake, was how such a building (and others like it) came about. Such buildings were produced because unrestricted land speculation created such enormous pressures that no land in American cities would remain undefiled unless the nation decided that the land belongs to all, not just to a few. Blake buttressed his argument with specifics. The price of land in the Grand Central area at the time was about $250 per square foot. The Pan Am Building would stand on a site measuring around one hundred fifty thousand square feet. Thus, a builder in the Grand Central area had to spend close to $40 million to get a piece of land of that size, either by borrowing the money and paying it back as rent to a bank, or by renting the site directly from the railroad. Given what it cost just to acquire the land, one was forced to build on it the biggest building possible in order to reap a profit. In a small building surrounded by parks and plazas, one would have to charge extraordinarily high rentals for office space—two to three times the amount charged in other office buildings around— to cover costs. If the basic cost of the land were nominal, however, every site in the city could be developed in the best interest of the city as a whole. Indeed, he says, many builders had a difficult time raising the money needed to build these huge buildings, which they were being *forced* to build by land speculation. His example: the Pan Am, for which Wolfson had to take in Cotton, a wealthy British investor, for the cash.

Among the other "remarkable performances" Blake cited was one by the noted modernist industrial designer George Nelson, who provided the most cynical, but also the most realistic, statement of all. As Nelson described it, a typical investment building was designed as follows: First, the plan was determined by rental experts; second, the exterior shape was determined by zoning and building codes; third, the floor-to-floor height was determined by structural and mechanical engineers; fourth, the exterior was determined by competitive bidding among curtain wall manufacturers; fifth, the cost per square foot was determined by mortgage bankers; and sixth, the stamp was put on the necessary drawings and specifications by some architect who might also, if his client let him, design the front door and lobby. Nelson was trying to shock, Blake said, and he hoped he had, because his description (which fit the Pan Am almost perfectly) was surprisingly accurate.

Blake's conclusion was that the situation was pretty depressing. "But unless architects and artists are willing to face up to the grim facts of today's building boom, they will be left behind," he said. "The only time the average investment builder calls upon a good architect is when he thinks this may pay off in terms of publicity, or when he thinks this may pay off in heaven."[39] The allusion to Wolfson and his hiring prominent modernists Gropius and Belluschi was clear.

Perhaps the sharpest rebuke came that August from Wolf von Eckardt, architectural critic of the *New Republic*. "Twenty new office buildings have risen in the past two years to scrape the sky of New York," von Eckardt wrote, "but only two of them stand out: the Pan Am Building, which straddles Park Avenue, virtually on top of Grand Central Station, is conspicuous for its ugliness and arrogant disregard of its surroundings. It is the world's largest of the mushrooming crop of so-called investment buildings erected by speculators to yield rent profits, which inundate our cities with bad architecture." Comparing it to the Chase Manhattan Building, which he liked, von Eckardt continued: "The Pan Am building has been criticized and attacked from the day Wolfson announced the project three years ago. What bothered planners, architects and others who care about such things, was not aesthetics so much as the prospect of adding some 30,000 office workers plus their visitors to the already badly congested mid-town Manhattan. The building's realtors now tell me that the actual working population will only be 17,000. . . . The trouble is that the estimated 250,000 persons who will push their way through Pan Am's underground concourse, which will connect the station with 45th Street and upper Park Avenue, will have to keep walking. Nowhere in this skyscraper jungle is there a place for a bench, a tree, a fountain, or, for that matter a breath of fresh air, until you get up to Bryant Park behind the Public Library or that delightful little plaza in front of the Seagram building."[40]

But Wolfson was undaunted by the charge of reckless crowding, von Eckardt continued, and New York authorities raised no objections to the scheme, which was aimed solely at delivering the greatest possible amount of rentable office space for the money his backers put up: "So there it stands, bang! A $100 million slab which looks as though some malicious seven-league monster had nailed up one of our finest avenues with Gargantuan boards just to spite us." Von Eckardt zeroed in on the building's aesthetics: the huge two-blocks-wide, fifty-nine-stories-high slab, tapered slightly on both sides in an attempt to make its width seem less brutal. The attempt failed. Seen from the avenue, the beveled planes which in plan gave the building the shape of an elongated octagonal were too shallow to be discernable. The attempt was further frustrated, he felt, by the strong horizontal emphasis of ribbon after ribbon of small windows, the monotony of which was broken only by the two bands or grooves of recessed stories which girded the building and served only to emphasis its bulk. The building, was, in short, "a disgustingly fat, complacent giant which seen from uptown, seems to take sadistic pleasure in dwarfing the gilded spire of the New York General [Central—the name changed] Tower" and appropriated the historicizing facade of the Grand Central Station as though it were its own. This insult, however, was a trifle compared to the injury the building did to Park Avenue in blocking the vista. This he thought particularly true of upper Park Avenue, which since the war had been turned into the most exciting metropolitan thoroughfare modern architecture had yet created. The Pan Am now cast an inescapable shadow over the lively shimmer of soaring glass facades, and that shadow included some of New York's finest modern structures.

Von Eckardt then focused his attack on Gropius and Belluschi. Noting Park Avenue's new consistent architectural style and pleasing harmony, he continued: "It is therefore a bitter irony that the leading proponent of that harmony and one of the fathers of that style, together with one of the most sensitive younger missionaries of modern architecture, should have participated in perpetrating the Pan Am folly. None less than Walter Gropius and Pietro Belluschi acted as consultants to Wolfson's architect." He sketched Gropius's past (which he knew well, ironically, having written a long, comprehensive article on the Bauhaus the year before): the Fagus factory of 1911, eight years before he founded the Bauhaus, marking the beginning of glass curtain wall structures since labeled "International Style"; his introduction, after being driven from Germany by the Nazis, of the new architecture to Americans as head of architecture at

Harvard; his continuing to contribute, since his retirement, to its dynamic evolution. Belluschi, von Eckardt continued, now dean of the architecture school at MIT, had adopted the new architecture particularly in the Northwest, which proved it capable of regional inflections. "Surprisingly," von Eckardt observed, "this team departed from its own lithe glassy style when it designed Pan Am," whose design, von Eckardt thought, leaned toward the more fashionable "new brutalism," which viewed architecture not as lightly enclosed space, but as abstractly sculptured mass. The design did so, he thought, "with little conviction." Suspecting Belluschi and Gropius were smarting under the criticism of "international style glass boxes," he thought their primary aim was to be different at all costs. At any rate, he concluded, they couldn't possibly be happy with their work, "which unfortunately will outlive their apologies."

Architect Roth was frank about it all, von Eckardt said, quoting him: "'In a free enterprise economy, architecture mirrors the society in which we live. Why don't we admit that we are living in an uncontrolled society—or at least one controlled only by money and the tax structure . . . The architect designs to his client's specifications.'" Gropius in turn reportedly said that he yielded only to the temptation to do his first big skyscraper. And Belluschi maintained it was the architect's duty to give assistance to any client who asks for it.

Not much of their advice had been heeded, von Eckardt quipped. Their first scheme was rejected as uneconomical because it didn't yield enough rentable space; they wanted window frames articulated, but the kind of sash they wanted would have cost $60,000, and the builder decided they wouldn't be seen high up anyway, so the building has sashes only on lower floors; the architects wanted round columns in the lobbies, but square ones proved $100,000 cheaper. "And so it went, throughout the job," von Eckardt observed.

Luckily, he said, there were clients—such as Chase Manhattan or Union Carbide—who took a more responsible view of building economics and the art of architecture. This was where speculative building investors with their cheap designs made their mistakes. "They may get their money back faster. But in the long run they depress their environment and ours. And everybody loses."[41]

Still a year before the building was to open, the controversy over the Pan Am, which had begun in narrow architectural circles, had by this time expanded to include the broad public. The *New Yorker* and *New York Times*, but also *Fortune, Harper's, Saturday Review, New Republic, Dun's Review, Business Week*, and *Time* all ran articles on the new structure.[42] The article in *Business Week*, illustrated by a photograph of Park Avenue looking south toward the Pan Am and bearing the caption "Eight Roth buildings crowd Park Avenue photo, including Pan Am" (figure 3.3), focused on the Roth firm, "the undeniable favorite of builders in Manhattan's postwar building boom," and the "barrage of criticism" that had accompanied the firm's expansion. The article pointed out that since the war the Roths had designed sixty Manhattan office buildings containing twenty-eight million square feet of space, many of them on Park Avenue, including "the massive Pan Am," and that builders had spent $1.1 billion to put them up. The criticism stemmed not from their daring designs but the routine formula that the Roths turned out "almost on a production basis." The general theme was that the Roths paid more attention to economics than aesthetics. It was a long article, which included a response from Roth, who was impatient with the criticism, as it failed, he contended, to understand how buildings got built today. Most of these were built by speculative builders, *Business Week* pointed out, whose main interest was in turning a profit. The typical speculative builder began by finding tenants, a site, and financing, ideally all at once; almost as an afterthought, he found an architect. In one out of three jobs in Manhattan's office boom, this had been Emery Roth & Sons. Why was the Roth firm such a favorite among speculative builders? "They design for the client who has to rent the building on the basis of a place to work in, not as a monument to posterity," according to one builder. "We're in the business of designing buildings for businessmen who put up buildings for other businessmen" was the way Roth put it.[43] Nothing was said in the article about the aesthetics Gropius and Belluschi were to provide or about the Pan Am design itself and its departure from the Roth norm.

Time, focusing on new construction in the city, was more pointed. Addressing the continuing building boom that "in volume, value, and variety is unmatched in the history of the human race," it raised the question whether New York, given its congestion, had become a better place to live than in the past. Citing the "monster octagon, . . . that still-unfinished midtown giant, the Pan American Building, an elongated octagon that stands athwart Park Avenue between the Grand Central Terminal and the once-proud Grand Central Building, now diminished to a small shadow against the looming white concrete slab of the Pan Am" as a particularly egregious example of the new buildings

FIGURE 3.3   "Eight Roth buildings crowd Park Avenue photo," 1962

adding to the congestion, it pointed out the Pan Am's primary asset: its site. "No building ever had a more accessible location," the article said. "It can be reached by train,
car, subway, taxi, air. Its roof will be a heliport equipped to handle 25-passenger, twin-
turbine helicopters; through its cellarage rumble some 400 trains daily; and in between
63 elevators will carry some 25,000 office staffers and executives up and down. It is
these 25,000—and the countless thousands more in other new buildings, plus those
who come to do business with them—that are posing a problem for New York as big
as the Pan Am Building itself." New York was a tidal city, the article asserted, with the
tide human. Some 3.3 million people entered its nine-mile-square central business district each day. It was a major port of entry into the United States, with Idlewild the
busiest airport in the world. And even as it seemed about to choke on its own traffic,
the city had become the preeminent "headquarters city" for major U.S. businesses, according to the article, and a center of culture and entertainment.

 "But more and more architecturally conscious Manhattanites think that some sort
of order should be imposed on heedless builders, who exercise their free-enterprising
right to build, with little thought for neighboring buildings and still less for sentimental
architecture," the article continued. It quoted Gordon Bunshaft, chief designer of SOM,
as saying that architecturally, the standards in the city were lower than anywhere else
in the world; and Arthur Drexler, director of architecture and design at MoMA, as saying, "The bulk of the commercial buildings is only packaged space. About all that can
be said of them is that they function mechanically."[44] That the Pan Am Building had
been used to prove the point was telling. It epitomized free enterprise's right to build,
regardless of public opinion, and called into question the city's unrestrained growth.
With its massive intrusion, the sense was that things had gone too far.

Even those who worked on the building were not surprised at the spate of criticism. Schiff, the project manager, did not think much of the building. Nor did members of the Ruderman office, which did the structural engineering, who said they never expected good reviews of their buildings, because the developers they worked for were "not interested in anything except how much money they could make out of the particular building on the particular site." They were hired to engineer the building, hence remained aloof from the criticism; like the Roths, they simply wanted the job.[45]

THE DEFENSE

A short article in the real estate section of the Sunday *New York Times* in June 1960, based evidently on a press release from Wolfson aimed at deflecting criticism, trumpeted the pedestrian circulation in the new Grand Central City building. It described how the new building would contribute to the city by easing traffic problems by providing a nearly two-block-long, seventy-six-foot-wide indoor public pedestrian thoroughfare that was to run through the center of the building at street level and connect the railroad terminal with East 45th Street; two floors of the building—street level and the second floor, the Park Avenue ramp level—would be open to the public. Sidewalks too were to be widened, with wide entrance arcades on both the Vanderbilt and 45th Street side. A network of twenty-one escalators would be provided for people using Grand Central subways and commuter lines, as well as four extra-wide escalators, which would rise from the terminal's main concourse to the pedestrian thoroughfare through the new building and onto upper Park Avenue.[46]

The improved circulation system, not aesthetics, was to provide Goble with his main line of defense. Goble was a staunch proponent of modern architecture and had long been a close friend and ardent defender of Gropius and especially of Belluschi. As criticism of the Grand Central City project mounted, he remained loyal, regularly publishing adulatory articles on their work and providing a forum for their own essays. In one editorial, Goble summarized Gropius's address, "Unity in Diversity," delivered on the occasion of Gropius's receiving an honorary degree of doctor of humane letters from Columbia and part of the "Four Great Makers" of contemporary architecture series sponsored by the Columbia School of Architecture. It was a talk, as Goble described it, that addressed "whether such unity and order [found in the Piazza San Marco] could be achieved in our time, and how we might undertake it." The problem, as Gropius saw it, was one of confusion and chaos. "'It seems that the inherent tendencies of an architecture of the twentieth century as they were born 50 years or so ago and appeared then as a deeply felt, indivisible entity to their initiators, have been exploded into so many fractions that it becomes difficult to draw them together to coherence again,'" Goble quoted him as saying in his address. Technical innovations, at first seen as means to an end, had become ends in themselves; differing approaches to design had solidified into hostile dogmas; a new awareness of the lessons of the past had led to a revivalism; financial affluence had eroded a sense of social responsibility and resulted in an art-for-art's-sake mentality. Rather than inspired by the wealth of means at their disposal, the young were bewildered. In short, architecture seemed to have lost direction and confidence, and, as Gropius put it, "'everything goes.'"

The solution, as Gropius saw it, lay in architectural collaboration. It was an idea that had "'become almost suspect since so many of my colleagues are still wedded to the 19th century idea that individual genius can only work in splendid isolation. Just as our profession 50 years ago closed its eyes to the fact that the machine had irrefutably entered the building process, so now it is trying to cling to the conception of the architect as a self-sufficient, independent operator,'" he lamented. Instead of simply throwing a few prominent architects together in the hope that five people will produce greater beauty than one, resulting more often as not in an assemblage of unrelated architectural ideas, Gropius urged collaboration that led to "'the development of related expression rather than of pretentious individualism.'" "Thus the image of the architect," Goble summarized Gropius's talk, "by one of our greatest living practitioners."[47]

Gropius's speech, which was long on abstractions but short on specifics, made no mention of the collaborative effort in which he was currently engaged on the Pan Am, or of the maelstrom swirling around it. The text of his speech was printed in toto in *Architectural Record* that June.[48]

As the Pan Am Building continued to come under attack, Goble was one of the few to come to its defense. As criticism mounted, in May 1962 he wrote a feature article, "Pan Am Makes a Point," which was prepared with help from both Gropius and Belluschi and reflected their thinking.[49] Subtitled "A plea for the vertical city as a planning principle, a three-dimensional city planned for pedestrians instead of autos," the article provided what Goble called "a fresh word on what may be the hottest current controversy of all, the impact of the Pan Am Building on New York's Grand Central area." Architects don't like the Pan Am, Goble stated bluntly, because they feel it is too big. Skeptical about one's "normal intuition" on this score, he believed the Pan Am represented "the necessities of its time and site," and not just financial necessities. It was important, he felt, that architects come to grips with the development of New York as a vertical city and to understand the forces that form the business community. The Pan Am Building *was* big, he acknowledged, but he thought its bigness should be considered an asset— not as a visual focus (as Gropius had argued), but as a contribution to city life (which was Belluschi's point). Deliberately skirting the issue of the building's architectural merits or visual fit with its neighbors, Goble focused on its implications for city planning. The point, he maintained, was simple. The business community worked best in a vertical, three-dimensional city. Comparing the vertical to the horizontal city, he posed the question: Would one rather conduct business in New York or Los Angeles? In the Grand Central district, one makes business calls on foot; in Los Angeles, one drives. The difference was that New York was a city of pedestrians, Los Angeles a city of cars. One had to plan for either one or the other. The Pan Am, he argued, was geared to New York.

The skyscraper was not only America's distinctive contribution to world architecture, Goble contended, but its contribution to the function of the city. It took advantage of verticality to concentrate or congregate people, which was, after all, the principal function of the city.

The arguments against the Pan Am could be wrapped up in a single word, Goble asserted: "congestion," which was simply a negative way of describing "concentration" or "congregation." The building will increase congestion, so the argument against it went; it will be a frightful monster added to an already congested city, will bring thirty thousand people, will crowd the subway and the terminal. Cities shouldn't be that crowded, the architects and builder were guilty of violating principle, the site should be left vacant, private enterprise has gone too far, there ought to be a law. It was easy to get emotional, Goble maintained, when this line of thought got started, and the building was seen as violating laws of human welfare. It was natural to defend the little man.

But doubting that the little man needed champions in this case, and doubting also that the building violated any laws of human nature, he suggested a calmer look.

The building *would* bring more people to the location, he acknowledged, but that was its function (again, Belluschi's point). It would also aid circulation (Gropius's point) and was specifically planned for pedestrians. Opening the Grand Central Terminal to the north where it was formerly blocked by the old terminal office building, the huge pedestrian concourse would extend from the heart of the station through the building to 45th Street and upper Park Avenue. Defending the building's height, the importance of the Pan Am was its very verticality, he argued, which would concentrate people in just the right spot, convenient not only to transportation but to other office buildings in the Grand Central area. Moving people up and down rather than horizontally, it would keep them within walking distance of their business contacts and thus in fact would *cut down* traffic exactly *because* it would concentrate so many offices in the heart of the district. Goble dismissed the notion of converting the site into a city park, as some had suggested, arguing that if the area needed a park, a better site than that of the Pan Am could be found. The belief that we should open up our cities with parks and plazas, limit the height of buildings, break up congested areas, disperse office and business concentrations, and limit crowds, he maintained, was nice, but wishful thinking, as growth was inevitable (Belluschi's point). He defended the modernist concept of zoning, then being challenged by Jane Jacobs and others, believing that the distinction between working and living quarters was important, as "what was good for one might not be good for the other." Cities mean congestion, Goble concluded. City planners should accept it and plan for it, with measures such as the separation of vehicular and pedestrian traffic taken by the Pan Am.[50]

Goble's article was illustrated by a bird's-eye view of the Pan Am model, now with a heliport on top, as well as diagrams of Pan Am's circulation (figure 3.4). Accompanying it were excerpts from an address by city planner Charles Abrams maintaining that high-density office areas held automobile transportation to a minimum, an address Belluschi had sent him.[51]

GROPIUS'S OWN DEFENSE

Throughout the storm, Gropius and Belluschi avoided talking publicly about their work on the Pan Am. In the wake of Moholy-Nagy's searing attack targeted particularly at him and the strident articles in *Harper's* and *Fortune,* however, Gropius especially was feeling

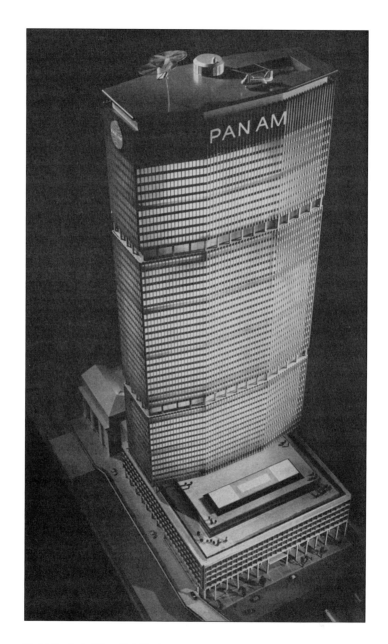

FIGURE 3.4   Model, Pan Am building with heliport

the heat. In a televised interview, he was asked by popular television commentator Dave Garroway what justification there was for adding such a gigantic building to Manhattan's most congested area. Gropius's response only added fuel to the fire: "Every citizen has the right to use the law as far as he can." New York City zoning permitted a tower of unlimited height on 25 percent of the site, Gropius explained: thus they could have built a much taller tower but were limited by practical reasons such as the number of elevators, which consume interior space. The site was the best in the region, he noted, the focus of the market, the center of everything. He could not imagine a park or green space there, as the site was "really where a large building belongs." He described how the building would improve circulation by allowing people to go through the building instead of around it; more difficult was the problem of traffic congestion, but that, he said, was the city's problem, not theirs. Gropius's interview with Garroway was exerpted in *Architectural Forum* without comment.[52]

Though shunning any mention of his work on the Pan Am, Gropius continued to write essays and articles on his thoughts and philosophy throughout the years the building was under construction.[53] At one point, however, he felt critics were entitled to a response and asked Paul Zucker, on the faculty of the New School, who had spoken positively about the project at the New School conference the year before, to write an article in its defense. He was pleased to hear that he had agreed to write something on the Grand Central, Gropius wrote Zucker in March 1961, because "the publicity went completely astray. Instead of discussing the whole matter on an objective professional basis, the opposition tries to make a moral issue of it. I would like to state that it has never occurred to me to refuse this commission because I see it as a positive, proper solution, and I believe that Dean Belluschi takes the same positive stand. All the pros and cons have been very carefully considered from all sides, and of course there are various points which are debatable."

Maintaining that the suggestion of using the site for a landscaped park rather than a high building was unrealistic, he told Zucker of their original proposal for a low, two-story base with an open courtyard on 45th Street, putting all the massing into the tower, which the client had vetoed, as large floor areas on a single level rather than stacked smaller spaces were what were in demand, and this was why they raised it to a broad, eight-story base. On the other hand, they had widened 45th Street, added a broad arcade, and improved pedestrian traffic through the building. And although improving the vehicular traffic was beyond their control, he had suggested improvements that could be made. They were "puzzled," he added, as to why their building had been so attacked, observing that Zeckendorf's scheme, which had called for a much higher building, had been criticized not for its size, but because it would have meant the demolition of the terminal, which their proposal saved. Nor had there been criticism of the Union Carbide Building, which Gropius thought was awkwardly sited. "There is no power in existence which could control the relationship of the building masses in and around Grand Central besides the existing zoning laws," he concluded, which was of course exactly what much of the whole Pan Am debate had pointed out. Gropius enclosed a copy of his remarks made at the New School, as well as the comments by Moholy-Nagy, Parry, and Kaufmann, which he found "full of sour grapes in a verbal jungle," and indicated he hoped Zucker would be able to put the criticism on "an objective and professional level."[54]

Belluschi had thought it wise for him and Gropius to avoid getting embroiled in polemics but agreed with Gropius that it was time for "a fair appraisal of the merits and motivations" behind the Pan Am project. In a letter to Zucker that followed closely on Gropius's, he began disarmingly, saying how impressed he and Gropius had been with Zucker's comments at the New School and wished they could have been published in full. To Gropius's comments, which Belluschi said stated their position quite well, he wanted to add only two points. One was to remind readers that New York City was the commercial and financial capital of the world and "a city like no other. Anyone who ponders on the complexity of nerves and sinews which feed and support the body of our modern society," he wrote, "will understand New York as a city and will also discover that the lines of personal contact which are still needed to function cannot be overextended without making present things much worse. The attempt to diminish the density by introducing green areas or low-building areas would only accentuate the already acute vehicular traffic problem."

The other point, he said in his characteristically thoughtful way, "is that perhaps most of the criticism springs from a nostalgic idea of what the city should be. Surely Venice or Stockholm or Paris are better places to live in, but what is important is the unique character of each; that character is the result of the complex forces and circumstances which gave it form in the first place." New York, he emphasized, "by the nature of its role, is a unique city—exciting, exuberant, unforgettable; it is the real showcase, not only of America in its full explosion of growth and activity, but a symbol of what the world, whether it admits it or not, aspires to be. Perhaps some people, and I am one of the millions, don't like to live in the 20th century; it is our prerogative to complain, but we must be clear in our thinking."

"New York is continually growing and growth has its consequences," he continued. "At the meeting held that night at the New School, you may remember I stated rather glibly that when a baby grows and his shoes get too small, one doesn't cut off his feet but buys new shoes. In a sense I was alluding to the real and worsening problem of mass transportation and the importance of finding new ways to make it work; it is expensive but possible, which cannot be said of automobile traffic." Belluschi acknowledged that critics had a point in their objection to the visual relationship between the new Pan Am and the existing buildings but pointed out that a good relationship between big buildings in a city was possible only when they were designed integrally, as a complex, such as Rockefeller or Lincoln Center.[55]

However cogent their arguments may have been, there is no evidence that Zucker ever wrote or published the article Belluschi and Gropius had hoped for.

Interviewed that spring for an article in the *Architectural Record,* Belluschi was asked in an obvious reference to the Pan Am project about the architect's responsibilities to the context in which he works. Belluschi replied that though some architects felt their responsibilities ended with their own building, he believed the architect needed to take both siting and the environment into account. Materials, height, width, and color should all be considered part of the visual whole. Placing a building among trees, on Park Avenue, or among a group of low structures—each required a different solution. He cited the Pan Am. "We have been criticized, perhaps justly, for dropping too big a building into too small a lot. But after all, that is New York, and there are certain advantages to it. If you're looking for the country, that area is not the best place to look."[56]

Like Gropius's, Belluschi's arguments struck people as lame.

HELIPORT PROPOSAL

The heliport that was placed on top of the Pan Am Building, providing quick transportation from the heart of Manhattan to the city's three major airports, was an *après coup,* added well after the design of the structure was largely completed and steel framing begun. The concept of aircraft landing and taking off from the tops of buildings itself was not new. It dated back at least as far as turn-of-the-century futuristic fantasies such as guidebook publisher Moses King's *Dream of New York* (figure 3.5) and was part of the thinking involved in equipping the Empire State Building with its dirigible mast. Helicopter transportation as a substitute for cars in the city had also been talked about in the 1950s, and its potential role as a means of transport between airports recognized by New York Airways, which hoped to operate "skybus" service as soon as facilities were available. It opened a heliport at the foot of Wall Street in 1953.[57] A heliport had also been included in both the Fellheimer and Roth Grand Central City proposals of 1954. The idea had been dropped, though, evidently for financial reasons, when the plans were revised in 1958.

In the fall of 1960, shortly after Pan Am signed on as the building's major tenant, and well after construction was underway, the idea of incorporating a heliport was revived. It seems plausible that it was Trippe who insisted upon it in his lease negotiations with Wolfson, as expanding the concept of the Pan Am/Grand Central Terminal as the city's major transportation hub to include the component of flight, linking his building to airports in the outlying area, would fit the company vision.[58] The idea apparently, however, was not his. According to Robert L. Cummings, president of New York Airways, the

FIGURE 3.5   "The Cosmopolis of the Future," *King's Dream of New York*, 1908

notion occurred to him one morning in September 1960 upon reading in the *New York Times* of the Trippe/Wolfson deal and their plans for the new Pan Am Building, and he promptly wrote Trippe about his thoughts.[59] Whatever the origins of the idea, the heliport had never been part of the Gropius/Belluschi scheme and called for considerable retrofitting. Work on it was begun later that fall, by which time the steel for the framing had been ordered and paid for, and much of it was already in place.[60] It meant adding three hundred extra tons of steel to the framework from the twentieth floor up to support the heliport's twelve-inch-thick concrete landing pad, as well as modifying the roof of the building, installing airfoils, or wind-deflecting aluminum vanes, along the edge to overcome the turbulent winds at the top of the building.[61] Most of the design work took place in the Roth office, though Gropius insisted on being included. He was particularly concerned about the impact of the heliport on the building's roofline and whether incorporating airfoils would disrupt the flow of projecting mullions, which he had wanted to continue unbroken into the sky.[62] Irked about not being informed about the negotiations with the lighting specialist for the building, in February 1961 he sent Colcord a strongly worded letter about the lighting solution for the roofline, which, as he put it, "unfortunately destroys the effect of the open mullions silhouetted against the sky. The whole upper silhouette of the building is so important," he wrote, "that all the items resulting from the heliport have to be checked up from the design point of view. I feel it to be the duty of the designers to see to it that the integration of all parts should function well. I ask you, therefore," he concluded, "to let us always know about your steps which may have any consequences on the design effect," and he promised that the next time he was in New York, he would see that the problem of the heliport was solved so that it did not interfere with the building's overall design.[63]

In March 1961, news of the proposed heliport broke in the *New York Times*. A service making it possible to fly to the heart of Manhattan was to be built on top of the Pan Am Building, the *Times* article reported, with twenty-five-passenger, twin-turbine helicopters already on order by New York Airways, operators of the service. It was hoped that the line, offering four- to seven-minute flights from the skyscraper to the city's main airports, would be ready to begin operation by December 1962, the date the building itself was scheduled to open. Although plans were already advanced, approval had to be obtained from the city, the Port of New York Authority, and the Federal Aviation Agency, which needed to be satisfied that the operations could be conducted safely and at a tolerable noise level. "Those behind the heliport plan realize that the public may blanch at the thought of sizable aircraft maneuvering on and off a roof in one of the most crowded sections of the city," the *Times* blandly commented. The landing area on the east end of the building was to be only 135 feet on its longest side, but aviation experts pointed out that with a two-engine craft, the heliport operation should be as safe as any other aerial operation over the city's streets. Moreover, if one of the two engines of the Vertol 107 helicopters planned for the operation were to fail, the craft would still be able to fly to a safe landing area on the one remaining engine.[64]

By the following fall, construction of the heliport was well underway, still without formal approval from city and federal agencies. The public was again assured that based on extensive wind tunnel and flight tests, "an extremely high level of safety" could be obtained, with helicopter performance being improved, which would in effect transform the Vertol 107 helicopter into a true vertical takeoff craft, and new flight techniques worked out so that operations could be conducted with minimal risk of "unplanned" landings in the congested streets below.[65]

As backers of the Pan Am heliport anticipated, the public was not pleased with the plans. Letters began pouring in to the *Times,* as people began expressing concern, then dismay, then outrage. One of the first, while focused on the issue of noise, raised the larger issue of public interest versus private gain: "As if the new helicopters were not already a nuisance as they fly across Manhattan, we will now be forced to inconvenience hundreds of thousands as two dozen passengers come and go from the top of the Pan Am Building. When will the city learn that there may be a level of noise beyond which any increment will do more harm than good?"[66]

Objections to the heliport were not limited to the noise it would generate. A year later, after the building had formally opened but the heliport had not yet received federal approval, public concern mushroomed about its safety. The heliport did not begin operations until December 1965, long after the building opened.

CONSTRUCTION CONTINUED

In the meantime, construction of the building continued. Framing had begun in March 1961 and by November was well underway (figure 3.6).[67] To satisfy "sidewalk supervisors," Wolfson had a closed-circuit television system installed on the main concourse of the Grand Central Terminal, enabling the curious to watch the construction of the building, much of which was below grade, hence out of sight. Also in the concourse was a six-foot-high "Directomat" that provided answers to 120 frequently asked questions about the new building, with information on general facts and figures, exterior and

interior design, special features and construction details. The machine responded to some two thousand questions per day.[68]

By this time the building, not scheduled for completion until December 1962, was over 60 percent rented.[69] In October 1961, installation of the textured masonry Mo-Sai panels was begun, with the first of nine thousand panels bolted into place (figure 3.7).[70] As winter was about to set in, the construction process was described as going so smoothly that in the words of a construction worker, "it sometimes scares me."[71] The flooring, a mark of Morse's ingenuity in adapting a technique used by bridge builders to create lightweight spans in which steel floor panels were bonded with concrete floor slabs, adding to the structural strength of the building, went up in February (figure 3.8).[72] The first set of the four-foot-wide escalators leading from the Grand Central concourse to the pedestrian promenade running through the Pan Am building were installed at the same time.[73] The multimillion-dollar worldwide electronic reservation and communication system designed by IBM specifically for Pan American World Airways, another technological "first," was installed in the new building the following month.[74]

While an enraptured nation watched astronaut John Glenn launch into space on his five-hour flight around the earth in March 1962 and some nine thousand people gathered in the Grand Central concourse to view the event on a huge television screen (figure 3.9), steel work continued on the Pan Am Building within arm's reach next door (figures 3.10–3.13). Construction was slowed only briefly in early March by a trade union dispute over the installation of the telephone central office on the building's twenty-first and twenty-second floors.[75]

The Pan Am Building's fifty-nine-story steel frame was topped out in May of that year. The occasion was celebrated in the *New York Times* with a photograph of the American and British flags, symbolizing the building's British-American sponsorship, along with the Pan American World Airways flag, affixed to two steel girders that were hoisted to the top of the building amidst the cheers of workman and a shower of confetti from buildings nearby (figure 3.14).[76] The event was also written up in *Business Week*, which noted again the controversy the massive building had aroused and, even as the building was being celebrated, was still alive.[77]

FIGURE 3.6   Pan Am Building under construction

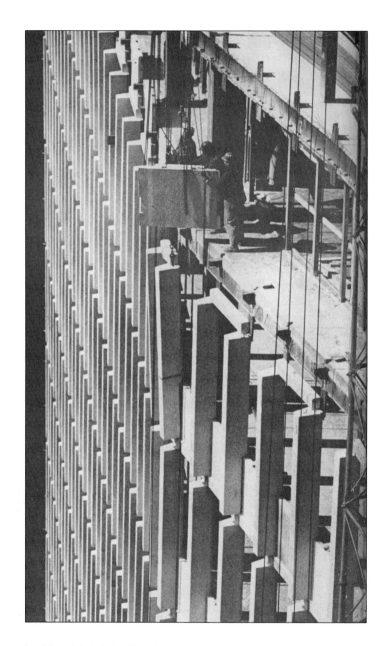

FIGURE 3.7   Mo-Sai panels being hoisted into place

R #V4823-26
AM BUILDING
YORK CITY
EMFER 10, 1962

FIGURE 3.8   Steel framing, with Mo-Sai panels below, September 1962

FIGURE 3.9   Watching John Glenn's launch into space, Grand Central concourse, March 1962

FIGURE 3.10   Steel framework under construction

FIGURE 3.11   Precision work on steel framework, upper reaches of the building

FIGURE 3.12   Steel framing going up, with Chrysler Building on right, Union Carbide Building on left

FIGURE 3.13   Dancing on top

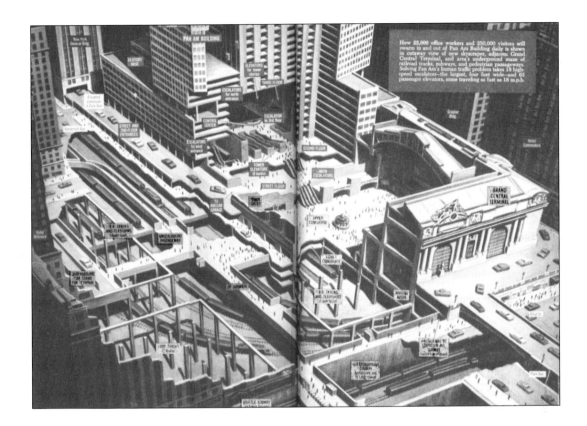

How 25,000 office workers and 250,000 visitors will swarm in and out of Pan Am Building daily is shown in cutaway view of new skyscraper, adjacent Grand Central Terminal, and area's underground maze of railroad tracks, subways, and pedestrian passageways. Solving Pan Am's human traffic problem takes 18 high-speed escalators—the largest, four feet wide—and 63 passenger elevators, some traveling as fast as 18 m.p.h.

FIGURE 3.14   Topping-out of steel frame, May 1962

FIGURE 3.15   Cutaway view

WOLFSON DIES

Wolfson died the following month, after a short bout with cancer. By time of his death, the "energetic, urbane" Wolfson, who was then sixty, had become one of the leading builders in Manhattan's postwar boom; the Diesel Construction Company, of which he owned 51 percent and was chairman of the board, had a backlog of $265 million in projects, including the $100 million Gateway Center office complex in Chicago, scattered throughout the nation. His success in construction was matched by his success in real estate; his real estate company, Wolfson Management, was owned by him alone. Among some sixty major construction projects of his in Manhattan alone since the war, the Pan Am was his baby, unique not only because of its size and location, but in being so highly personal. It was Wolfson who had originally conceived the idea of developing the Grand Central site, then had his own company, Diesel Construction, build on it. It was he who sought the financing, attracting British funds when conventional financing proved difficult for a building of the Pan Am's size, he who personally negotiated the lease with Trippe—the largest lease ever at the time for office space in Manhattan—saving over a million dollars in brokerage fees by handling the deal himself. His success was due to a combination of personal charm and hard business savvy, of an ability to get along comfortably with others coupled with a one-man rule. After his death less than a year before the Pan Am was scheduled to open, James D. Landauer, by then one of the nation's leading realty consultants, who had worked on the Pan Am development, took over the real estate arm of the Wolfson enterprise, becoming president of Grand Central Building, Inc; Morse took over the construction.[78]

BUILDING NEARS COMPLETION

Construction continued throughout the summer and fall of 1962.[79] As the building neared completion, its extraordinary engineering feats were written up in numerous publications, from *Life* to *Popular Science* (figures 3.15 and 3.16). Called "the most complicated building ever built," the Pan Am was touted for its many record-breaking features: Its multidimensioned circulation system consisted of eighteen escalators and sixty-three high-speed elevators, among the fastest in the world, that would transport passengers from the railroad tracks below it to the heliport on its roof; adjoining the Grand Central Terminal and rising over its maze of underground tracks yet shielded from the vibration of trains, it was "a city within a city," a single building whose population

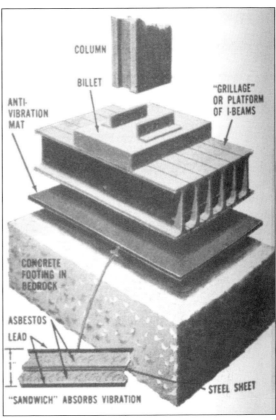

BEDROCK

NEW BRACING AVOIDS
TAKING UP VIBRATION
FROM OLD COLUMNS
BY STRADDLING THEM
WITHOUT TOUCHING

NEW COLUMNS
before being covered with
concrete fireproofing

OLD COLUMNS

COLUMN

BILLET

ANTI-
VIBRATION
MAT

"GRILLAGE"
OR PLATFORM
OF I-BEAMS

CONCRETE
FOOTING IN
BEDROCK

ASBESTOS

LEAD

1"

"SANDWICH" ABSORBS VIBRATION

STEEL SHEET

FIGURE 3.16   Structural detail, old and new columns

of twenty-five thousand almost equaled that of Urbana, Illinois, or Butte, Montana; its 2.4 million square feet was exceeded only by the Pentagon in Washington and Merchandise Mart in Chicago; its occupants would consume enough electricity for ten thousand homes, and their phone calls required a new telephone exchange all of its own—all on one of the most congested sites in the world, with a 450-train-per-day railroad station, three subway lines, buses, taxis, cars, and throngs of people. Accommodating arrivals by air, the heliport on the roof would be the first in the heart of the city, providing a shuttle from the building to the city's outlying airports. It marked a succession of remarkable engineering achievements, among them the razing of the old six-story building that formerly occupied the site while the new building was begun underneath, and the interweaving of its footings and columns between the two layered tracks of the Grand Central, all without disrupting train service. And the building was to be floodlighted at night, transformed into a brilliant shaft of light.[80]

PAN AM OPENS

Amidst much fanfare, the building opened March 7, 1963 (figure 3.17). The ribbon-cutting ceremonies were attended by city, state, and federal officials, who spoke at the opening, stressing the international scope of the building. Among the dignitaries were New York Governor Nelson Rockefeller, who was quoted as saying the building "rose over the city as a symbol of the genius and the creativity of the free enterprise system," and the city's mayor, Robert F. Wagner, who declared it "an expression of faith by the business community in the city's future." Among other speakers were U.S. Secretary of Commerce Luther H. Hodges, U.S. Senator Jacob J. Javits, and Frederick J. Erroll, president of the British Board of Trade.[81] For some it was a celebratory occasion. No evidence suggests, however, that either Gropius or Belluschi was there.

FIGURE 3.17   Pan Am Building opens

4

THE BUILDING'S IMPACT

ECONOMIC SUCCESS

"Pan Am Building, Called a Huge Gamble, Is Opening 91% Rented, 100% Financed," the *Wall Street Journal* announced on the building's opening.[1] To the surprise of some and the dismay of many, the building proved to be a remarkable financial success from the moment it opened. Skepticism abounded as to whether it would ever be built, according to Landauer. Unlike most office projects, the *Journal* pointed out, the building was started in 1960 without any firm leasing or financing commitments (which was not quite the whole story, as Cotton had signed on as co-owner in August 1959, providing the financial backing to enable Wolfson to proceed with construction). Moreover, the building came at the end of a postwar skyscraper splurge that saw 150 new buildings rise in Manhattan, adding about fifty million square feet and doubling the city's office capacity.

The success of the Pan Am contrasted strikingly with the problems of the 102-story Empire State Building. When the latter opened in 1931, near the end of Manhattan's last big skyscraper boom in the 1920s, it was three-quarters empty and did not approach becoming fully rented until a decade later, in the early 1940s. On the other hand, the Pan Am's developers never considered the project risky, as the site was "a natural, in about the best location in the country." Thus far, despite a higher average rental rate, rentals in the Pan Am were running well ahead of those in other new buildings available for occupancy—a success rate that was due, according to real estate brokers, to its prime location.[2]

Ironically, as the *Journal* pointed out, it was the building's location that had provoked much of the criticism from architects and planners. Chances were, the *Journal* predicted, the outcry would grow as the building became fully occupied in the coming months. The massive octagonal tower set on its ten-story base blocked one of the largest and last "open spaces" in the heavily congested Grand Central area, and both the city and the area would have been better served, according to some city planners, by a large park. It *was* "a wonderful spot" for a park, the *Journal* article quoted Wolfson as having said, but "who could afford to dedicate a $20 million plot to a park?" Critics also faulted the tower, which many found ugly, as an example of prosaic commercial architecture. The article quoted Huxtable as suggesting that its huge size simply precluded beauty and that the attempts of "its distinguished architectural consultants" had done little to ameliorate the problem. The biggest complaint, however, was the congestion the building would create, which was expected to severely strain facilities in the area. The article quoted Charles Colbert, dean of Columbia University's School of Architecture, as saying, in reference to the congestion, "[the building] just doesn't belong there." The Pan Am's owners had responded to the criticism by calling fears of overcrowding exaggerated, pointing out the staggered hours of some of the tenants, company cafeterias located in the building, its wide promenades, and noting that the recent opening of another express stop on the subway line seventeen blocks north of Grand Central would ease the traffic squeeze.[3]

Other articles on the opening of the building similarly noted the criticism but focused on the building's financial success. *Business Week* called it New York's newest and largest executive landmark, 70 percent filled and 92.5 percent rented only three months after its opening, and quoted Gordon I. Kyle, one of New York's most highly respected skyscraper appraisers, whose judgment Zeckendorf pronounced "never wrong," as predicting that it would be more than twice as valuable as the Empire State Building.[4] Wolfson and his British partner had paid Kyle (whose opinions were evidently unfazed by the escalating criticism) $50,000 to appraise the Pan Am, believed to be the highest fee ever paid an appraiser.[5] While noting some problems that were already emerging with the building, such as the difficulty of simply getting there, given the traffic, or of finding a place to eat in the noontime jam, *Business Week* listed some of the building's tenants: in addition to the Katherine Gibbs School, one of the earliest tenants, and Pan American World Airways, its biggest, there were such blue-chip companies as Westinghouse Electric, Reader's Digest Association, and Aluminum Company of America, as well as a number of foreign companies, among them Mitsui & Company, Ltd., British Iron & Steel, and Compagnia Tecnica Industrie Petroli.

Architectural Forum observed the building's opening matter-of-factly, saving its critical comment for a later date, and used it as the point of departure for an article on the end of the postwar building boom. Begun in New York, the boom had by that time spread to other parts of the country. Real estate had been "a wonderful business" in New York the previous fifteen years, the *Forum* said, with 147 office buildings going up in Manhattan, containing 50,632,000 square feet of rentable space, to which the Pan Am would add still another 2.4 million. Noting too that the current rate of addition to the available rental, estimated to be seven million square feet per year, was somewhat inflated "by a rush to build" before a new tightened zoning ordinance in New York, among other things reducing allowable densities in certain areas, went into effect, people were wondering how long the boom, which began in 1947 when the Tishman brothers put up the Universal Pictures Building at 445 Park Avenue, New York's first big new postwar office building, could go on.[6] Though many had predicted big tenants would start a mass exodus to the suburbs as a result of rising rents, it didn't happen, and instead, there had been an epochal rush to build in Manhattan's mid- and downtown cores. Dire predictions of oversupply of office space followed, which curiously hadn't happened either. Some thought now with the opening of the Pan Am, finally an oversupply would occur, and that 1964 would be the year when things would start to slow down.[7]

CONTINUED CRITICISM

By this time, academia had joined the chorus critical of the Pan Am Building. Scully had jumped in early on with his oft-quoted critical comment on the building and its effect on Park Avenue, later published in *Perspecta*.[8] His essay, "Death of the Street," began with the history of Park Avenue and was illustrated by views of Park Avenue pre– and post–Pan Am (figure 4.1). It was in 1950, he wrote, that the old avenue began to be destroyed. Lever House was the first to break the line of the street, created by the regular wall of facades that defined and channeled the flow of Park Avenue space, then the Seagram Building, which Scully said was fine in itself, but when its shimmering glass walls were mimicked by neighbors to the north, it lost its identity and needed traditional buildings to play off of. Park Avenue received its final blow, Scully said, "from the fat, wide slab of the Pan Am," which ballooned like a cloud beyond Whitney Warren's late 1920s New York Central Building. Unlike Warren's building, which allowed the eye to go beyond and space to flow around, the Pan Am blocked the view, Scully said, denying the continuity of the avenue, shutting off the avenue's axis of movement, and smothering its consistent scale. "In any terms other than those of brute expediency, it should not be there at all," he concluded.

Like the Lever House and Seagram, the Pan Am was a move of self-centered aggressiveness, Scully asserted. What do such buildings, in their self-centered aggressiveness, portend? Le Corbusier suggested as much: If skyscrapers were to become the basic building type of the city, they had to be spaced far apart, and the street would have to go. So, Scully concluded, on Park Avenue the street was going. But in contrast to what Le Corbusier had envisioned, the new skyscrapers were being placed close to each other following the principle of who owned what lot, rather than in accordance with a higher order. A new pattern was emerging, Scully believed, that could be significant, but the old Park Avenue had its virtues, and he regretted seeing it go. There was no reason why the street had to be destroyed, why buildings could not be designed to frame spaces, why "the decisions taken by elected authority [could not] be larger ones, disciplining anarchy in order to make the city what it has always been, the ultimate work

FIGURE 4.1   Park Avenue pre- and post-Pan Am, from Vincent Scully, *American Architecture and Urbanism,* 1969

of human art." Portraying the problem as urbanistic in scale, Scully placed the blame on the men involved: "The times do not make us, but we the times."

In the interest of scholarly impartiality, *Perspecta* also invited Richard Roth to give his perspective on Park Avenue. Addressing the forces he believed shaped Park Avenue—the economic, political, and legal forces with which the architect had to contend—he pointed out that art critics and historians often discussed urban planning from an unrealistically narrow point of view. Architecture as an art, now more than ever, was determined by the interaction of economics, politics, and law, and the architecture created was but a reflection of society. In the past, it had represented the image of the patron; today it expressed the desires of the masses. Whereas this may not be good for art, he said, it was not bad for people. Alluding to Scully's status as merely an academic (and an art historian at that), Roth pointed out his own long experience as a practicing architect in New York and added that he had been recognized as (or accused of, depending on whose side you were on) having done much to change the face of the city. He thus felt he could speak "with some authority" on the whys and wherefores of the changes.

The transformation of Park Avenue, he contended, had come about as the result of basic laws of supply and demand. In the past, large apartment houses met the demands of a rich moneyed class; after the war and with a new tax structure, modern office buildings met the demands of a corporate society needing modernized working spaces. The Uris brothers gambled and built a commercial building; "monuments" such as the Seagram Building followed. Things change. Initially investment builders, such as the Urises, erecting buildings for multiple tenants were interested only in appropriate size and layout; once they had proved successful in building commercial structures and their financial gamble had paid off, they could entertain aesthetics, which was where Roth felt the situation was at the time. With the way paved for him, the architect now had a chance to enhance the design. Nonetheless, his creative freedom was still limited—by zoning restrictions, by building codes, by the function of the building, and above all by the building's budget. He must not forget that he is creating and designing a building for people: the investor, the tenants, and the general public. If the cost of construction was too high, the rent would be beyond the means of the tenant, regardless of how attractive the structure might look to the layman. These are the basic facts of the society, Roth maintained, in which we live.

New York was not the same as Boston or Baltimore, Roth asserted. There wasn't room in New York City for low, rambling office buildings surrounded by parking space.

In New York, space was gained by building up, and no matter how much critics carped, that was the way New Yorkers wanted it. New York was congested, but congestion was good for business. New York architects created buildings and spaces to suit the needs of tenants and to give profit to the owner. Once again, architecture mirrored the society in which one lived. To produce a truly humanistic city, Roth said, the architect had to be concerned with more than just the design and plan of his particular building: He had to take into account public transportation, restaurants, places of relaxation, and shopping facilities.

Illustrating his points, Roth cited, as had Scully, the Pan Am Building, whose large size, he contended, was determined mainly by its proximity to public transportation and its location in an area where it could be easily reached by rail, subway, bus, even air— the bustling center of a busy district. In sum, Roth felt that for the most part buildings were simply the reasoned, pragmatic responses to societal conditions. If the public wanted more visual distinction, it had to be willing to pay for it, as given the price of land, cost of construction, and the rental rates tenants were able to pay, that is, the basic economic realities of society at the time, one could not expect such refinements to come from the developer.[9]

Convincing as Roth's argument may have seemed to some, condemnation of the Pan Am continued. An editorial in the *New York Times* just after the building opened was sharply critical. Commenting on the opening of "New York's most controversial" new building, which had been marked by ceremonies of much fanfare, souvenirs, and brass bands, the editorial pointed out the loss to the public, never mind the private gain, that had resulted from the building. "Now that we have the $100 million building," *Times* editors asked, "just what have we got? We may have gained the world's largest office building, but we have lost some of the world's most impressive urban views, now that Pan Am's massive bulk blots out the sky and reduces the silhouette of the New York

Central Building to an ineffectual shadow." Also lost with the Pan Am's construction was the opportunity to plan sanely and efficiently the city's most congested commercial area. Nor in exchange for these losses, the editorial said, had New York gained an architectural masterpiece. "What the art works [in the Pan Am lobby] cannot hide is the painful fact that monumentality has been confused with mere size, and that the important public spaces are pedestrian in spite of their scale." Even more serious, the editorial continued, was the building's impact on the neighborhood, as it promised to crowd twenty-five thousand more people into an already crowded area. "In promoting a project of this size," the *Times* concluded, "private enterprise assumes some of the responsibilities of public planning. Whether it has lived up to those responsibilities is another matter."[10] The implication was clear that in the case of the Pan Am, it had not.

Time magazine was equally harsh about the building's architectural and urbanistic impact. The Pan Am "rises like a giant tombstone above the skyline of Manhattan's East Side," *Time* said.[11] "It has been described as ugly—and undoubtedly it is not beautiful. But it claims to be the world's largest commercial office building." The building was not as high as the Empire State Building, nor did it sprawl over as much acreage as the Pentagon, but located where it was, adjacent to one of the world's busiest railroad stations, it was bound to command attention. By the previous week, the article said, 91 percent of the building's space had been leased, with tenants—among them top U.S. corporations as well as branch offices of Canadian, British, Italian, Mexican, and Japanese companies, and of course Pan Am—drawn to the building for its location: on Manhattan's most convenient site, handy to trains depositing employees right on the corporate doorstep.

"Few buildings have been built over so many protests," *Time* concluded. "Esthetes argued it would ruin views down Park Avenue (it does). Commuters were fearful it would overtax already swarming Grand Central Station. Yale professor Vincent Scully believes that 'Except for brute expediency, it shouldn't be there at all.' Yet despite all the protests, the Pan Am got built."

New York Times articles on the building, which by this time was beginning to acquire symbolic significance, continued in the same vein as tenants moved in. A front-page article illustrated with four well-sized photos of the building referred to it as the "controversial Brobdingnagian structure that looms over the Grand Central Terminal" that had been "described variously as a monument to greed and irresponsibility, a towering achievement, an ugly building, and a man-made Mount Everest."[12] It listed the building's records: 93 percent of the space already rented; the lease with Pan American World Airways the largest ever for space in Manhattan; its $70 million mortgage, held by the New York State Employees Retirement Fund, the largest ever in the city for a single piece of commercial property; its single internal transportation system the largest ever installed in a building; at 808 feet high, the seventh-tallest office building in the world; its heliport the world's highest. Even the building's inception was big, the *Times* said, with Kyle paid $50,000 for his appraisal to help establish the feasibility of building the huge building. The article then described the complicated logistics in constructing the building, its design, and the subsequent criticism. The architects as well as the builders had been under attack from planners and architectural critics, who lamented both the decision to build it where it is and the final design of the building. On the other hand, the *Times* pointed out, the building did have a few defenders. A spokesman from the Transit Authority pointed out the added cars to the subway system, the widened platforms, and the new express subway stop on Lexington Avenue at 59th Street, which would offset the large influx of Pan Am employees. There were also restaurant facilities planned in the building to ease noontime congestion. And there was the art.

The most pointed remarks in the *New York Times,* however, were from Huxtable, whose career as an architectural critic had begun with her article on the transformation of Park Avenue and who had continued to follow the Grand Central City/Pan Am project closely. As the Pan Am neared completion, she was also on the eve of being appointed the first architectural critic on the *Times*'s staff, an appointment her incisive articles on the Pan Am helped bring about. In an article "Architecture Stumbles On" on recent buildings in the city, she singled out the Pan Am, "the city's most monumental addition since the Empire State Building," which had made its official debut "with brass-band ceremonies worthy of a Presidential inauguration."[13] President John Kennedy was missing, however, from a distinguished list of speakers in business and government "who paid tribute to the fulfillment of an economic, if not aesthetic dream." Among the other new buildings she cited, the Pan Am had "far the greatest impact on the city scene." Criticism, which had been considerable since the building's inception five years previous, had been directed largely at its physical and sociological implications. But now that the building was virtually finished and functioning, she wrote,

something else becomes distressingly apparent. Bigness is blinding. A $100 million building cannot really be called cheap. . . . But Pan Am is a colossal collection of minimums. Its exterior and public spaces used a minimum of good materials of minimum acceptable quality executed with a minimum of imagination (always an expensive commodity), or distinction (which comes high) or finesse (which costs more). Pan Am is gigantically second-rate. . . . At best, Pan Am is an impressive demonstration of the number of square feet (2.4 million) of completely standard rentable office space that can be packed into one income producing structure; a lesson in how to be mediocre without really trying. For its bulk, its importance, its effect, and its ballyhoo, it had an obligation to be much better. Size is not nobility; a monumental deal does not make a monument.

HUXTABLE ON QUALITY

Huxtable's comments on the Pan Am Building were even more stinging in a weighty, richly informed address to architects at an AIA conference on quality in architecture (figure 4.2), later published in the *AIA Journal.*[14] Acknowledging the loss of quality in recent architecture, which had precipitated the conference, she reminded listeners of the legacy of great buildings in the past that had provided a standard and pointed out that although there were some good buildings being built at the time, most were appallingly bad, and that architects themselves, especially those who were distancing themselves from the "art" of architecture, were "not without guilt" in the matter. She chided them (presumably with architects such as Roth in mind) for their "near-total abdication of aesthetic responsibility." Times had changed; economics and technology, thought to be the saviors of the new architecture in the twentieth century, had in fact resulted in a standardized mediocrity, as buildings had become "pedestrian in concept, routine in design, tasteless in detail, ordinary in material, inferior in execution, disastrous in the aggregate." One spoke now, she said, not of the art of architecture, but of the economics. The cost of good materials, of good design, of labor, supervision, and upkeep had eliminated the craftsman and pride in craft, enforcing conformity and dictating minimum standards. The *art* of architecture, and the philosophical attitudes and accepted aesthetic

FIGURE 4.2   Ada Louise Huxtable at AIA meeting, 1963

principles that were its base, had been lost, and all that remained were the pressing needs of an expanding industrial society, and the promise—undelivered—of new technology to solve them.

There were still other factors at works, she noted, such as a new clientele. Taste once informed and aristocratic was increasingly democratic, as lower classes moved up and acquired economic power, demanding multilaned bowling alleys, mauves and magentas, the "stainless steel and plastic architecture of the tailfin age." This, she said, had led to a new set of standards, which the architect defied at his risk; the building had to be big and up to date, impressive by its size, modernity, and cost. Or it could be pseudo-scientific, which might look strange at first but could be justified with mathematical equations proving that the solution was the most economical engineering means for maximum structural efficiency. Or it could stress integration with the arts, promising quality and culture in one package. And if all else failed in the quest for quality, one could talk about it. She cited the AIA-sponsored symposium on aesthetic responsibility held the previous spring, which she said had come to an interesting conclusion: Beauty, in our dollars-and-cents culture, like whitewall tires, was an optional extra.

Having talked thus far in generalities, Huxtable then turned to a specific example of what passed for "quality" at the time: the Pan Am. She ticked off the points: It was the biggest office structure in the world and cost $100 million, which took care of point 1. It passed up the familiar glass wall for the newest wrinkle—Mo-Sai precast concrete panels—and its shape was octagonal rather than square. Okay on point 2. It had the world's largest air-conditioning system and every modern mechanical amenity—point 3. Leading painters and sculptors were commissioned for art in the lobby—point 4. And as an extra added attraction and guarantee of success, the prestige touch of big names was given by distinguished architectural consultants. The results? A monument to mediocrity.

"The attainment of quality comes down to two factors," she concluded, "the attitude of society, or its tolerance of and desire for excellence, and the ability and desire of the architect to produce it." On the first, she was optimistic, as the public was increasingly aware of architecture. Standard publications like *Time, Look, Life,* and *Business Week* were all now including architectural coverage and reflected a growing public interest in the arts, part of an American cultural boom. An aware public would give the architect his due and might even ask him to do his best, which threw the responsibility for quality back to the architect. But it was a gullible audience, she pointed out, one that accepted charlatans and pitchmen as easily as geniuses, guaranteeing only a receptiveness. "The rest, gentlemen," she said, "is up to you."

Several months later, Huxtable was to write again, this time on changing architectural values. Again she cited the Pan Am Building as "a package for profit." This time she specifically mentioned the Roths. "It is a stunning fact, if you stop to consider it, that Emery Roth, the most efficient of the investors' architects, is as responsible for the face of modern New York as Sixtus V was for baroque Rome." New York, she observed, had become a Roth city. The Roth firm had lined Manhattan streets and avenues with the Roth style of financial expediency. Richard Roth, she said, was "an honest and engaging man who says frankly that this is what he understands, and discussions of aesthetics leave him grimly disconsolate. He makes a good weathertight cost formula, and that is enough for him and his clients. But is it enough for New York?"[15]

THE ARCHITECTURAL PRESS

Earlier that spring, just after the Pan Am Building opened, as architectural critics seemingly emboldened by Huxtable's outspokenness became more trenchant in their attacks on the building, James Burns wrote a blistering article in *Progressive Architecture*.[16] "The rightness or wrongness of the siting and position of the new Pan Am Building—and the subsequent traffic pattern—can, in this writer's opinion, be summed up very briefly," he asserted: "It's wrong." Noting that the concept of vertical stacks of office space in the center of cities had much to recommend it, if sufficient space between high-rise structures were provided, he noted that in the case of the Pan Am Building, the "world's largest commercial office building" had been jammed into a spot "where day-to-day rush hour traffic already resembles one of the more delirious student demonstrations on Tokyo's Ginza." Observing that the public relations counsel for the building had revised its figures, maintaining that the permanent working population of the building would be 17,000, with some 250,000 persons using its facilities or walking through the building daily, and that in addition there was a four-hundred-car parking garage, Burns concluded dryly, "Enough said on that score."

The design of the building itself was another matter. "With a powerhouse of consulting design talent—Dr. Walter Gropius and Dean Pietro Belluschi—and in control, the most knowledgeable firm in New York when it comes to commercial builders—Emery Roth & Sons—Pan Am is an architectural design failure. Had lesser lights been involved, this could be overlooked, and it would be a curiosity merely for breaking the rules of decent city planning. But the obvious effort on the part of the late Erwin S. Wolfson, his professional team, and noted artists to make this a gem of the first water makes the failure all the more significant."

Seen from either north or south on Park Avenue, Burns continued, the building broke the continuity of the thoroughfare, where previously the Grand Central Station and the tower of the New York General (originally Central) Building had served to point it up. The new building formed a vast, anonymous backdrop for the older structures, but it also dwarfed them with its immensity, rendering them insignificant. Since the building sat on such a crowded site, one had to move some distance away in order to see it as a whole, at which point it became apparent that the precast, three-dimensional elements, introduced onto the facade for light and shadow, blended into each other, forming just another plain curtain wall. Approaching the building through narrow side streets, he observed, one lost sight of the structure as a visual composition and was overwhelmed by the square ten-story base; from the elevated ramps bringing Park Avenue around the site, the juxtaposition of elements was inexcusably jarring, with the base, tower, parking garage entrance, and Grand Central Station meeting in a most unfriendly manner (figure 4.3). On clear, sunny days, the building's octagonal shape read, but when seen from even a short distance away on a hazy or smoggy day, it became one-dimensional, a flat screen.

Burns then turned to the building's lobby and its "taste for monolithism." The spaces he found too big and heavy handed, the surface materials too numerous. Great care was said to have gone into the selection of artists and artworks for the public areas, he noted; he nonetheless found them disappointing. The aluminum and stainless-steel screen by Kepes behind the elevator control desk, he said, had a "meretricious '1930ish' look," and the flashy tile mural by Albers over the exit to the station was too loud, adding yet another jarring note to the whole.

FIGURE 4.3   Juncture between Pan Am Building and Grand Central

Hoping that some of these defects could be made up for by tenants' interiors, Burns concluded that the best thing about the building was its views from the upper floors.

Several *Progressive Architecture* readers found the article unduly harsh. One of them was Edmund Bacon, executive director of Philadelphia's City Planning Commission (and, it should be noted, a good friend of Belluschi, with whom he was working on the Rohm & Haas Building in Philadelphia at the time), who thought the Pan Am was "a distinguished addition to the design structure of New York" and was "remarkably successful in giving a visual background to both of the great historic vistas of Park Avenue." He thought that the building fit into the Grand Central complex remarkably well, found its circulation system and connection with mass transit "highly rational," and summarized his remarks by saying that there was so much else worthy of complaint that energy should not be wasted on criticizing the Pan Am.[17]

Most readers, however, applauded *Progressive Architecture*'s publication of Burns's article. "The Pan Am Building deserves all the *P/A* said about it—and more," wrote Albert Bush-Brown, a colleague of Belluschi's at MIT before becoming president of the Rhode Island School of Design. "What was said sufficiently provokes the further moral questions, to be addressed most of all to the architects."[18] "Howard Roark, hero of *The Fountainhead,* was right—blow it up," suggested Earl Carbin from New Haven, Connecticut.[19] "Congratulations on your article on the Pan Am Building," wrote Paul Kirk from Seattle. "It is my opinion that the individuals responsible for drawing up zoning regulations must begin to think of our cities as totalities, rather than individual pieces of property. The present approach permits an owner to erect a building that puts an undue load of vehicular and pedestrian traffic on streets unable to support it. The Pan Am Building exemplifies the incorrectness of this approach."[20] "The Pan Am Building is an excellent example of overjamming an already overjammed and complicated complex," wrote Edgar A. Tafel in New York.[21] Particularly damning was the letter from Herb Greene from Norman, Oklahoma, who admitted to having seen the Pan Am in photographs only: "A recurring impression is that the building represents a moral lapse on the parts of Dr. Gropius and Dean Belluschi. That the building would have been done anyway—and worse—if they had not participated, is the sentiment of any architect serving Mammon." He found the architects, relegated to mere stylists, unable to cope with the aesthetic challenges of a huge structure. Assuming that so much office space had to be erected on the site, the architects could have incorporated important open spaces through the center of the building so disposed as to avoid the damlike impediment of Pan Am, which would have resulted in a taller, thinner structure. Greene acknowledged that this might not have met the economic equation set by the financiers, but "imagination might have found a way." He also thought "the solid profile and uniform set of Pan Am utterly lacked a sympathetic relationship to the environment of forms and circumstances" in which it was placed.[22] There was also this rather cynical view from C. J. Wisniewski in New York, targeted directly at Gropius: "Dear Editor, Lest you suggest some form of 'socialist' control, remember that one of our inalienable rights (Number 13½, to be exact) is that each man has a God-given right to make his own uglies—if he can afford to pay for them."[23]

"It is time that someone blew the whistle on horrors of this kind," wrote Thomas Stauffer, president of the Chicago Heritage Committee. "There is far more admiration expended on the new and huge without any questions being asked from the point of view of architecture, social policy, or human needs. These new structures are not thoughtful efforts to contribute to the greatness of cities or the richness of their human life; they seek, instead, to exploit the greatness that others have built. The tenants of such a building do not live better or work more efficiently for it, nor do their neighbors. Such hulks put an unreasonable—if not insupportable—burden on public services and the engineering of the city. They are contrary, or should be, to public policy. . . . In this, as in other matters, if private enterprise does not meet the needs of society, society will have its say. . . . Even the works of art, commendable in the abstract, here seem to be merely a form of face-saving or apology."[24] "The Pan Am Building is not much to write home about," began another letter aimed squarely at the building's two top designers. Calling the building "a social *faux pas*," the letter's author wondered if it was conceivable that the consultants didn't know the rudiments of design. "Certainly not; as leaders of good taste in matters of architecture and as educators of our young, they are expected to set an example of high professional standards. I conjecture that one or both of the following factors may have been responsible for their failure: either the terms of employment were such that the architectural giants could not give the project the required attention, or the client was unreasonable in his demands, and the consultants did not have the intestinal fortitude either to educate the client or to quit. Too many architects," the writer noted, "are willing to do anything for a buck."[25]

The barrage of letters continued to pour in to *Progressive Architecture* the following month. Gunnar Birkerts wrote to say that the "necrology" on the Pan Am reminded him of a similar case in Rimini, Italy, a few years prior in which the Italians "tore the rascal down."[26] Said Raniero Corbeletti, a professor of architecture at Pratt Institute: "The Pan Am Building illustrates again, for the benefit of the general public, the great gulf that exists between the City Planning Commission's zoning constraints and a visually accept-able result. The negative influence of zoning is producing a negative city scene, and will continue to do just that until city planning enthusiasts decide to give to design and aes-thetics equal billing as to sky-exposure planes and floor-area ratios. Timidity, nothing more or less, is responsible for this Paul Bunyan."[27] Leonard K. Eaton, an associate pro-fessor of architecture at the University of Michigan, was in full sympathy with the ar-ticle. He had "long been pained that professional leaders such as Gropius and Belluschi lent their names to this enterprise," and was not surprised that the structure was "a failure in architectural design, because the men who worked on it must inevitably have had qualms of guilt about their participation in the entire affair. No architect can work well if he isn't convinced that what he is doing has at least a fair degree of validity."[28] "Dear Editor," wrote still another reader, "My reaction to the Pan Am Building is more one of shock, recoil, and curiosity than of satisfaction. In spite of dear old Gropius's *apologia per vita panamericanus,* which he delivered at a Cambridge luncheon on the occasion of his eightieth birthday, the building-shaped cake that was presented him was mercifully not in the shape of Pan Am."[29] And yet another reader, evidently un-aware of Haskell's long campaign and Huxtable's concerted efforts, commented: "Your criticism and comments on the colossal Pan Am Building are startling and provocative. Unfortunately, had the same criticism been made before the building was erected, it would not have prevented construction, since the city authorities, even if they had agreed with you, would have been powerless to act. . . . Private enterprise and uncon-trolled civic planning are generally accepted as aspects of our democratic way of life. There apparently was no way of preventing the erection of this 'new city' short of an in-junction by city authorities (who, it should be recalled, were there celebrating the build-ing upon its opening) following studies of the possible consequences."[30]

The letters supporting Burns's article continued from across the country throughout August and September, including another long, thoughtful one from Carl A. Bystrom, an architect in Seattle, acknowledging, among other things, the role of the press. By-strom thought Burns's article was "a superlative job of architectural criticism" and com-mended *Progressive Architecture* for publishing it, adding that the profession had a need for succinct, insightful analyses. As he was a continent away, he was reluctant to comment on the building's finer details, but he agreed that the project was a failure and posed conceptual and philosophical questions that demanded analysis. The project was doomed at the start, he said, doomed "from the very moment when it was conceived of as situated on that site, at that great scale, and in that more or less standard office building form." From that point on, he continued, *only* a complete rethinking of the program or a radical rehandling of the building mass could have saved it. Abstractly considered, the tower wasn't bad, its massing rather subtle and pleasant, but when placed in its site, it became "a great scaleless, hulking, omnipresent colossus." From it one might learn that there was "a point in building size and scale where subtle changes of form and refinements of details become ineffective and inadequate. . . . Perhaps also limits should be placed on the economic exploitation of a limited site, of which the Pan Am Building seems to be the consummate and, I hope, ultimate example."[31]

In the meantime, Belluschi, writing eloquently in *Architectural Record* about simplicity in church architecture, and Gropius, basking in the glow of his celebratory party in the Harkness Commons at Harvard in honor of his eightieth birthday, seemed oblivious to the criticism.[32]

ARCHITECTURAL RECORD AND MILDRED SCHMERTZ

On the face of it, *Architectural Record* seemed to concur with the faultfinding. "The Pan Am Building is now open. . . . All have pronounced the building ugly, of course, for how could it be otherwise?" Mildred Schmertz began her article, "The Problem of Pan Am," as if the building's ugliness were preordained.[33] Schmertz's article was, however, in effect, an apologia for the Pan Am's two key designers. Her contention was that the architects had achieved "an excellent architectural solution," despite "tough economic imperatives." Written, as was Goble's earlier article, in close collaboration with Gropius and Belluschi, who provided the material for it, the article set forth the two architects' arguments in defense of the building, taking issue not with them, but with the press, which she felt had dealt with them unfairly. Included among the illustrations to her article was a hitherto unpublished drawing of the Pan Am as it would have appeared had Gropius had his way and the 1929 New York General Building (formerly New York Central, later the Helmsley) been removed and its site made into a park (figure 4.4).

The building was now open, she wrote, larger than any other, its entrepreneurs celebrating the fact that it was already 95 percent rented and fully financed. Were it also acclaimed as a work of art and gift to the citizens of New York, its owners would be happier still. As it was, the building had received much derision, but little praise—criticism, she maintained, that was "ill-informed and unfair." Newspapers had been blasting away at it with holy zeal; for the public, the Pan Am was "the last straw." The concerned citizen, prompted by the press, saw the building as "a monstrous symbol of the greed

FIGURE 4.4   Gropius's early scheme, with site cleared for plaza

of real estate speculators in dark collusion with city hall." It was faulted for its callous indifference to the welfare of the common man, crowding an already crowded area, slowing his taxis, jamming his restaurants, and blotting out his sky. "All have pronounced the building ugly, of course, for how could it be otherwise?"

The universal disparagement of the Pan Am she found unfortunate for two reasons. So far, the journalistic criticism had done nothing to enhance understanding "of the real forces which shape cities and buildings." Equally serious was its unfairness to the architects, Gropius, Belluschi, and Roth, and to the building's late owner, Erwin Wolfson. If a painting or sculpture fails as a work of art, we can simply disregard it, she wrote; if a building, however, is "less than a total aesthetic success, it may be a brilliant compromise with incontrovertible forces which reasonable criticism must consider." The Pan Am, she felt, was just such a brilliant compromise. She repeated the by-now familiar arguments: Most of New York's postwar office buildings were ziggurats whose form was determined by the maximum allowable rental space that could be packaged on the site. Wolfson, however, had "sacrificed" six hundred thousand square feet of the allowable rentable space so that his architects might achieve an architectural, meaning an aesthetically laudable or at least acceptable, solution. (Schmertz made no mention of the economic factor here, and the anticipated difficulty of renting a larger building, which had been pointed out by Kaufmann.) Contrary to others, she found the Pan Am "decisive in form and explicit in its relationship to its site" and its link to the Grand Central Terminal (which Burns had found awkward) "carefully studied."

She noted that Gropius and Belluschi, who, she said, had been brought in at Roth's suggestion (which was, again, not quite accurate; they were brought in, as Kaufmann again had pointed out, at Wolfson's insistence), wanted the tower sited in such a way as to avoid visual ambiguity. A setting of glass skyscrapers of different heights and varying setbacks along the Park Ave building line presented a shifting aspect at best, and in a city that is continuously transforming itself, only the old street patterns are fixed. To these, she said, relying on the information Gropius and Belluschi had provided to her, the Pan Am related. Both design consultants believed that the axis of Park Avenue should be closed by Pan Am (the suggestion was, of course, Gropius's, and Belluschi concurred with it), with the building serving as "a strong point of reference for the unbalanced building masses" north and south of Grand Central Station.

She described the building in by-now familiar terms and the architects' motivations for doing what they did: It was an octagon to catch different intensities of light, subdividing the building and diminishing its apparent bulk. This was not, she pointed out, economically sound, as it increased the cost of construction and resulted in a loss of rentable wedges, but Wolfson had "made this concession to the aesthetic recommendations of his design consultants" (concessions that in hindsight were for naught, given the disappointment, even hers, in the building's aesthetics). Gropius, she says, was responsible for the design of the exteriors as well as the public spaces; he had also been entrusted with leadership of the whole design process in the interest of visual unity.

Schmertz continued on not as a detached critic, but as an advocate for the designers. The broad face of the tower was made to face north and south, she said, not to reduce air-conditioning loads, but for aesthetic reasons; although the building could be seen as a backdrop for the New York General Building looking down Park Avenue from the north, it was not conceived as such, as ownership of the building might change, and older (meaning prewar, premodern) office space might some day become as obsolete as the prewar apartments that once graced Park Avenue. In a perfect world, she declared, Gropius would have had the New York General Building site turned into a park.

The days were numbered, too, she contended, for the old concourse. The station had been thus far spared "not through the force of anybody's architectural conviction, nor 'save the concourse' pleas a (snide swipe at *Architectural Forum* here), but only because Boisi had not included it in the three-and-a-half-acre air rights parcel offered Wolfson for development. When asked about earlier schemes for the Grand Central redevelopment that had included the station, notably Pei's proposal, Boisi had replied that as the Zeckendorf scheme involved ten million square feet and fifty thousand people, it was "too big" and that there was no purpose served "in making grandiose plans." His aim simply was to encourage more-limited development schemes that would provide income as soon as possible to the railroad. And this, Schmertz said, had led to the disappearance of "all the elegant, much lamented but not very profitable apartments" on Park Avenue that were being replaced by office buildings. Would the terminal too go in time? According to Boisi, it was not "inviolate," and he considered it "a burden." What would replace it? Boisi wasn't sure.

The Pan Am architects all revered the terminal, she maintained (which, though politically expedient, was again not true; neither Gropius nor Belluschi thought much of the building and had made no effort to help save it), and the new building respected its elderly neighbor, aligning, for example, the height of its base with the cornice height of the terminal (this, it should be remembered, was neither Gropius's nor Belluschi's original intention; they had wanted a much lower base building to serve visually as a forecourt for their sculptural tower, which Wolfson had insisted on heightening for economic reasons). Moreover, the entrance to the new building from the concourse was deliberately underplayed, she indicated, so as not to violate the station's great interior.

Both Gropius and Roth, she said, believed that Wolfson was determined to put up the best building he could, consonant with a reasonable return on his investment, which meant costs had to be held to $25 per square foot, compared to the $40 per square foot of the Seagram Building. She quoted Roth as saying (irony of ironies), "Erwin wanted to put up a building he could be proud of that wouldn't hurt the city or him."

Noting that Boisi was now projecting even fewer occupants, seven to ten thousand, in the Pan Am, rather than seventeen thousand, she concluded that the building could "hardly be accused of drawing new hordes to the Grand Central area," and defended the principle of vertical rather than horizontal circulation espoused by Goble in *Architectural Record* the previous year. The concentration of office buildings in the area contributed to the city's economic life, she asserted, "and these structures are great taxpayers as well." Adding that "[A]ll the Pan Am architects agree that the city must increase its transportation facilities to accommodate them," she quoted Belluschi, who tried again to make his point about growth and babies' feet: "'There is one point that you cannot gloss over, and that is the congestion in the subways. But when a baby grows out of his shoes, you don't cut his feet down or cut off his toes, you just buy new shoes. And we are used to growth in this country.'" She ended by quoting Roth, who thought the whole Grand Central area, like Wall Street, should be pedestrian only. He predicted the building's most serious impact on its surroundings would occur at lunch time, admitting that the building and area lacked adequate restaurant facilities. "We will have to wait and see what happens; the full force will be felt by next Christmas when everyone will be in."[34]

This "wait and see" attitude—"we build and let the city cope"—was exactly what critics like Haskell were fuming about. *Architectural Record*'s uncritical, weak-kneed acceptance of the status quo no matter what the consequence only contributed to the sense of outrage.

While in a decided minority, *Architectural Record* wasn't completely alone in defending the Pan Am. An architect in San Francisco responded to Burns's stinging criticism in *Progressive Architecture* by challenging critics to come up with a better design, asking what *they* would have done under said circumstances, and suggested a design competition.[35] Another maintained that although no one would argue about the undesirability of the building's size, siting, and parking, more of the criticism should have been aimed at the City Planning Commission.[36] Yet another letter, this one in the *New York Times,* voicing an opinion the writer would later retract, was from August Heckscher, former art commissioner of New York and President John F. Kennedy's special consultant on the arts, who chided the *Times* for its editorial in which it "once again" referred to the Pan Am Building as "a cut-rate monument." "I have been wanting to say a word in its defense," Heckscher wrote. "Almost nobody else has done so, either in print or in private comment. People who have not heretofore shown a concern for the cityscape wax voluble in opposition to this particular building." Heckscher then waxed eloquent himself on behalf of Pan Am's interior spaces: There was no more enchanting a series of spatial experiences in New York today than that through 230 Park Avenue, through the lobby, out across the intervening street and into the Pan Am, which was what civic architecture was all about. . . . The most common complaint about the Pan Am was that it blocked the view. But the view, he pointed out, had long been walled in by the Grand Central building, whose base was the same height as the apartment houses that formerly bordered the avenue; as these apartments were replaced after the war by office buildings of an entirely different scale, it was "natural," he said, to have the vista closed by a wall of comparable height. Without the backdrop of the Pan Am, the Grand Central building in its present context, he thought, would look "grotesquely dwarfed," and the space around it "like that of a missing tooth."[37]

This was Gropius's argument, which few found convincing at the time.

HASKELL'S ARGUMENT

Scathing as the criticism of the Pan Am had been in magazines such as *Harper's, Time,* and *Fortune,* which were aimed at the general public, none was so acidic as Haskell's in *Architectural Forum.*[38] In a long, richly illustrated article, "The Lost New York of the Pan American Airways Building," Haskell expressed both his outrage that the building, so wrong for its site, could and did get built, and his profound disillusionment with its two modernist architects, Gropius and Belluschi. Written on the eve of his leave of absence as *Forum*'s editor, the article was the outpouring of an anguished soul. "Now that there has been time to think about it," he began one draft of the article, "the real sadness in the story of New York's new 59-story Pan American Airways Building, situated at the very center of that commercial capital, is how brutal and pathetic were the conditions that shaped it. Pan Am marks the end in a whimper of a mighty drama of enterprising ideas."

Haskell's *Architectural Forum* had never been the unabashed propagandist *Architectural Record* was, but Haskell did have a great deal of respect for both Gropius and Belluschi. He had corresponded frequently with Belluschi, in whom he had confidence as a spokesman for the profession, about his views on numerous architectural issues, and he shared with the profession at large a high respect for Belluschi's design abilities.[39] Haskell also knew Gropius personally, though he respected him less as a designer than as an educator, and made a point of keeping in touch with him throughout the Pan Am affair.[40] Haskell conceived of his role as the *Forum*'s editor as that of a watchdog of the public environment: not an insider, promoting the activities of professionals, but an outsider, providing information vital to an informed community of individuals connected with the building industry. Thus, early on in the Pan Am project as criticism was beginning to swell, Haskell wrote James Marston Fitch, whose book on Gropius was about to be published, about running something in the *Forum* on Gropius's philosophy to bring it up to date, as he believed the team concept in particular needed clarification. A big gap, Haskell thought, existed between design by committee and Gropius's notion of collaboration, which was based on the conviction that the design process is facilitated by the various performers' understanding what others were doing. "Unfortunately," Haskell added, "Gropius himself as a designer doesn't seem always to be the most inspired."[41]

Haskell had a long investment in the Grand Central project and cared about it passionately. His involvement in it dated back to the early 1950s, not long after he had joined the *Forum* as its editor, when talk first began of redeveloping the Grand Central area.[42] After his campaign in 1954 to save the concourse, he followed the railroad's plans closely, tracking the Grand Central City project through the early Roth scheme, Wolfson's hiring of Gropius and Belluschi, the New School debate, and the bowling alleys proposal. In 1959, in a lecture to the Michigan Society of Architects, he recalled J. P. Morgan earlier in the century, who, in speaking of the Grand Central Station, a purely business institution for the making of money, declared that it "must nevertheless be built as 'the gateway of the city.'" It was the loss of this civic dimension, this sense of civic responsibility and pride among corporate rulers, the successors of the Vanderbilts and Morgans, that anguished Haskell. "By now the corporation itself, in which these men put their heart and soul, has reached stature," Haskell said in his talk. "They are a new aristocracy and they mean to give their own institutions, like the corporation, a worthy face."[43] As construction of the new building got underway, Haskell met with Wolfson and Boisi repeatedly to urge a broader perspective and to assure them that architects were not against their making money but simply wanted the project done in such a way as to enhance, not spoil, the city. As a self-appointed guardian of the built environment, Haskell continued to monitor the situation, especially the expanding commercial exploitation of the terminal building. As he expressed it in a letter to Joseph Watterson, editor of the *AIA Journal,* he thought action was needed to make sure the Grand Central complex was not turned into a "ramshackled shopping bazaar with a few commuter tracks under its adjacent tower." Fearing that Wolfson still had not grasped the real principle of the matter and that "poor Boisi" was simply trying to cut New York Central's losses in any way he could, Haskell thought perhaps a national effort on the building, "which was once a national gateway of major importance and which is still a great room as a focal point of the world's greatest metropolis," was called for.[44]

FIGURE 4.5   Aerial photograph, from Douglas Haskell, "The Lost New York of the Pan American Airways Building"

When the building finally opened, Haskell was simply outraged. Long in gestation, his article in the November 1963 *Forum,* over six months after the opening, began not with text but with a full-page aerial view of the densely packed Grand Central area: Park Avenue to the north and south, the Chrysler Building on the right, Rockefeller Center to the left, the Union Carbide, Lever House, the Seagram, the Grand Central, and the Pan Am (figure 4.5).[45] Describing the mammoth new building and how it was representative of what was happening to New York, and by extension cities everywhere, Haskell, in his customary learned, insightful way, zeroed in on what he saw at the core of the matter: public versus private interests. "In every vigorous growing city there are buildings and building groups which although privately owned were developed as public institutions," he wrote, as the spot or the function demanded it. Outstanding in New York were four: the Stock Exchange, Rockefeller Center, and the two great railroad stations, Penn Station and Grand Central. Of these the most interesting by far, in his opinion, was the Grand Central complex, "for its construction not only contributed the most to New York's growth but gave the world the great prototype pattern of the Futurist City." That was fifty years ago, he said, and what the railroad got out of it was not only a magnificent terminal, but also a rich, continuous realty holding in New York, which it still owned. One used to hear a great deal about the "Grand Central City," he said. But those who were not aware of what this "city" once meant "have no measure for the degradation of great ideas which is involved in the recent handling of the property, including the manner of developing, atop the station, the new 59-story Pan American Airways Building." The same degradation, he noted, was affecting other aspects of the city: Penn Station, for example, was now being torn down, and the Stock Exchange moved. "Thus the decline of New York has been set in motion," he noted, "not by communists or enemies, but by the city's unastute business leaders—its latest expatriates."

Given the city's waning splendors, he thought the situation of the Grand Central and the Pan Am demanded scrutiny. "Actually what is wrong with Pan Am is not that it is so very big or that it might produce such extreme congestion or that the forces which produced it are so very formidable," he said, cutting through the trivia. "The trouble is, on the contrary, that its underlying ideas are so inadequately small, and are formed to the lowliest kind of business imagination. The program for the building renounced the central impulse by which New York lives and has to live; and this kind of renunciation is spreading." To understand this, one needed to understand what made New York great when it was great, and "the organic connection between great architecture and great ambition." And this, he thought, involved understanding why New York led America with its greater imagination, energy, and comprehensiveness and the greater speed of its commercial *and* cultural leadership. He then delved into the rich history of the Grand Central Terminal, pointing out what made it so magnificent: It was not simply the terminal itself, in his eyes, but the futurist city the whole complex presented. What New York contributed to citycraft, he said, was not congestion, but congestion with movement, and it did this on the very spot the Pan Am now occupied. It was this achievement that was summed up at the turn of the century under the title of "Grand Central City," even though the only part of that "city" visible was the above-grade terminal. What gave New York, a commercial capital on a constricted island, its edge over its Atlantic-seaboard competitors Boston, Philadelphia, Baltimore, and Washington was its transportation, its "free swift movement," which, in Haskell's words, was what commerce was all about. First it was with canals, then with the railroads, and after the Civil War, in internal city circulation. New York was the first with elevated lines, fast elevators, subways, and commuter trains, like those of London. Tubes were dug under the Hudson for the Pennsylvania line, then for truck and bus routes. New York invented the parkway, then the freeway, and had the world's longest span for a suspension bridge.

Anybody can congest a city, he pointed out. "What New York did in its creative days with congestion was to make an art of it." What made it an art was the imagination and simultaneous development of adequate movement to go with it. The brilliant breakthrough of the Grand Central Terminal project came from the fact that during the first decade of the twentieth century, New York wove together its two major achievements—concentrated building and swift urban transportation—into a single operation, which was, in Haskell's words, "majestically fantastic," representing a "pinnacle of creative effort. Here was compounded the great movement of urban futurism—and all that Sant'Elia did in his famous futurist railroad station schemes for Milan a decade later was to draw up another Grand Central with its covers off."

The New York Central Railroad started all this in 1902, Haskell maintained, when it began the redesign of Grand Central, sinking the four tracks carrying six hundred trains per day underground south of Harlem. As the tracks approached the terminal, they splayed out, ultimately into more than a hundred tracks, divided between an upper (for long distance) and a lower (for suburban trains) level, both underground. Above the rail yard was Park Avenue, carried on steel posts, in effect a miles-long bridge, burying the noise and pollution of the rail yard underground and out of sight, Haskell marveled, as New York's civic-conscious, City Beautiful Movement–minded Beaux-Arts architects and engineers, squeamish at time about such utilitarian forms, covered over this bare-bones structure with more civic-minded fare.

Then, Haskell said, as Thomas Wolfe sang in his poetry, big buildings began rising out of those deep wells in the interstices of the tracks: hotels, clubs, office buildings, and apartment houses, some of which (such as the Commodore, Biltmore, Roosevelt, Park Lane, Barclay, Ambassador, and Waldorf-Astoria) still stood. Then after the war, came a spate of office buildings, including the Union Carbide.

The railroad yard thus, Haskell pointed out, became a huge realty holding, concentrated in a single hand. The boundaries shrank some, but the yard itself still extended up to 58th Street, with a total of forty-eight acres. Already by 1925, even before the 1929 New York Central Building was built at the head of the compound, the value was a third of a billion dollars. This was the first Grand Central City, with its two levels of tracks below grade and streets above. But this was not all. Park Avenue itself was elevated where it split to go around the terminal as an elevated ramp, and the complex was bound to the rest of New York by means not only of surface streets, but of the old elevated lines; plus new subways and pedestrian passageways tunneled in all directions, linking the terminal with wide areas of midtown. Concession-lined, he pointed out, this network established a precedent for the Rockefeller Center later.

On top of all this, the monumental, sumptuous, costly, architecturally nonsparing $75 million station (the equivalent of $225 million in 1964, Haskell added) was built. It was a noble architecture—not just for the station, but for the whole city-within-a-city, about which Warren, as architect, had final say on all facades and cornice lines. "Such are the money-magnetizing characteristics of big ideas," Haskell observed. "Such is the way of creating a great metropolis, calculatedly urban."

There were three major theoretical breakthroughs here, Haskell contended: first, a new transportation theory that maintained that modern commerce no longer had terminals, but rather transfer points between one transportation system and other (in this case, from railroad to city traffic); second, the segregation of different transportation modes by level to keep them linked without colliding; and third, the integration of traffic and congestion enabling them to function together. As a dividend, he said, there was the splendid architecture that could be both stimulated and paid for in the pride and excitement of generating great exploratory urban ideas.

How different the current state of affairs! Against this rich, glorious portrait of the Grand Central's past, Haskell depicted the present, describing how the establishment of the new Interstate Commerce Commission began a sequence of events that left the railroads weakened, and how similarly, the tax system of cities was changed to place the highest values on areas where development was most dense, which inhibited progress in the most critically important spots. Rent control, retained after the war, had also had drastic consequences for the area, leaving the New York Central compelled, Haskell said, to tear down the unprofitable residential constituents of its Park Avenue Gold Coast and replace them with more profitable modern office buildings.

This could have been the signal for creative ideas, a new vision drawing on the newest techniques to create an unprecedented kind of new urban precinct, a major development that demanded of government—city, state, or federal—a series of public improvements to go along with it. It could, for example, have requested a link with other New York railroad stations (for example, Penn Station). As it was, he pointed out, it took as long for a commuter to get from the Grand Central Terminal to Penn Station as to get to Stamford, Connecticut; by the same token, such a link would have saved Penn Station from demolition.

None of these possibilities were realized, Haskell said. Instead of addressing these issues, New York Central "hired a real estate butcher" to carve up the site like a gigantic carcass into individual lots that then sold or were leased for individual office buildings, "mostly cheap." In the end, the choicest piece of all, which should have given the correlated "New Grand Central City" its urban style and crown, was leased to Wolfson, to see what he could do with a speculative building. And Wolfson, Haskell said, "built the Pan Am."

It was, in Haskell's words, a sad procedure for so pivotal a site. Wolfson (who had obtained the land at an inflated rate and was unable to treat the empire—the whole site—as a whole, to leverage out his costs) proceeded to get a massive rental volume out of his one building by setting rental rates low enough to attract large numbers.[46] And this meant putting up a huge—but low-cost—building, instead of the more flexible, well-distributed, modestly high complex that could have been built instead. Wolfson then, Haskell said, hired two well-known modern architects, who were to give this procedure the best face and their names, and persuaded the more elderly of the two to think of this as a "megalopolitan reality," while the other, the dean of a planning school, declared in favor of building first and letting somebody do the planning afterward. Gropius, he said, "was touchingly proud that 600,000 square feet were cut away from the permitted legal bulk for the sake of a shape," for which he claimed moral credit. The consequence was the Pan Am.

Haskell acknowledged that the opening of the building had not created the calamity critics had predicted and that there weren't the twenty-five thousand occupants and quarter of a million visitors daily that had been foreseen. Nonetheless, the building procedure that led to the Pan Am, on a spot precious to the city, "was corrosive to the core."

Regarding traffic, the only advantage Pan Am could offer, Haskell believed, was that commuters might be able to step from train to office under one roof. But even this was not very inspiring, as they would arrive by one of the filthiest, ugliest subway stations in the world, then come up through the once noble, now honky-tonked Grand Central concourse, whose magnificent interior was hacked up (by the same realty butcher, Haskell noted) into concessions.[47] From here, they would rise on escalators into an imposingly tall Pan Am lobby, with its grandiose, badly blemished granite piers.

Haskell was no more impressed with the art placed in the building's interior than he had been with the building, which he said made a fair try but little more than that. He found the same true too of the building's masonry exteriors, aimed at offsetting all the glass of neighboring office buildings; there too the effort only half-succeeded, as the deeply textured wall pattern might read well from far distances, but not from close up. There was also its "insistent parade of little sticks," which ate away at and destroyed the silhouette of the richly sculptural building masses both to its north and its south, older buildings above which Pan Am now rose as an enormous backdrop. Its faceted form, though new to the city, was in fact not new, but pilfered, only "a clumsy copy of a Le Corbusier building of 1931," on one of the best corners in New York. Moreover, the architects turned the building so it spanned across the avenue, shutting off all further views on either side. "Thus," he observed, "the Pan Am gives two leading transportation companies a symbol consisting of a major roadblock." By doing this, Haskell said, instead of inviting or inspiring exploration, it blocked it, shutting it off. This made the situation even worse, Haskell lamented, interjecting a note of respect for cultural history that must have cut Gropius to the core, "for when the freedom-loving Greeks made it their rule that every great civic composition must leave at least one clear view into infinity, this sprang out of their sensuously based gift of curiosity and mental speculation, upon which was reared Western civilization itself."

It was sad to see, a clearly disillusioned Haskell said, especially in New York, which had "made itself America's free-enterprise capital." It was "pathetic to have things go thus with a realty empire in which even before the Pan Am was built, the railroad owners and their subsidiaries had an estimated half-billion dollar interest, and on which all buildings include those on land lease ran into the billions in value." Grand Central City first, then the Rockefeller Center after, demonstrated how New York, as a metropolis, depended on being built as a series of large, tightly planned enclaves, dependent on space and variety and free movement within them, as well as free movement in and out of them. Other cities, he noted, had seen the point and modeled themselves on

Grand Central City, New York's magnificent Futuristic achievement of swift movement amid tall, tightly grouped, crowd-accommodating buildings.

"Now this is lost in New York," he concluded. Leadership was needed, and for this Haskell turned, significantly enough, in light of his comments about Gropius, the "elder statesman," to the younger generation. Great architecture, he summarized, rode on great ideas, which were not present here.

It was a long, poignant article in which Haskell marked the Pan Am as a turning point, a symbol of the city's decline, emblematic of what had gone wrong with the modernist vision.

Clearly aware of the article, which followed on the heels of a major critical appraisal of transportation planning in American cities in the October *Architectural Forum,* William F. R. Ballard, chairman of the City Planning Commission, Department of City Planning, who had earlier defended congestion in the Grand Central area, wrote Haskell several months later.[48] He and members of the Commission were planning a symposium aimed at developing a master plan for the city and wanted him to serve as a member of the planning advisory committee to develop the symposium's content and select its participants. The timing, he thought, was propitious, and the event, apparently prompted by Haskell's article, had the potential of becoming a landmark in the field of city planning. "Over the last several years," Ballard wrote to Haskell, "this nation has witnessed an extraordinary new public awareness that the U.S. is not only becoming overwhelmingly urbanized and suburbanized but that this development is taking the form of great new metropolitan areas posing an array of the most difficult challenges to planners. As the nation's principal city, New York itself confronts on a vast scale most of the problems involved." Which was, of course, one of Haskell's main points.

JACK COTTON DIES

As Haskell continued to fulminate, things elsewhere went on. Cotton, whose business partner Wolfson had died at age sixty just one year before the Pan Am Building opened, died at age sixty-one just one year after. For both of them, the building had been their biggest and most challenging project ever. It was a productive partnership, as complementing Wolfson, whose background had been in construction, was Cotton, with a background in architecture. A practicing architect before he became chairman of City Centre Properties, he left it one of the world's richest development companies by the time he died and the Pan Am "a financial, if not a critical, success."[49]

By virtually all accounts, this was true: Although almost universally acknowledged as an architectural failure, the building was a stunning business success. Moreover, the strangulating traffic that critics had envisioned as a result of its operation never materialized.[50] Credit for this, however, was due, according to Fitch, a historian and preservationist, less to the design skills of Gropius and Belluschi than to Wilgus's vastly more complicated, brilliant scheme for the Grand Central Terminal and its ability to absorb huge new crowds.[51] Richard Whalen, author of a September 1964 article in *Fortune*, had a different explanation. "Traffic still moves," he wrote. "The thousands of workers have been absorbed in the morning and nightly flood of subway riders. The noontime scramble for lunch-counter space is more frantic, but somehow the mob gulps hamburgers in 15-minute shifts. All that has happened, really, is that life has become more unpleasant for countless people. The critics were not wrong to attack the Pan Am Building as an architectural and sociological atrocity; they simply underestimated the capacity of New Yorkers to endure inhuman pressures."[52]

CRITICISM ELSEWHERE

As criticism of the Pan Am continued in both popular and professional magazines and newspapers, it began appearing in other venues as well. Condit's 1961 text on American building techniques, reviewed by Wayne Andrews in *The Reporter*, was one of the first, two years before the building was even open. It was followed by Blake's, written just after. In 1964, Blake, managing editor of *Architectural Forum* since 1961 and author of *The Master Builders*, came out with *God's Own Junkyard: The Planned Deterioration of America's Landscape*. It was a book written not in anger, Blake wrote, but in fury, "though not, I trust, in blind fury." It was, he said, "a deliberate attack upon all those who have already befouled a large portion of this country for private gain." A fierce di-atribe against uncontrolled free enterprise, which he felt was ruining the American landscape, the book contended that the major factor determining the shape of the American city was unregulated private profit, with buildings largely built without the slightest regard to urban design, "solely for the purpose of making a fast buck faster." As an example, Blake cited the Pan Am Building. Astride Warren and Wetmore's "beau-tiful" 1913 Grand Central Station, the building exemplified "the ruthless disregard for structures of the past in the quest for money." Noting that planning commissions were typically ineffectual, as variances were easy to come by if the developer had the right political connections, Blake again used the Pan Am to prove his point. Its size, he main-tained, had been limited not by zoning regulations, but by pure pragmatics and the prob-lem of accommodating more elevators in a much larger building. Zoning regulations in New York City were so feeble, he noted, that even after they were made more strin-gent in 1961, Pan Am developers could have built bigger, had they desired. "Every single planner or urban designer of any note in the United States," Blake maintained, "is convinced that the Pan Am Building is a massive disaster for midtown Manhattan—the giant cork that will finally, and forever, plug up that particular bottleneck." Blake's book, excerpted in the January *Forum,* was illustrated by a series of comparisons, the most compelling of which was one of Park Avenue pre– and post–Pan Am (figure 4.6).[53]

Although Blake had not mentioned him in his comments on the Pan Am, Gropius felt personally attacked. He was furious. "Dear Peter Blake," he wrote in long, verbose let-ter in February 1964. "So far I had taken the criticism on my work for the Pan Am Build-ing quietly in my stride. But after I have read your new book, *God's Own Junkyard,* it is time that I speak up. After I have been for a lifetime in the forefront in fighting the dis-figuring and ugliness of our environment, just as you do today, and have actively con-tributed towards improvement for two generations, it is a very curious experience to see one of my major works thrown by the wayside into the junkyard." Now claiming the building as his own, Gropius continued, "It makes me indignant and angry that you count me *by implication* among 'the latter-day vandals' who 'befoul the country' and create 'uglification.'. . . I am writing in the mood of an offended friend who, I think, de-serves respect and consideration. I certainly welcome constructive criticism which can be argued on an objective basis. Instead I find myself facing an exaggerated, emotional campaign which has lost all proportion. . . . Could I not expect that critics would as-sume that a man of my experience has given careful thought to all the problems in-volved in this difficult task? But my well-founded reasons were disregarded by the

FIGURE 4.6   Park Avenue pre- and post-Pan Am, from Peter Blake, *God's Own Junkyard,* 1964

critics. I confess that I had expected that from you would come a balanced critique, weighing objectively pros and cons which would stop the current band wagon criticism." Assuming somehow his name alone guaranteed a quality building that was above criticism, Gropius took issue with Blake's statement that "every planner or urban designer of any note in the U.S. was convinced the Pan Am Building was a disaster" and cited Bacon's letter in *Progressive Architecture,* as well as Ballard's in the *New York Times,* as evidence to the contrary—two examples, he thought, from which one could assume "that quite a few others" felt the same.[54]

Accustomed to a more purely promotional treatment at the hands of the architectural press, Gropius pressed Blake for "an honest answer," maintaining that in the photograph he had used to demonstrate the impact of the Pan Am on Park Avenue, Blake had failed to point out all the other high-rise structures which had already changed the avenue and its scale. As for the "bottleneck," Gropius pointed out that in fact the Pan Am had *improved* pedestrian circulation and that he had suggested ways the city could improve the vehicular traffic the building would generate. And as for aesthetics, why did none of the critics realize "the necessary consequences which have arisen from the complete change in height and magnitude of the buildings on Park Avenue, which condition has dwarfed the old Tower and called for a 'new focus,' a 'new point of reference' in keeping with the new, greatly enlarged scale of the neighborhood?"

"In the face of these realities," Gropius concluded, evidently unaware of how strongly people felt about the issue, "what is the sense of this emotional campaign, condemning me wholesale and accusing me almost of having committed an immoral act by tackling this job at all?"[55]

Blake's response to Gropius was a good deal more conciliatory. "I can only tell you that I am sorry I offended you so deeply," he wrote. Assuring Gropius that the Pan Am Building was probably better for his participation in it, and that taken by itself it seemed a fine building, Blake said his objections had only to do with its relationship to its surroundings. "You know, of course, that there are a great many people who admire you as much as I do, and who agree, substantially, with me on this issue, and disagree with you."[56]

Among the issues raised by the Pan Am, beyond the aesthetic (its "uglification") or sociological (the crowding or congestion) was the deeper, more fundamental question Haskell had raised of private versus public interests. It was the focus of a long, six-part series of articles, "Who Owns New York?" published in the *New York Herald Tribune* in February and March 1964. The series was written by Daniel M. Friedenberg, a longtime Manhattan realtor and occasional writer, who was clearly not happy about the state of New York City's architecture. Gresham's law, he pointed out, applied to architecture as well as money: Cheap architecture drives out good architecture. Regarding buildings built by real estate speculators, and their quality or conspicuous lack of it, he posed the following question: What have they contributed to the growth of New York? Builders, he noted, took enormous risks, and hence expected high profits from their investments; although there were various kinds of builders—individual entrepreneurs, syndicates, public corporations—they all had one thing in common: profit as their single guiding factor. While not always deserving it, public corporations were usually credited with the better buildings, individual builders with the worst. As examples of the latter, Friedenberg cited the Uris brothers and most especially Wolfson, with whom "profit has been practically the sole motivation, to judge from the final product." Pointing out that some individuals start out intending to build well, but that costs thwart those intentions, Friedenberg again cited as an example Wolfson, whose Diesel Construction Company brought costs and aesthetics down to a competitive level. Most builders were not interested in "mere beauty," Friedenberg said, and quoted Richard Roth, whose firm, Emery Roth & Sons, was the one "most often identified with New York architecture at its least inspired level. . . . In a free enterprise economy, architecture mirrors the society in which we live. Why don't we admit that we are living in an uncontrolled society—or at least one controlled only by money and the tax structure?" Speculators such as Wolfson, Friedenberg concluded, dominate the realm of those who made good in New York real estate, giving the public "ugly boxes divided like eggcrates by paper-thin walls with faulty air conditioners and inadequate elevator service. And they say forget about aesthetics—that's something for women's committees and the editors of high-falutin' architectural magazines."[57]

By this time, too, the general public, including its youth, was involved in the debate.

NEW YORK is an
ARCHITECTURAL
DISASTER

was the content of a lamppost-size poster sticker affixed to the side of the Pan Am Building by "a squad of junior terrorists" operating, according to an editorial in *Architectural Forum,* out of a Greenwich Village basement.[58] Ironically, a letter Gropius had sent to the journal's editors regarding its article "Education and Architecture" in which he maintained he was motivated not by a "passion for education," as the journal had asserted in the article, but by a "love of architecture," appeared in the same issue.[59]

By this time, the Pan Am Building was figuring in discussions in other, more highbrow circles as well. In a famous debate in *Architectural Forum,* Scully rebutted the arguments novelist Norman Mailer had set forth in a two-part article in *Esquire,* in which he attacked modern architecture as 'totalitarian.' Totalitarism, Mailer had written, "has haunted the twentieth century. . . . And it proliferates in that new architecture which rests like an incubus upon the American landscape." People who admired such architecture did so because it obliterated the past, Mailer contended, people who were sufficiently totalitarian themselves to want to avoid the consequences of the past and were looking to inject into their environment and landscape the same deadness and monotony life has put into them. "A vast deadness and a huge monotony, a nausea without spasm, has been part of the profit of American life in the last fifteen years," Mailer asserted. Scully responded by denouncing Mailer's equating modern architecture, which was banned, he pointed out, by all of the most totalitarian countries, with totalitarianism "as the Big Lie at its most majestic" and went on to dismiss him as being simply uninformed. Both men in their verbal duel cited Park Avenue in the context of "a vast deadness and a huge monotony" and the Pan Am building as "killing the vista," with Mailer getting the last word.[60] By this time, Park Avenue and the Pan Am had become emblematic of modernism's deadness and monotony, of destroyed vistas, and of the aridity of modern life.

Well after it opened, the Pan Am continued to be cited as a notorious example of modernism gone awry. "The news that New York is to have another blockbuster like the Pan Am Building . . . stirs fears of a dismaying new plunge in the city's unrelenting postwar movement toward architectural mediocrity," wrote the *New York Times* in an editorial in August 1964. As plans were being made to raze the Savoy Plaza Hotel for a new General Motors headquarters building, fears were roused that the city would suffer the loss of another open space. "The tragedy, of course," the editorial maintained, "is that New York, unlike Paris or Washington, has no review rights on its main avenues or plazas. It is now up to the conscience, capabilities and sense of public responsibility of a group of private investors . . . to make or mar the city's face. New York needs no more cut-rate monuments like Pan Am."[61] It was a hard lesson the *Times* hoped the city had learned.

HASKELL AND THE DEMISE OF *ARCHITECTURAL FORUM*

In the summer of 1964, a little over a year after the Pan Am Building opened, *Architectural Forum,* unable to make ends meet, folded. It marked the end of an era. Haskell, for whom the Grand Central Station—and by extension, the Pan Am—had been a cause célèbre, in a final essay, brilliantly summarized the three-quarters of a century that had passed since 1892 and the magazine's inception as *The Brickbuilder.*[62] Every decade brought change, he said: In the 1890s, it was the steel frame office building and the skyscraper, which multiplied to bring about a new skyline, a development that left architecture unprepared and Beaux-Arts City Beautiful concepts simply irrelevant. Of the next two decades, 1900–1920, some historians, he said, exalt the Beaux-Arts masterpieces, whereas others trumpet the rising "machine age" and its "machine esthetics." The victory of the machine, however, Haskell contended, was not formal, but technological and social, a "vast popular liberation" providing people with new instruments of transportation that gave them a new power over speed and motion, over taste and access to land, fundamentally changing planning patterns. But first had come the railroads, which did more than stir aesthetic admiration for their locomotives. Vanderbilt on an urban scale, with his futurist city, worked together with Wilgus, Reed and Stem, and Warren and Wetmore to develop the Grand Central City under, around, and above the Grand Central Terminal. The Italian Futurists were the only ones to emulate it, when Sant'Elia drew up his proposed station for Milan, stealing, as Haskell put it, "all the Futurist credit." Then three years after Vanderbilt finished his futurist terminal came

Ford and the car, resulting in another unexpected revolution in city patterns. Meanwhile, in Europe during the 1920s, emperors were gotten rid of, and with them their stale, sentimental architecture. Europe went "modern." Only the United States hung back, "still entranced with the afterglow of the Beaux-Arts."

By this time, Haskell said, deftly weaving the history of architectural publishing into that of architecture and the architectural profession, Michael Mikkelsen, publisher and editor of *Architectural Record,* who had grown up with the *Record* back in the early days when it was a general magazine for cultivated readers and had notable critics such as Russell Sturgis and Montgomery Schuyler on its staff, brought Frank Lloyd Wright back into the discourse. By that time, however, architectural magazines in general had settled into being narrowly professional. Then in 1917, *The Brickbuilder* took a broader approach, changing its name to reflect what in fact it had already become: an architectural *forum.*

With the 1930s came the Depression, Wright, Fallingwater, and Johnson Wax, but also Gropius, who brought new continental ideas to students at Harvard, and Mies. Rockefeller Center took shape, and Tennessee Valley. But architecture needed more than these stunning exceptions to get back on its feet. Howard Myers, editor and publisher of what was now *Architectural Forum,* stepped in, breaking rules. Magazines were supposed to stick to art reporting and aesthetic discussion fringed by news and technological research. Myers treated architecture as not only an art but also a cause, in which a magazine's job was to give all possible aid. This became possible in 1932, when together with Luce, publisher of Time Inc., he forged the *Forum* into a new instrument.[63] New departments such as "Building Money" and research were added; "hidden" architects doing significant work were sought out for recognition.[64] Rather than simply reported, news was treated analytically. Readership jumped from about seven thousand in 1934 to over thirty thousand in 1936. The *Forum* henceforth was first among the world's paid-circulation architectural magazines, read not simply by architects but by their allies: engineers, contractors, lenders, and owners.

After the 1930s came the Second World War, and after the war, the triumph, eventually worldwide, of modern architecture; a new body of aristocratic patron-clients rose out of industry and gave five or six "modern"' pioneer architects their star status. As the world grew more complex, modernism splintered, as Saarinen described in the *Forum* in July 1953.[65] Mies's leadership declined as his work was parodied by a new class of "builder-scroungers" manipulating the income tax and challenged by a group of younger men. History was brought back, and eclecticism, and fantasy, as well as the new plasticity of concrete. These all enriched the scene, but even as they competed for the limelight, architecture "for the troops" still lagged.

The *Forum,* conceived as an aid to architectural leadership, was by this time, Haskell said, interested in more than simply showing exceptional cases, and instead raised issues of broad concern to the architectural community such as exposing the hidden censorship of the FHA in ruling out modern houses, challenging entrenched clichés of school planning, and arguing for wider use of curtain walls. By this time (the early 1950s), the magazine had its hands full of "crusades."

Its biggest new venture, however, was yet to come. The Depression, then the war, had left cities and slums unattended. The *Forum* was the first, Haskell contended, to be heavily engaged in urban redevelopment, housing the poor, and changing city patterns due to the car. All architecture could be divided into two, he said: the splendid, glorious, star architecture that "mankind needs so badly, for the nourishment of his soul, and cannot live without," and also the rest of it, beyond the wealthy patrons, the architecture of the "vast, underdeveloped though affluent, middle class with its overwhelming land-shaping and landscaping-destroying activities and its untutored taste," and the architecture of the poor. A "total" architecture (Gropius's term, of course, though Haskell made no mention of him) would demand the hands of all nations, at different levels. . . . And the work, without someone in command, had to mesh, and was dependent on understanding, consensus, common purpose, adaptability, and good will.

"Such, then," he summarized, "are the concerns of those who deal with architecture day by day, not alone as contemporary 'art history' but also as the contemporary history of an art; who are interested in current architectural criticism, yes, but also in architectural statesmanship; who are looking toward the future on both counts." As the *Forum* was leaving its job of addressing not just architects and engineers, but all those involved in building activity, Haskell voiced his hopes that another medium would be found to step in. "For despite the pettinesses and parochialisms of those who can exalt only their own part," he concluded, "history has already made architecture the art of all man-made surroundings. And it is a glorious thing that, whether to humanize a former slum or to create a high place on earth or to seek a habitat on the moon, the man with the magic, to whom so many have given a helping hand, can bring inert materials to life and occasionally make the very stones sing."

Haskell's essay was part of a special issue of the *Forum,* its last as a separate Time Inc. publication before it was absorbed into *Fortune.* Accompanying it were scores of letters affirming its importance, influence, and quality. "Your magazine has been of immeasurable importance to our profession, both as a source of information on leading architectural work in the U.S., and as a forum for serious architectural criticism. I thank Time Inc. for having made it possible for the *Forum* to be published in spite of its financial losses through the years," wrote one individual. Wrote another: "*Forum* has been a big help in dispelling the notion that the architect's main function is merely adding window dressing to someone else's layout." From Richard M. Branham, director of marketing for the National Concrete Masonry Association, came this: "It is a grave loss to the entire building profession that *Forum* will no longer exist. Through the years . . . it has consistently represented the highest editorial standards and has exercised a definite influence on matters requiring both foresight and courage. . . . *Forum*'s service will be sorely missed." From George Danforth, a professor in the Department of Architecture at the Illinois Institute of Technology: "Inasmuch as *Forum* has been the only critical publication at a time in architectural development when strong, objective editorial leadership is vital, it is pitiful to think it cannot be continued." From Colin Boyne, executive editor of *The Architects Journal,* based in London: "It was so encouraging to countries limping after the U.S. to feel that the major American architectural journal was addressed to builders and clients as well as architects and engineers. Here are the makings of a seed-bed for civilization." And from still others: "*Forum* has always been in my mind the 'top of the line.' In this critical time when economics seems to be prevailing over culture at every level, *Forum* was a beacon in the dark." "Your distinguished magazine is an essential cultural bond between America and the world. It has set architectural and critical standards." "For so long a time *Forum* has been the prestige publication in the field that it is the loss to the nation more than to architecture that is lamented. The U.S. needs *Forum*. . . ." "The *Forum* has contributed immeasurably to the quality of our buildings and our cities." "*Forum;* . . . a real journal of considerable social and cultural significance." And there were more.[66]

Of even greater significance was the editorial in the *New York Times*.[67] "When a professional periodical fails," the *Times* said, "it may be of considerable concern to specialists, but it seldom has much impact on the world at large. The demise of *The Architectural Forum,* a publication directed at all who build or are interested in building, is a different matter, however, since it played an influential and broadly beneficial role that went higher and deeper than most people realized. . . . When cities are being rebuilt and wilderness invaded, the end of a force for better building is dismaying. We are all a captive audience of our physical environment, and need every means possible to shape it to better ends."

FALLOUT IN THE NATIONAL PRESS

Architectural Forum's architectural coverage, which had followed the Pan Am story closely, was continued in *Fortune,* at least for a while. Whalen's "A City Destroying Itself," in *Fortune*'s September 1964 issue, again conjured up the Pan Am as an image of things going awry: "A chaotic Sixth Avenue, the overweening walls of the Pan Am Building, the abysmal reaches of a Queens housing development" comprise "this angry view from New York's streets."[68] The headquarters city for U.S. industry was not being built for people, Whalen noted, but for various independent economic units, and its failures "cast a portentous shadow over all urban life in the U.S." The blame, he said, must be distributed: City Hall had neglected the mass-transportation system; speculative builders and mortgage lenders encouraged by tax laws and zoning and building code inadequacies had been profitably manipulating the land. In the process they "have produced towers that block out the vistas of the city's landmarks and hulk brutally over the streets."

Whalen described the city's complexity, the millions of people who were fed, housed, clothed, transported, and organized for work. But how was the human spirit faring in this great metropolis? he wondered. It functioned only with growing difficulty and inefficiency: "Concentration is yielding to strangling congestion." Economic disorder, however, was not the problem, as he saw it. The truly terrible costs were social and spiritual: "New York is frowning, tight-lipped, short-tempered. It is a city without grace."

Whalen spoke of the city's increasingly inhuman scale and the usual explanations (such as those that had been provided by Goble and Schmertz in *Architectural Record*) that the shortage of space on the island had caused high land prices, which in turn necessitated high density. But the city's increasing ugliness was not foreordained, he argued (taking issue with both Goble and Schmertz): Men were making New York the eyesore that so much of it was. Whalen spoke of the city's business district with its lifeless architecture, most of which consisted of buildings that were, he asserted, the "standardized products of builders who are strictly in the business of manufacturing space." Through their collective decisions, speculative builders and, even more importantly, mortgage lenders had reshaped the contours of the city, determined how it functioned and how its inhabitants lived. Provided with incentives by every level of government, these private decision makers of great public power had feverishly torn down, rebuilt, and expanded, profitably manipulating the land beneath buildings and even, Whalen said (in another veiled reference to the Pan Am Building) the air above.

Hitherto relying on allusion, Whalen then got specific, quoting Morse that the difference in costs between an aesthetically pleasing building and an ordinary one was nominal, as structurally and mechanically most buildings was pretty much the same. In a $15 million office building, Morse estimated, "1 to 2% additional is all that is needed to give a feeling of quality." (No mention was made of what had gone awry with the money spent on "aesthetics" in the Pan Am Building.) Whalen described the tax laws that allowed New York builders to appreciate the entire cost of their buildings at accelerated rates, providing them with a comfortable cushion even if rents fell short of expectations, tax laws that favored speculative building and real estate syndication. "It's state socialism for the rich," Whalen quoted another individual, whom he identified only as "an experienced, unusually candid operator," as saying.

Whalen went on to describe zoning regulations, their supposed function in protecting public interest and improving the city's physical environment, and their actual effect, citing Jacobs and her conviction that New York's 1916 zoning code had served in fact to open up endless possibilities for the use of government power to further private gain. He mentioned the rewriting of the city's zoning code in 1960, largely as a result of rising complaints of so many tawdry buildings being built, and how this had led to a torrent of new buildings all trying to meet the December 1961 filing deadline to come in under the old, more lenient code. The new code, he said, was aimed at replacing the ziggurat skyscraper with a new, theoretically more pleasing tower rising from a block base. But the change was more apparent than real as, if a builder assembled a large enough site and left open space at street level for a plaza, he could in effect consider the sky the limit, building vertically to gain *more* square feet of rentable space than would have been possible on the same site under the old code.

The new megalith style of skyscraper, Whalen said, was exemplified by the Pan Am Building, the "world's largest commercial office building, which hulks brutally over Grand Central Station." Whalen mentioned, as had others, Wolfson's regret that the site couldn't have been left as a park. "You have to agree with that," Whalen quoted Wolfson as adding wistfully: "It would be nice if it were possible." The only real restraint operating on Wolfson was self-imposed, Whalen said, citing Wolfson's contention that he legally he could have built a much larger building that would have dumped twice as many workers into the Grand Central area than the Pan Am Building currently did.[69] With municipal agencies powerless to protect their interests, Whalen pointed out, New Yorkers were forced to rely on such mercies.

Zeroing in on the main point of his article, Whalen pointed out that Wolfson's wistful remark aside, from the perspective of its owners and developers, the Pan Am Building was overwhelmingly successful: The New York Central Railroad, which owned the land, would receive $1 million annually over a seventy-seven-year lease, the building was already 98 percent occupied, and Pan American World Airlines' lease alone called for a payment of $117 million over an unspecified term in excess of twenty-five years. The mortgage holders were pleased with their $66 million investment in a conspicuous "prestige" structure. The only interest that could not be expressed in economic terms, he said, was that of the people.

"What, after all," Whalen asked, "is a vista worth?" referring again to the Pan Am Building, which had raised the issue. "Can a citizen who once derived pleasure from the tracery of the old New York Central tower against the sky sue someone for the loss he suffers because the south end of Park Avenue is walled up? The signs he is now forced to view have commercial value, as Pan American fully realized."

The truth, Whalen asserted, was that the real power in New York was not political, but economic. Ordinary New York office workers had given up, "convinced of the futility of individual protest," and lived elsewhere; the men above them on the corporate ladder, too, were insulated from the problems of the city, sequestered in expensive East Side cooperatives, aloof from the actual life of the city by choice. Citing the example of a businessman and his wife from Cincinnati who found New York, albeit the dirtiest, most violent, noisiest city they'd ever lived in, to be free of the civic responsibilities they had felt in cities where they had lived before, Whalen concluded that the responsibility U.S. business owed to New York was "perilously overdue."[70]

Over the years, the Pan Am continued to be cited as exemplifying the problems of modern architecture and urban design. A *New York Times* editorial in 1967, "Design for a City," cited the Pan Am Building as a familiar example of a mistake to avoid. Applauding the city's new established Urban Design Council, the editorial quoted Le Corbusier,

who had once called New York "a beautiful catastrophe," and noted that over the en-
suing thirty years since Le Corbusier had made his remark, there had been "more catastrophe than beauty. . . . As an exercise in what-might-have been, there is the
appalling General Motors Building [1968; Edward Durell Stone, with Emery Roth & Sons
as architects], destroyer of scale, space and standards. . . ." This was not just a matter
of design sacrificed by the builders to economic expedience, "but, like the Pan Am
Building, it is a matter of brutality of size and in addition a perversion of open-space
planning."[71]

Five years after the Pan Am opened, opinions still hadn't changed. At a national AIA
convention in Portland, Oregon, in June 1968, a young architect (a local Belluschi fan?)
donned an oversized lapel button with the inscription "Save the Pan Am Building." The
architect's sentiment "was scarcely unanimous," according to Glenn Fowler, reporting
on the convertion in the *New York Times,* though the example he used and what it stood
for was well known, even on the West Coast. It was revealing, Fowler maintained, of a
"substantial undercurrent" among U.S. architects of the day, who were keenly aware
that their fellow Americans regarded them "as prime culprits in the disfiguration of the
urban landscape," even as they looked to architects "as the likeliest saviors of whatever beauty is left."[72]

Criticism of the Pan Am Building continued to come in from all sides, from academics as well as from practicing architects, critics, and the general public. In his *Modern
American City,* published in 1968, Yale professor of city planning Christopher Tunnard
referred to it as "a giant slab over Grand Central Terminal's platforms" that might have
gained the company publicity but had done little for city planning.[73] Scully, his colleague
at Yale, was far more pointed the following year in his textbook *American Architecture
and Urbanism,* in which he praised the Grand Central as a grand achievement, urbanistically more intricate and subtle than Penn Station, and lauded the "slender tower of the
Grand Central Office [sic] Building," which rose on the axis of the avenue, high enough
to draw the space to it and narrow enough to let the eye slide around it on both sides,
then slammed the Pan Am Building for later smothering that movement, faulting the
building on urbanistic grounds. Scully came down even harder on Gropius, describing
the Pan Am as "Gropius' own *coup de grâce* to Park Avenue."[74]

William Jordy of Brown University, a more temperate scholar, similarly blamed the
Pan Am, in his text on American architecture, for defacing Park Avenue.[75] As a visual
entity, the avenue was impressive, Jordy maintained, particularly from the 1920s until
right after World War II (figure 4.7). "If the silhouette of [the New York Central] tower

bulked sufficiently to provide a picturesque focus for the corridor," he observed, "it still did not wholly barricade the long vista (as does the Pan Am cliff at present) and thus prevent its extension by imagination into the infinity of the sky." And later in the same work: "On Park Avenue, the ragged manner in which unrelated plazas have chewed the boundaries of the street have also eroded its unity. The château tower of the Grand Central office building, which once shown as the climax of the Avenue, now exists as a wraith, making a dim appearance against the ponderous Pan Am wall behind."

Huxtable, too, remained unkind. In 1968, she began her article "Architecture by Entrapment," on a proposed new post office building (at a cost of $100 million), as follows: "The new General Post Office announced for New York last week will be just about as big as the Pan Am Building laid on end—if anyone would want to do it. Most New Yorkers have a hard time accepting it standing up."[76]

CRITICISM ABROAD

Criticism of the Pan Am Building was hardly confined to home. News of it and Gropius's involvement had spread quickly throughout the world, well before the construction on the building was begun. In Italy, in September 1959, while the building was still in the planning stage, *Domus* ran a three-page, largely descriptive story on the project illustrated by renderings and full-page photos of the Gropius/Belluschi model.[77] Response from readers was immediate. "Gropius probabilmente erra a New York" (Gropius Probably Bungling in New York) was the headline of a letter to the editor from Martin Pinchis, a Romanian architect, in *L'Architettura Cronache—Storia* the following month, accompanied by a sketch of Park Avenue and Pinchis's proposed solution (figure 4.8).[78] Pinchis described the proposed building (which he attributed to Gropius alone) as a two-hundred-meter-tall elongated octagon in the heart of New York that promised to cut off the perspective of the avenue, forming a colossal shield or folding screen. The building struck him as too static, blocking rather than opening up the vista. He proposed instead two solid lateral towers connected by a transparent central body set on a square base, which he believed was a far more sculptural and dynamic solution. Pinchis sent a similar letter to *Werk* in Berlin that was printed not only with Pinchis's sketches but with an aerial of the Grand Central area with the proposed Grand Central City montaged in. Again Pinchis described the challenges of designing a tower on such a pivotal, central site, and again he suggested his own solution, which would allow the vista to remain open. Rather than Gropius's proposed building, which he likened to a solid wall that

FIGURE 4.7   Park Avenue in the 1940s

FIGURE 4.8   Pinchis proposal, Grand Central City

arrested the movement of the business district, one of the most dynamic in the United States, Pinchis's proposal would let sun and sky as well as the avenue pass *through* the structure, a far more appropriate solution animated by freedom of construction and movement.[79] Pinchis's letter, printed in French in *Werk,* was reprinted again, this time in German, in *Bauen + Wohnen* the following month. This time it was accompanied by an essay by Gropius, "Unity in Variety—A Cultural Paradox," which was illustrated by several TAC projects, the foremost of which was the Grand Central City.[80] The essay, addressing what Gropius believed was at the core of the problem in American culture and his proposed solution, namely, a broad humanistic education, was general and abstract and made no reference to his own work. The captions for the photographs that accompanied Gropius's essay, however, were evidently provided by the magazine's editors, as they were unmistakably critical in tone. "As with the Lever House," a caption to one of the photographs of the Pan Am Building said, "the basis of the structure is formed by a lower building. The skyscraper itself is, however, not significantly separated and the transition from the horizontal to the vertical movement is obscured. Moreover, the building is squeezed into a tangle of other buildings, so there is not enough air around it. The high building will, moreover, cause further density of traffic which, in our opinion, will be increased by an unbearable amount."[81]

With word of the project spreading quickly across Europe, the issue was picked up several months later in *L'Architecture d'Aujourd'hui,* which included extracts from Pinchis's letters and sketches of his "contre-proposition."[82] Construction of a new skyscraper, the largest commercial structure in the world, in New York, posed urbanistic problems that had prompted an alternative solution from one of the journal's readers, said the article, again amply illustrated by photos of the model, renderings, and Pinchis's sketches. Several months later, *L'Architecture d'Aujourd'hui* published Gropius's response.[83] Both the criticism and the counterproposal, he felt, showed a total lack of comprehension of the specific conditions under which the building would be constructed and the problems its design posed. How, he asked, could Pinchis imagine a client's agreeing to build, on the most expensive land in the world, such an absurd skyscraper as the one Pinchis had proposed with a budget of $100 million? Pinchis's counterproject was elegant, to be sure, Gropius said, but it lacked any consideration of the specific functional demands of an office building. In an enterprise of such magnitude, economic problems were obviously decisive, and the architect had to conform to limitations of space in plan and volume. Gropius mentioned his design team's success in persuading their client to reduce the building's size, as well as his initial proposal for a slender tower on a base with an open courtyard that would have visually isolated it from surrounding buildings, a solution that the client had deemed unrealizable on economic grounds. Gropius then added that he found Pinchis's argument that the circulation in the area demanded a dynamic solution unconvincing. On the contrary, Gropius contended, it seemed to him desirable to close the perspective of the very long Park Avenue with an imposing structure "d'une forme prismatique puissante."

The controversy about the Pan Am and Gropius's role in it was aired again several years later in *L'Architecture d'Aujourd'hui* in an article on current American architecture by Moholy-Nagy.[84] Although the achievements of leading European émigrés in education were laudable, Moholy-Nagy maintained, their architectural contribution seemed stagnant. She cited Gropius specifically and The Architects Collaborative, whose work expressed the profound difference between Gropius's built work and his "projets d'école." She was particularly harsh in regard to the Pan Am Building, which despite Gropius's avowed aims of its being integrated with its social and urban milieu, she said, failed to create even a single space truly architectural. It was a denial of all of Gropius's principles and "seemed like a betrayal of the evangelist of functionalism." Included in the same issue was Gropius's essay "Tradition et Continuité de l'Architecture," in which he defended his work on the Pan Am by arguing, as he had elsewhere, that the responsibility for the deterioration of Park Avenue lay with the city, not the architect, for failing to regulate developers with new and appropriate laws.[85]

News of the building struck British quarters as well. In an address to the RIBA in June 1960, Ely Jacques Kahn spoke critically of the Pan Am tower, then about to be built behind one of New York City's main railroad stations, and of the added mass of people it would bring to the already crowded spot. He, like Huxtable, placed the blame squarely on the architect, who was the key person in solving such complex problems as those the building had generated.[86]

More strident was "Outrage: Counter Junk" in the London *Architectural Review* several years later. The article, a review of Blake's *God's Own Junkyard,* was illustrated by the book's full-page photographs of Park Avenue before and after Pan Am. Describing the newly awakening urban sensibility in the United States, which the review's author, Michel Santiago, believed would be counted as one of the achievements of the Kennedy era, it noted how the urban mess had worsened since the war: "In 1950 there was no outrage to report that was half as monstrous as the Pan Am Building [would prove to be] in New York."[87]

ZEVI CRITIQUE

Most stinging was the criticism from Bruno Zevi, a former student of Gropius's who had received his degree in architecture from the Harvard Graduate School of Design while it was still under Gropius's direction. In 1955, after leaving Harvard, the influential Italian architectural historian and critic founded the architectural journal *L'Architettura*. In the fall of 1963, six months after the Pan Am opened, Zevi published an article, "Gropius on Park Avenue," in the Italian magazine *L'Expresso,* which was reprinted in translation in *Atlas,* published in the United States.[88.] "Nothing could be sadder than the weariness which overcomes our aging luminaries," Zevi wrote. "Walter Gropius, a leading light of the Bauhaus, was not a great creative artist, but his impassioned teaching and his loyalty to the principles of city planning and modern construction sufficed to make him a sturdy and reliable guide. Among conflicting personalities and ambitions, his objectivity and soundness have inspired three generations of architects. But now the Gropius myth, too, is in decline. The Pan Am Building, which rises above New York's Grand Central Station, is an absurdity in city planning which no dialectic could ever justify," he declared, mincing no words. Smack in the most congested part of the city, its offices were to hold seventeen thousand employees and attract an estimated additional two hundred fifty thousand people daily, yet its garage had space for only four hundred cars—which reduced the whole program, Zevi maintained, to utter insanity. Given this, comment on the aesthetic validity of the skyscraper was superfluous: Gropius himself had taught that in this age, architectonic values were one with those of city planning, and that any attempt at poetry was pointless if based on an antisocial design.

Zevi enumerated "the sophisms" on which the Pan Am defense was based: (1) that most of the office buildings erected in New York since the war were built like ziggurats in order to maximize available space yet adhere to the letter of the building code, but in the case of the Pan Am, the owners renounced hundreds of thousands of square feet of usable space to give the skyscraper a regular, well-defined geometric form; (2) that the widest sides of the prism faced Park Avenue south and north while the narrow sides marked the east-west axis of 44th Street to accommodate the checkerboard pattern of New York's streets; (3) that the tower's octagonal form was uneconomical, but Gropius planned the shape to reflect the changing intensity of light, articulating the volume of the structure and reducing its mass; (4) that the visual consistency of the building was derived from the prefabricated concrete panels, whose plasticity was distinctly superior to that of the usual glass-and-metal facades; (5) that the location of the building had been carefully studied, so that seen from the north, the skyscraper served as a neutral background for the Gothic lines of the New York General Building, and from the south, the Grand Central Station rose ten floors to form a harmonious base for the tower; (6) that urban centers had certain economic requirements—if a child's shoes are too tight, we buy him new ones, rather than cut off his feet (Belluschi, who also knew Zevi personally and of course would have read the article, must have winced at this)—and it was vital that business offices be concentrated; traffic problems had to be subordinated to and resolved to function within this concentration; Gropius had envisioned, though he considered it only a remote possibility, the razing of the New York General Building and its replacement by a park; and lastly, (7) that urban centers should be free of automobile traffic; were the Grand Central area limited to pedestrians, as it should be, the increased population generated by the skyscraper would present no problem.

To refute these arguments, Zevi wrote, was "child's play." Acknowledging that employing Gropius and Belluschi as consultants to Emery Roth & Sons "avoided the worst in architectonic horrors," nonetheless a crime had been committed both visually and in terms of city planning. The continuity of Park Avenue had been violently disrupted by the immense structure, which brutally flattened the buildings around it. One had to be at a distance to appreciate the tower, at which point the plasticity of its textured panels was lost and the octagonal prism seemed two-dimensional. The errors of the building program were only compounded, Zevi said, by the building's offensive, pointless architecture.

As they looked at pictures of the Pan Am Building, Zevi asserted, thousands of Gropius's disciples scattered throughout the world would wonder: Why did he give in? For years, Zevi said, Gropius was involved in teaching; then, when his teaching mission was finally over, he continued in the profession with TAC, in association with former students, and the quality of his work declined. Gropius was out of touch with the American businessman. Then Wolfson appeared, inviting his participation in what would be New York's most conspicuous skyscraper. And for the first time Gropius did not have the courage to say no.

Perhaps he was thinking of the unrealized projects of his youth, Zevi surmised, of the Bauhaus, of the colleagues and students who had deserted him, of the powerlessness of the message of rationalism in a skeptical and vulgar world. Gropius felt like a survivor from another age, Zevi conjectured, outside the mainstream of the present. As Wolfson had said, the Pan Am Building was an opportunity, a chance for a comeback. In any case, Zevi quipped, "it served to help him forget old age and declining powers."

Gropius retaliated the following March with a two-page letter contending that Zevi's article contained "misleading statements on [his] personal attitudes and on town planning aspects which are of general interest."[89] Zevi's general comments on the early history of the Pan Am Building and Gropius's motivations were "just so much hearsay and speculation, and not based on actual facts," Gropius said. Zevi's professed disappointment at his "alleged desertion" of his own city planning principles showed little understanding of them in the first place. "Nobody twisted my arm in the design and placement of the Pan Am Building, nor did I twist my own," Gropius insisted. "I followed consistently my planning principles for business centers which I had already formed and predicted in various publications in the '20s."[90]

Zevi was out of date, Gropius maintained, on present trends in city planning, which called for vertical business centers with high density and accordingly short pedestrian distances. The Pan Am Building within the dense Manhattan banking center was the "the natural and practical outcome of the facts of life" rather than "utter insanity." The owner of the Pan Am Building had renounced 20 percent—six hundred thousand square feet—of usable office space permitted by the existing zoning law not "to give the skyscraper a regular well-defined geometric form," Gropius maintained (contradicting not only Belluschi, who had said the octagonal form was an aesthetic decision, aimed at reducing the apparent bulk of the building, but his own statements earlier), but because of a very practical and important consideration: namely, to greatly increase the pedestrian traffic spaces in and around the building by means of arcades and to reduce the building to its economic limits. Zevi's characterization of the skyscraper's octagonal form as "uneconomic" Gropius simply dismissed as amateurish. On the contrary, he asserted, the large bank of elevators in the building necessitated a widening of the center part of the building, which "automatically" led to the octagonal plan as the most economic solution.

If Zevi found it "child's play to confute the arguments" on which the design of the Pan Am was based, his remarks sounded just like those of a child, Gropius said. The old New York General Building, originally well balanced in scale with the other medium-high buildings lining Park Avenue, no longer was, and the balanced entity of the old Park Avenue was now lost in a medley of shapes and sizes. A new focus large enough to be in balance with the flanking new skyscrapers north and south of Grand Central Station was badly needed. Rather than "brutally flattening" the adjacent buildings and "violently interrupting the continuity" of the avenue, quite the contrary, it reestablished the former balance by recognizing the new scale of larger and higher building masses along Park Avenue.

Quoting again at length the letters of Bacon and Ballard on the Pan Am's urbanistic merits, he also cited Zucker, a professor of art history at the New School, who had spoken out in defense of the building at the New School symposium in 1960 and had praised it for providing a new unifying factor, a point of reference to which all the individual buildings in the area were visually connected.

Finally, Gropius concluded, "May I correct Mr. Zevi's uninformed and confusing statements about the activities—or inactivities, as he would have it—of my firm, The Architects Collaborative. In view of the extent of these activities, I certainly do not feel 'like a survivor from another age, outside the mainstream of the present,' as Mr. Zevi would have it, but rather in the front line of things to come."

Rivaling in vitriol, if not pettiness, the exchange of letters between Moholy-Nagy and Natalie Parry over the Grand Central City project years earlier, the Zevi versus Gropius duel did not stop there. Zevi responded by immediately translating Gropius's letter into Italian for publication in *L'Architettura,* believing that readers were entitled to know of Gropius's objections. He also replied to Gropius's rebuttal in a letter to *Atlas*. Initially, Zevi wrote,

My impulse was to discuss, phrase by phrase, both Prof. Gropius's social and aesthetic considerations. The principle of planning densely built business centers, to which I subscribe, has very little to do with perpetuating and aggravating the congestion of an unplanned metropolis in which it is already so hard to live. The argument that the Pan Am Building is "the natural and practical outcome of the facts of life" is not convincing. Professor Gropius has taught us a professional ethics, which includes refusing to accept the "facts of life" when they are socially negative. And I cannot accept the idea that Park Avenue must be destroyed simply because there is a new zoning law. If we accept new zoning laws passively, Rome, Venice and Paris as we know them will soon disappear. A conscientious architect—Professor Gropius told us at Harvard—must have the courage to oppose bad zoning laws, and in any case should never be co-responsible for their application.

But on reflection, Zevi said in his *Atlas* letter, he decided not to respond to Gropius, believing that although his duty as an architectural historian was "to criticize mistakes, independently of their authors and unpleasant as it may sometime be," out of respect for Gropius, whose student he still perceived himself to be, he felt he owed him the last word.[91]

True to his promise, Zevi reproduced his original "Un testamento che non convince," along with Gropius's reply, in *L'Architettura* the next month without further comment, trusting the arguments to speak for themselves.[92]

THE ARCHITECTS

THE ARCHITECTS' REPUTATIONS: EMERY ROTH & SONS

All the criticism of the Pan Am Building had a profound impact on the reputations of the architects responsible for its design. For Emery Roth & Sons, the Pan Am Building was a plus—a clear affirmation of the firm's worth to the business community. A feature article devoted to the Roth office, "Architect for Business in a City of Towers," in *Business Week* in September 1962, as the Pan Am Building neared completion, said as much.[1] Illustrated by a view of Park Avenue dominated by the Pan Am, the article pointed out that despite the criticism the Pan Am Building had generated and its reputation for an emphasis on economics at the expense of aesthetics, the Roth office had become the "undeniable favorite" of builders in Manhattan's postwar building boom. By 1962, Roth buildings dominated the Manhattan skyline; there were sixty Roth-designed office buildings in Manhattan containing twenty-eight million square feet of space, with builders having spent $1.1 billion to put them up. The Roth office had also grown, having moved quarters four times over the decade prior to the article's publication, and had expanded internationally, with projects in Paris and Caracas as well as New York. In sum, though uninspired, Roth architecture satisfied builders.

Another article in the *New York Herald Tribune* the following year confirmed this view. "There must be a time when, looking at New York's oppressively dull forest of skyscrapers, a sightseer gets the impression that there is really only one architect in circulation. This impression cuts painfully close to the truth. One firm, Emery Roth & Sons, has had a phenomenally large say in shaping the city's post-war architectural profile—about as much of a say as all other architects put together," the article began.[2] Of fifteen office skyscrapers completed or slated for completion in Manhattan that year, nine were by Roth, and the total space of those nine buildings was roughly the equivalent of all the commercial space available in downtown Dallas; the firm had also manage to pepper the city with some forty apartment buildings, a couple of hotels, and three public schools, plus stores, garages, and warehouses. The *Herald Tribune* followed its account of the firm's successes with the criticism it had generated, citing the disparaging neologism "Rothscrapers," which referred to the many boxy, glass-walled buildings overrunning the city, as well as the anecdote about Frank Lloyd Wright's refusal to allow his taxi drivers to use Park Avenue when he visited New York because he found the buildings so appalling. And it quoted Richard Roth as dismissing most of the criticism as sour grapes, but having to agree with some of it: "I've designed buildings I don't like myself. So has every other architect. Unfortunately, buildings are not like drawings. You can't just erase them."

Which was just why there was so much hand-wringing, the *Herald Tribune* maintained, over the Pan Am Building, which had opened that March. "Nowhere, Roth's critics say, is the conflict sharper or more visible between what is best in 'old' architecture and what is worst in 'new' architecture than on the fabulously expensive chunk of Manhattan where Grand Central Terminal and the Pan Am Building sit side by side. The one . . . is monumental and gracious in scale and detail, the other is monumental only in the amount of rentable space it provides and in the lack of judgment that put the building there in the first place." No one argued the point that the Pan Am was the largest commercial office building in the world, the *Herald Tribune* said. Almost everything else about the building, however, was a point of contention. It was attacked by planners, critics, and writers as a hideous example of overcrowding, irresponsibility, and greed. Its size and location, astride and towering above Park Avenue "like some arrogant, faceless Colossus, makes it impossible to dismiss or ignore." The article then pointed out that if the truth be known, Roth alone was not responsible for the Pan Am, but that Gropius, "venerated founder of the famed Bauhaus school of design" and Belluschi, "dean of the School of Architecture at MIT and a practicing architect of towering stature," had also been involved. The rest of the long article, devoted to Roth's phenomenal success, described the history of the office (founded in 1903 by Emery Roth, an émigré who left his native Budapest to gain a professional training in architecture denied Jews in Hungary), its clients (big competitive builders—the Uris brothers, Wolfson, the Tishmans, Samuel Rudin, Joseph Durst, the Minskoff family—with ties to Roth in several cases that dated back to the 1920s); its work (it didn't invent the glass curtain wall, but "merely gave it to the masses"); its approach (not known for its sentimentality, solidly behind arithmetic not aesthetics); its operational practices (the office factory); and its key to success (its focus on the "belly" rather than the "face" of architecture, since it is the "belly" that attracts the paying customers; a facade cannot be rented, it only covers rentable space). "'Roth designs a building as a place to work in,'" the article quoted one satisfied client. "'You can't rent monuments,'" said another. "'The Roths give you maximum utility without losing an inch of rentable space,'" the article quoted another as saying.

Five years later, another article in the national newsmagazine *Newsweek* demonstrated that the firm's success showed no signs of diminishing. "'An office building is a machine to make money with,'" it began, quoting a New York builder in rebuttal to

Philip Johnson's contention that office buildings were built for people and therefore should be aesthetically pleasing. Such polar views—between the simultaneous claims of function and form, economics and aesthetics—represented the dilemma of the modern urban architect, with no U.S. firm encountering this dilemma more frequently or with more controversial results, the article said, than Emery Roth & Sons. By this time, the number of buildings the firm had designed in Manhattan since the war had risen to seventy, containing more than thirty million square feet of space, half of all the office acreage created in Manhattan since the war. The "glittering new face of Park Avenue" was almost entirely Roth-fashioned, with no fewer than twelve glass-skinned Rothscrapers reflecting each other along a twenty-block stretch. The firm was also deciding the shape of things to come: Of the thirty-eight office buildings currently planned for the city, the article noted, twenty-one would be designed by the Roths, with their draftsmen (now 120) currently working on the sixteen-acre World Trade Center (in association with Minoru Yamasaki) and the forty-eight-story General Motors Building (with Edward Durrell Stone). It quoted Huxtable saying Emery Roth & Sons was "'as responsible for the face of modern New York as Sixtus V was for baroque Rome.'" Much of the firm's current workload had come about in the wake of the Pan Am, the first instance, it should be remembered, of the Roth's collaboration with leading designers in an associate role, a role they had only reluctantly accepted. Clearly successful, it henceforth became their modus operandi.

Again *Newsweek* mentioned the pervasive criticism of the Roth style, which it could hardly ignore. "New York's face, of course, puts off more than a few discriminating observers—as does the name of Roth," it said. Indeed, the firm's standard product drew as much criticism as its "cookie-cutter approach" to architecture. The Roths shrugged off the criticism. "Architecture reflects society and this is not a great age," it quoted Richard Roth, who "presided over [the firm's] empire with the paternalistic congeniality of corner grocers," and referred to its cavernous drafting room as "the factory." The motto on the office envelope: "Architecture—Art Adapted to Human Needs," meant, in effect, the article's author said, giving the customer what he wanted.[3]

BELLUSCHI

Belluschi fared considerably worse, though not with his corporate clients. In response to a letter from Landauer, who clearly respected Belluschi and was dismayed only about his waning interest in the project, Belluschi apologized for being unable to attend the

building's dedication but assured him that "[t]o have participated in this magnificent enterprise is and will be a great source of pride for me," promising Landauer that his services would always available should Landauer need them.[4] Despite criticism from
professional and public quarters that grew more heated as the building neared completion, Belluschi was nonetheless asked if he wanted to be considered for the design
of the World Trade Center, an invitation he declined, with the job subsequently going to
Yamasaki, with Emery Roth & Sons as associates.[5] Other corporate commissions continued to pour in.[6]

Fully aware which side of his toast was being buttered, Belluschi retired from the
deanship of the School of Architecture and Planning at MIT in January 1964, to devote
himself fully to his large-scale projects, which were growing in number.[7] Among these
were the Rohm & Haas Building, which was nearing completion in Philadelphia, the Juilliard School of Music at Lincoln Center, and the Bank of America Building and St. Mary's
Cathedral in San Francisco.

Throughout the Pan Am debacle, *Architectural Record* remained loyal to Belluschi,
regularly publishing articles on his work and essays. In 1961, it published an interview
with Belluschi by Jonathan Barnett, an architecture student at the time, providing Belluschi with the opportunity to voice his own thoughts about his professional practice,
which was then under question.[8] As criticism of the Pan Am swelled in the wake of the
New School debate in 1960, Goble and Schmertz, the *Record*'s editors, had each spoken up in the architect's defense.[9] Several months after the building opened, the
Record published Belluschi's essay "Eloquent Simplicity in Architecture," on his church
design, and it continued throughout the decade to publish articles on his churches and
synagogues.[10]

Within the architectural community, however, particularly among academics on the
East Coast, Belluschi lost credibility in the wake of the Pan Am controversy. In 1972, he
received the AIA Gold Medal, the highest award granted by the twenty-four-thousand-
member institute, but it was largely through his West Coast connections. A brief biography of him in the *New York Times* on his receiving the award told of his designing over
a thousand buildings, churches, and residences, among them the landmark Equitable
Building in Portland, Oregon, and more recently, the Juilliard School of Music. Conspicuously absent was any mention of the Pan Am.[11]

An incident at the University of Oregon shortly after the Pan Am had opened was revealing. Belluschi had been invited to speak to architecture students on the beauty of
simplicity, a subject suggested by Walter Gordon, an old friend and former employee in

Belluschi's Portland office, then dean of the college. The auditorium was packed. After Gordon gave an introduction, but before Belluschi had a chance to speak, a student interrupted, asking belligerently how Belluschi could possibly justify defiling the old, beautiful Grand Central Station by building the mammoth Pan Am. The student's question, clearly touching a nerve, was met with thunderous applause. According to Gordon, Belluschi handled the question with grace, and instead of his intended talk spent the hour regaling students with lively tales about how the real estate people and bankers dominated the discourse in determining the number of floors, the bidding process with the window industry, the complicated dealings with all the multifarious factions of the construction business, and finally how they, the architects, were allowed to design the entrance lobby and connecting link to the railroad station. It was, Gordon recalled, a fascinating, but disillusioning, account.[12] And of course Belluschi's riveting stories served to divert attention from the moral issue the student had originally raised.

In 1990, long after the Pan Am controversy had died down and New Yorkers had come to accept the building as fact of life, in an interview with Jim Murphy published in *Progressive Architecture,* Belluschi, who was then ninety, was asked a series of penetrating questions about his professional practice: how as one of the pioneers he got into the consulting role, what he thought other architects felt about him in this role, and specifically, about his involvement in the Pan Am. That involvement had been very difficult, he responded, in part because of the building's very visibility, in part because there were so many other competing interests. There was the owner, who was investing millions of dollars, plus the tremendous technical difficulties the designers encountered, all of which forced compromises. For a building of that sort, even one involving Gropius, he said (as if Gropius's name alone should have been enough to quell it), there would obviously be opposition. When asked how the Pan Am collaboration came about, Belluschi admitted frankly that his and Gropius's role was largely one of public relations, and that the developer needed help overcoming opposition to what he knew would be a difficult project to defend. Belluschi went on to rebut Murphy's points, such as that the building blocked the view down Park Avenue—there was no view, he maintained—and as for the highly lauded Grand Central Terminal, he confessed that when he first arrived in this country from Italy, he had thought it terrible.

The Pan Am was intrinsically an impossible job aesthetically, Belluschi asserted. On a highly valuable piece of land, but faced with difficult circulation problems, with thousands of people and multileveled railroad tunnels, it was a nightmare. As the building had to house eighty elevators, the architects gave it what he said was the most logical form, fat in the middle to handle the large elevator banks. He was never very proud to have worked on it, he admitted, contrary to what he had told Landauer years earlier, but looked at it "as something that you take and make the best of it." Asked finally about his views on the role of the architect at the time of the interview, and whether architects were understood and appreciated in the United States, Belluschi replied that he thought they were but did not think they had much impact on the environment, or as much as they should or could have on the real life of cities: "They are still the tailor of fancy clothes for pretty ladies."[13] It was this kind of cynicism that students and academics found repellant, a cynicism that surfaced in Belluschi, who by then was known as a leading representative of corporate modernism, with his work on the Pan Am.

GROPIUS

The impact of the widespread negative reaction to the Pan Am Building fell hardest on Gropius, to whom the building was largely credited, both within the profession and without. In 1950, long before the Pan Am Building, Haskell wrote an article in *L'Architecture d'Aujourd'hui* on Gropius's promise and his influence in America.[14] Now that modern architecture was well established in the United States, Haskell wrote, it was time to reappraise the Gropius legacy; he called Gropius, admiringly, "almost our only modest genius" among the many leaders in architecture at the time.[15] Recognizing the complexity of the problems of the time, Gropius called for a team approach, well aware that one man could not handle them alone. By temperament, Haskell noted, Gropius hated "the exclusiveness which ends by limiting growth" and he cited the like-minded Wassily Kandinsky who, years before Robert Venturi, was "loath to accept 'either-or' statements, always searching to see whether, instead of choosing between this *or* that, it might not be possible to have this *and* that," as it made life so much richer.

When one thought of bringing architecture into an industrial age, Haskell said, one thought of Gropius, more so than Wright, Mies, Le Corbusier, and other modernist leaders. Gropius's thinking focused on moral issues of method and responsibility, showing how to proceed so that the forces of industry worked for rather than against one, how architects could escape being dilettantes while at the same time their work, even at large scale, could remain an art, not merely a cold science. Haskell described Gropius, whom young Americans had known of as head of the Bauhaus even before he came to Harvard, and his basic idea that architecture in an industrial age must partake of the nature of industrial design. He discussed the notion of collaboration, training students to work together sympathetically on buildings and their furnishings, and the influence of this kind of thinking on American architects such as Saarinen and Charles Eames. The Bauhausian notion of learning by doing whereby students became engaged in actually building, becoming part of the process rather than aloof from it, by working against contractors or builders on the owner's behalf, had also taken root in the States. A clear analysis of the problem presented by a proposed building, and the use of forms that spoke of industrialization—smooth surfaces rather than rough-sawn "natural" ones, a repetition of regular elements rather than informal irregularity—were other Bauhausian influences, Haskell noted, as was the collaborative association with painters.

Regarding large planning schemes and development projects, Haskell thought Gropius's keen analytic thought process had been especially valuable, as was the fact that Gropius was thoroughly conversant with industrial aims and ideals. "Just as the concern with architecture as a field of industrial design deals with the central fact of 20th century production," he observed, "the concern with land planning deals with the central facts of 20th century distribution." If some found Gropius's own architectural designs unexciting and sober, there were other architects who could bring in fantasy and personal expression. No wonder, Haskell concluded, his feeding station was attracting so many different kinds of birds.[16] This was the promise of Gropius.

Gropius himself was to heighten this sense of expectation, this sense that the best of him was yet to come, with his views on the role of the artist in society, which he began propounding in the mid-1950s to counter a growing hostility to the "machine aesthetic." In an address at the opening of the new Hochschule für Gestaltung in Ulm, Germany, in October 1955, later published in *Arts & Architecture,* Gropius contended the artist was necessary for the healthy development of a progressive democracy.[17] In our scientific age, he said, as America drew closer to the Sputnik era, voicing a theme he was to repeat throughout next several decades, the artist had been almost forgotten, derided, his true value to society underestimated, and his work portrayed as a luxury. It was time, he urged, to recognize "the significance of the magical in contrast to the intellectualized thinking of our time" and to restore the artist to his legitimate place and leading role in the modern production process. "The hypertrophy of science," Gropius continued, "has cast aside the magical in our life; the poet and the prophet have become the stepchildren of the over-practical men of action as a result of the unprecedented series of victories of rational science." He saw this development as dangerously one-sided, as given the great changes in the modern world, man sought an anchor, something to hold on to. What was desperately needed, he said, was "a new orientation on the cultural level," a spiritual direction provided by the thinker and artist "whose creations stand beyond logical usefulness. To them we must always turn." The irony here, given his message, and the promise it held out, was surely not lost on those who remembered, years later, the contribution he made to society, which was seen as anything but spiritual, with the Pan Am.

In June 1959, less than six months after the Gropius/Belluschi proposal for the Pan Am Building, then still called Grand Central City, was published, Gropius received the AIA Gold Medal, as Belluschi was to do a little over a decade later. To mark the occasion, *Time* ran an article on "the lawmaker," making his a household name. Calling him "the high priest of the famed Bauhaus, acknowledged shrine of modern architecture," the article cited, among his many new commissions, Grand Central City. "I was possibly too Puritan," the "lawgiver" was quoted as saying. "Too much storming against the old traditions. Now I have, with the same conceptions, I hope, a more subtle, more delicate expression."[18] This again raised expectations.

FITCH ON GROPIUS

By the end of the decade, however, the reverential tone began to change. In 1960, Fitch, a former editor of *Architectural Record,* then *Architectural Forum,* who had in 1954 been appointed professor of architectural history at Columbia, published a short monograph on Gropius as part of the Braziller series "Masters of World Architecture," which appeared (upon his suggestion) in a somewhat condensed version in the May *Forum.*[19] The book, for the most part a sympathetic, perceptive assessment of Gropius and his contribution to architecture, was not without a critical undertone. Like Einstein, Shaw, Matisse and Wright, other prophets who had overrun their prophecy, Fitch said Gropius was a shaker and maker of the modern world whose work had come to fruition in a particular set of historical conditions that had changed; he was still alive, surviving not merely to see their predictions come true, but to live on into a world in which their works had become commonplace, "the very warp and woof of everyday life." No mere legendary hero, Gropius was a practicing architect whose work continued to evolve. His work, Fitch observed, was grounded in the factual, the objective; his perennial concern was with the impact of industrialism. Calling Gropius (ironically, in light of the criticism that was about to appear, calling into question this very thing) "a principled man who always chose the principled (rather than merely expedient) course of action," Fitch noted that in 1925 Gropius had chosen to move the Bauhaus to Dessau, rather than submit to the reactionary demands of the Weimar government, and that when differences arose between him and the city government in 1928, he resigned rather than wreck the school; in 1934, rather than face life in Adolf Hitler's Germany, he left. He was also a man not afraid to speak his own mind: It was in the *Saturday Evening Post,* "that bastion of middle-class American complacency," Fitch noted, that Gropius had written on the "curse" of American conformism, and at the national AIA meeting in New Orleans the previous June, which many had boycotted, Gropius had spoken out against segregation. The quality that distinguished Gropius's career mainly from that of Wright or Mies, Fitch contended, was its explicit social responsibility, which affected architecture not just in terms of the types of projects he took on, such as housing and town planning, but also its expression. Fitch stressed the rational, dispassionate, objective, and most importantly, collective nature of Gropius's work. Unlike Mies, Le Corbusier, and Wright, Gropius saw architecture as "an impersonal instrument," and the work of collaborators not individuals. Gropius drew his analogies, Fitch said, from the world of science and technology, in which design by the individual genius was no longer possible. This commitment to collaboration, Fitch maintained, was a matter of principle, not insecurity about his own talent, as evidenced by his early work when he worked alone in the 1920s; as a result of this conviction, Gropius had done much to discover and develop the talent of others.

According to Fitch (again, not without irony, given Gropius's work on the Pan Am, then under construction), Gropius always thought in terms of the whole, the larger arena, rather than the individual building. "'My idea of the architect as the coordinator—whose business is to unify the various formal, technical, social and economic problems that arise in connection with building—inevitably led me on, step by step, from the study of the function of the house to that of the street, from the street to the town, and finally to the still vaster implications of regional and national planning,'" Fitch quoted Gropius as saying in *The New Architecture and the Bauhaus.*

Among the works of Gropius illustrated in Fitch's book were the Boston Back Bay Center, built in 1953, the project Gropius had done with Belluschi as well as others, and Grand Central City. Fitch commented specifically on neither but noted that the quality of some of Gropius's later collaborative work was not always the highest. He concluded his text on an equivocal note, observing that Gropius had, on a trip to Japan in 1954, found for the first time a modern architecture which he spent much of his life trying to create. It was there, confronted with that great body of traditional architecture, that for once he felt at one with the majority. "It is sad," Fitch concluded, "to think that he should ever have felt so isolated, for he has always tried to act in the interests of the many, the multitude. Few creative personalities in our period have sought as consistently as he to speak for the majority."[20] Published in 1960, just as criticism of the Pan Am and especially of Gropius's role in designing it began to burgeon, Fitch's tribute pointed up the irony of the situation.

Fitch's monograph was reviewed in the *New York Times Book Review* by Allan Temko, architectural critic for the *San Francisco Chronicle*, who thought it one of the best of the Braziller series. Like Fitch an ardent Gropius enthusiast, Temko believed that at age seventy-seven, Gropius was just "coming into his own as one of the chief creative spirits of the age," and Temko applauded the fact that Gropius's "magnificent accomplishments, not only as a daring designer but also as a fervent democrat and educator," were finally receiving recognition. A die-hard protagonist for modernism who staunchly defended Gropius and his legacy, Temko carefully avoided, as had Fitch, any mention of Gropius's involvement in the Pan Am and the controversy then gaining momentum.[21]

More bluntly critical was the Italian critic Gillo Dorfles in the Milanese architectural magazine *Zodiac.*[22] Acknowledging Gropius's role as "a powerful catalytic agent in the evolution of the modern architectural idiom" and his considerable historical legacy—the 1911 Fagus Factory, the Dessau Bauhaus in 1925, his house using prefabricated elements at the Weissenhof in 1927—Dorfles addressed Gropius's current work and what Dorfles saw as a "limited capacity for innovation." He began with the Pan Am Building, which together with the Hanscom Elementary School in Lincoln, Massachusetts, the U.S. embassy in Athens, and the University of Baghdad masterplan, suffered, in Dorfles's opinion, "from a lack of stylistic and formal inventiveness, and from the absence of any novelty in spatial modulation capable of giving them autonomous vitality. . . ." Addressing specifically the Pan Am, Dorfles continued: "A truly decisive work cannot help standing out from its pre-existing architectonic setting, stylistically, if not planimetrically, or volumetrically. . . . In the case of the New York skyscraper, this does not happen." Seemingly bound to remove one of the most interesting characteristics of the "old but curious" Grand Central Station, Gropius's new Park Avenue skyscraper promised to be a building that lacked Grand Central's "fantastic and balancing characteristics of space," and appeared instead—"for all the rigorous harmony of its masses and volumes—stylistically 'neutral.'" Knowing the question would be raised as to whether these recent works were really the work of TAC rather than Gropius, Dorfles brought up one of Gropius's great merits: his humility, which "neutralized" him among his group of disciples rather than distinguishing him from the team. Although this was admirable ethically, Dorfles felt, its results were questionable aesthetically; indeed, given the master's latest work, "one realizes how easily he has bowed to the needs dictated by environment and by collaboration." Dorfles concluded, sadly, "that the present-day works of the TAC are no more than the excellent and very dignified achievements of a professional group which graduated from a highly enlightened and honest training: a training however, betraying concerns and impulses which can hardly be considered a starting point for future experiences." In summarizing Gropius's work, Dorfles thus underscored Gropius's tremendous historical legacy but raised the question of teamwork and whether it did or could work. Given the growing strength of the "star system" in architecture at the time, Gropius and the collective team approach he advocated appeared to be a dead end.[23]

Cranston Jones, in *Architecture Today and Tomorrow,* a "major monuments and their makers" book typical of the time that included Gropius, was similarly dismayed at the Pan Am and similarly saw the team approach as being at fault. His belief that design could be a cooperative effort was widely disputed, Jones said, concluding that architecture was "perhaps not a matter for a committee. This conviction that the act of giving form in any art must finally depend on one artist's hand has become the rallying point for a significant sector of the younger generation to whom the Bauhaus is the New Academy." Jones's book included a photo of the Pan Am model, with a caption referring to it as "a 59-story behemoth atop the Grand Central Terminal," and "Manhattan's largest single building," which, Jones wrote, reflected "the cult of bigness, introducing a scale of building that may tax existing traffic facilities."[24]

When Gropius received the Kaufmann International Design Award for 1961, a $20,000 award granted by the Institute of International Education for achievement in design education, it was mentioned in both the *New York Times* and *Newsweek.*[25] Neither article said anything of his current involvement in the Pan Am. Describing the results of an interview with Gropius, who spoke "with traces of a German accent and a mixture of autocracy and humility," *Newsweek* said Gropius saw the rectangular glass-and-metal facades of the buildings lining Park Avenue as a reflection of the overcommercialism that he felt was an American plague, while admitting he felt partly responsible, as he himself had built the first curtain wall building in Germany in 1910. But it had gone too far. To the untutored, Gropius said, Park Avenue and similar building complexes rising across the country might seem the height of "modernity," but in many instances the buildings were flat and uninspired. Tellingly, Gropius blamed this on "ignorant politicians" and minimal zoning laws that allowed such buildings to be built and urged as a solution, as he had in the past, a broad, general education that stressed aesthetic and spiritual values. "It seems to me unimaginable that human nature should not rebel against the conspiracy to replace the 'tree of life' with a sales spiral. I hope this generation will, by the great power of education, produce men who eventually will blaze a trail out of the commercial jungle." In the long run, he said, only a better-educated public, with a better and deeper sense of aesthetic values, could "correct this cultural lag."[26] Again, Gropius made no mention of the Pan Am project and the golden opportunity it afforded him to do something about the current "chaos in city planning and construction" he deplored. The contradiction between his theory and practice was glaring.

On his eightieth birthday in May 1963, commemorated by a party at the Gropius-designed Harkness Commons that was written up in *Architectural Record,* Gropius was asked, as had become customary, his thoughts on the state of modern architecture.[27] "We are not sure at this point of what is permissible and what is destructive for our society," Gropius said, "and the architect and planner, who is supposed to create the physical structure for this vague situation, can only proceed from his personal conviction with no assurance that *his* will be the right kind of contribution for making a new pact with life which mankind so badly needs. This is the great risk and adventure we all have to face." Surprisingly, or perhaps not surprisingly, given the heated debate going on in architectural circles, no mention was made of the Pan Am Building, which had opened just two months earlier.

Ignored by *Progressive Architecture* as well as *Architectural Forum,* the party for Gropius was also written up in *Arts & Architecture.*[28] In describing his views on collaboration and its difficulties for the article, Gropius himself this time brought up the Pan Am, presenting what one listener called an "apologia per vita panamericanus": "Under the pressure of a practical task, of course, opinions may differ widely regarding what fits and what does not fit into an existing environment. As the Design Coordinator for the Pan Am Building in New York, I have been attacked for lending my hand at all in put-ting such a large building mass into an overcrowded area. One critic even went so far as to suggest that this site—cost $40 million—should have been made into a green plaza."[29] This suggestion, Gropius said, is indicative of a prevailing urbanistic senti-mentality, a blindness to new trends and to the changing order of scale and of magni-tudes of building masses in cities. For the problem is not how to *stem* the tide of these new trends, but how to find proper *solutions* for them. The region around the Grand Central Station and Park Avenue, he said, had, after the war, been converted rapidly into a vertical business district—a world marketplace—with short horizontal pedestrian dis-tances. In that area, he said, was happening *exactly* what had already happened in the bank district in Manhattan, and he wondered why the new Chase Manhattan Building there, which was even more densely surrounded by skyscrapers than the Pan Am, had not been attacked for overcrowding the area.

From an urbanistic and aesthetic point of view, the massing of the new building cor-responded, he contended, to the completely changed scale of the area in which it was located. The old 1920s tower, once well related to the ten-story street walls of Park Av-enue, had been dwarfed by the rows of high-rise buildings shooting up on either side of Park Avenue. What was needed now, he asserted, was a large structure above Grand Central that could take over the role of providing a dominant visual focus and unifying element within the new range of scale.

"There is still in the public mind much confusion and uncontrolled sentiment about desirable densities," he claimed. "But what may be considered as congestion in one district, may be just right for another. From the Wall Street area, we have learned the obvious advantage of verticalism for business with its wholesome consequence of re-duced vehicular traffic. The same trend, vigorously and consistently promoted in the Grand Central area by the City, would decongest it in spite of its building density. We have to develop our *own* significant new standards from the vigorous realities of Amer-ican life, and we should not let our minds be sidetracked and confused by the nostalgia we may feel for the beautiful European cities of the past."

At a convocation that fall at Williams College, where Gropius had given an address on the occasion of his receiving another honorary degree, he again deplored the state of society, bemoaning the fact that the "vast development" of science had thrown so-ciety off balance, overshadowing other components that were indispensable to har-monious life.[30] Again conspicuously making no mention of the newly opened Pan Am Building, which many had envisioned as the crowning achievement of his long, celebrated career, Gropius stuck to generalities, blaming others for a "slip-cover" civilization that valued quantity over quality, calling for a "reorientation on the cultural level" with a renewed emphasis on the humanities, and urging teamwork to bring the artist into the community, as "prerequisites for a creative development of architecture and design." Acclaimed as one of the great masters of modern architecture, Gropius delivered his grandiose pronouncements as the audience sat enraptured, too awed or too polite to challenge him on the Pan Am.[31]

Gropius's address again was written up in *Architectural Record*.[32] The article coincided with Haskell's outpouring of rage and disillusionment with the Pan Am, in "The Lost New York," in *Architectural Forum* the same month, underscoring the vast differences between the two architectural magazines—the one glowing, adulatory, focused on the great master, the other analytic, critical, addressing the larger issues embraced by Gropius's work and its impact on society. Whereas the *Record* ignored the gulf between Gropius's pearls of wisdom and his built work, Haskell, in the *Forum,* focused on the contradiction.

GROPIUS'S "TRADITION AND CONTINUITY"

Seemingly unperturbed by the critical maelstrom swirling around him, in February 1964, less than a year after the Pan Am opened, Gropius delivered another address, "Tradition and Continuity in Architecture," at the Boston Architectural Center. Seen as one of the most important essays of his later life in which he summarized the great themes of his career, it was published in toto by *Architectural Record* in a three-part series beginning the following May.[33] The United States was still young, still new, Gropius said in the address, a melting pot of different races and nations without a collective consciousness or tradition of its own, and it needed visually educated individuals to help define a shared identity. Since his Bauhaus days, he had also urged architects to embrace industrialized forms of production, seeing this as the only appropriate direction for architecture. These were goals he had tried to pursue in the United States, he said, bloodying his nose in the process. Fifty years later, architects still turned a blind eye to the problem of prefabrication, and visual training was still far from constituting a significant part of general education. He chided architects for bemoaning the ordinary citizen's lack of taste, for wallowing in the exalted role of "arbiters of taste," and for continuing "to guard immutable aesthetic concepts" while ignoring more fundamental problems.

Noting that since the early 1920s he had been identified with functionalism as the only line of direction for architecture, this line, interpreted by those with "sectorially developed minds," had become so straight and narrow that it had led to a dead end. Its complexity and psychological implications, as he and his Bauhaus colleagues had understood them, had become eclipsed, and it was seen as a simple-minded, purely utilitarian approach to design, devoid of the imagination that would lend grace and beauty to life. The explorations he and his colleagues had made in architectural design had been followed "by a wealth of new conceptions and refinements in the field of space relations," and Gropius now thought the stage was set for positive development, if only architects could "keep from straying into a new eclecticism" or some sort of "super-functionalism that borders on mysticism."

"Our very real need to develop an understanding for historical continuity," he said, employing his customary "we" as a means of identifying collectively with his audience, "is not helped by flights into make-believe." The problem of what to protect or destroy, he maintained (in a statement loaded with irony, given his well-publicized desire to demolish the New York Central Building to make room for a park that would also serve as a spacious forecourt for his new building), haunted all cities with a proud past. Venerable landmarks should be incorporated into the changing fabric of a city as far as possible, but less famous buildings were more problematic, as divested of their original contexts, they seem inanimate. The concern for preservation per se "should not mislead us into creating lifeless, museal islands divorced from the life of the city." In one of the few (albeit oblique) references he made to his own work on the Pan Am, Gropius maintained that the idea of freezing certain urban patterns that had outlived their usefulness just because they were pleasing would inevitably lead to grief if the public did not share the tenets that made the particular setup possible, and if the citizens of Manhattan had been serious about wanting to save Park Avenue's spacious former appearance, he said, they should have protested when the first skyscraper went up.

Shifting fault from the citizen to the city, Gropius contended that the loss of continuity and tradition on Park Avenue was a result of the city's failure to replace the old zoning law with one that imposed a new, unifying height limit and building line geared to the new scale that had resulted from the city's transformation from residential to business and trade. The city's irresponsibility here, he argued, had sanctioned a commercial development in an uncontrolled free-for-all spirit, and unless the public wanted to challenge the very notion of free enterprise, with its vested interest in the property value of land, it was pure hypocrisy to complain when the system asserted itself. It was, he said, "inconceivable that it should be expected to refrain from using its privileges and assume instead a noble attitude of financial sacrifice when nothing in our national book of conduct taught it so." It was also futile and self-deceptive, he maintained (in another allusion to his work on the Pan Am), to expect from the system more than "an occasional gesture toward better town planning" at the present time. Once it was apparent that good business was not necessarily identical with the common good, attitudes might change, but that time, he said, had yet to come.

Gropius then turned to the role of architect, contending that for more effective urban design, architects had to strengthen "the fading image of the architect as a man" (Betty Friedan's *Feminine Mystique,* the rallying point for the feminist movement in the 1960s, had been published only the previous year), geared to help the community in this area, and chided the architect superstar who "rushes on stage with a fancy proposal that promises nothing so much as to be a monument to his own ego." In the past, he observed, a centralized governmental power had been able to exercise an autocratic control over the environment, and unless comparable means of creating order out of chaos through the voluntary will of an educated public could be found, cities of the day would never rival those of the past.

Alternating between blaming "the brilliant soloist" and the general public for what was wrong, Gropius turned next to preservation. After watching the comings and goings of over half a century, he confessed (in a statement replete with implications in light of the Pan Am project, Grand Central Station, and the still embryonic Historic Preservation Movement) that he was "impatient with our inertia and the recent tendency to stand wailing at the grave of the 19th century. Why, for instance, do we dissipate our strength by fighting battles for the resurrection or preservation of structures which were monuments to a particularly insignificant period in American architectural history, a period which, still unsure of its own mission, threw the Roman toga around its limbs to appease its nagging doubts?" Barely concealing his contempt for the legacy of American architecture, especially the old Beaux-Arts buildings of the City Beautiful Movement, he called Penn Station "such a case of pseudo-tradition," noting that now that the spotlight had shifted from the railway gate to the jet airport, the building had become a liability. "Cities whose health is robust are never content to live, as it were, on their funded capital of achievement in buildings or anything else," he said (ignoring European cities such as Rome, increasingly dependent on their architectural past for their growing tourist industry); "they push on, thinking more of building well than of not pulling down." Gropius's remarks, accompanied in *Architectural Record* by a photograph of the Pan Am filling entirely the Park Avenue vista beyond the New York Central Building, continued to blame the system and ordinary citizens for the problem of urban ills: "The courageous act of creating new cities on virgin ground has been deplored as a presumptuous attempt at cheating the slow course of a natural development. . . . Confusion and paralysis have arisen because the average citizen, ignorant or uninterested in the visual aspects of his civic background, does not participate in the attempts to solve environmental urban problems, and is unaware of his own responsibility, his own power in a democracy, to make his own voice count."[34]

One wonders how Gropius could have been oblivious, if indeed he was, to all the letters from the public published in places like the *New York Times,* which had tried to make their voices heard in protest of the Pan Am. One wonders, too, whether in outlining an approach to design that emphasized the integration of each new building with its environment of which it was a part and giving it a character commensurate with its place in the social order, he believed he had accomplished this with the Pan Am; as apt as it was to prove or disprove his point, he never mentioned it.

By this time (summer of 1964), things had changed. Penn Station had been demolished, a historic preservation committee created, and the Pan Am had opened amidst more criticism than acclaim. Attitudes in architecture too were shifting, with Philip Johnson in New York continuing to chip away at the modernist edifice, Vincent Scully promoting historicism at Yale, Robert Venturi in Philadelphia working out his theories to be published two years later in *Complexity and Contradiction in Architecture,* and Aldo Rossi abroad drawing on the past and focusing on collective identities in a wholly new approach to the design of the city.

Seemingly unaware of these changing trends, in 1965 *Architectural Record* ran a series of articles, "Presentation Details of Significant Architecture by Master Architects," among whom was Gropius. The article devoted to his work began with a statement by Gropius, significantly enough, on scale: "The effect of a building will be intense only when all requirements for human scale have been fulfilled for any potential distance or point of view. From far away the silhouette of a building should be simple so that it can be grasped at a glance as a symbol even by an ever-so-primitive spectator, as well as by people passing in automobiles. When we approach more closely, we start to distinguish protruding and receding parts of a building, and their shadows will serve as scale regulators for the new distance. And finally, standing close by and no longer able to see the whole edifice, the eye should be attracted by new surprises in the form of refined details and textures." Though Gropius was clearly describing his aims in the design of the Pan Am, he made no specific mention of it. During the nineteenth century, the resolute modernist continued, "such refinements of buildings had deteriorated into added-on adornments. In contrast, the modern architectural revolution demanded that details and refinements be constituent parts of a building's structure and derived from functional considerations, in both the practical and psychological sense." His remarks were followed by details illustrating the development of the curtain wall in his buildings, which included the Pan Am (figure 5.1). Regarding the building's urbanistic context, Gropius said, as he had before, that the design team had learned from Wall Street the advantage of vertical growth, which they thought would decongest the Grand Central area in spite of its density. Tacitly acknowledging Zevi's attack on the Pan Am on the grounds of illegibility as well as the more broadly based criticism of the congestion it added to the Grand Central area, Gropius continued his defense undaunted on both scores.[35]

Gropius remained in the public eye as a spokesman for orthodox modernism throughout the 1960s. His essay "L'architetto e la socìettà" was published in Italian in *Casabella* in the fall of 1965.[36] Two years later, as talk about participatory planning gained momentum, he was interviewed for an article in *Connection* on whether designers should have the moral right to decide how people should live. With his characteristic combination of humility and condescension, of equality and paternalism, Gropius replied that they should, as the inertia and herd instinct of the average man "is so strong that he never steps out of his confinement—since he hasn't got the imagination and the understanding to think further. He must be guided." When it was pointed out that planners thought architects had done too much of that—that the people themselves ought to decide how they should live, Gropius responded that he didn't believe "a laissez faire attitude" would lead to positive results. Americans, he said, were "afraid that they may be told from above to do it this way and not that way—and they don't like that—but what I meant here is something else, namely, that we should quietly use our professional know-how to fulfill the inarticulate, unconscious wishes of our clients."[37]

FIGURE 5.1 Precast concrete curtain wall, Pan Am Building

Just how far out of step Gropius by that time had become with current trends in architecture can be measured by the comments of Colin Rowe, who, in a review of Venturi's *Complexity and Contradiction* that fall, spoke of the ideals of modernism and the disillusionment that had set in. "Not so many years ago, when modern architecture was allegedly no more than an objective approach to building, implicitly it was much more," Rowe began. "Implicitly it was a prophetic illustration of the shape of things to come, the revelation of a world in which difficulties would vanish and conflicts be resolved. . . . This future of yesterday, one might suggest, is the present which we now occupy; and evidently, it is not quite the anticipated future. Modern architecture now exists in abundance, but the hoped-for utopia has scarcely ensued."[38]

Gropius was again honored in an article in *Architectural Record* in 1968, on the occasion of his eighty-fifth birthday.[39] This time it was on his having been awarded yet another honorary degree, the doctor of fine arts, by the University of Illinois. Leonard J. Currie, dean of the College of Architecture and Art at the University's Chicago Circle campus and a former student of Gropius's, reminded listeners of Gropius's momentous contributions to the profession: the uniting of art and technology; the emphasis on method or process rather than form; the importance of teamwork, not only intraprofessional but broadly interdisciplinary as well; the aim not of designing elegant buildings for individual clients, but of embracing an attitude of responsibility to the community and to society as a whole. The Pan Am Building, Gropius's eagerly awaited capstone to his long and brilliant career, was again not mentioned. Nor was it mentioned in the write-up of the birthday celebration in the *AIA Journal.*[40]

It was, however, in Peter Blake's tribute to the "old master of design," published in *Life*. Pointing out his own complexity and contradictions, Blake noted Gropius's "compulsion to collaborate—and be first" and described his work with TAC. He stated Gropius's basic ideological premise, that buildings must be designed to serve their users and surroundings, not the architect's ego. He chronicled his work as one of the four modern masters, along with Le Corbusier, Mies, and Wright; his association with Breuer (who was then much in the news in regard to *his* proposed tower over the Grand Central Terminal); and the Bauhaus philosophy *and* style (which, Blake emphasized, contrary to Gropius's convictions, *was* a style). He outlined Gropius's concept of teamwork (as opposed to "prima donna architecture"), which, to Gropius, was what the twentieth century was all about. But teamwork had its pitfalls, too. The buildings that result from it may turn out to be good, bad, or indifferent, depending on the quality of the other members of the team. Alone or with others, Gropius had done some good buildings, but he had also done "some rather pedestrian jobs, presumably under the influence of less inspired teammates." As an example, Blake cited the Pan Am, "a dull clod of a building, heavy-handed and rude to its street," which chopped Park Avenue in two, interrupting "the swift flow of space so characteristic of the American street." By comparison, Gropius's light, airy structures of an earlier time seemed to have come from an entirely different hand.[41]

Apollo in the Democracy, a collection of Gropius's essays written over the years, was published the same year. In the preface, Gropius made his increasingly outdated, but unflinchingly modernist, stance clear. Illustrating the first essay, which spoke of the need for art and beauty in contemporary life, was the Lippold sculpture in the lobby of the Pan Am.[42]

Peter Collins reviewed the book, none too kindly, in *Progressive Architecture.* Collins, then professor of architecture at McGill University and editor of the *Journal of the Society of Architectural Historians,* maintained that its vague title reflected the fact that it was a collection of miscellaneous essays, mainly speeches on festive occasions such as birthdays or receipt of honorary degrees. All, he said, manifest "that same basic conceptual unity that may be said to characterize the essence of Walter Gropius's legendary prestige." While others revised their theories or searched for new forms, Collins noted, Gropius had been advocating "the same panacea for all architectural ailments over nearly half a century." It was hard to find a parallel for "such single-minded persistence." For Collins, the book exemplified, to some extent, the same Madison Avenue technique Gropius himself derided in one of his essays, namely, how to sell the notion that the product one has been trying to market for the past fifty years is even more relevant today. Each ailment, each diagnosis, met with the same cure, to wit, a regular dose of Dessau.

Opinions differed, Collins wrote, with thinly veiled sarcasm, as to how useful the Bauhaus method was after kindergarten, where Gropius himself acknowledged it was already widespread. But he thought few readers would "share Gropius's optimistic as-surance that the traditional universal instinct for environmental harmony will inevitably be reestablished once the electorate (Gropius's "citizen") has been properly imbued with the mysteries of nonrepresentational art." Collins then pointed out Gropius's nu-merous contradictions, that essay 2 blamed urban conformity for environmental ills, whereas essay 6 placed the blame on urban chaos; essay 1 lamented modern society's refusal to cooperate with the creative artist, yet essay 6 decried the refusal of creative artists to cooperate with one another (especially the inability of architects to work in teams); and so on.

The text was suffused, Collins observed, "with prophetic optimism expected in the set speeches of a professional pioneer" but was clotted with "chinks in the outworn and threadbare slogans" in which one saw all too clearly "a new nostalgic awareness of the past, and of the Orient, far removed from the complacent contemporaneity of Gropius's earliest writings. His new enthusiasm for the persisting aboriginal traditions of Japan; his willful insistence (despite well-publicized historical evidence to the con-trary) that the rue de Rivoli exemplifies 'anonymous prototypes of a public spirit of de-cency and propriety'; his use of illustrations of the Parthenon, Vigevano, Venice and Bath in juxtaposition with his own designs—all seem to indicate that the dreams of Dessau were irretrievably shattered by the traumatic experience of the Pan-American controversy."

Given the occasions on which the speeches had been made, much of this was to be expected, Collins concluded. The book, he observed, was basically a memorial to Gro-pius's prestige as an inspiring teacher.[43] Ironically, Gropius was to die three months later.

GROPIUS'S DEATH

Scores of articles appeared around the world in the wake of Gropius's death on July 5, 1969. Most were positive in tone; few mentioned the Pan Am.[44] The front-page article in the *New York Times* was typical, heralding Gropius as the founder of the Bauhaus and one of the century's leading architects and designers and "one of those rare accidents of history, a man who became a legend in his own time."[45]

The few that did mention the Pan Am were less adulatory, weighing his merits against his failures. *Newsweek* called Gropius the "founder of the revolutionary Bau-haus school of design and one of the brilliant fathers of what we now call 'modern archi-tecture'" and noted his many accomplishments and firm convictions, especially that of teamwork—which had, however, shortcomings. Gropius "never seemed to grasp that the quality of his buildings hinged on *the quality of his collaborators*," the article said. "The Pan Am Building in New York is one such disappointing collaborative effort, bulky in appearance and oppressive to its neighboring Park Avenue buildings."[46]

An editorial in *Design,* published in Bombay, called Gropius one of the great teachers of his time, a "man of powerful convictions" whose "ideas and influence instigated a revolt the banner of which simply said: form follows function." It described the Bauhaus, the Nazis' rise to power in Germany, Gropius's disgust with the climate of intolerance, his departure, Harvard, and his impact "not just on students at Harvard but on the entire field of architectural education in America." The editors, however, thought less highly of Gropius as a designer. "While Gropius was able to pull down from their pedestals the idols sanctified by the plagiarizers of Gothic, Baroque and Renaissance forms, few of his personal contributions were as heroic as those of his great contemporaries. By a sardonic twist of fate Gropius was unable to create as great an impact with his architecture as he was able to with his powerful logic and design philosophy. His buildings lack the grandeur and power which the buildings of Wright, Corbu, and Mies have. . . . His acceptance of a position as consulting architect to New York's Pan American building earned him considerable criticism for lending his name to a tasteless project."[47]

An article in the *New York Times Magazine* the following September was devoted to two events marking the fiftieth anniversary of the Bauhaus, "that long-defunct but still legendary German school of architecture and design," founded with the aim of reconstructing society by reshaping the environment it lived in: a mammoth exhibition sponsored by the Federal Republic of Germany in cooperation with several other international institutions, and "an equally ponderous" undertaking, the publication of *Bauhaus,* a massive, documented history of the school. The article described the founding of the Bauhaus, Gropius's aims, the faculty, and the exodus of Bauhauslers—among them Josef Albers, Laszlo Moholy-Nagy, Marcel Breuer, and Herbert Bayer—to the United States, pointing out that the "Bauhaus in exile" was in fact responsible for much of the design that surrounded Americans in the late 1960s: the furniture they used, the architecture they worked in, the ads in the newspapers in they read. As a hothouse for the International Style in architecture, the Bauhaus promoted that taste for systematically produced, straight-sided, glass-walled buildings that was still very much evident— though too often, the article noted, reduced to the ubiquitous office crate. In the 1920s, the article said, "Bauhaus directors dreamed of constructing American-type skyscrapers; years later, translated into reality, the results have not been laudable in every case. Gropius's Pan Am Building, lording over the architectural jumble surrounding New York's Grand Central station, throws up a wall against what had been a lovely prospect down Park Avenue."[48]

An editorial in *Casabella* noted Gropius's death, but in a clear sign of the renewed interest in history that had begun in the late 1950s and early 1960s, used the occasion to focus on the role of the past in his thinking. The July issue, in proof when editors received news of Gropius's death, was devoted to the dilemma of either rejecting history or employing "an exasperated" historicism. Though it was challenging to do so with the issue so close to publication, the editors thought it important to include Gropius in the discourse. He rejected history, as he had to. But while the rejection of history was useful for those already steeped in history, it proved to be "a wasteland" for those who were not. One could not forget that once in the United States (a country that, *Casabella* pointed out, "had no complex about history"), Gropius himself found that he had to turn once again to the lessons of history, rediscovering it in Japan. The conclusion was that "notwithstanding all the dangers, we cannot avoid a relation to history."[49]

In her tribute to Gropius in the *New York Times,* Huxtable, with her usual critical acumen, seemed most on target.[50] "The death of Walter Gropius last week did not mark the end of an era," she wrote; "the era was already over." Together with Wright, Le Corbusier, and Mies, Gropius had changed the world, Huxtable said, turning the solid brick and stone cities of the nineteenth century into the glass-and-steel, sky-piercing miracles of the twentieth, a physical and structural phenomenon unparalleled in history. "But the world they changed has changed again," she noted. "It has moved into absurdity, tragedy, chaos and decay. The intellectual and aesthetic battle that established modern architecture has taken on the aspect of a Pyrrhic victory. At the feet of skyscrapers are the slums. Monuments are measured against human misery. By any sensitive standard, the city, man's most sophisticated work, is his most conspicuous failure. And the problems of an urban society are a greater challenge than the art of building has ever known." It was against this background, she said, that we should measure Gropius. He was not a great architect in the sense that form givers Wright, Mies, and Le Corbusier were; their buildings were "testaments to our highest aspirations and achievements." Gropius's work was uneven, seemingly influenced in quality, she said, by the men with whom he collaborated. His early buildings with Adolf Meyer come closest to his best; the late projects done in this country ranged from the consistently competent to the disappointedly pedestrian. But he did not produce buildings that shattered stylistic norms with the imprint of personal genius.

At the core of his philosophy, she noted, was his concept of teamwork. The necessity of teamwork in the control of today's exploding environment, she wrote, was now acknowledged in a way that went far beyond anything he had visualized. She described Nazi Germany, his migration first to England, then to the United States and chairmanship at Harvard, where he trained a generation of modernists "at a time when they helped turn the tide of American architectural thinking." One of his students recalled that through him, they felt they could "reach the roots of the modern movement. We looked for dogma, but found liberal unitarianism."

Ironically, Huxtable said, liberal unitarianism was inadequate for the task. Gropius's response to the challenges of the time was that of a nineteenth-century utopian rationalist, still rooted in the idea of a collective art practice suited to a more placid time. This was the flaw, she said, in his prescience. But only a madman or an oracle could have anticipated the crisis conditions of the 1960s.

"The final irony," she observed, "was the betrayal of his own teachings of social and urban responsibility in one of his late jobs where he acted as consultant with Pietro Belluschi for the 'smoothing up' of the urban outrages of New York's notorious Pan Am Building." It was something, she said, that still saddened his admirers.

Several years after Gropius died, more-scholarly assessments of his life and work began to appear. One of the first was by Wolfgang Pehnt, who wrote on the expressionistic stage in Gropius's career (1918–1919) and the formation of the Arbeitsrat für Kunst, which had been all but forgotten in art historical literature.[51] Pehnt's article focused on Gropius's early, pre-Dessau years and made no mention of his later career. Other books and articles began appearing, such as Marcel Franciscono's *Walter Gropius and the Creation of the Bauhaus in Weimar,* which again focused solely on his earlier work.[52] In 1972, a retrospective exhibition was staged by his widow, Ise, with documentary material and editorial assistance from TAC, which had instigated the exhibition in an attempt to redeem Gropius's by-then tarnished reputation. The introduction to the catalogue by Fitch, long-time Gropius champion, added little to Fitch's own 1960 monograph on Gropius and again said little about Gropius's later work. The Pan Am Building—its inception, the commission, the initial Gropius/Belluschi proposal with a slender tower over a low two- (described here as eight)-story base building enclosing a courtyard which was chucked for financial reasons—was mentioned in a catalogue entry only, with text evidently provided by TAC. Acknowledging the controversies that had erupted over the building, the catalogue entry credited Gropius for the positioning of the tower, spelling out his reasoning that the accumulation of high-rise buildings on Park Avenue "called for a monumental focus astride the Avenue, corresponding in height and scale to the changed townscape around it and giving the endless row of buildings a point of reference." Clearly on the defensive, it added that no traffic jams had occurred in the wake of the building and that in fact the area had become less congested despite the additional volume of traffic the building brought to the area.[53]

As Huxtable, a staunch defender of modernism in the 1950s when she attempted to persuade the American public of its merits, pointed out in her review of the Gropius show, it offered little that was new. Faulting it for its wholly adulatory, uncritical view, she noted that as it was staged at Columbia University, the exhibition credited Gropius solely for the works included in it, omitting the names of collaborators, an oversight that was corrected in the catalog. Despite its reverential tone, she observed, the show "raised all kinds of naughty questions—about why some buildings were better than others, and to what degree established and essential physical and psychological relationships of people and buildings, developed over centuries, were scuttled for the messianic promise of a new technology and the great aesthetic revolution of the International Style." The price we pay today for "those intellectual miscalculations," she pointed out, was awful. With due respect to the master and his achievements, she concluded, it was no longer possible at this "troubled moment in time" to look at his work with the uncritical awe with which they had all been indoctrinated in school. An objective and thoughtful reevaluation had now become a historical necessity.[54]

A decade later, during which time Charles Jencks published *The Language of Postmodern Architecture* (1977) and the *Harvard Architecture Review* came out with its special issue "Beyond the Modern Movement" (1980), Harvard in May 1983 was still perpetuating the long-standing tradition of celebrating Gropius's birthday with festivities, staging a series of exhibitions, lectures, symposia, and seminars to commemorate Gropius's 100th birthday. Filled with mostly nostalgic reminiscences and a special memorial lecture by Professor Emeritus Reginald Isaacs, a Gropius disciple who had continued the Gropius tradition at Harvard after Gropius left and was currently engaged in compiling a comprehensive biography, the "Gropefest" was described as "rich in anecdote if thin in analysis," with the "current disenchantment with Gropius dismissed with an insouciance which illustrated the unquestioning loyalty of former associates to his principles." A solid historical account, as opposed to a sentimental celebration of the sort the Gropefest represented, was still needed.[55]

Vittorio Gregotti tried for some historical perspective. In a provocative article in *Casabella* later that year, the Italian historian and theorist compared Gropius's career to Adolf Loos's. The year 1983 marked an important date in modern architecture, the fiftieth anniversary of Loos's death and the hundredth anniversary of Gropius's birth; between the two of them, Gregotti pointed out, they spanned a large part of the history of modern architecture, leaving a legacy on the level not so much of style and form as of ideology, which Gregotti defined as the relation between thought, society, and architecture. Whereas Gropius enjoyed many years of critical success with Loos in relative eclipse, there had been "a curious inversion" of tendencies in the previous twenty years (twenty years before would have been around 1963, the year the Pan Am Building opened), and Gropius's fortunes had undergone an eclipse as the importance of Loos, especially among the young, had risen. Underscoring the persuasive role of architectural magazines, particularly those of a theoretical bent, and their powers to sway minds, especially those of students, Gregotti thought that it was his generation, and particularly the *Casabella* group of the 1950s, that was largely responsible for this reversal. And since Loos's fortune had not stopped growing, he thought it was time for a more realistic, historically accurate perspective, pointing out that Loos was not alone or the first to do a lot of what he had been credited as doing. Gropius too, Gregotti concluded, like Loos, had opposed the formalistic aspects of the avant-garde, emphasizing method rather than a particular style. Loos, however, was right in maintaining that the ills of industrial production could not be corrected by the forces of architecture but rather had to be remedied by the deeper forces of culture: not by the modernist prophet Gropius called for, Gregotti contended, but by underlying structural forces largely beyond his control.[56]

Reflecting the growing disillusionment with the great master, Winfried Nerdinger's comments on an exhibition of Gropius's work several years later were still more critical in tone. In his catalog of drawings, prints, and photos drawn from the Busch-Reisinger Museum, Harvard, and the Bauhaus-Archiv in Berlin, Nerdinger described the Pan Am and the controversy it had raised in blocking off Park Avenue, a storm of protests led, he said, by Gropius's former student Zevi. It was criticism, he said, targeted particularly at Gropius, and it had severely damaged his architectural reputation.[57]

Nerdinger's catalog caught the eye of Boston architectural critic Jane Holtz Kay. It was time, she said in an article in *Progressive Architecture* in November of the same year, for a balanced reassessment of this "archetypal Modernist," and the exhibition of some 150 photos, drawings, and models, held at Harvard's Busch-Reisinger Museum though visually stunning, had captions and commentary that were less than positive, transforming the exhibition "into a critical biography." Nerdinger, a German architectural historian who was head of the architectural collection at the Technical University in Munich, had "virtually rained on his Gropius parade," Kay said, with pages of commentary pinned to the exhibition's walls. TAC members called them "gossipy, opinionated put-downs" and basically insulting; Busch-Reisinger Museum curator Peter Nisbet responded by saying that the point of Nerdinger's commentary was to counterbalance the prevailing Gropius myth. The show's "countervailing criticism" not only repeated by-now familiar attacks on the failure of modernism to provide social housing, Kay maintained, but also "excoriated Gropius's design ability, his capacity to get work, and his unembarrassed use of the team-work slogan to appropriate projects by others to himself." Tom Wolfe (whose outrageously scathing assessment of Gropius in *From Bauhaus to Our House* had come out in 1981) "was no more relentless."[58]

Then there was Franciscono's review in the *Journal of the Society of Architectural Historians* of Isaacs's massive, 1,292-page, two-volume "official biography" of Gropius, published in 1983 and 1984.[59] Noting the total absence of a critical stance on the part of the author, who had been Gropius's friend, student, and collaborator, Franciscono pointed out that the biography had been started before Gropius died, and indeed Gropius himself had written the introduction. Based largely on Gropius's private correspondence and conversations, as well as information and documents supplied by Ise Gropius, including her own personal journal, the tone of the book was wholly reverential, and although it provided an abundance of material especially about his years in England and the United States, there was no interpretation of the material, which was simply presented without comment. The work, Franciscono said, raised no important or significant questions and offered no analysis. This was unfortunate, Franciscono maintained, because readers had a right to some recognition of the questions Gropius's career had raised. The function of Isaacs's publication was simply to ratify the work and ideas of its hero, and as a piece of "special pleading," it could have been published in the 1950s, along with the monographs of Sigfried Giedion and Giulio Argan. Gropius's

place in history as an educator was assured, and no one had done more than he to pro-
mote the cause of modernism in architecture, Franciscono asserted, but his reputation
as an architect was far more problematic, and he had been controversial for many years.
Few today would grant him the stature of a Mies or a Le Corbusier.

The single most important disclosure of Isaacs's biography, according to Franciscono,
was that Gropius could not draw. His much-vaunted notion of teamwork was thus a
strict necessity. (Although Franciscono did not point this out, if indeed he knew of it,
Gropius's wanting Belluschi as a collaborator on the Pan Am lends weight to his assertion.) That Gropius always worked with design partners was now recognized as proof
of his creative weakness, and more than one critic had pointed out that the designs of
his buildings were due in significant part to his collaborators. This revelation lent credence to the suspicion that he was less an architect than idea man and organizer.

Gropius's reputation as an architect and planner would probably never again be what
it had been in his lifetime, Franciscono concluded, and was certainly not likely to be restored in the present climate of opinion. As Nerdinger's study had been sharply critical
of Gropius as a planner and unduly dismissive of the defensible in Gropius's work,
Isaacs's work should have addressed the issues it raised and corrected the balance. It
did not, and as a result, "the case has gone to Gropius's critics largely by default."

Isaacs's biography, which had been, in his own words, "a continuing preoccupation
and goal for many years," an all-consuming "labor of love," and a project to which he
had devoted the last years of his life, had, in fact, mentioned the controversy surrounding the Pan Am.[60] As Isaacs saw it, Gropius, saddened by an autobiography written by
his former wife, Alma Mahler Werfel, which he thought had inaccurately portrayed their
relationship, "fortunately had other things on his mind" in his architectural practice,
namely, the Pan Am Building, which later became, as Isaacs put it, his most controversial commission. Everyone involved—the owner, the architects, the tenants, even the
city officials who had approved the building—was both praised and vilified, the building
was declared "a visual crime against city planning, a rape of its environs." Critics com-
plained that the flow of space around the building had been interrupted by the Pan Am
Building, although evidently not by the Grand Central Terminal, which was similarly
sited. "In view of Gropius's lifelong fight against the disfigurement of the environment," Isaacs observed, "it was not surprising that he was amazed by the criticisms."

Gropius was far from alone in defending the building, Isaacs pointed out, citing
among "its many supporters" Goble (who wrote about the advantages of the vertical
city), Heckscher (who praised the series of spatial experiences created by the Pan Am

Building, the play of light upon its faceted sides, its silhouette, and the appropriateness of its scale), and Bacon (who refuted the criticism regarding access, transportation, and congestion and praised the building's contribution to Park Avenue's vistas and the design structure of the city). Time had also weighed in on their side, Isaacs observed, as no crisis had occurred in either pedestrian or vehicular traffic as a result of the building's existence. The building had become a visual landmark and a prototype "imitated many times in school and practice," Isaacs maintained, though he provided no evidence to back up the assertion.[61]

The Walter Gropius Archive, 1945–1969: The Work of the Architects Collaborative, volume 4 of the Walter Gropius Archive series, published in 1991, was in much the same adulatory vein as Isaacs's biography.[62] In his introduction to the volume, which dealt with "a lesser known phase of the work of one of the world's most famous modern architects, during the final period of a long and immensely productive career," when he was a partner in TAC, Fitch said it was, in a very real sense, the last of three careers Gropius had. "In this last and probably happiest career, Gropius was acting precisely the role that he had always advocated for architecture and industrial design—as a collaborator among equals, working with other architects and technical specialists." The buildings illustrated (among which was the Pan Am), were "those with which Walter Gropius was most closely associated" and most clearly reflected his own tastes and predilections in the closing years of his career, a taste that was "serene, secure, conservative." In his preface, TAC member John Harkness wrote of how rewarding working on the archive had been, reminding him of the principles to which Gropius had dedicated his life, his conviction that the living conditions on this earth could be improved through architectural design, and the "deep social conscience" his work represented. The work, however, was not truly an archive, as it did not include drawings actually made by Gropius. His method of working, Harkness said, was to present a basic philosophical approach to design and to work with others, on a give-and-take basis, to develop specific solutions for particular projects. Those projects selected for the archive, each written up by the partner with whom Gropius worked on it, were the ones most important for him and had had his greatest participation.

Written thus by members of the firm and decidedly *parti pris,* the descriptions of the projects varied in quality. That on the Pan Am Building, written by Alex Cvijanovic, who worked with Gropius mainly during the later stages of design, was sketchy, defensive, and at times misleading. Naming Pan American World Airways as the client (Pan Am did not sign on as the building's major tenant until the design was all but completed) and giving 1958 as the building's date (it wasn't completed until 1963 and meanwhile undergone changes), it cited as architect "TAC Principals Gropius, A. Cvijanovic, N. Fletcher, with Pietro Belluschi and Emery Roth & Sons, associated." Wolfson and Cotton, the developers, it said, had made a special effort in 1958 (Cotton was not brought in until summer of 1959, and in fact had very little to do with it, other than to put up the money) "to secure the participation of the best architectural minds for the design of the controversial project" (no mention of why at this point it was controversial, or, of course, of the public relations role Wolfson hoped the two leading modernists would serve). They commissioned Gropius and TAC (Wolfson in fact engaged Gropius and Belluschi, not TAC) "to provide the design leadership and collaborate with the office of Emery Roth of New York, who remained the architects of record." Belluschi, according to Cvijanovic, served "in a design advisory capacity" (which was not the role he was brought in to play, though it may have ended up that way). Gropius, who "had joined in the polemic between the urbanists, artists, architects, media, and developers" about the appropriateness of the development adjacent to the Grand Central, persuaded the owners, Cvijanovic maintained, to reduce the building's size from 5 million to 2.5 million square feet. According to Cvijanovic, Gropius did not hide behind the argument that regardless of the unsuitability of the site, a building on it was going to be built anyway and therefore ought to be designed by good architects; on the contrary, Gropius believed that the location was indeed appropriate for a large-scale development. Gropius considered the site as a rare instance of an urban node where several modes of transportation came together—a railway station serving the suburbs, two major subway lines, bus lines, and private cars—"an eminently suitable location for a commuting destination for several thousand employees" (the original estimate was for twenty-five thousand, with two hundred fifty thousand visitors daily). Much time was spent, Cvijanovic said (it was spent mainly, in fact, by the Roth office), on the pedestrian circulation on the ground level and the link with the Grand Central Terminal. As of the time he was writing, some quarter of a million people went through the Pan Am lobby every day on their way to or from the station, and twenty-five thousand people worked in the building, without congestion. The prismatic shape of the tower, Belluschi's design contribution, was intended to visually reduce the bulk of the building (there was more to it than that, such as Gropius's elevator argument); a heliport was incorporated on the top of the building to provide a connection to airports and complete the cycle of transportation modes. The heliport, Cvijanovic noted, "was later considered too hazardous and was closed" (not exactly what happened: Despite public protest over its noise and safety, the heliport service was approved with full official assurance of its safety; it was closed only after a fatal accident a decade later). "In the Pan Am Building, as in all the buildings he designed [no mention of the collaborative process at this point], Gropius succeeded in integrating arts [no mention of the virtually universally negative reviews the Pan Am's art had received]. Kepes's sculpture was unfortunately torn down during the remodeling of the lobby," Cvijanovic concluded, replaced "by tasteless post-modern kitsch."

A 1992 review of Isaacs's biography in *Progressive Architecture* was more balanced, putting Gropius and his work into perspective and pointing out his merits without ignoring his mistakes. "Walter Gropius always said Modernism was not just a style," began author Jonathan Hale, whose own book, *The Old Way of Seeing,* was then in the making. "But these days Modernism is nothing but another box in the architectural grab-bag, and the pedestal Gropius used to occupy has long been empty. Still, there lurks a sense that in the process of demoting Modernism, architecture has pushed aside something important. The movement Gropius came to personify broke its promise to make the world beautiful. But it is worth noting that the vision Gropius pursued went beyond Modernism or Post-Modernism or the other current isms. Architecture is again looking for principles. That is what Gropius was looking for." It was a good time to reappraise Gropius's successes, Hale maintained, as well as his failures. Isaacs's biography, however, was not such a reappraisal, though it might serve as a stimulus for one. Indeed, "the book is almost an incitement to a reconsideration, for it is so complete, so authoritative, yet so maddeningly uncritical." To read Isaacs's work, Hale said, was to look at Gropius and modernism across a divide, to an era when modernism was the answer and Gropius had yet to topple. It read as if the last twenty-five years had never happened. This was not to belittle the work, which he said belonged on the shelf of anyone who cared about the history of modernism. On Gropius's personal life, it was exhaustive, but all the frankness about his personal life, Hale maintained, "merely underlines the book's great unasked questions about his work."

In summing up his goals in *Scope of Total Architecture* (1955), Gropius claimed that he sought the harmony in design that he found in the preindustrial era and wanted to maintain that harmony in the machine age. In a way, Hale observed, Gropius himself acknowledged the possibility that something might be going wrong. "A 'Bauhaus Style' would have been a confession of failure and a return to that devitalizing inertia," Gropius wrote in *Scope,* "that stagnating academicism which I had called [the Bauhaus] into being to combat. . . . There is no such thing as an 'International Style.'"

But there was a Bauhaus style, Hale pointed out. It was the style of the century, and "it was Gropius's baby, like it or not." In denouncing the use of styles in the past, Gropius could hardly propose a new one, which is why he so disingenuously denied the existence of the International Style. But it is also why, Hale said, Gropius still counts. While the International Style might have solved the problem of how to express the machine in architecture, expressing the machine wasn't the central problem. The real problem was, and is, Hale argued, how to express life in buildings and cities in an age of machines. What continued to make Gropius still valuable was his belief in the deeper principle.

There was a strange sort of self-betrayal in Gropius's story, Hale maintained. Although he had the opportunity to build his dreams, after about 1940 his designs became stale. Halfway through his career, at the peak of success, he declared victory and seemed to give up the fight. The buildings of his last thirty years had little of the energy of his previous work. But Isaacs, Hale said, was complacent, trotting out one drab project after another. Of the Pan Am Building, Isaacs had written: "'Time has come to the defense of the design.'" Well, Hale responded, "perhaps Time has had the last laugh: the building is still there and Pan Am isn't." There was room for another look at Gropius, Hale asserted, a critical look at where he went wrong, but also one that took in, without the old adulation, what he did right.

Whatever the weakness of modernism might have been, Hale said, was not the immediate cause of Gropius's problem as a designer. Modernism was no weaker in the 1950s than in the 1920s, Hale pointed out, noting the successes of the Seagram Building and Ronchamp. Yet the later work of Gropius lacked its previous fire. Was he just a minor talent? The Fagus factory (1911) and the house Gropius designed in Lincoln, Massachusetts (1937) suggested he was not. He had been accused of relying too much on codesigners. But a Gropius building was no less fine, Hale pointed out, because it came out of a collaboration with Meyer or Breuer. Gropius brought in people to help, which was consistent with the old medieval craft approach he sought to revive. Hale recited the story about the Lincoln House, one wall of the deck that Gropius wanted painted a magical pink, the color of reflected light at dusk. The hue wasn't coming out right, so Gropius called in the painter Lyonel Feininger to mix it. It was that kind of pink and that kind of house, the result of collaboration and not a noble single artist, that was Gropius's method. He demonstrated time and again his ability to lead a committee to come up with a horse, not a camel. Why then did Gropius produce, with his later collaborators, not just the occasional camel of his earlier career, but a regular caravan? It was an open question, and the answer was worth waiting for, because what happened to Gropius, Hale maintained, had its parallel in what happened to modernism itself.

"The relevance of Gropius today is the priority he put on expressing age-old principles in ways that would work for our time," Hale said in conclusion. "Our time is a little different from his time—the Bauhaus goes back 70 years now—but we could do no better than to pursue his goal."[63]

Pivotal as the Pan Am Building was in Gropius's career, and by extension, in the history of modernism itself, there is no mention of it in John Peter's *The Oral History of Modern Architecture,* a series of recorded interviews with "the greatest architects of the twentieth century" published in 1994.[64] Opening with a two-page photo of the Bauhaus building, the book aimed at telling the story of modernism from the inside, that is, "what the founders of modern architecture thought and said they were doing." Peter defined modern architecture as the predominant trend of a forty-year period, and the characteristic architecture of the twentieth century of the Western world, arbitrarily setting the onset of modern architecture in 1923 and ending it equally arbitrarily with Venturi's *Complexity and Contradiction in Architecture* of 1966, which heralded, as Peter put it, postmodern architecture (a time span that in essence bracketed Gropius's Bauhaus building at the beginning and the Pan Am Building at the end). Though Peter interviewed Gropius on at least two occasions, once in 1956, two years before the Pan Am was commissioned (at which time Gropius was grumbling about being "nobody's baby"), and again in 1964, just after the Pan Am opened, the building was not mentioned. In a telling remark made in the context of a discussion about collaboration and Gropius's concept of teamwork, Gropius gave his customary line, that the times were so complicated that no one individual could do it all, and that only by creating a well-oiled team could one make the design process work. It was easily said, but not easy to do, as to function well, teamwork had to be done voluntarily, with much give and take. On the other hand, Gropius said, "the spark always comes from the individual." This prompts the great unasked question: What happened on the Pan Am, which had, from all accounts, a superbly formed, well-oiled team? Who provided the spark, or was there one? Peter did not ask, nor did Gropius volunteer an explanation.

Nor was the Pan Am, heralded as the largest commercial office building in the world at the time, built on one of the choicest urban sites in the world, a building many thought would serve as Gropius's magnum opus, mentioned in 1995, when the office of TAC, on the verge of bankruptcy, finally closed its doors.[65]

6

AFTERMATH

HELIPORT

The heliport on top of the Pan Am Building was an important part of Trippe's vision. Harking back to early-twentieth-century Futurist dreams, it promised to complete the concept of the Pan Am/Grand Central complex as the city's major transportation hub, linking it to the rest of the nation underground by rail and to the rest of the world, with flights to the city's outlying airports, overhead by air. Businessmen and well-to-do commuters applauded, as it promised to cut travel time amazingly, with helicopter flights from the Pan Am Building in the heart of Manhattan taking only four minutes to La Guardia, six to Newark, and seven to New York International (Idlewild) airports. It thus skirted one of the major drawbacks of air travel: navigating through congested highways to and from the airport by bus, taxi, or car. The heliport was not popular with the public, however, and the animosity it raised only compounded that generated by the design and sheer presence of the Pan Am Building itself. Letters of protest began appearing in the *New York Times* in March 1961, immediately after plans for the heliport were announced.

Fears were voiced about the safety of helicopters landing on a tiny airstrip fifty-nine stories above the street in the heavily congested area. While the heliport was under construction, a group of owners and managers of nearby buildings urged those federal and city agencies whose approval was still needed not to endorse it, arguing that although it provided Pan American promotional benefit, it would present serious dangers to the public, and the noise would disrupt occupants of nearby offices, residences, and hotels; the group also pointed out that the heliport violated city building laws, claiming that it was illegal for the city's Department of Buildings to have granted a building permit for the heliport's construction, as the area was not zoned for heliports.[1]

The *New York Times* initially supported the heliport, pointing out that rooftop heliports were in use in other cities, and that based on scientific research, airflow vanes, installed to control air turbulence, assured safe, all-weather operation.[2] Few seemed reassured, however, and the debate became acrimonious as more and more private citizens spoke out. They were not against a midtown heliport; they only wanted it in a safer location, such as on the East River, which would not involve the public "in the unnecessary gamble with human lives" posed by the rooftop heliport in the Grand Central area. No "scientific research" could guarantee operating safety involving problems of mechanical failure, visibility, and pilot error. Critics also accused the *Times* of failing to address the heliport's illegality. Construction of the landing pad had proceeded without the necessary city permits from the Department of Buildings and Department of Marine and Aviation. Did the *Times,* one letter asked, condone this method of constructing "what was really a civic facility"?[3]

As plans for the heliport proceeded despite public concern, another civic controversy was predicted as the City Planning Commission confirmed in March 1964 that the owners of the Pan Am Building had applied for permission to operate the heliport.[4] Again the *New York Times* endorsed the project, noting that Pan American World Airways was also building a heliport at its airline terminal at Kennedy (formerly Idlewild, its name changed in the wake of President Kennedy's assassination the previous November) Airport. Citing again the "impressive" safety record of New York Airways' helicopter service, the *Times* renewed its expression of confidence in the safety and desirability of the Pan Am heliport. "It will be a good thing for the city, for aviation," the *Times* asserted in an editorial the following month, "and serve the traveling public as no other location could. Ways must be found to bring our airports closer in travel time to the cities they serve."[5]

This drew acid response from readers, who accused the *Times* of not reading its own columns. Citing examples of helicopter accidents, including one fatal crash and two failures requiring emergency landings of the supposedly safe twin-engine type of helicopter planned for use on the Pan Am, one such opponent quoted headlines in his letter to the *Times:* "22 Safe, Helicopter Down in Bay" (July 17, 1962); "28 Safe, Copter Lands in East River" (July 27, 1962); "Idlewild Crash Kills 6 in Copter" (October 15, 1963). This hardly constituted "an impressive safety record," the writer said, a record that was even less impressive considering that those crashes had occurred in areas where safe emergency landings were immediately available, not on top of a skyscraper in the heavily congested Grand Central area.[6]

More letters arrived in protest. "The location of a heliport atop the Pan Am Building is sheer madness," the author of a particularly prescient one wrote. "It is impossible to justify it by the small social and economic benefit it will afford. . . . It is a promotional idea, pure and simple, foisted upon our city at huge risk to the public safety." That the helicopters had twin engines was irrelevant, the letter's author pointed out, as fatal crashes in the past had occurred because rotor hubs, rotor blades, rotor shafts, or gear boxes failed, throwing the aircraft off balance, and hence out of control. Such failures resulted from metal fatigue, to which helicopters, because of their vibration during their operation, were especially prone.[7]

When city planners approved the project, making front-page news the following month,[8] the battle heated up, with then Republican Congressman John V. Lindsay urging that proceedings be delayed on the grounds that approval of the Pan Am heliport "would put the private interests of a few before the public needs of the city," a position he would, upon becoming mayor, later reverse.

Taking a similar stand, the former commissioner of marine and aviation voiced his concern.[9] He endorsed the city's traditional policy on helicopters, which was to limit them to over-water routes, adding that the advocates of the heliport on top of the Pan Am "were asking for an unsound and dangerous thing for the sake of private interests," and called for the city to undertake development of a comprehensive heliport plan.

All the protest was to no avail. A front-page news article in the *Times* on January 5, 1965, announced that the New York City Board of Estimate had voted unanimously to approve heliport operations, giving all but final city approval.[10] Service was tentatively set to open in April. New York Airways was to start with twelve takeoffs and landings an hour from the Pan Am roof and build gradually to twenty or so an hour, with service starting at 8 A.M. and continuing until 10 or 11 at night.

Final flight tests were conducted that March.[11] The political dimensions of the controversy widened as President Lyndon B. Johnson recommended severing federal subsidies for helicopter service; Senators Jacob K. Javits (Republican) and Robert F. Kennedy (Democrat) urged continued federal support; more letters poured in denouncing the *Times* for its endorsement, including one from Walter Strickland, Chairman of the Board of Best & Co., that called the heliport "an affront to public peace and privileges"; and state assemblyman William F. Passannante from Manhattan introduced a bill that sought to block the heliport operations, claiming that he had been flooded with telephone calls and letters from people terrified about a possible crash. Were a blade from one of the helicopters ever to break off, it was pointed out, it could easily plummet through the thin vault of the Grand Central.[12]

In the meantime, however, the *Times* marveled at the spectacle (figure 6.1).[13] "What's it like to fly off the roof of a 59-story skyscraper was demonstrated yesterday by New York Airways. And those who took the ride agreed it was like nothing else," the

FIGURE 6.1   Heliport

article began. It described the experience in the twenty-five-seat Vertol 107 helicopter, the "breathtaking view of Manhattan 800 feet below," and the six-minute-and-twenty-second flight to Kennedy, provided by the heliport operators as part of their promotion.

"The view of Manhattan to helicopter riders above the Pan Am Building, as described by your reporter, may well have been breathtaking, but the infernal noise made by this latest addition to air traffic is anything but heavenly to the people living and working below," was the response to the article in yet another letter to the *Times*.[14] "The *Times* itself has for years vigorously supported campaigns to reduce the din of the city. Yet here we are blithely about to add the monstrous, clattering roar of helicopter rotors to what many consider an already intolerable daily assault upon our ears and nerves. Passengers served each day by the helicopter line will probably be counted in the mere hundreds, whereas tens of thousands of people in the midtown section will be subjected to this new harassment." Such letters reinforced public perception of the arrogance of Pan Am, both the airline sponsoring and promoting the helicopter service and the building itself, whose name it bore and off whose rooftop the service operated.

Amidst as much protest as fanfare, the heliport opened in December 1965.[15] Members of "the aviation clan," an assortment of political figures, journalists, and photographers were expected to attend the grand opening, marked by a cutting of ribbons as well as the commencement of the scheduled helicopter service. Initially flights were only to go to and from Kennedy, landing next to the Pan American World Airways terminal. Passengers using the midtown heliport would be afforded all the amenities of air travel, as Pan American World Airways had a ticket office and waiting room on the first floor of the building, enabling cars, taxis, and buses to pull up to the office doorway; there the Pan American staff would process passports, tickets, and baggage, which passengers would not see again until they arrived at their foreign destination. Once ticketed, passengers would walk but a few steps to an express elevator for a thirty-second ride to the fifty-seventh floor of the building, then take an escalator to a heliport lounge one flight up and a short elevator ride to the boarding lounge next to the control tower and roof pad. The speed, travel, convenience—it was all pretty futuristic stuff (figures 6.2–6.4).

Robert L. Cummings, president of New York Airways, which had provided journalists with their free ride, saw the new service as "the coming of age in America of the commercial helicopter"; such service was already established in Europe, he said, and in regular use by the American military. The wholehearted acceptance of the operation by Pan

FIGURE 6.2   Entrance, Pan American World Airways Ticket Office, Pan Am Building

FIGURE 6.3   Heliport, Pan Am rooftop

FIGURE 6.4   From helicopter to Pan Am jet

American World Airways, whose chairman, Trippe, had invested $4 million in the operation, was also an economic endorsement of "the maturity" of this type of flight. Pan American had also, Cummings added, purchased three new helicopters listed at $635,000 each, which it planned to lease to New York Airways for the operation, in addition to the $1 million that Pan American had spent on the heliport passenger terminal, lounges, and other related facilities, in the Pan Am Building itself.[16] These were only the first of a series of expenditures that were to cripple the powerful airline, then one of the world's largest, years later, after Trippe stepped down as chairman.

Signaling the occasion's civic importance, attending the opening celebration were not only New York Mayor Wagner and Governor Nelson Rockefeller, but also Cardinal Francis Joseph Spellman, who had flown in from the Vatican for the occasion (figure 6.5). Vice President Hubert Humphrey joined them by telephone. Speaking from his home near Minneapolis, Humphrey gave the signal to turn on the helicopter's lights, calling it "the first such helicopter in the world," and predicted it would soon prove indispensable. Trippe, the governor, and the mayor cut the red ribbon, then passengers, including Cardinal Spellman, who was later to depart by a Pan American jetliner for Vietnam, where he would spend Christmas with U.S. troops, boarded, and the aircraft took off. The second of the two inaugural flights left an hour and a half later, both flights connecting with Pan American World Airways jetliners flying overseas.[17]

Important as the Pan Am heliport was in the eyes of politicians, the public remained unconvinced. Letters to the *New York Times* opposing the heliport's operation continued. "Those who are thrill-seeking and stout of heart would do well to peer at the rooftop of the Pan Am Building," said one. "Now that the age of progress is upon us they will see monstrously large helicopters hopefully descend to the tiny rooftop pad, and then bravely rise again, diagonally over the city streets and buildings below, with their thousands of innocent and unconcerned people. Somewhere there was a promise that these machines would rise straight up to a height from which they could safely glide to the river, or drop down to the roof, if failure occurred. But not these brave monsters! You need not a pilot's license to tell that failure on these lift-offs could plummet tons of metal into Grand Central Terminal. . . . This time and a thousand times there will be a successful landing and another successful take-off. But . . . one time a rotor blade will break or a pilot will miss in this crazy operation. For indeed this is an incredible exercise in public irresponsibility."[18] Another, more plaintive letter addressed more mundane concerns: "I would like to express my concern with the noise created by the scheduled flights of helicopters whose terminus is the Pan Am building. . . . Pan Am

FIGURE 6.5   Ribbon-cutting ceremony opening Pan Am heliport, with Mayor Wagner, Cardinal Spellman, Governor Rockefeller, and Juan Trippe (rear), December 1965

may be serving its customers; it is not making a good part of mid-Manhattan a pleasant place to live or work."[19]

In response to the continued complaints, the city instigated a study that found that although heliport flights presented no danger to residents and employees in the area, the noise was indeed excessive and had to be reduced; it also recommended that the forty-five daily flights (decreased from the twelve per hour originally projected) start later than 8:30 in the morning and cease earlier than 10:10 at night.[20]

Under increasing political pressure, Lindsay, who had by then become mayor, had called upon his Transportation Administrator to study the situation. Several months later, he concluded, based on the administrator's report, that the controversial Pan Am heliport was a "sound operation and a safe one," though flight hours should be curtailed and flight patterns changed to minimize noise. He also pointed out that tests had shown that if one of the engines failed the other would enable the craft to glide safely to the river. This was a reversal of his position, when he had been a congressman; as noted previously, he was at that time one of the heliport's most outspoken critics and maintained that approval of the heliport "would put the private interests of a few before the public needs of the city."[21]

Not everyone opposed the Pan Am heliport. Although in a decided minority, proponents felt equally strongly about it. "Recent *New York Times* articles relating to the controversy over the heliport atop the Pan Am Building indicate an organized opposition to city center air service," began one such letter from a commuter in Long Island. "This raises the question as to how the thousands of airline passengers (who have found the service to the Pan Am Building one of the greatest blessings a harried air traveler has received) may also have their voices heard. The airline passenger has no voice in Federal, state or local government and is not organized to petition the authorities or to seek support for his needs. Furthermore, the local community, its workers and shops, are often the direct beneficiaries of the thousands of business trips made by air. . . . Certainly the value of a New York City center transportation service, measured in minutes not hours, must somehow be weighed."[22]

That the writer of the letter lived outside the city did not escape the *Times* readership. Observing that the author of the letter was a commuter, another writer responded by saying that as a New York resident, she spoke on behalf of others in the midtown. The noise was a constant source of irritation and distress to those in the area, who greatly outnumbered those who helicoptered from the Pan Am to the airport. It was, in her eyes, "a great public disservice."[23] Despite more complaints about the heliport din, however, and mounting frustration as the efforts of those opposed to the heliport proved of no avail, the city in December 1966 renewed the heliport license for another year.[24]

Just over a year later, the *New York Times* began to soften its editorial stance in support of the Pan Am heliport. In light of a new heliport proposed by Pan American World Airways and approved by thc city on the East River at 61st Street, any new heliport, the *Times* said, must strike a balance between the convenience of travelers and that of apartment dwellers living nearby. "The heliport atop the Pan Am Building, which we welcomed, has proved to be a mixed blessing."[25]

Operations of the Pan Am heliport were finally suspended, but not because of citizen complaints. As Pan American's fortunes began to wane in the late 1960s, in part because of Trippe's reckless spending, a dispute arose between the airline and New York Airways over the airline's continued subsidizing of the operation. Word was that Pan American sought control of the service, a report lent credence by recent disclosure of Pan American's order for five Sikorsky S-61L thirty-passenger helicopters at a cost of $1 million each. An article on the operation's suspension in the *New York Times* added that opponents of the heliport were no doubt pleased.[26]

Indeed they were. "I write this following the first blissfully quiet helicopterless weekend since December 21, 1965, when the Pan Am heliport was opened," wrote one. Since then, the writer noted, the din had been practically continuous. "Now, due to a squabble over the size of the Pan American World Airways subsidy to the helicopter operator, New York Airways, flights to and from the Pan Am pinnacle have been suspended. The fact that the Department of Marine and Aviation has allowed this to happen, and so capriciously, gives lie to the much-vaunted claim that these helicopters provide a viable necessary transportation 'service' to the city. They do nothing of the kind. Instead they are essentially not much more than an advertising and public relations 'gimmick' for Pan American for which thousands of New York residents and workers have suffered noise harassment and potential danger for more than two years."[27] Opponents lobbying for permanent closure of the heliport cited more accidents—such as the crash in California of a Sikorsky S-61L helicopter, the same kind Pan American planned for the Pan Am heliport, killing all twenty-three passengers aboard.[28]

Despite public opposition, the heliport taxi service operated by Pan American World Airways near East 60th Street was begun the following year.[29] It also looked at that point as if the helicopter service from the Pan Am Building, which had been halted since February 1968, because of the Pan American and New York Airways dispute, would be resumed. The airline, which by this time, according to the *New York Times,* owned the building, had reached an agreement with New York Airways under which the airline would invest $1 million in the helicopter service, increasing its interest in New York Airways from 16 to 45 percent and subsidizing its operations with up to $260,000 a year. Before the Pan Am heliport was reopened, however, it needed safety clearance from the FAA, in light of two crashes in California involving the same type of helicopter that Pan American proposed to use.[30]

This time the *New York Times* opposed the reopening of the Pan Am heliport.[31] "The tragedy that would result if a 28-passenger copter were to plunge through the roof into Grand Central Terminal or into one of the busy adjoining streets is too great for a project of such minimal community benefit," the *Times* now said. Even if the risk of a crash were reduced to zero, there was still the noise. Noting that the helicopter service at best served only a tiny fraction of the passengers who used the airports, it concluded that in any case the one place a heliport should *not* be was in the densely populated center of midtown Manhattan.

Operations of the Pan Am heliport were subsequently suspended, ostensibly because of community opposition to the noise magnified in the deep canyons below the facility and the dangers it presented in flying over the densely populated area.[32] They remained suspended until test flights in preparation for a resumption of the helicopter service were held (figure 6.6).[33] Not surprisingly, opposition resumed as well. "The resumption of helicopter flights from the roof of the Pan Am Building is incredibly absurd from the standpoint of public safety," one opponent wrote. "No doubt the flights will provide a measure of convenience for the handful of travelers who will use the service. . . . But from the public standpoint it is ridiculous. Perched over the fragile roof of Grand Central Terminal, used daily by thousands of commuters, and located in the very heart of our crowded city—one could not choose a more dangerous place. . . . Helicopters do fail."[34]

Ignoring such objections as well as charges that the city's Environmental Protection Agency had failed to conduct noise tests on weekends and had used faulty equipment to conduct the tests, the New York City Board of Estimate again unanimously approved the Pan Am Building helicopter service in February 1977, and the service resumed later that month.[35]

Opposition escalated after the heliport reopened. "Why ban two or three Concorde flights daily way out at JFK and permit the helicopters to fly over 100 times a day from the Pan Am Building? . . . It is an expensive convenience for only a tiny handful of plutocrats," wrote one individual. "Furthermore, since most users must be businessmen on

FIGURE 6.6   Flight tests, March 1977

tax-deductible travel, we are in effect subsidizing this maddening irritation with our tax dollars. The sky over the heart of town is a public asset, which New York Airways should not be allowed to defile."[36] "Are we writing off New York City as a decent environment in which to work and live?" asked another.[37] And another commented: "All this Concorde agitation makes me wonder why somebody interested in environmental protection and noise pollution doesn't draw a bead on New York Airways, that private outfit which now uses midtown Manhattan as its flyway to and from the Pan Am heliport something like 100 times a day. . . . And for the benefit of whom? Its stockholders, I guess, and a handful of well-heeled travelers, most of them out-of-towners. . . . And at what cost to hundreds of thousands of us locals in terms of noise pollution, air pollution, rasped nerves? And at what an incalculable risk? For one fine day, one very sad day, because of somebody's carelessness or a little unanticipated metal fatigue. . . ."[38]

Ironically, less than a month later, the inevitable happened. On May 16, 1977, a helicopter arriving from Kennedy Airport keeled over on broken landing gear, snapping off a rotor blade, which slashed four people to death as they were boarding the craft. The broken blade then plunged over the roof's parapet and crashed through a window into an executive office about halfway down the tower; a portion of it continued to fall, killing a fifth person on the street below (figure 6.7).[39] Seven people were injured. After years of public protest, the service was finally discontinued and the heliport abandoned.

The heliport affair sullied still further the image of the building, as well as the reputation of its namesake company, Pan American World Airways, in the eyes of the public. The airline was already by this time experiencing financial difficulties, and its days were numbered; two years after the accident, New York Airways, nearly half the stock of which Pan American owned, filed for bankruptcy.[40] The Pan Am Building itself would go on the block the following year.

HISTORIC PRESERVATION

The heliport was only one of many controversies plaguing the Pan Am. Historic preservation and the Grand Central Station was another. The movement to preserve Grand Central Terminal for historic reasons dates back at least to 1954, well before Penn Station became a cause célèbre, when Young first made plans public to redevelop the Grand Central area by demolishing the old 1913 Beaux-Arts Grand Central Terminal and erecting an eighty-story, sixteen-hundred-foot tower in its stead, prompting Haskell to launch his "Save the Concourse" campaign. As American attitudes toward their archi-

FIGURE 6.7   Fatal accident, May 16, 1977

tectural past began shifting in the latter half of the 1950s, Haskell's views changed as well, as reflected in his 1957 *Architectural Forum* article "The Value of Used Architecture," in which he pointed out the merits of historic buildings.[41] At the same time, Huxtable was still trying to persuade a skeptical public to accept the new stark steel-and-glass forms of modern architecture, in articles such as "The Park Avenue School of Architecture."[42] Aptly representing the two factions, those seeking to replace aging buildings with progressive new modern ones versus those urging their preservation in the fight over the Grand Central, were Boisi and Haskell. In calling for Grand Central Terminal's preservation, Haskell was not alone, nor was the terminal the only historic building being threatened at the time. In 1959, Philip Johnson spoke out in defense of an 1890s Richardsonian Romanesque post office in Omaha, Nebraska, which was threatened with demolition to make way for a new ten-story federal post office;[43] several years later the *Forum* ran an article on A. B. Mullett's 1860s post office in St. Louis, which was then being threatened, urging preserving rather than demolishing "used" buildings.[44] Even as concern for the nation's dwindling architectural heritage grew, however, threats to the integrity of the Grand Central Terminal continued, with the New York Central filling the terminal's interior space with concessions, television screens, and Kodak signs, and then proposing bowling alleys. All this fanned the fires of preservationists. Then came the controversy over Penn Station.

A front-page article in the *New York Times* in July 1961 announced plans for a new Madison Square Garden project, to be built on the Penn Station site.[45] The plans called for replacing the 1910 McKim, Mead & White Pennsylvania Station with a $75 million "garden and entertainment center" by architect Charles Luckman.[46] With the threat to the Grand Central ever present, preservationist forces were primed. Among the first to react, reflecting undoubtedly the presence of Huxtable, was the *New York Times,* with an editorial on the imminent demolition of the station, describing it as "a tragic loss."[47] The Committee for the Preservation of Historic and Aesthetic Structures was established; it was later disbanded, and in April 1962, a permanent twelve-member Landmarks Preservation Commission was appointed—too late, however, to save Penn Station.[48] The Action Group for Better Architecture in New York (AGBANY) was formed the following August to protest the demolition of the "venerable neo-classic structure."[49] Another *Times* editorial addressed the demolition of Penn Station and the formation of the protest group. "One of the city's strangest and most heartening picket lines appeared in New York recently. It wound its way around Pennsylvania Station led by upper-echelon architectural professionals carrying signs of protest [against the demolition of the station] to make way for a $90 million redevelopment scheme of dubious grandeur. The marchers were members of Action Group for Better Architecture in New York, local counterpart of Britain's Anti-Uglies. They call themselves AGBANY, which sounds a lot like agony, the state of mind of many over current changes in the New York scene." The demonstration was joined by about twenty leaders in the architectural field, including designers of some of the city's newest buildings. What they were protesting at the moment was the increasing loss of New York's irreplaceable architectural past through irresponsible speculative building. "If professionals find the situation serious enough for this kind of action, something is very wrong," the *Times* asserted. "With minimum controls, New York's builders are well on the way to turning the city into a bottomless—and topless—morass of mediocrity." With the all-but-completed steel frame of the Pan Am Building towering over the Grand Central several blocks away, the magnitude of what could happen was obvious. Something can and should be done, the *Times* concluded. It applauded the appointment of the Landmarks Preservation Commission, which it urged to take a clear position on threatened buildings of historic or artistic, as opposed to strictly economic, value: "Progress and change involve more than profit and loss. The city's investors and planners have aesthetic as well as economic responsibilities. New Yorkers do not lack civic pride. If AGBANY springs to the barricades the public will not be far behind."[50]

There were more editorials, including Haskell's in *Architectural Forum,* reminding readers what had almost happened to the Grand Central and urging constructive measures to prevent further losses.[51] To the surprise of few, in February 1963, the New York City Planning Commission approved the Madison Square Garden Corporation's redevelopment plans for the Penn Station area. All that remained for the project to go ahead was the final ruling of the City Board of Estimate.[52] The following month, as the *Forum* put it, "the crash of the wrecker's ball was heard across the land, and the sound was accompanied by cries of outrage," which were growing in volume. Out of the effort to preserve several old buildings, a new public consensus was emerging that Americans were not totally committed to erasing their architectural past. In New York, however, Penn Station appeared lost, as the city granted approval to tear down the old building for the proposed sports arena and office-building complex. The City Planning Commission contended that it was powerless to weigh the value of the old building against that of the new, and under existing ordinances could only decide whether the new building was justifiable per se in terms of public revenue, traffic problems, and the like. An incensed band of architects and cultural leaders stormed the public hearings but "were armed only with idealism," the *Forum* noted, "a commodity not listed in the city budget."[53]

Meanwhile, with a clear impact on the historic Grand Central site, the Pan Am was nearing completion, Belluschi was voicing his antipreservationist views, and Gropius was contending that Penn Station was "a case of pseudo-tradition . . . only a throwback to the empty mannerism inspired by the dependence of the American businessman on European prototypes of the so-called 'ageless masterpieces,'" and not worth saving.[54]

PHILIP JOHNSON

Johnson, whom Huxtable identified as "a top tastemaker" and "a powerful influence in the market place where all cultural styles wind up," played an important role in the historic preservation fracas.[55] He and Belluschi were long-standing adversaries who had squared off in the early 1950s in a Yale symposium on architectural practice and the responsibilities of the architect, with Johnson coming down on the side of the *art* of architecture, Belluschi on the side of its practical and social functions.[56] Their views continued to polarize throughout the Pan Am controversy, with Johnson firmly on the side of preserving the Grand Central, Belluschi indifferent or opposed to it.[57] The enmity between Johnson and Gropius was no less intense. A year after the Pan Am debate at the New School and several weeks after the framing of the Pan Am Building had begun, Johnson presented his views on the changing architectural scene in "The International Style—Death or Metamorphosis," an address sponsored by the Architectural League of New York at the Metropolitan Museum of Art.[58] As Robert Stern, then a young New York architect and Johnson disciple who had written a thesis in architectural history under Scully at Yale, was years later to maintain, Johnson articulated the differences between "two streams of late modernism, commercialized Miesian and the brutalized Corbusian," and between a native pragmatism and European idealism. Johnson's talk was, according to Stern, also an endorsement of historicism, a return to the history spurned by the Modern Movement. It was, he said, expressive of Johnson's desire to *épater* the masters of the Modern Movement, Walter Gropius in particular. Gropius's antihistorical biases, his naive belief in program-as-form-generator, and his philosophy of materialistic as well as social progress were not only crippling to his students at Harvard, Stern wrote in his commentary on Johnson's talk years later, but also grossly contradicted in his own highly commercialized practice, as typified by his use of "onion domes" in the University of Baghdad complex and his elaborate circumlocutions in defense of his very mediocre Pan Am Building.[59] Johnson's talk was in fact far more mild than Stern's comments, published in 1979, suggest. Johnson mentioned Gropius only briefly in his 1961 address, in the context of what the founders of European modernism were currently doing, maintaining that Gropius had "kept to International Style architecture with his team until recently, when we have onion domes . . . in the Moslem mode, part of a much larger neo-Historicism which is all over the country."[60] Johnson made no mention here of the Pan Am Building or of a "commercialized Miesian" trend, which appear to be part of Stern's retrospective editorializing.

Johnson's views on Gropius and modernism were indicative nonetheless of changing attitudes toward the architecture of the past, a change with which both Gropius and Belluschi were out of touch. Writing to European scholar Jürgen Joedicke later that year, Johnson challenged the modernist notion of structural honesty, attacked its moral basis, and suggested the entire Modern Movement was "winding up its days."[61] Elsewhere, Johnson was more explicit about his views of the Pan Am, calling it "oppressive" and an example of "distressing visual ugliness and ungraceful cost accounting functionalism."[62]

HUXTABLE AND OTHERS ON PRESERVATION

Advocate of modernism that she was, Huxtable, too, was quick to embrace the preservationist cause. An article in the fall of 1961, citing the interior of the Grand Central Terminal as one of the nation's "near misses" in the fight to preserve the city's architectural legacy, was devoted to saving New York City monuments. Preservation, Huxtable argued, would sustain "those values without which a city becomes a sterile and unattractive place: a sense of history, the retention of local personality and color, the presence of familiar landmarks, and the pleasure of esthetic variety and richness in the architectural scene." She called for a judicious mixture of old and new and said the city needed laws "through which buildings or neighborhoods of permanent value are acknowledged and protected"; otherwise, preservation was "left at the mercy of competitive economics."[63] As the article appeared not long after Huxtable's "Marvel or Monster" article on the Gropius/Belluschi proposal for the Grand Central site, in which she had pointed out how little creative room the architects had been allowed because of competitive economics, her allusions were clear.

Haskell, whose own views on the merits of the Grand Central and Penn Station were equally clear, similarly continued to speak out on issues of historic preservation. In an address at the annual meeting of the National Trust for Historic Preservation held later that fall, he applauded the meeting, "Preservation Planning for the City of Tomorrow," as it was high time the historic-preservation movement looked to the future as well as the past, and pointed out the importance of preservation in economic terms, as it constituted a major part of the total construction program in the United States. Characteristically assuming a broad perspective, he stressed the importance of cultural and physical continuity: "In the tight times ahead when we have so many other burdens to bear, the U.S. can no longer afford the inefficiency of its totally unrelated past building efforts. Individuals must continue to reign, but an individualism in sensible voluntary agreement that there has to be leadership and continuity."[64] It was the absence of a civic consciousness, an awareness of the city's cultural heritage and its past as well as its economic future, that Haskell, as he later made clear, found so deplorably lacking in Wolfson's vision and the Pan Am Building project as a whole.

Architectural Forum, which was revived in 1965 after its demise in 1964, continued to be a leading force in preservation issues in the 1960s, warning readers about the threat to the 1890 Reliance Building in Chicago, an architectural landmark that was proving uneconomical, as well as Irving Gill's 1916 Dodge House in Los Angeles, whose future looked grim unless a "more economic" use for the land it occupied was found.[65]

Meanwhile, as the wrecking ball continued to swing, the staff of the Landmarks Preservation Commission began compiling a list of New York buildings for a comprehensive architectural history of the city and recommended landmarks legislation to protect the city's architectural heritage. It recognized, however, that until such legislation was passed, its work was no more than lip service.[66]

Protective legislation was finally approved in 1965, providing the New York City Landmarks Preservation Commission established in 1962, legislative teeth. "Landmarks are not merely a matter of interest to historians and antiquarians," the report recommending the legislation read. "They are the heritage of all the people and provide the inspiration for civic pride and respect, the foundation of good citizenship. For the preservation of this heritage certain limitations on private property rights are proposed in the public interest and for the public welfare." Just as zoning represented the exercise of a sovereign power over individual interests, so it was proposed "to protect the public interest in our common heritage."[67] The wording the report used, echoing much of the "private rights versus public interest" rhetoric generated by the controversy over the Pan Am Building, was telling. Telling, too, was the fact that in 1967, the first building the Landmarks Preservation Commission designated, providing it with legal protection against alteration or demolition, was Grand Central Terminal.[68]

Less than a year later, in 1968, Penn Central, owners of the Grand Central Terminal after the New York Central merged with the Pennsylvania Railroad the same year in what was, at the time, the largest corporate marriage in business history, wanting to enhance still further the revenues of the valuable mid-Manhattan site, announced plans to build a second tower in the airspace over the Grand Central. The $1 million, fifty-five-story tower with just under two million square feet, to be designed by Marcel Breuer and backed by British developer Morris Saady, was to be located directly above the terminal, just behind its landmark 42nd Street facade (figure 6.8).[69] Penn Central's plans brought an outcry from architects and preservationists, who believed a second tower would amount to an even greater desecration of the Grand Central than the Pan Am. With the Landmarks Preservation Commission's landmark designation blocking their plans on the grounds that the new tower would compromise the terminal's landmark stature, Penn Central and its allied real estate interests sued. After a decade-long succession of court cases that pitted the proponents of the Breuer-designed tower against preservationists, in 1978 the U.S. Supreme Court upheld the city's position, protecting the Grand Central and validating the landmark law.

The story of the proposed tower and its eventual defeat—the railroad company's increasing financial problems, its negotiations with Saady, Breuer's design, the series of court battles, Breuer's redesign of the tower, and finally the U.S. Supreme Court decision upholding the landmark status of the building—has been told before and need not be repeated here except as it bears on the Pan Am.[70] Among the Landmarks Preservation documents prepared in the process of securing the landmark design was a report on the Grand Central Terminal that maintained that the terminal exemplified "more completely than any other building in New York City all the elements that comprise the best of the Beaux-Arts style of architecture."[71] Pointing out the importance of the terminal's location—at the heart of the city and exposed to thousands of people who passed through it daily—the report said the that the terminal was, in a literal sense, "the gateway to New York City," a symbol of civic pride, a tourist attraction, and the focus of one of the most vital centers of business and commerce in the world. The document described the Beaux-Arts style, its history and importance, and the building itself—its rich sculptural ensemble crowning its main entrance on 42nd Street, providing the building a compositional climax and giving it its expressiveness. The facade was, in essence "a triumphal Roman archway" which faced down the long axis of Park

FIGURE 6.8   Marcel Breuer tower proposal, 1968

Avenue and expressed the idea of "welcome." It opened onto the great waiting room, the report noted, which itself served as an introduction to something still bigger beyond, the main concourse. The third element of the composition, according to the document, before the Pan Am Building was built, had been a discreet colonnaded 6-story office building housing administrative offices extending northward over the tracks (figure 6.9); its low profile, however, had been replaced "by the overpowering mass of the Pan Am Building," the report went on to point out. Analyzing the building's multileveled circulation, which it said represented "one of the world's great triumphs in the solution of an extremely intricate problem of circulation" and its urban planning, the report told of how New York Central had been able, at the time the building was constructed, to plan a group of well-related, highly profitable hotels and office buildings that not only provided a visual enframement for the great terminal but also supplied an auxiliary income to the railroad. In language suggesting Haskell's involvement, the report said the Grand Central marked a fine balance "between public responsibility and maximum acquisitiveness, later upset by the erection of the Pan Am Building." Wholly out of scale and character with its surroundings, the Pan Am destroyed, the report asserted, what had until then been one of the few monumental vistas in the city: the view down Park Avenue. "If the view up Park Avenue towards the Grand Central Terminal still carries the message of 'welcome,' the view down Park Avenue towards the Pan Am Building states unmistakably, 'the public be damned.'"

Monumentality, the document observed, was not synonymous with bigness. Monumentality resulted from the handling of scale, relating the size of the building to the size of the human being, and in so doing exalted the viewer. Regarding terminal vistas, the report pointed out that New York City had few of them because of the uninterrupted grid plan of most of its streets. Most street views led on indefinitely, into infinity. Trinity Church at the head of Wall Street was one exception; the triumphal south facade of the Grand Central, filling the full 140-foot width of Park Avenue and visible from a mile away, was another. The report concluded with a comment on the Landmarks Preservation Commission of New York City, which was now responsible for the designation and protection of buildings of historical or aesthetic interest, which had been found to be "a matter of public necessity, among other purposes, to safeguard the city's cultural heritage."[72]

This cultural heritage, the report said, had been compromised by the Pan Am Building. It was, for the city, a bitter lesson.[73]

FIGURE 6.9   Grand Central Terminal and Grand Central Office Building, with New York Central Building tower in the background

HASKELL'S ROLE

Preserving the Grand Central Terminal had long been one of Haskell's major crusades. From his 1954 "Save the Concourse" campaign, embarked on shortly after he joined *Architectural Forum* as editor and carried on throughout the bowling alley debacle, he continued to battle the railroads and their real estate profits. His 1963 essay "The Lost New York of the Pan American Airways Building" had focused on the marvel of the Grand Central Terminal, which had been denigrated by the Pan Am. As landmarks legislation got underway, Haskell remained closely involved. The son of Congregationalist missionaries, Haskell was infused with missionary zeal; his academic background—a bachelor's degree in political science, with a minor in the Fine Arts, active participation in debate and in his college's Liberal Club over which he presided his senior year— complemented this missionary inclination, preparing him for a prominent civic role.[74] He was also highly respected in architectural circles for his scholarship and the breadth of his knowledge: He contributed entries on architecture to the *Encyclopedia Britannica Yearbook* for a number of years and taught seminars at Columbia for seniors and graduate students in architecture and planning.[75] He had in the early 1960s planned to write a book on democracy and architecture, in which he intended "to pull together the results of 40 years of observation and reflection on what might be called the statesmanship of architecture." Had the book been written, Haskell's notes in the Haskell Papers, Avery Library, suggest, the case of the Pan Am Building, its effect on the city, on public morale, and on the Grand Central Terminal and historic preservation, would have loomed large.

"Long ago I found myself gravitating in thought toward the 'policy' side of architecture as a cultural undertaking," he wrote in a long, ardent letter to August Heckscher describing the planned book in March 1962, a year before his "Lost New York" article on the Pan Am. "As a young man I was among the first in America to join up with the twentieth-century modern architectural movement. Not only were its design concepts thrilling, but it seemed to have a chance to capture the country for a noble kind of building. Since then I have watched with distress how the purpose and the accomplishment have seemed to shrink and shrivel, at the very moment when opportunity seems greatest." How had it happened? he queried. "The destructive forces came from a quarter whence they were least expected. I have been a fighter for architecture myself, and down in the trenches. . . . The reason for struggling with 'democracy' is that the way architecture is commissioned today, and the way it has to be executed, and the kind of competition it must carry on with the other things which people may prefer to do, has so very much to do with the chance for quality. Sure, architectural genius has found its way through under all sorts of circumstances, and still does, but in architecture very little comes through without substantial patronage." With speculative buildings such as the Pan Am in mind, Haskell noted that most current building was not for institutions, but for an amorphous mass market served by builders who would never use or run their buildings under their own names and built them with other people's money "for faceless purchasers known only as statistical data."

"All my life as such new situations have manifested themselves," he continued, "I have been trying to find who, what, where, can be appealed to for what action that could redound to architecture's advantage. For my faith is quite sublime that architecture, that ancient love of mankind, will start putting itself through once again, more and more, because of its own intrinsic appeal, once we get it fairly mounted. As businessmen put it, the problem is leverage. Leverage to put the deal over, with plenty of 'exposure' to be sure, but with a fair chance for a handsome profit. And if democracy has done not always so well with architecture, let's remember that the problem is new." The book, he envisioned, would be "an experience record of battles lost or won," with or without his participation. New York's loss with the Pan Am, about which he was to write so fervently the following year, clearly weighed heavily on his mind.

Among the five elements Haskell believed needed to be considered in a discussion of architecture in a democracy were the building industry, the client, the architects (whose position, he said, was changing faster than they realized), the "persuaders" (which included everybody from newspapers and television down to grade-school teachers who could persuade people to "make this way or that way" with their architecture and their cities), and perhaps foremost: architecture's vision. "Never before" he said, "have ultimate aims been stateable so big and bravely, in terms of architecture qualifying all of mankind's man-made surroundings to make them into a noble setting; but never has achievement been further short of vision."[76] Haskell was one of the American journalists who as early as the late 1920s had followed closely and written about the avant-garde ideas emanating from the Bauhaus.[77] He himself had met Gropius even earlier, on a student tour in 1923, while the Bauhaus was still in Weimar, and had written about the powerful impact of its still-experimental educational system on his thinking.[78] He had continued to pin high hopes on the European modernist well into the 1950s and wrote ardently of Gropius's essays on architecture and democracy, with their noble aims and solid moral principles. On the other hand, by the early 1960s,

Haskell was also all too aware of the nobility of the Pan Am site, its rich cultural legacy, and the poverty of the vision of it in the postwar era, about which he was to write with such fervor the following year. He never wrote the book on democracy and architecture that he had planned; instead, he poured his passion and his own thoughts on the subject into the article on the Pan Am.

In his introduction to a panel discussion, "New Dimensions in Architectural Knowledge," at the annual AIA convention in Dallas several months later, Haskell reiterated a view he had articulated elsewhere: that others besides architects were responsible for architectural failures. Considering the tiny price of architectural services in the larger scheme of a building's costs, he maintained, the architecture that was produced was one of civilization's miracles. Though its costs were usually less even than the annual interest charges on building loans, architecture nonetheless made the difference between barbarism and culture, between haphazardness and planning, between surroundings barely fit to exist in and surroundings that reflected mankind's aspirations, and it had done this wherever allowed. Most of the time, however, economics blocked it from carrying out this function. The presence in Haskell's files of copies of a series of articles Manhattan realtor Daniel Friedenberg had published in the *New York Herald Tribune* in 1964, in which Wolfson and the Pan Am Building were cited time and again, as well as Haskell's own notes for the "Architecture and the Entrepreneur" course he was teaching at Columbia, indicate that the Pan Am figured prominently in his thinking on the subject.

Architecture was "being blamed for an ever-spreading cancer of non-architecture," he told the AIA. But architecture was effecting only half a revolution, he said, because it neglected building economics—not simply costs and budgets, but economic factors on a much larger scale. Great chunks of the American environment had slipped out of the architect's control (a conclusion, it should be remembered, that had been drawn from the New School debate on the Pan Am the previous year). In large measure, he observed, this was because economic control was shifting away from client as owner to client as managers, employees, and business technicians working with other people's money. "Under the heading of 'private,'" he noted, "we have the new entrepreneur, the canner of office space under 100% financing. These people operate with an apparatus of leases, leasebacks, overlapping commitments, separate sales of land and buildings which are physically inseparable, syndicates, the swapping depreciation accounts." Responsibility and decision making were dispersed and hidden; financing was fragmented and floated on vast pools of accumulated savings, the control of which lay again not with the owner, but with banks and insurance companies. The issue hinged not on the "so-called question of taste" or architectural quality, but on money. "My contention to you," Haskell concluded, "is that so long as architecture deals only in a haphazard way with this revolutionary new world of economics, it will continue to get a beating"[79]—which is exactly what Haskell believed had happened with the Pan Am.

Haskell's choice not to mention the Pan Am specifically in his AIA talk may have been more than simple professional discretion, as the month before, Wolfson had been diagnosed with the cancer that was to kill him two months later. But that Wolfson, the Pan Am, and Haskell's high hopes for the project were indeed on Haskell's mind at the time is suggested by a letter Haskell sent to Landauer in July 1962, conveying his condolences on Wolfson's death. They at *Architectural Forum* had been fond of Wolfson, he said, adding "It's a sad thing not to have him around as a guy you kept hoping would do better."[80]

Haskell took a leave of absence as editor of the *Forum* following his "Lost New York" article on the Pan Am in 1963. The Pan Am by that time was a fact, a physical presence that he and other New Yorkers lamented but now had to live with. Its presence drove home a hard lesson, however, and he wanted it well learned. He remained involved in architectural issues, and as the threat to the Grand Central Terminal cropped up again in the later 1960s with the Penn Central's proposal for the Breuer tower, Haskell poured his energies into retaining what was left of the old Beaux-Arts building's original integrity. His passion remained undiminished. In February 1968, as the battle with Penn Central over the second tower heated up, urban designer Frank Williams published an article on the Grand Central City in the newly revived *Architectural Forum* as part of an issue devoted to urban transportation.[81] The article left Haskell fuming, as in his mind Williams addressed solely the issue of circulation, ignoring the other, more urgent and more serious part of the Grand Central story. Nor did it make any mention of the *Fo-*

rum's role in the preservation of the Grand Central Terminal or of Haskell's "Lost New York" article, in which he had traced the history of the Grand Central concept, pointing out not simply the analogy between the Grand Central and what the Futurist Sant' Elia had done in Italy several years later, but also the likely historical connection between the two, underscoring the Grand Central's significance not just to current New Yorkers but to history and an understanding of the historical process.

Williams had focused on the 1913 Grand Central as a laudable example of urban transportation, applauded the heliport currently perched on top of the tower built atop the 1913 station, and portrayed the Pan Am as an addition to the Grand Central that in some ways might have aggravated foot traffic but had also improved it; moreover, he accepted the still-contested, yet-to-be-approved Breuer proposal for yet another tower over the Grand Central as inevitable. His detached, uncritical approach, which ignored so much cultural history, infuriated Haskell, who expected more of the magazine in which he had so much invested. Lacking was any discussion of the ethical issues the Pan Am had raised, as well as any sense of history. "The famous Grand Central Concourse would not even be in existence today," he wrote *Forum* in protest, "had there not been imaginative, creative, thoughtful and strenuous work by a number of people to see to it that at least the shell of this magnificent facility be preserved. It needed to be retained somehow, to await the time when the proprietors would at last wake up to railroading as their primary business and to the obligation toward urban progress that is involved in moneymaking on a prime public building site." This, to Haskell, was the main *moral* point in the Grand Central story that could not be ignored. And if one accepted the "latest projected debasement of the Terminal itself—again with the assistance of a high-standing architect as before" as a fait accompli, as Williams seemed to, the job still remained, Haskell said, of getting the Penn Central operation "to re-establish the Grand Central City dream in modern terms, instead of simply aiding the enrichment of owners who are giving foreign speculators a chance to destroy New York a little more."[82] Furious, and disillusioned with the *Forum*, Haskell redirected his energies elsewhere and turned to preservation.

Haskell remained involved throughout the long Landmarks Preservation Commission battle to have the landmark designation of the Grand Central upheld, consistently couching his concerns not in narrow stylistic terms, such as "modernism" or "Beaux-Arts" or "postmodernism" (which was, at that point, several years after Venturi's *Complexity and Contradiction in Architecture* was published, still embryonic), but in terms of the larger issues—moral, economic, social, political, cultural—involved in architecture in the broadest sense. As the tumultuous decade drew to a close, well aware of how important the subject was, he wrote Fitch, whom he had talked to about doing a book on Grand Central, to say that he was pleased that "a real architectural historian" was going to write up the whole Grand Central story, as much of it seemed in danger of being lost. He filled Fitch in on what had transpired while he was editor of the *Forum,* provided him with references, gave him copies of Friedenberg's articles in the *Herald Tribune* on the economic value of the Grand Central area, "Manhattan's real gold mine," the civic responsibility the railroads were shirking in pursuing real estate profits rather than addressing the problems of running the railroad, and the *cultural* role the Grand Central played in the history of the city as well as architectural history. As there was a great deal more to the story, he promised to send Fitch "a full memo," if Fitch needed.[83]

The case of the Grand Central Terminal and Pan Am's role in it, as the two were irrevocably intertwined in his thinking, remained a pressing concern for Haskell throughout the 1970s. In a letter to attorney James Nespole, he demanded, with obvious indignation, "Why the hell does Penn Central et al. enjoy the *only* piece of land that straddles what was formerly a major thoroughfare (formerly Fourth Avenue, now Park Avenue)?" An old map of 1879 Haskell had found suggested that the first Grand Central Station did not straddle Fourth Avenue but was alongside it to the west, as was the yard. "The only excuse for *anybody* being allowed to straddle a major avenue and thus gain special privilege was that it was a *public utility.* I don't know the legalities," Haskell wrote, "but obviously the public utility was the city's purpose. It was *not* the purpose to give a favored group the chance to put up three skyscrapers in a row blocking the thoroughfare more and more and more. Maybe there is something legal you could make of this. A public utility that scandalously neglects its public utility job is not to be rewarded with miscellaneous real estate profits. And the profits made on Pan Am have improved railroad service not one whit, but only enriched the directors."[84] To him the issue was clearly a matter of civic responsibility, of the moral obligations involved in privately owned public space.

Haskell continued his campaign to preserve Grand Central Terminal until the end of his life. The long, carefully crafted testimony he prepared but was not allowed to make before the Grand Central preservation hearings in the spring of 1972 argued on behalf of the terminal's *meaning,* as part of a great civic transportation concept operating together with Park Avenue, which he felt would be destroyed, rendered meaningless by the proposed Breuer tower. He again focused his attack on the railroad with which the city had shared its streets. In exchange for letting the railroad use valuable city property, the city had the moral and aesthetic right to expect that the railroad should perform not only efficiently, but safely and agreeably, in its public-utility role.[85] "There is tremendous special reason, your Honor," he wrote in another draft, "why the full duty of the railroads, from the very start, was to make their terminal building both aesthetically and practically a building of pronounced civic character, non-discriminatory, and public-service, not private enterprise use. The reason is that the public made to the railroads an enormous gift to that end. The city allowed the railroads to block a major public thoroughfare."[86]

He delivered a talk on the subject at the College Art Association in 1973, then dealt with it again in a long article in the London *Architectural Review* the following year.[87] Describing the long, rich history of the Grand Central, the sinking of the tracks, the first depot, electrification and the brilliance of Wilgus's invention, and the Grand Central City concept, which combined convenience with beauty, he pointed out that in the days when the Grand Central Terminal was conceived and built, "the citizen was a King." Though not all could afford to live in the luxurious apartments that lined Park Avenue, anyone could walk through the station complex with its grand vistas and stately promenades. It was, in his words, "a Palais du Départ, a Palais d'Arrivée, a Palais de Vivre—architecture as a celebration, lifting up the ordinary daily sensible facts of life." Then, as the railroads' income faded and rent control knocked the economic base from under the Park Avenue Gold Coast, imagination too seemed to flee. And with the Pan Am Building, Haskell concluded, things changed again, the original concept of the Grand Central City was lost, and with it the sense of civic grandeur it had brought to the area it occupied.

THE LATE 1960s

The Grand Central was by this time a nationally recognized public arena in the heart of nation. Just as thousands had jammed into the Grand Central concourse to view John Glenn lift off into space in February 1962, so too in the late 1960s, the concourse served as a forum for a newly emerging political activism. It was there in the concourse's cavernous space that three thousand "chanting youths" met in March 1968, signaling a new militancy among demonstrators against the war in Vietnam (figure 6.10). Whereas the demonstrators had hitherto been seen as peace-loving dropouts alienated from life and aimlessly "doing their thing," policemen, clergymen, and social workers now sensed a new militancy on the part of youth. Allen Ginsberg, "the bearded poet, guru

FIGURE 6.10   Demonstrators and police in Grand Central concourse, March 1968

and cultural hero of many hippies," denied, in a *New York Times* article about the growing activism, that being a hippie meant a complete withdrawal from life. "These people are simply seeking another form of social cooperation," he said of the new crop of political activists. "They are trying to start a utopian society, in the midst of a locked-in, technological society."[88] "What sphinx of cement and aluminum bashed open their skulls and ate up their brains and imagination? Moloch! Solitude! Filth! Ugliness!" he had written over a decade earlier, as work on the Pan Am began.[89]

It was a sign of the times, a poet's finger on the pulse of the times. By the late 1960s, youth riots coupled with police violence were regular fare in the news, polarizing public sympathy between a rebellious young and the conservative backlash that resulted from their outbursts.[90]

As the raucous dispute over the railroad's plans for the Breuer tower above the Grand Central continued, Huxtable spoke up, pointing out that the new tower would stand just 221 feet south of the Pan Am Building and rival it in size and impact on the city scene. "The latest Fun City Special is a project for a $100 million, 55-story building to sit on top of the Grand Central Terminal—a bizarre scheme that could only be conceived in and for New York. . . . The architectural curiosity may seem like an unreal or surreal super-Pop vision, but it is actually superreality, New York style. Reality in this case consists of the following ingredients: the apparently insatiable demand for expensive office buildings, the astronomical value of air rights in midtown Manhattan, the financial troubles of the Penn Central Railroad and its desire to capitalize on the air rights over the terminal as a real estate investment, and the terminal's status as a protected landmark."[91]

"Hitler's Revenge," a fiery article by Sibyl Moholy-Nagy in *Art in America* that fall, also lambasted the Breuer proposal, this time drawing Gropius and the Pan Am Building into the fray.[92] Subtitled "The Grand Central Tower Project Has Dramatized the Horrors Inflicted on Our Cities in the Name of Bauhaus Design," her lively, strident essay recalled the lofty ideology of German functionalism, with its roots in Ruskinian morality, and of its transformation on American soil as it swept through American architecture schools, with a whole new curriculum based on mass production. "In 1933 Hitler shook the tree and America picked up the fruit of German genius," she began. As in the best of Satanic traditions, some of this fruit was poisoned, although it looked at first sight to be pure and wholesome. "The lethal harvest was functionalism, and the Johnnies who spread the appleseed were the Bauhaus masters Walter Gropius, Mies van der Rohe, and Marcel Breuer. . . . The function of German functionalism was ideology. In a straight line of descent from Ruskin's 'morality in architecture,' Gropius's Bauhaus

Manifesto of 1919 called for 'the new building of the future . . . which will rise toward heaven as a crystalline symbol of a new future faith," she wrote. By the time the Bauhaus was closed in 1933, the "building as prophetic" idea had undergone a radical transformation. Gropius identified functionalism with anonymous teamwork "relating only to the life of the people"; Mies celebrated technology, indifferent to the fate of the individual, as the only valid architectural expression of the zeitgeist, and Breuer, carrying the functionalist torch into the second Bauhaus generation, spoke of seeking the typical, the norm, relying on scientific principle and logical analysis. Hannes Meyer, Gropius's successor as Bauhaus leader, summed it up, she said: "'Building is social, technological, economic, psychological organization, product of the formula: function times economy.'"

Bearers of "this peculiar brand of ideological pragmatism" had arrived in the United States at an auspicious moment, Moholy-Nagy maintained. The Depression had shaken the newly won self-confidence of the United States and revived the hereditary national disease of looking for imported solutions. A gradual realization spread that the careless boom-and-bust times were over and that organized skill and research were needed to guide manpower and urban reconstruction. Architecture schools, she noted, were still mired at the time in nineteenth-century Beaux-Arts academism. The new functionalism entered America through university appointments, with Harvard, MIT, and the Illinois Institute of Technology establishing through their European design teachers a totally new curriculum that was eminently mass-producible.

Perhaps America would have awakened to the plain paucity of actual buildings turned out under this formula by Mies van der Rohe and the Gropius-Breuer team, she theorized, had the financial straits of the 1930s continued. But after the nonbuilding war years, the greatest building and speculation boom since the 1850s sent city cores sprouting upward. Architecture schools proliferated as the building tide spread across the continent, their curricula derived from the Harvard program, which combined, she maintained, three unbeatable prestiges: Ivy league pedigree, a genuinely imported ideology, and the adaptability of a credit card system: Everything that was "functional" could be charged to Harvard. The Gropius TAC team, "so anonymous that it has left to its leader the glaring spotlight of world publicity," Moholy-Nagy continued, "dutifully turned its pencils in the same groove of a stuck conceptual record." But it was only fitting that Breuer, youngest of the "Grauhäusler," should present to the world an apotheosis of the functionalist era. The Grand Central tower he had designed, she said, "has the architectural relevance of a Harvard Design Thesis of 1940. . . . And now, across the generation gap of a mere city block the disciple shouts at his old master, who commit-ted the Pan Am Building, that he can be more functional at any time—no facetious hexagonal facets to relieve the 309 by 950 by 152 feet concrete pullover—and he cares even less for 'regional' environment. While the Pan Am discreetly hides its feet of con-crete block behind arcades, the Saady-Breuer teamwork crushes the last remnant of the past era of extroverted design responsibility under the monstrous load of profit dic-tatorship." A typical Moholy-Nagy bombastic blast, it was also revealing of changing at-titudes toward modernism at the time.

As attitudes toward modernism continued to shift, so too did those toward privately owned public spaces, questions about which had been raised by the Grand Central/Pan Am controversy at the beginning of the decade. In April 1969, architect Arthur C. Holden published a pamphlet, "The Lessons Learned from the Threat to Grand Cen-tral," based on his testimony at a public hearing before the Landmarks Preservation Commission the same month.[93] The case of the Grand Central had importance beyond the question of demolition, he asserted in the document. In addition to aesthetics, it in-volved the nature of ownership of property, especially real property. As monuments of historic value were being torn down, disillusioned New Yorkers were at a loss as to what to do about it. The purpose of legislation authorizing municipalities to set up land-marks preservation commissions, he noted, was "to give statutory recognition to the fact that a public interest exists in objects of art and beauty, and that no owner who may come into temporary possession may destroy without public consent, the historic or esthetic values of an object or site designated by a competent authority as worthy of preservation in the public interest."

Pointing out that American individualism had peaked in the last quarter of the nine-teenth century, Holden delved into the underlying principles that had established the right to private ownership and control of real property, going back in history to the ori-gins of the feudal system, evolution of property rights in the United States, American individualism, and the concept of land ownership. In the United States, he said, the state, representing the people, had taken over the fundamental position of a feudal lord with discretionary power. This was the issue, he asserted, on which the fate of the Grand Central Terminal depended. Beyond the question of the preservation of a single building, it had to do with the right to exploit real property for the owner's private ad-vantage, a right, Holden pointed out, claimed as one of the most fundamental rights of an American citizen. (This, it might be remembered, was Gropius's claim—that citizens have the right to go as far as they want within the letter of the law—which he articulated at the New School debate over the Pan Am Building in 1960.) It is not, however, and never has been, Holden maintained, a right that is not subject to abridgement for the general good of the community. The transient owner or controller of a parcel of property does not possess the right to exploit real property to the detriment of the public interest that continues to reside in all real property and for which the American state of the time, as theoretical successor to the feudal lord, was bailor or protector. By refusing to participate in intelligent planning, Holden concluded, the Penn Central Railroad had, in the case of the Grand Central, defied those public rights that reside in all property.

What might be seen as particularly significant about Holden's essay, apart from its implications for New York Central's pursuit of its Grand Central City development in 1960 despite widespread public opposition, were Holden's comments about "transient owners." Already by this time, Trippe, who had acquired 10 percent of the stock in the Pan Am Building as part of his negotiating package with Wolfson in 1960, had been quietly increasing his ownership interest in the building, buying an additional 45 percent from the Jack Cotton estate in 1968. The company was to buy out the rest, as well as purchase the three and a half acres of land on which the building stood, from the Penn Central Corporation, a decade later.[94] It was an ownership transfer loaded with symbolism, from the then bankrupt Penn Central Railroad to Pan American World Airways, the nation's fourth-largest airline and one of the biggest in the world. Ironically, Pan American was itself to go bankrupt in turn, and two years later would be forced to sell the building.

SALE OF THE BUILDING

In February 1980, Pan American World Airways, whose fortunes had waned under the influence of Trippe's brash spending, a slack economy, the financial environment of the airline industry in general at the time, and then government deregulation of the industry in 1978, announced it might sell its headquarters building.[95] Close to a decade earlier in the early 1970s, at a time of a soft office-leasing market in Manhattan, Penn Central had put up for sale twenty-three properties and buildings in the Grand Central area, a sign of its increasing financial woes. The Grand Central Terminal itself was not for sale, as the railroad, which had filed for bankruptcy the previous year, planned to continue its railroad operations; the 1.7 million square feet of prime air rights above the building, however, were. Among the properties up for sale were New York City landmarks such as the Waldorf-Astoria Hotel, the Yale Club, and the Pan Am Building.[96] In 1978, Pan American, which by then had acquired 55 percent of the stock of the building, bought up the remainder mostly from the Wolfson estate and at the same time purchased the land the building occupied from the Penn Central Corporation.[97]

In contemplating the sale of the building two years later, the company announced its intention, however, to remain in and possibly expand its offices in the building. The building, still the world's largest private office building, which originally had cost $115 million to build, had recently been assessed to have a value of $93 million. The company's asking price for the building had not yet been set.[98]

In May of that year, the Pan Am Building was put up for sale in what was seen as one of the biggest deals of the time. Calling the building "one of midtown Manhattan's most conspicuous landmarks," *Business Week* quoted the price as likely to exceed $200 million, believing the sale would test where the real estate equity market was headed—specifically, how badly the turmoil in the financial markets at the time and the spreading recession would reverse a two-year spree of rising prices and lower investor yields for properties. The Pan Am Building (as well as certain regional shopping centers) were, in *Business Week*'s words, "the kind of high-quality properties that top institutional investors scramble to get."[99]

Two months later, it was announced that the Metropolitan Life Insurance Company would acquire the building for a $400 million, a record price at the time. The sale was major news (figure 6.11). According to William T. Seawell, who had taken over as chairman of Pan American after a series of weak successors to Trippe, who had stepped down from the position in 1968, the company planned to use some of the proceeds from the sale to retire part of its debt, which at that point totaled $874 million. Pan Am would stay in New York and continue occupying at least 350,000 square feet of the building, which would remain its headquarters. The building would also retain the Pan Am name as well as the airline's logo. Metropolitan Life, which bought the building as an investment and a hedge against inflation, did not intend to occupy the building but planned to modernize the concourse, lobby, elevators and other public areas (those portions, it might be remembered, that Gropius had designed). Metropolitan Life was one of nine candidates (another of which was Donald Trump) in the opening round of bidding for the building, which was in the range of $325 to $350 million. A key factor in the record price was the strong outlook for the office rental market at the time. Perhaps a more significant factor, was New York City's recently announced plan to rezone parts of midtown Manhattan to reduce the allowable density of construction, which would restrict the size of future buildings in the area, thus making existing buildings more valuable.[100]

Metropolitan Life Plans to Acquire Pan Am Building for $400 Million

The New York Times/Chester Higgins Jr.

The Pan Am Building

Price Apparently a Record — Airline Is Preparing to Retire Some of Debt

By ERIC PACE

Pan American World Airways announced yesterday that it had reached preliminary agreement to sell the Pan Am Building on Park Avenue for about $400 million to the Metropolitan Life Insurance Company. The price was reported to be the highest ever for a single building.

Pan Am's chairman, William T. Seawell, said his company planned to use part of the proceeds from the sale, which would be completed about the first of next year, to retire part of its debt. The company's current liabilities total $874 million, a Pan Am spokesman said.

Mr. Seawell said Pan Am, which has been operating at a loss, had not decided how to invest the rest. But he suggested that it might put part of the money into two subsidiaries — the Inter-Continental Hotels Corporation and Pan American World Services Inc., which offers aviation, engineering and other services.

A strong outlook for the office rental market was a key factor in the price for the Pan Am Building, according to Manhattan real estate experts. [Page D4.]

The Pan Am Building will retain its name, Mr. Seawell said, and it will still bear the airline's nickname emblazoned high on its angular exterior. Pan Am is to

Continued on Page D4, Column 2

FIGURE 6.11   Front-page article on sale of the Pan Am Building, *New York Times,* July 29, 1980

John R. White, a real estate expert and chairman of Landauer Associates, which had become by this time an international consulting company specializing in the real estate transactions of large corporations, negotiated the deal. He maintained that the price, the largest ever for a single building in recorded history, was a reflection of the building's "unusual size." The sale price of $400 million worked out to $177 per square foot, also a record, largely reflecting the fact that leases for about half of the space in the building would be coming up for renewal in 1983 and 1984. As a point of comparison, the *New York Times* cited another Park Avenue landmark, the Seagram Building, which had sold the previous February for $85.5 million, or $135 a square foot.[101]

Aviation Week also carried the news of the sale. One condition of the transaction, it pointed out, was that the building would retain its name so long as Pan American remained a principal tenant. Though Seawell had refused to say what the corporation would do with the (before taxes) cash infusion of $340 million it expected to gain from the sale, it needed it to balance its books. Pan American was a troubled company, and part of a troubled industry. The company's net loss had been $66.3 million in the second quarter of 1980, a loss the corporation blamed primarily on the escalating cost of fuel and on the company's inability, in accordance with U.S. law, to implement fare increases in international markets to offset those costs. According to the *Aviation* Week article, Metropolitan Life technically would acquire the Pan Am Building and the underlying land by acquiring all the stock of Grand Central Building, Inc., by this time a wholly owned subsidiary of Pan American.[102]

An article in *Time* the following month confirmed the sale. "The rumors that real estate prices might have peaked received a setback last week," the article began, "when Pan American World Airways announced it was selling its octagonal tower that looms over Park Avenue for $400 million, the largest price ever paid for a single urban building." Metropolitan Life, which the article noted was the nation's second biggest insurance company, had been pouring large chunks of its $46 billion in assets into real estate as a hedge against inflation. Large institutional investors like pension funds and insurance companies had been looking closely at big-city office real estate, the article said, as they considered it a better investment than stocks and bonds, citing as an example the Teachers Insurance and Annuity Association's recent purchase of the Seagram Building. Current office building owners were eager to sell, as they wanted to pull their profits out of the long-depressed but now booming downtown real estate market to direct cash elsewhere. As an example here, *Time* cited Pan Am, which wanted to retire some of the $1.1 billion in long-term debt it had racked up in acquiring new, fuel-efficient jets. It was also looking for cash to offset the huge operating loss ($108.5 million) it had sustained during the first half of the year. In addition to canceling service to two dozen international cities and projecting management layoffs, Pan Am, the article noted, was selling its headquarters building. As part of the deal, MetLife had agreed to retain the Pan Am name on the building, the article reported, in addition to leasing the airline company 15 percent of the building's office space at about 30 percent below the going market rate. According to Trump (who, as noted previously, was one of the losing bidders), it was an extremely generous deal for Pan Am but would probably turn out to be a good deal for Metropolitan Life as well, which *Time* observed was already happy with its "proud tower." As MetLife's chairman put it, "In terms of prestige, location and quality of tenants, there is no more attractive building in the City of New York."[103]

Still other articles appeared in *Business Week* and *Forbes* describing how Pan American had acquired the building, why the airline was in such bad financial straits, and why it now was selling the building. Top Pan Am officials had seen trouble coming and drawn up an operating and financial plan for 1980, the article said, but then in April the recession had hit, and it was now expected that Pan Am would suffer the worst loss in its history. Fares and fuels were blamed, as Congress forced the Civil Aeronautics Board to permit international airlines such as Pan Am to pass along climbing fuel costs by increasing fares. Because of the delay in approval for such increases, however, Pan Am had been unable to get a new pricing structure in place in time for the peak summer travel season. In the second quarter of 1980, its fuel bill had been 81 percent higher than the combined bills in the previous year's second quarter of Pan Am and National Airlines Inc., which Pan Am had acquired in January 1980. Pan Am's acquisition of National Airlines was another part of the problem, as it meant that Pan Am faced the cost of putting together two airlines in the midst of a deep recession, a process complicated further by labor disputes. Still other problems stemmed from the airline's inability to sell two of National's long-range McDonnell Douglas DC-10s and one of Pan Am's old Boeing 707s. And though other airlines were also suffering, Pan Am had had by far the steepest net loss of any airline thus far, as its most profitable overseas routes had lost ground in the face of foreign competition.[104]

Decades later when White died in 1995, his obituary noted that despite his long experience in Manhattan real estate, he was unprepared for the complexities he encountered in the Pan Am building sale. Assessing the value of the fifty-nine-story landmark on Park Avenue in the 1980 New York real estate market at the time of its sale had proved daunting. According to the obituary in the *New York Times* at the time of White's death, in order to project the value of leases and factor in other financial considerations, White's company had had to design its own computer program, and simply to describe the conditions of the private sale took a sixty-five-page brochure. To guarantee confidentiality, White himself received and handled bids, which had to be hand-delivered to him by top executives of the bidding institutions. Nine of the bids had exceeded $325 million, for a building that had cost just $115 million to construct seventeen years earlier. In addition to setting a sales record, the *Times* pointed out, the $400 million Pan Am/MetLife transaction added its mark to legal history. Because the transaction had been set up so that not the building, but the stock in its single-asset corporate parent was sold, Pan Am avoided all but $125 of the $4 million New York City real estate transfer tax that would have been due on the sale of the building. As a result of the resulting furor, the article noted, the law had been changed to close the loophole.[105]

LOBBY REMODELING

In 1985, five years after the Pan Am Building was sold, MetLife remodeled the building's lobby, as it had announced it planned to do at the time of the sale. As most of the building's original long-term leases were about to expire, the new owner wanted to update the building's spaces and services, especially the main lobby, with the hopes of attracting upscale tenants.[106] It was also concerned that although almost everybody in New York could identify the Pan Am Building, few knew where its main entrance was, and it needed enhancing. The lobby was also dark and dismal, and MetLife wanted it remodeled, according to an article in *Interior Design* on the remodeling project, to give Gropius's original spaces "a more human scale and to relate them better to human sensibilities, as well as to increase the value of the commercial building's rentable space."[107]

The $15 million remodeling, which included upgrading the twenty-two-year-old building's services as well as its public spaces, included the addition of a large, sweeping marble staircase from the public street-level lobby to the tenants' lobby one flight up. Large triangular stone planters were also added to the floor of the lobby, as well as huge, gold-plated metal disks suspended from the ceiling (figure 6.12). Fire sprinklers, not required by the fire code when the building was first built, were installed, and a second computer, controlling the building's energy and emergency systems, as well as other upgraded facilities were added, with the aim of drawing new tenants.

The results were, in the eyes of those at the time, mixed. This was well after Johnson had made waves in 1978 with his whimsical, Chippendale-topped American Tele-

FIGURE 6.12   Remodeled Pan Am Building (MetLife) lobby , 1985

phone and Telegraph Company (AT&T) Building. On the other side of the continent several years later, one of his protégés, Michael Graves, had made an even bigger splash with his strident Portland Public Services Building, festooned with swags and other colorful ornamentation, another milestone in postmodernism. "Coming at a time when many designers are obsessed by the debate between modernism and postmodernism, between abstract severity and decorative delight" the *Interior Design* article said, "the Pan Am remodeling clearly opts for the latter, and installs it in a building that is the epitome of modernism—a huge commercial skyscraper that boasted the design services of arch-modernists Pietro Belluschi and Walter Gropius." Knowing that opinions would differ, the magazine included a broad spectrum of reactions from critics, representatives of the clients, and laymen who used the lobby. From the perspective of the client for the design services in this case, the problem was image. MetLife had been told that the Pan Am Building was "the perfect location for an office building in Manhattan, at the geographic and transportation center of the city," which was why the company had bought it. But the building had no image. It was not perceived as a high-quality business address, and it did not command the highest commercial rental rates. According to the owner, the building had a rather dowdy image, if it had one at all.

"In fact," the article said, "public perceptions have always been rather a live issue where the Pan Am Building is concerned." The building had been controversial from the start, the article noted, and its location above the Grand Central had raised issues of urban planning; its mass and volume were seen as overpowering, even as "a bald act of unmitigated greed," and its design, a collaboration between Gropius, Belluschi, and Roth, had been called "ugly." The public interior spaces, primarily Gropius's work, were plain and austere, notable mostly for their art.

In addition to the new curving stair, aimed at countering the severe rectilinearity of the original lobby, a new security desk in the tenants' lobby was added, the lobby's retail spaces were expanded, the Vanderbilt Avenue entrance was redone, the lighting was revamped with new light fixtures, and the graphics were redesigned. "Unequivocally decorative ornament," as the article put it, had also been added, including gold-leafed arcs with hanging ferns echoing the arches of the Helmsley Building across the street and serving as capitals on "streetlamp-like decorative columns," as well as gold-leafed standards that were to "bridge the volume and height of the space and connect it to human form." It was, in the words of Warren Platner, the designer responsible for the remodeling, an intentional departure from the building's original interior, which Platner said, "'had no ornament, and was severe to the point of being banal. It was a void.'"

The Lippold and Albers artworks were left in place; the Kepes mural facing 45th Street on the mezzanine level, however, was removed.

In response to critics who felt his design lacked any connection to the original building, Platner drew upon a then-fashionable postmodern palimpsest notion: "'A city like New York is really many layers of building. Our intent was to make it a more attractive and livelier place. The owners asked us to have an effect on the building, so everything we added was intended to have visual effect. We *wanted* people to notice it.'"

That people did. Their reactions ranged widely, *Interior Design* reported: "'A poor performance, even by Platner standards . . . with a striving for effect stretched even to the details. . . . No music here; even Liberace would have blushed at the vulgarity'" (Carter Wiseman). "'Five years ago, the lobby of the Pan Am Building could only be described as a dark, cold passage,'" which Platner had "'dramatically transformed into something fresh and visually exciting'" (Thomas J. Sheehan, executive vice president of Metropolitan Life subsidiary Cross & Brown Company, managing and leasing agent for the Pan Am Building). "'The problem was to breathe new life into the old lobby, which was somber, undistinguished, and wasteful of space. . . . The centerpiece is a dramatic staircase, where none existed before, suggesting a Flo Ziegfeld movie set'" (Marilyn Hoffman, a New York–based staff correspondent for the *Christian Science Monitor*). "'The Pan Am Building was very functional, but it was a bit on the drab side. The renovation . . . all in all without doubt a decided plus for the Pan Am Building'" (Thomas Kyle, director and general manager of the Pan Am Building). "'When the Pan Am Building was first built, I became enamoured with the ground-floor restaurant, Trattoria. . . . Gradually, however, I "forgot" about Trattoria, possibly because the forbidding lobby of the Pan Am Building was considerably less than hospitable, not to say downright off-putting. . . . The now very hospitable lobby [has] flowers, plants, whimsical sculptures. . . . Even the original Richard Lippold sculpture in the west lobby now looks beautifully placed. . . . It was a shame that the lobby was so uninviting for so long'" (Richard Torrence, executive chairman of the Creo Society, a New York–based nonprofit educational organization).[108]

In the eyes of John Belle, of Beyer Blinder Belle Architects, responsible for restoring and remodeling the Grand Central Terminal in 1999, the original Pan Am lobby (figure 6.13) "was a stark, modernist space, the starkness of which the art work reinforced." Though he did not intentionally disparage Platner's work, it was clear Belle did not think much more of it than he did of Gropius's original. (figure 6.14).[109]

FIGURE 6.13   Park Avenue entrance, Gropius original, 1963

FIGURE 6.14   Park Avenue entrance, Platner remodel, 1986

DEMISE OF PAN AMERICAN WORLD AIRWAYS:
FLIGHT 103 AND PAN AM'S FINAL DESCENT

Pan American World Airways, which had pioneered global aviation and was the first to fly Boeing's 707 commercial jetliners, launching the jet age, retained its ascendancy among the nation's top airlines up to the late 1960s. Earlier in that decade, in December 1962, barely a year and a half after Pan American signed on as the main tenant of Wolfson's new building, the directors of Pan American World Airways voted to merge with TWA, its major competitor on international routes, a merger that, had it been approved by the Civil Aeronautics Board, would have created the world's largest airline.[110] The airlines' merger request was rejected on antitrust grounds.[111] The building, Pan Am's headquarters since the building opened in 1963, had become the focal point of the close-knit aviation community, with the Sky Club on the fifty-seventh floor replacing the Chrysler Building's Cloud Club as the bastion of the industry's male corporate executives. Until the late 1970s, when the airline industry as a whole began to splinter in part as a result of the 1978 deregulation of the industry, four of the country's five largest airlines were based within a few blocks of each other in midtown Manhattan, with Eastern headquartered at Rockefeller Center at 5th Avenue and 49th Street; American and TWA across the street from each other at 3rd Avenue and 40th Street, and Pan American in its namesake building, of which it occupied the top nine floors as well as the ticket lobby on the street floor[112] (figure 6.15).

Under Trippe up to time of his retirement in 1968, Pan American World Airways remained one of the world's largest airlines. The year 1966 was a record year, with the airline scoring all-time high profits. By then, however, its troubles had already begun. Buoyed by his successes, that year Trippe purchased twenty-five Boeing 747 jumbo jets, with a passenger capacity of 350–400 each and flying just under the speed of sound. Three years earlier Trippe had taken an option on eight supersonic airliners, then as soon as a commercial supersonic program in the United States was approved, Pan Am was the first of the U.S. airlines to sign up for fifteen of the supersonic jets. Unwilling to wait until the 1970s, when the supersonics were scheduled to begin flying, he talked Boeing into manufacturing the huge 747, and in April 1966, he signed a contract with Boeing for twenty-five of the jets—the largest single order for a single aircraft

FIGURE 6.15   Juan Trippe and the Pan Am Building

model in the history of commercial aviation. Adding the 747s to a previous order for the 707 and other Boeing jets, Trippe committed Pan Am to spending close to $1 billion for new aircraft.[113] It was one of several lapses in judgment on Trippe's part, as the company had agreed to a strict payment schedule that involved paying a quarter of a billion dollars for the planes even before they had been granted FAA approval and obviously well before they could start flying and begin to repay the huge investment. Then, in 1968, just as Breuer's proposal for a second tower atop the Grand Central Terminal was arousing the ire of preservationists, Trippe suddenly retired, leaving no strong successor to carry on his solo management style.

By 1971, when Seawell took over as president of Pan Am, becoming chairman in 1972, Pan Am was already deep in debt. As the economy began to weaken and international travel slowed, tensions in the Middle East sent the price of fuel soaring, as the Organization of Petroleum Exporting Countries (OPEC) quadrupled oil prices; late in 1973, Middle Eastern oil was embargoed, which resulted in further price increases and fuel rationing that hurt Pan Am, mainly an overseas carrier, in particular.[114] As the U.S. economy continued to falter, with Pan Am losing about $70 million on its international operations in 1973, the airline faced real trouble. In late summer the following year, Pan Am asked the White House for $10 million a month in emergency aid, which according to Barbara Sturken Peterson and James Glab, authors of a book on deregulation's effects on the U.S. airline industry, sounded to the president's advisors "ominously like the recent bailout of Penn Central Railroad: a billion-dollar fiasco."[115] Denied the handout, Pan Am was forced to cut back, terminating some key routes and swapping others with competing airlines. The strategy worked for a while, but then as deregulation of the airline industry appeared likely to become law and Pan Am anticipated increased competition, especially from abroad, it sought a merger with National Airlines in the hopes of gaining a foothold in domestic routes that would help feed its international flights. It was another major mistake in judgment, as not only did Pan Am pay far too much for the smaller domestic company, but the debt it incurred in the purchase could hardly have come at a worse time. After deregulation was signed into law in October 1978, giving airlines the right to enter new routes without Civil Aeronautics Board permission as well as lifting price controls, other airlines began merging in the greatest wave of consolidation the industry had ever seen. By this time the close-knit aviation community in mid-Manhattan had begun to disintegrate. Eastern moved its headquarters from New York to Miami in 1976; American planned to leave Manhattan for Dallas.

By 1980 it seemed clear that the U.S. economy was heading into a recession, fuel prices continued to climb, and the airline industry as a whole was hurting. Then problems developed with the Pan Am/National merger, as the two companies had very different operations, incompatible aircraft, and labor contracts, which made it difficult for the two companies to work together effectively. As a result, both airlines declined, with Pan Am suffering a record operating loss of $129.6 million in 1980.[116]

To continue operating, the airline needed money. It was at this point Seawell turned first to its real estate, as the New York Central and Penn Central Railroads before him had done, then to the airline's international hotel company, both of which had been profitable investments. According to Peterson and Glab, deregulation's first victim was the Pan Am Building. By the end of the 1970s, they wrote, the building "had become a fitting metaphor for the company's festering problems. When the Walter Gropius-designed structure had gone up in 1963, blocking what had been a sweeping vista along Park Avenue, it was derided as a 'monument to greed and irresponsibility.' Those were the days when Trippe and his Yale cronies literally looked down on their competition, secure in the knowledge that the logo emblazoned atop their aerie was the best-known corporate name in the world after Coca-Cola. Now this dubious landmark would have to go on the block."[117]

After agreeing to sell the Pan Am Building to MetLife for $400 million in 1980, the company sold its Inter-Continental Hotels for $500 million the next year. Eight of Pan Am's 747s also were sold for $200 million, but immediately leased back so the airline could continue using them. This helped Pan Am to stay aloft but had no impact on the now-combined airlines' operations. Operating costs sank even deeper into the red, with the company sinking into a record deficit of $359 million in 1981. By this time Pan Am was out of cash.[118]

From that point, Pan Am continued to deteriorate. With the Pan Am/National alliance deemed a failure, in 1981 Seawell agreed to step down and a new chairman, Ed Acker, was appointed. But by 1984, Pan Am still had a long-term debt of $1.2 billion. In March 1985, as labor problems in the industry grew and mechanics and ground workers walked off the job, the company's reserves dwindled. His back against a wall, Acker sold to United not only Pan Am's routes from the United States to Japan, but its entire vast Pacific network, the company's crown jewel, from the Philippines to Australia, from Korea to Singapore and Thailand, including all the jets required to fly the routes, as well as all of Pan Am's stations and equipment in the Pacific—fully a quarter of Pan

Am's airline business, a big chunk of the company's empire. The $750 million deal was the biggest in the history of the airline industry.[119]

By the end of the 1980s, as the dust from deregulation began to settle and "merger fever" in the industry subsided, scores of smaller companies had been eliminated, leaving huge megalines in their wake. The competition, now international, took an especially heavy toll on Pan Am and TWA, still the nation's two top overseas airlines. As the United States opened more and more of its airports to service from foreign countries, with British Airways alone doubling the number of cities it served in the United States over the course of the decade, the impact on Pan Am and TWA was obvious. Before deregulation they had controlled just under half of the transatlantic passenger market; by 1988 they were down to a combined market share of 30 percent.[120]

As competition in the airline industry increased, with giant domestic carriers like United and American, which dominated the home market, continuing to expand internationally, in December 1989, American negotiated to take over all of Eastern's Latin American routes, which represented a direct threat to Pan Am's survival, as its Latin American route network was the one area that was proving profitable. Eastern had always been a weak competitor, with Pan Am carrying twice as many passengers as it did. With Eastern absorbed by American, Pan Am faced a much larger, more powerful Latin American competitor.

Labor problems continued in the late 1980s, with Teamster strikes threatening and the airline's quality of service deteriorating. The heightening conflict in the Middle East led to a wave of terrorist attacks, resulting in public fears of flying that hurt the company even more. Then on December 21, 1988, Pan Am Flight 103 was downed over Lockerbie, Scotland, the result of a terrorist bombing. All 259 passengers aboard the plane died. In the words of Peterson and Glab, "The Pan Am name, once a valuable asset because it was so closely linked to the U.S. flag in the minds of the world, had become a deadly liability by making the airline a symbolic target." The impact on Pan Am's transatlantic traffic was swift and severe, as bookings dropped off dramatically, the toll devastating in economic as well as human terms. In the first three months after the bombing, Pan Am lost $151 million, according to Peterson and Glab, who estimated that the Lockerbie incident had a direct cost of $44 million to $60 million in lost revenues. It marked a turning point for Pan Am, which was, as the investigation of the bombing continued, widely criticized for inadequate security, thus raising in the public mind the possibility that the airline itself bore the responsibility for the tragedy.[121]

Problems continued to plague Pan Am in the wake of the Lockerbie bombing. Even though international passenger revenues gradually began to increase, fuel costs shot up by a third in the first quarter of 1990. And on its domestic system, revenues declined. By March 31 of the year, Pan Am was down to its last $90 million in cash. As competition from American, which had gone ahead with its plan to take over Eastern's Latin American routes and was also adding more flights to Europe that summer, increased, Pan Am attorneys began preparing bankruptcy papers. Since Trippe's retirement in 1968, the company had lost nearly $3 billion and sold off assets worth $1.2 billion. In May, Pan Am sold its shuttle service and agreed to turn over its Berlin-based German route network to Lufthansa. The situation continued to worsen. In August, Iraqi President Saddam Hussein's invasion of Kuwait aroused fears of renewed terrorist acts, especially against U.S. flag lines. Pan Am's symbolic position as the premier international airline served again to work against it. That fall, the company sold a number of its transatlantic routes, including its coveted London route network, to United.

On January 8, 1991, Pan Am's lawyers filed for bankruptcy. "It was," in the words of Peterson and Glab, "an ignominious, although long-expected, fate for the airline Juan Trippe had built into a huge, globe-spanning empire that dominated international aviation for decades. While the man in the street may have looked upon this as just the latest in growing number of corporate failures, Pan Am's 1991 bankruptcy filing was a portentous event indeed for the millions of people who worked in the airline, travel, and tourism industry, not just in the United States but all over the world. Pan Am had been more than a U.S. institution; it was a global institution."[122] It was one thing for a small, regional airline like Braniff or Continental to go broke, Peterson and Glab noted, but quite another when it was Pan Am.

In the summer of 1991, Pan Am, trying to pull itself out of Chapter 11 bankruptcy, turned to Delta Airlines, transferring its remaining European operations to Delta for $260 million. Pan Am, at one point one of the largest airlines in the world, now having shrunk to a small portion of its former size, was kept aloft as a Miami-based regional airline operating into Latin America and the Caribbean.[123]

"This is not a story about planes. It's about romance," an obituary on Pan American World Airways in *Newsweek* in July 1991 began, calling the airline a national institution. "The death knell for Pan American Airways was imminent last week, as the airline had agreed to sell its major European routes, its East Coast shuttle, and 45 planes to Delta Airlines, America's largest carrier. "It may be hard," the article said, "for today's frequent fliers to remember that once, air travel was an adventure; that airlines once had a soul. Pan Am certainly did. It ushered in cross-Pacific air travel in the mid-30s with its China Clipper and commercial jet travel with its Boeing 707. The carrier came to stand for a questing American spirit—and sound business sense. The entrepreneur who built Pan Am, Juan Trippe, was perfect for the role: part swashbuckler, part tyrant, he made the airline his toy and his obsession. Trippe saw the competitive advantages in going global, often negotiating personally with foreign officials for landing rights. . . . The airline was also a point of civic pride in New York," the article said, "where the unabashedly ugly headquarters building had almost the star status of Chrysler's nearby skyscraper."[124]

Pan American World Airways symbolized a lot of things to a lot of people—world travel, international aviation—its planes "still a symbol of America's global reach."[125] Its headquarters building, however, never drew the same acclaim, and in the end symbolized as much as anything the company's bust.

"Today we see the end of an airline whose name will be forever forged in American history," wrote the *New York Times* on December 5, 1991. The future of the airline, which had been founded in 1927, and pioneered global aviation, was uncertain. After selling its prime assets to Delta, Pan Am had hoped to emerge from bankruptcy court protection as a smaller airline, the *Times* noted, and had begun a small domestic system with its hub in Miami with help of a financing package from Delta. But even Delta's backing was not enough to reassure travelers and travel agents, the *Times* said, citing as an example the president of a travel agency in New Jersey who, although not avoiding Pan Am outright in her bookings, usually chose other options. Many of her clients were reluctant to fly Pan Am, she maintained, mainly because of memories of the Lockerbie explosion.[126] Her comments said much about public perception in the airline industry and the role of collective memory.

Under Delta, the now considerably downsized Pan Am kept flying for several more months, but then Delta's financial support ceased. On December 4, 1991, Captain Mark Pyle piloted a Pan Am 727, the "Clipper Goodwill," on an early morning departure from New York to Barbados, arriving at the island before noon. As he and his flight crew walked off the aircraft, they saw the local Pan Am station manager waiting for them with a message: At 9 that morning, while they were somewhere over the Atlantic, Pan Am had gone out of business. The station manager asked Pyle to return the plane to Miami for storage, and at 2 P.M., the plane took off again. As it approached Miami, the dispatcher sent Pyle a message to make low pass over the airport, a symbolic gesture of sorts. It was Pan Am's last flight.[127]

PAN AM SIGN CHANGE

"Will Pan Am Building's Logo Go Way of Airline?" asked the *New York Observer* in January 1992. The article's subtitle was telling: "More Eyesore Than a Landmark, but One New Yorkers Now Like."[128] In the wake of the airline's demise, many wondered whether or for how long the Pan Am sign on the building would remain, as the terms of the building's sale to Met Life required the sign to be retained only so long as the airline continued to lease its 225,000 square feet of office space in the building. But as of January 1992, when Pan Am vacated its offices, Met Life had the legal right to remove the corporate name and logo from the company's erstwhile world headquarters building and either replace it or leave it bare. There were those, the *Observer* article noted, who hoped the dead company's logo would not fly much longer, "like a white flag over a financially ailing city." There were others, however, who wanted the sign to remain "as a monument to the early, glory days of an airline pioneer and to a company that, in its domination of international travel, seemed to embody modern corporate America's achievements." Though MetLife was under no obligation to retain the sign, many to whom it was a landmark hoped the company would. As the building itself had not been designated an official landmark, however, legally MetLife was not bound to preserve the name.

A movement to save the sign was spearheaded by Christopher McLaughlin, a British Air pilot who planned to become a U.S. citizen. "I love that sign," the *Observer* quoted him as saying. "I would have preferred to see Pan Am planes and pilots still flying, but at least the sign should stay in recognition of all the company achieved." McLaughlin had first turned to Jacqueline Kennedy Onassis, who had joined the cause to save the Grand Central Station several decades before. He made little headway with her, the *Observer* said, as she was "an unlikely supporter for the building that dwarfed the train station" she had helped save. Her assistant referred him to the Municipal Art Society, which, clearly wanting no part of McLaughlin's campaign, referred him in turn to a local community board, suggesting that a public body such as it might be more receptive to his request than a private, academic organization. Had he looked into it, the *Observer* went on, McLaughlin would have found that organizations like the Municipal Art Society had "little affection" for the Pan Am Building or its signs and that many preservationists had opposed the building's construction to begin with. The building, "likened to a garage door pulled down on Park Avenue," blocked Park Avenue's north-south prospect, a view that had been previously "cluttered but not obscured by" the Helmsley Building tower. McLaughlin's discussions with the community board, too, led nowhere, since though the board could advise the Landmarks Preservation Commission, it had no legal authority itself to decide which buildings to protect.

Undaunted, McLaughlin took his case to the Landmarks Preservation Commission and filled out forms for landmark designation, only to learn that signs were not protected unless they were affixed to a designated landmark. Moreover, by law, the commission had no jurisdiction over buildings less than thirty years old. The Pan Am Building was only twenty-eight. Hearing this, McLaughlin expressed his hope that in two years, when the building turned thirty, the commission would recognize its architectural merits. Laurie Beckman, chairman of the Landmarks Preservation Commission, however, showed little interest in saving it, suggesting instead that the whole building be torn down. "What a great gift for the next century to open up the north-south vistas up and down Park Avenue," the article quoted her as saying.

Others, however, agreed with McLaughlin. A spokesman for Mitsui & Company USA, one of the original tenants of the building, said the company was saddened by the possibility that the building might lose its name. "Everyone knows where the Pan Am Building is," the spokesman noted. "If you suddenly said we're in the MetLife building, people won't know where it is."[129]

McLaughlin persevered. In a letter to the Landmarks Preservation Commission several days after the *Observer* article was published, he spelled out his argument.[130] Pan Am represented and meant a lot to the country, he maintained, and its name should remain as a memorial. Pan American World Airways had done more than any other to pioneer international and intercontinental air travel at a time "when every new step and every new route crossed hitherto uncrossed boundaries," he asserted. Pan Am "pioneered the flying boat routes across the Pacific Ocean and into South America, growing globally until at its peak in the 1960s, the name Pan Am was synonymous with that of the United States." It was painful, he said, to watch its slow disintegration over the years, and even more painful to see it finally cease operations altogether. "It is my feeling," he said, "and I'm sure the feeling of many others both inside and outside the airline industry, that to leave the Pan Am sign up would be an appropriate way of honoring one of this country's great corporations and great exploring endeavors."

"From the City of New York's point of view," McLaughlin continued, "the building will always be known as the Pan Am Building to many, and the sometimes expressed feeling that to leave the sign up would draw attention to bankruptcy at a time of recession, I believe is far outweighed by the richness in history, bravery, teamwork, and pioneer spirit that was Pan American World Airways. We celebrate and remember Byrd and Lindbergh, and those who opened up the west, so let's leave up this memorial to those who opened up the whole world and brought it right to our fingertips." Replacing the sign with a MetLife sign or with nothing at all, he argued, "would make a rather dull and uninteresting building even duller. The Pan Am sign brings the building to life, particularly at night, and gives it the only color and character that it has. It also, like it or not, has become a Manhattan landmark that is known and recognized internationally. To change it would change the face of Manhattan."[131]

Despite McLaughlin's appeal, the Pan Am sign—or signs, as there were four of them, with the two logos on the building's east and west ends—were removed later in the year and the name of the building changed (figure 6.16). The change shocked many New Yorkers. "Like a giant beacon of the Jet Age, heralding the sleek white-and-silver clippers that could breach the oceans in a matter of hours, the words 'Pan Am' have hung high above Park Avenue for a generation," wrote David Dunlap in the *New York Times*.[132] "Now, a year after Pan American World Airways left its namesake tower in mid-Manhattan and collapsed in bankruptcy, the Pan Am Building is to lose its familiar skyline signature in favor of something a little more stolid, but considerably more solid: 'MetLife.'" As Pan Am was no longer a tenant and was itself virtually out of business, it made sense, according to the president and chief executive of MetLife, "to replace the sign with a familiar name that symbolizes strength, stability, and long-term commitment to New York City." The fifteen-foot-high letters of the Pan Am signs, with their distinct windswept edges, as well as the twenty-six-foot-wide globes on the tower's sides were to be taken apart in pieces, hauled up over the building's edge to the abandoned rooftop heliport "from which true jet setters once embarked on worldwide journeys," and removed by means of the freight elevators. Like the old ones, the new signs would be illuminated, the words "MetLife" appearing on the north and south facades, and four interlocking M's replacing Pan Am's globes on the east and west.

What remained to be seen, Dunlap continued, was whether New Yorkers would cease referring to the building as the Pan Am and start calling it the MetLife. Were this to happen, it would result in confusion, as the company's headquarters remained in its landmark skyscraper on Madison Square. Pan Am's headquarters, which once occupied 15 floors of the building, were down to 4 floors by time it moved to Miami. "New Yorkers might have been fond of the globe-girdling airline," Dunlap wrote, "but they never liked the building, a behemoth that altered forever the vistas up and down Park Avenue.

'Couldn't they just leave the sign and take the building down?'" joked Robert Stern, one of the building's strongest opponents. Tama Starr, president of Artkraft Strauss Sign Corporation, an unsuccessful bidder for the dismantling project, said she approved of the sign removal. "Pan Am symbolizes failure, where MetLife symbolizes assurance and security. The emotional resonance of Pan Am is not holding. It no longer means flight. It means crash and burn."[133]

Memories of the airline and of its namesake building remained vivid. Several months after the Pan Am signs and logos were taken down, another article appeared on the loss of Pan Am, once the "sovereign of the skies."[134] Describing the demise of the airline and its fragmentary remains on display in a small store in Miami filled with Pan Am memorabilia, the comments of the article's author, Coleman Lollar, on the airline's headquarters building were telling. As editor of the popular travel magazine *Travel & Leisure*, Lollar had visited New York recently and had taken a mandatory walk over to Park Avenue to see what had been (and for him would always be) the Pan Am Building. The big blue logo with its stylized globe was gone, and workers were installing MetLife signs with the building's new name. The building "was never a notable piece of architecture," Lollar wrote, but "stripped of its signature blue-neon beacon, for decades one of the world's most recognized logos, the 59-story skyscraper looked plain—even seedy. There was nothing left to evoke the days when helicopters arrived at and departed from its rooftop helipad; when Pan Am generals huddled over maps in upper-floor strategy rooms, plotting their conquests of faraway empires; when kings and prime ministers regularly dropped by to pay homage to the undisputed sovereign of the skies." He wondered if some token remained, as a reminder, in the office in which Trippe had once "slammed his fist on a desk and demanded that Boeing add an upper deck to the 747, then ordered so many jumbos the reluctant plane builder had to comply."

FIGURE 6.16   MetLife Building

The emptiness he felt standing on Park Avenue had been deepened by memories of a far simpler building he had just visited in Miami, operated by a group of former employees bent on shoring up the airline's place in American history and folklore. "Pan Am was always America to me," a German woman told him. She recalled how Pan Am had run the Soviet blockade of Berlin in 1948 and served as the divided city's lifeline until the Wall fell, just a couple of years before Pan Am itself collapsed in 1991. He quoted a cab driver: "America can prop up a hundred foreign countries, but it couldn't save the Pan Am. A shame, I tell you, a dirty shame."

The passion for owning a piece of Pan Am ran deep, Lollar wrote. "It's not just because of all those audacious conquests that Juan Trippe pulled off: the first commercial flights to Latin America, the first across both the Pacific and the Atlantic, the first to go around the world, just about any first you can name." Typically, he said, it hinged "on an intensely personal memory which won't let the mind accept that the great old airline is gone." For him that memory was forged one day when he "stood on the tarmac at Monrovia, heading home from two years in the Peace Corps. As a 707 with a big blue globe on its tail fin slipped gracefully through the West African thermals, I knew how it must have felt to see the flag flying over Iwo Jima. I was already home."

PAN AM BUILDING: LANDMARK STATUS?

In the fall of 1988, several years before the question of removing the Pan Am signs from the building came up, the question of landmark status for the Pan Am Building had arisen at a New York Public Library symposium on historic preservation. According to Christopher Gray of the Office of Metropolitan History, architect Robert Stern had called the postwar office structures on Park Avenue a potential modernist landmark district, even singling out for designation (perhaps in jest) the 1963 Pan Am Building.[135] Stern later confirmed this, saying he had proposed nominating the whole district, but only informally, and not the Pan Am Building specifically. Clearly disliking the building (as much, one senses, for what it represented as how it looked), Stern added that since the building was larger than was now legally allowed, it would never be demolished and another, better building put up in its stead. The building *was* important, he agreed, "for all the right and wrong reasons. It was an important lesson of what *not* to do, a landmark of the mistakes we made."[136]

7

CONCLUSION

PAN AM AS SYMBOL

In August 1962, a few months after the topping out of the Pan Am's steel frame, several articles appeared on the Eiffel Tower. "Landmark on the Seine: Is It Ugly? Is It Sublime? The argument among Frenchmen will probably never end, but the Eiffel Tower has become the symbol of Paris," opened one in the *Saturday Evening Post*. It told of the tower's annual meeting of stockholders and recited the familiar story of the Frenchman (Guy de Maupassant) who morosely ascended its stairs day after day for lunch at the restaurant on the second platform of the tower. Asked why he always lunched there, he replied it was the only place in Paris he could be sure he wouldn't have to look at it.[1] Close to three-quarters of a century after the Eiffel Tower was built in Paris, on the other side of the Atlantic, as questions were raised and opinions shared about another new controversial tower, the Pan Am—"Marvel or Monster?" (Huxtable); "a massive burden" (letter to *New York Times*); "a major landmark in Manhattan . . . disastrous . . . a monstrous denial of urbane urbanism" (*Fortune*); "Something Less than Chartres," (Wayne Andrews); "dubious distinction of being [one of] the largest most spectacular failures that New York has seen in years" (Huxtable); "conspicuous for its ugliness and arrogant disregard of its surrounds" (Wolf von Eckardt)—the Eiffel Tower served as a reminder of how fluid attitudes could be. A second article on the famous tower shortly before in *Newsweek* remarked on its great success as a business venture.[2] "Holding stocks in the Eiffel Tower company is like having stocks in tranquility—no worries, no problems," quipped a member of its board of directors. As the Pan Am Building neared completion and articles ballooned congratulating its founders for their resounding business success but castigating its designers on aesthetic grounds, the analogy between the two monuments, both "gold mines in the sky," was clear.

Gropius had hoped his new towering skyscraper would stand as a symbol of progress, of the triumph of modern technology and the success of modern democracy, a symbol of the great metropolis of New York, which in the postwar era had surpassed Paris as the cultural capital of the world. Others saw it differently, as a symbol not of progress or modernity, but of greed, private interests at public expense, failure, crash and burn.

LATER CRITICISM

Criticism of the Pan Am continued well beyond the raucous 1960s and early 1970s. Almost two decades after it was built, in the wake of the 1975-1976 MoMA exhibition on the Ecole des Beaux-Arts, Paul Goldberger, another Scully student and Huxtable's successor as architecture critic for the *New York Times,* wrote an article on the newly restored 1929 New York Central Building in which he described it as a "splendid tower that sits like an exclamation point in the middle of Park Avenue," praising the Beaux-Arts building, which had for years commanded the vista of Park Avenue.[3] "Park Avenue at the end of the 1920s was a masterpiece of urban design—a row of buildings, each interesting in itself but each subordinated to a greater whole . . . their cornice lines almost matching, materials similar. . . . All of this," Goldberger continued, "went, of course, in the late 1950s, when new development led to a slew of confused, awkwardly placed glass towers. Some, like Lever House and the Seagram Building, are first-rate; others are mediocre," he wrote, "but the point is that all of them helped destroy the unified composition of Park Avenue. The final blow was dealt by the Pan Am Building . . . its enormous mass sitting astride the Grand Central Terminal completely blocked out the New York Central tower from the south and was a huge, boring backdrop for it from the north."

Goldberger was even less charitable in his description of the Pan Am (which he obviously disliked but could hardly ignore) in his guidebook to Manhattan architecture published the following year. The New York Central Building was "a perfect punctuation mark" on the grand, sweeping Park Avenue vista, he said, providing an ideal focus for the southward view from upper Park Avenue; it pulled the eye down the long line of Park Avenue apartment houses, gave it a moment of joy as it reached the exuberant top, then sent it on its way again, moving down the avenue. "All that is gone now," he said. "The building, of course, is still here . . . but the meaning of Park Avenue as it was created through the 1920s has evaporated. [Then] came the Pan Am Building, the precast concrete monster that was set in between the New York Central Building and the Grand Central Terminal; at fifty-nine stories it soars way above the pyramidal top and steals from the sky the role of backdrop. And it is wide, so wide that the eye can no longer travel around the older tower and have a sense of Park Avenue's continuity to the south. In short, it blocks everything."

"It is said", Goldberger continued, "that Gropius turned the building's great mass so that it would block Park Avenue, which makes his participation in this act of destruction of the cityscape even more disturbing; it is ironic that the apostle of Bauhaus social responsibility should have ended his career by collaborating on a building that is the epitome of irresponsible planning and design. If Pan Am, an arrogant, oversize intruder, represents the contribution one of modern architecture's great theorists could make to the city, it is hard not to call that entire theory into question."[4]

Goldberger was not alone in his views on the Pan Am. John Tauranac, in another guidebook on Manhattan architecture published the same year, wrote similarly of Park Avenue, the newly refurbished New York Central Building Tower (which was by this time the Helmsley Building), and the Pan Am. "Here's a piece of urban design that worked," he wrote. "For fifty blocks north of Forty-sixth Street you could see the New York Central Building straddling Park Avenue, its embracing arms continuing the cornice line and enclosing the vista, its thirty-five stories acting as the avenue's capstone and setting its tone. It was built to command, built to consume conspicuously, built to convey the power and the glory that was the New York Central Railroad. Now the railroad is bankrupt, the building's name is not the same, and the scale of Park Avenue has changed. . . . With the coming of the Pan Am Building in 1963, the New York Central Building was dwarfed almost to the point of obliteration."

On the Pan Am specifically, Tauranac was especially harsh. "The scale of the Pan Am Building brought the building little but outrage at first and firm resolve now never to let another like it happen again. One trip to Pan Am is enough. In a city whose resolve has always been to build 'em higher, wider, but not necessarily any more handsome, it is ironic that the Pan Am Building should have created such a storm of protest, a storm that has not yet subsided. If the reason for a city is concentration," he wrote, clearly cognizant of the arguments of its defenders at the time, "if the function of a city is congregation, and if the attraction of a city is multiplicity of choice, then the Pan Am Building should be beyond reproach. Here, after all, is a vertical building in a vertical city, built at a public transportation hub. . . . The façade is nothing more than one precast concrete panel after another, a marvel of expediency, no doubt, since the construction company only had to hoist up one panel, slap it into place, and go on to the next, taking the merest aesthetic to its grossest proportions. What is lacking is any sense of scale, any sense of grace. This mass, this behemoth, rises straight up and looms over Park Avenue to the north and Grand Central Terminal to the south, shouldering aside all sense of proportion and elegance in its gigantism." Tauranac described the heliport on the building's flat roof, pointing out its historical importance and the bad blood its helicopters generated. "Imagine the chill that ran through the neighboring offices when a helicopter took off or landed—first a blast of sound reverberating amidst the canyons, then a shadow across the desk." Pointing out the Pan Am's role in the historic-preservation movement, he added a note on Penn Central's subsequent plans to build yet another building over the terminal itself, plans fortunately aborted by the Supreme Court ruling in favor of Grand Central's landmark designation, thus "sparing us another Pan Am behemoth."[5]

That design professionals, caught up as they were in a post-AT&T, postmodernist reverence for sculptural rather than flat tops, thought no more of the building than critics geared to the general public, is suggested by the project, "A Pan Am Building Rooftop Addition" (figure 7.1), which won a *Progressive Architecture* Architectural Design Citation in 1982.[6] The proposed addition (which bears an uncanny resemblance to several 1922 Chicago Tribune Competition entries, such as those of the Dutch architect A. van Baalen, the Italian Saverio Dioguardi, and Swiss P. Hurlimann, each featuring a huge globe poised above a massive tower), consisted of a large glass sphere supported by a four-column steel frame on the by-then defunct Pan Am heliport.[7] The program for the project had called for a major space for varied public functions, such as a nightclub, a casino, bars, and restaurants; the site was the western portion of the Pan Am roof, which consisted of a large opening for air conditioning. The proposal was to add a new structure that would appear to "float" over the existing building and not divert focus from the Pan Am Building itself, but rather "create a sense of completeness by combining two structures of universal architectonic language, at once integrated and independent of each other." The comments of the *P/A* jurors adjudicating the design competition were revealing. George Baird thought the real question was whether the addition would improve the Pan Am. Alan Chimacoff thought that in elevation, it did that quite well. To this, James Stirling added, "On the other hand, if that's what we're into—improving the Pan Am—there are other ways one could do that." Baird found the sphere an interesting idea for elaborating the top of the building, with which Stirling agreed: "At the moment the building is just sort of cut off with a straight line. . . . Compared to the tops of such buildings as the Chrysler or Empire State . . . Pan Am is just the usual kind of bleak postwar effort." Stirling concluded, "At any rate, [the proposed addition is] an improvement on the Pan Am as it is now."

Professionals aside, the widespread popular dislike of the building was reflected in an informal poll by *New York* magazine in 1987, on buildings New Yorkers loved to hate. At the top of the list was the Pan Am, which was featured on the cover of the magazine, blasted by a wrecker's ball (figure 7.2). "New York's skyline is studded with bad buildings," the article accompanying the *New York* poll began, "banal buildings that ruin wonderful views, and abominations that should never have been built. Imagine what the city would be like if they could all be torn down." The magazine asked more than a hundred prominent New Yorkers to come up with a list of the ten buildings they'd most like torn down, with the Pan Am emerging as the top choice. "It's not *just* that the Pan Am Building is undistinguished—it's how this Bauhaus-inspired monolith totally gulps

FIGURE 7.1 "A Pan Am Building Rooftop Addition," Architectural Design Citation by *Progressive Architecture,* January 1983

FIGURE 7.2   "The Buildings New Yorkers Love to Hate," *New York,* June 15, 1987

down the skyline, ignores the scale and style of surrounding buildings, and, alas, blocks that once inspired vista up and down Park Avenue," the article lamented. Twenty-four years after Walter Gropius, Emery Roth & Sons, and Pietro Belluschi designed the fifty-nine-story concrete-and-glass curtain looming over the Grand Central Terminal, New York City Councilwoman Ruth Messinger condemned the building "not for what, but for where it is." Even August Heckscher, who had once defended the building, cited it as one he would now vote to destroy.[8]

Over a decade after *New York* held its poll, after the building itself had been sold and its name changed, *Progressive Architecture* conducted a similar poll, opening the pool of potential offenders, this time, worldwide. Illustrated by a figure of the Park Avenue vista fully walled in by the Pan Am, the article was a response to the question posed in the May issue: What building would you miss the least if it went away? The favorite response—not surprisingly, *Progressive Architecture* said—was the MetLife Building. "New Yorkers rue its presence—and the resulting damage to Park Avenue—as much as they do the absence of Penn Station," said the article presenting the poll results. It added that the building's recent change of name and ownership did not seem to have helped much.[9]

By the mid-1990s, by which time postmodernism as well as modernism were trends of the past, retrospective views began appearing on the modernist legacy. In a 1995 *New York Times* article on the preservation of modernist buildings in New York, Goldberger noted that the New York City Landmarks Preservation Commission had been signed into law thirty years prior, with the aim of stopping or at least slowing the city's tendency to sell off its greatest architectural works. The law had done much to avert the type of disaster that befell Penn Station, he said, and as such, it might be "the single most influential piece of legislation affecting land use in New York since the first zoning laws in 1916." But the city was evolving, Goldberger said, and so too the sense of what saving history really meant. In addition to the solid grand buildings of the haute bourgeoisie, representing the legacy of people mainly of European descent who built the city in the nineteenth and early twentieth centuries, the commission had begun to look at the poor, working-class neighborhoods of more recent immigrants. There was also the question of the city's newer buildings. Since the legislation made buildings eligible for designation as landmarks once they were thirty years old—the exact age of the commission at the time Goldberger was writing—the whole question of the architecture of the 1960s was just then coming into play. For years, he said, "it has been fashionable in architectural circles to denounce the skyscrapers and apartment buildings of the 1960s as worthless commercial trash—but the Art Deco buildings of the 1930s were once called that too. Will time mellow our views of the 1960s as it has our views of the 1930s? Will anything from the decade that gave New York Lincoln Center and the Pan Am Building be worth designating?"[10]

Well before Goldberger's article, the Pan Am Building had become a favorite modernist whipping boy, the target of a postmodernist backlash. But even as postmodernism too slipped into the past and a "neomodernism" began to emerge, disaffection with the Pan Am Building remained. A 1996 book on "the world's most famous and important skyscrapers" aimed at the general public included the Pan Am.[11] Scholarly disdain for the building aside, as it was the largest commercial office building in the world at the time it was built, the author, Judith Dupré, like others, could hardly ignore it. "In fairness, it should be stated at the onset that any building, by its sheer presence," the book's essay on the Pan Am, already on the defensive, began, "would have destroyed the Park Avenue streetscape now mourned in the toxic wake of the Pan Am (now MetLife) Building." Accompanied by a full-length, close-up view from the north of the Pan Am filling entirely the Park Avenue vista (figure 7.3), the essay gave a schematic history of the building and cited Gropius's aims in designing it ("a strong point of reference for the unbalanced building masses north and south of Grand Central Terminal"), but then added commentary decidedly critical in tone ("precast-concrete panels made for the Pan Am's broad prismatic façade that, though well-proportioned to the building's scale, increased its intrusive bulk"; "Gropius . . . decided the huge mass of the Pan Am should have an east-west orientation, one that effectively blocked all views up and down Park Avenue"). And as was now customary, Gropius alone was credited (or blamed) for the building; of the three architects involved, only his photo and biography were presented.

No more able to ignore the criticism of it than the building itself, the author quoted Goldberger on Gropius as "'the great apostle of Bauhaus social responsibility'" and his building "'that epitomizes irresponsible design.'" She also quoted Huxtable, who called the Pan Am "'a colossal collection of minimums,'" and who had observed about it that "a monumental deal does not make a monument." Pointing out that initially Gropius had wanted the New York Central Building razed to make way for a park, Dupré also maintained that the Pan Am had "appropriated the façade of the Grand Central as its own," yet another example of the arrogance of the design. "From the moment its design was unveiled through the present day, the Pan Am Building has met with nearly universal disparagement. For the visual damage it caused, it was derided as a 'seven-

The wrecks beside of many a city vast,
Whose population which the earth grew over
Was mortal, but not human; see they lie,
Their monstrous works...
— Percy Bysshe Shelley, Prometheus Unbound, 1815–1819

FIGURE 7.3 Pan Am Building, from Judith Dupré,
Skyscrapers: A History of the World's Most
Famous and Important Skyscrapers, 1996

FIGURE 7.4 Pan Am Building, side view

league monster,' a 'fatal blow,' and a 'bad joke.' Concerned New Yorkers, further in-
flamed by such press, saw it as the product of greedy real-estate speculators in collusion with city hall, and as inflicting yet another strain on the area's already jammed
streets." Some critics had been kinder, she pointed out, mentioning Schmertz's defense of the building in *Architectural Record,* in which the building had been depicted
as "less than a total aesthetic success," but under the circumstances "a brilliant compromise." Then allowing Manhattanites the last word, Dupré cited *New York* magazine,
with the Pan Am Building ranked first among buildings New Yorkers most wanted destroyed, on the cover.

In the later 1990s, as more and more postwar modernist buildings turned thirty years
old, thus qualifying for landmark status, the question of which of them merited preservation was again raised. Again the Pan Am Building was cited (not without facetious-
ness, as it was clear, the question of landmark status aside, that the building would
never be torn down and replaced), as an example of a building worthy of preserving as
a monument to what should *not* be done.[12]

The disagreement about the Pan Am was not confined to New York or even to the
United States. An article in the British glossy *Wallpaper,* illustrated by a view of the
building down 44th Street (figure 7.4), paid homage to the building. "Control Tower,"
the caption to the figure read. "Even though they've redubbed it the MetLife Building,
we will always know the superstructure that straddles Manhattan as the Pan Am Building. It is loved and loathed in equal measure, but whatever the jury's verdict to this vertical lozenge, it looks as if it's here to stay."[13] A lively literary account of "Party Girl,"
drawing on the main character of the 1990s movie by the same name, and why she
loves the building, a glimpse of which she gets each time she crosses the room in her
tiny studio apartment on the tony Upper East Side, the *Wallpaper* article described the
building, its tight site, the neighborhood, the crowds, the lobby, its host of shops and
services lining the mezzanine that no one seems to populate. "In fact," the article
noted, "no one ever seems to stop. Which is why people like Party Girl *love* this building. Although not everyone does. There was total bedlam when the view downtown
was abruptly cut off, and there's still a rabid contingent who'd like to see Metropolitan
Life, who bought the building after Pan Am went belly up in 1991, do the neighbourly
thing and tear it down. Even artist Claes Oldenburg thought a giant sculpture of a melting ice cream bar, with a bite taken out of it for traffic [figure 7.5], would be an all-around
better idea. But unlike the thousands that course through it every day," the author concluded, "the Pan Am Building is not going anywhere."

Claes Oldenburg, "Proposed Colossal Monument for Park Avenue, New York City: Good Humor Bar," 1965. Crayon and watercolor, 16¾ × 13½ inches.

The Pan Am Building continued to crop up in a wide range of different contexts: of what to do with modernist buildings in New York, the restoration of the already compromised Grand Central Terminal, the rebuilding of Penn Station. A *New Yorker* "Talk of the Town" on the proposed new Penn Station cited the Pan Am as a mistake made and a hard lesson it hoped the city learned: "A cultivated respect for public buildings that aspire to grandeur is behind the plan to spend $484 million to build a 'new' Pennsylvania Station across the street from where the old one stood. . . . Horrendous architectural mistakes are usually irreversible in New York. We have learned to live with the World Trade Center and the former Pan Am Building . . . because, well, we have no choice. This time, though, there is a chance to fix the very place that was broken."[14]

Some attitudes change; others are less fluid. Unlike Paris's Eiffel Tower, toward which views soon mellowed, by 2000 and the change of the millennium, a full generation after it was built, the Pan Am Building was still not "dear to the hearts" of New Yorkers. *Time,* as part of an article asking "What Will Our Skylines Look Like?" conducted yet another poll on which buildings deserve the wrecking ball. The MetLife (Pan Am) Building again topped the list. "To give some cachet to a crime against urbanism," *Time* said, "Modernist pioneer Walter Gropius was lured into designing this slab, originally the Pan Am Building, astride what was once the vista down Park Avenue. (The Berlin Wall is gone, but this we're stuck with.)"[15] It was a statement replete with irony, given Pan American World Airways' role as Berlin's lifeline during the Soviet years, prior to 1989 and the collapse of the Berlin Wall.

Even more damning was an Internet article on the MetLife Building that called it "probably the public's most detested midtown skyscraper." "Its immense bulk and height completely dominates and overshadows the former New York Central Building," the article's author observed. "By shrouding such a masterpiece in its shadow, the Pan Am desecrated a major icon of the city."[16] The article both reflected and propagated globally a still deeply felt view.

Then came September 11, 2001, the terrorist attack on the World Trade Center, and the realization of how abruptly attitudes toward buildings can shift, their meaning wholly transformed. A stonemason at work cleaning the facades of the MetLife Building on the morning of September 11 saw the Boeing 757s coming, and described what he felt:

The morning sky was a brilliant azure with whiffs of high sirrus clouds sun sparkled the deco chrome eagles of the Chrysler as tourists gathered at the Empire and Trade center observation decks. We can see them from our eagle aerie here at the 60th deck of the old Pan Am. . . . Eight am yesterday morning we were hanging rigs at the 57 floor; it's a busy morning we are on the Vanderbilt side with commanding view of lower Manhattan. . . . It's a Tuesday its warm yet you can feel a cool Canadian front upon us.

Up high my foreman Tiny grins with his missing eye tooth. His rig rests over the side of the 57th floor; appox half the distance in height of the twin tower. We are gamming on about the weather; and what we "gotta do". . . when Tiny (who weighs 275) breaks conversation and sez getta load of this asshole.

With that all eyes focus on this incoming 757 wagging its wings coming over the Pan Am just 200 feet from our deck. As the huge jet approaches it veered slightly to the right; the sparkle of the sun glistened its wings and the rays warmed its fuselage. Our men who hang precariously off the sides of buildings are outraged at the total disregard for safety; stand and yell obscenity at the pilot shaking their trowels as the jumbo careens over Broadway just broadside of us.

The sun is very bright just now we can see the white shirt of the pilot (?) and in the direct sun we can see the heads of passengers at their assigned windows—I distinctly see a blond woman at her seat.

This is unbelievable—perhaps another low level tourist ride; perhaps he came low to avoid another aircraft; perhaps . . . perhaps . . . as we watch the plane pass the Empire State Building and then diminish in size until . . . until . . . poof, a large ball of flame emerges from the twin tower. . . . all at once everyone is screaming.

We are slack jawed in disbelief; all at once everyone is screaming . . . radios crackle. . . . It hit the Trade Tower . . . Tower Hit . . . a plane just hit Trade Center!!! We are slack jawed in disbelief; there is a deafening silence as we glance at each other in momentary stillness; radio calls are coming in from below asking for information . . . we watch the burning and tug at cigarettes and hangnails . . . minutes pass and we observe what appeared to us an observer plane coming in for a look see. But suddenly it too plows into the other tower . . . explosion . . . fire ball . . . no mistake this time . . . that's deliberate . . . all of a sudden it becomes apparent that we are a potential target . . . everyone starts yelling . . . get down . . . get down like submarines under depth charge attack, huge hanging rigs and their crews drop down the sides of the building in fits and starts . . . cussing and yelling as they push off the building face and scale down in record time.[17]

Several weeks later, Christopher Gray of the city's Office for Metropolitan History questioned what effect the September 11 attack might have on views of the Pan Am;

as attitudes shifted about architecture of the 1950s and 1960s and as the facades of the Pan Am were being cleaned, he wondered whether in fact attitudes toward the building might have softened. Frank Sanchis, executive director of the Municipal Art Society, who remembered the initial controversy surrounding the building, doubted that the Landmarks Preservation Commission would designate the Pan Am as a landmark "anytime soon." John Jurayj, a painter from Brooklyn involved in preservation issues who was not yet born when the building went up, saw things differently, and regarded it as "very forward thinking, and not antiurban in bringing people back to the city, . . . a very high quality building." Robert Stern said he was now "ambivalent."[18] Attitudes elsewhere were more firm. A half year later, as decisions were being made about who or what architectural firm should be selected to redevelop the World Trade Center site, "The Wrong Stuff—Keep 'World' Architects Away from Ground Zero," sang out in the *New York Post* loud and clear. Arguing against a world superstar as architect of the redevelopment, the article reminded readers of the "geniuses" who scarred Park Avenue with the Pan Am (MetLife) building. "We have a right to be suspicious of international dreamers," the article asserted, "ever since Walter Gropius inflicted the Pan Am Building on us, and blighted Park Avenue with its hideous concrete façade."[19] Tastes change, but some memories last.

ARCHITECTURAL CRITICISM, CRITICS, AND POPULAR PERCEPTION

Given the powerful roles Vincent Scully at Yale and later his student Robert Stern, as well as their éminence grise, Philip Johnson at MoMA, served in generating and perpetuating unfavorable views of the Pan Am, the question might arise as to what extent the widespread disapproval of the building was simply a reflection of their own sometimes fickle taste, voiced in such influential books as Scully's *American Architecture and Urbanism* (1969) and Stern's *New Directions in American Architecture* (1969) and later *New York 1960* (1995); these were books that helped establish the aesthetic values, set the trends, determine the attitudes, and shape the tastes of a whole generation of architectural students, especially in the late 1960s and 1970s. But wholly independently of and well before them there was Huxtable in the *New York Times* and Haskell in *Architectural Forum*. And there were scores of other critics who viewed the building with chagrin: Wolf von Eckardt at the *Washington Post*, Edgar Kaufmann, Jr., in *Harper's*, Allen Temko in the *San Francisco Chronicle,* and Jane Holtz Kay in the *Boston*

Globe, as well as scholars such as Carl Condit at the University of Chicago, William Jordy at Brown, and Christopher Tunnard of Yale.

And there was Peter Blake, whose *God's Own Junkyard* (1964) was followed by *Form Follows Fiasco: Why Modern Architecture Hasn't Worked* (1977) close to a decade and a half later, in which he attacked the major premises of modernism: its "myth" of function, "myth" of the open plan, "myth" of purity, "myth" of total industrialization, and "myth" of the skyscraper, which he criticized for its effect on urban life. Illustrating his point were views of Park Avenue pre- and post-Pan Am. Then, a decade and a half later in *No Place like Utopia* (1993), his personal memoir on modernism, he specifically cited Gropius and Belluschi and the example the two architects had set with the Pan Am Building, which "more than any other one event" was the turning point in their thinking about modernism.[20]

Blake's mid-1970s diatribe against modernism was picked up by others as post-modernism gained momentum: Brent Brolin's *Failure of Modern Architecture* (1976), Charles Jencks's *The Language of Post-modern Architecture* (1977), and Paolo Portoghesi's *After Modern Architecture* (1982). Portoghesi dated the high point of modernism to the late 1950s with the Seagram Building, which he called one of the "undisputed masterpieces of orthodox modernism," and like others, he dated the end of modern architecture to the early 1960s.[21] The Pan Am Building, conceived in the fall of 1958 and opening in March 1963, spanned them both.

THE PAN AM BUILDING: THE VISION OF THREE MEN

Erwin Wolfson conceived of the Pan Am Building as a "Grand Central City," which promised to be his biggest, most challenging, and from a businessman's perspective, most successful enterprise ever. It was given visual form, or so he is credited, by Walter Gropius, who aimed at designing the ultimate modernist statement, a skyscraper then the largest in the world on one of the choicest sites in one of the world's pre-eminent metropolises. It was given its identity by Juan Trippe, who envisioned it as the cornerstone of his world-renowned aviation empire. All three men pinned great hopes on it, seeing it as one of their most important endeavors ever, a capstone to their long and successful careers. Their aims differed: Wolfson sought profit, Gropius fame, Trippe a fitting status symbol. In each case, their hopes were dashed, Wolfson dying amidst fierce criticism before the building even opened, Gropius attacked on both moral and aesthetic grounds for his role in the building, and Trippe retiring to leave the company he had all but single-handedly built up into one of the largest airlines in the world, headed toward bankruptcy and final demise, its name disgraced.

THE SIGNIFICANCE OF THE BUILDING

The Pan Am Building, however, remains, a testimony of their dreams as well as their miscalculations or outright failures. A conspicuous landmark and a testament to what many in New York felt should never have been built and should never be allowed to happen again, it is far more than just that. The Pan Am Building marked a pivotal moment in American culture. The largest commercial office building in the world at the time, a fifty-nine-story engineering marvel built over two layers of subterranean railroad tracks that triggered a postwar renaissance of truly tall buildings in the city, it broke a long list of records—the first major foreign investment in a purely real estate venture in the country; the biggest venture to that point undertaken in commercial building anywhere; the largest construction loan at the time ever placed on a single commercial property; a pioneer in construction management; its contract for forty thousand tons of structural steel said to have been the largest volume ever for an office building; the largest elevator contract for office building elevators, with the fastest elevators in the world at the time; the first centralized telephone service of its kind in the country; its lease to Pan American World Airways the biggest ever up to that point for commercial office space in Manhattan; the largest long-term mortgage ever made in New York at that time for a single commercial property—and on and on. Its history draws on that of the railroad: its rise in the nineteenth century, the sinking of its tracks, electrification, and monumental expression as the gateway to the city during the City Beautiful Movement, then its decline with the widespread use of the private car after World War II. It draws on aviation history, especially that of Pan American World Airways: originating in the 1920s, expanding during 1930s and 1940s, flourishing in the 1950s and peaking in the 1960s, then declining in the 1970s and 1980s and meeting its final demise in 1991. More than any other single thing, the Pan Am Building marked the shift from the railroad, over whose tracks it was built, to the airline, whose feats it symbolized, in the nation's long-distance transportation systems. It marked a high point in the career of James Ruderman, its structural engineer, constituting one of the most challenging, complex engineering projects of the time. A highly successful business endeavor, it gained Erwin Wolfson, who died before it was completed, the admiration of many. Once the corporate headquarters of its parent company, divested of its name, it marked the demise of Pan American World Airways, a pioneer in global aviation and once the nation's most powerful, most highly respected international carrier. And it marked a turning point in the careers of modernist heroes Gropius and Belluschi with their utopian visions, raising profound questions of professional ethics and artistic integrity, and forever tarnishing their reputations. Representing the corporate order the Beat poet Allen Ginsberg denounced in "Howl" in the 1950s, it raised still broader questions about private versus public interests and control over privately owned public space that burgeoned in the 1960s. After the Second World War, as architectural theorists and historians alike in time came to see, modernist ideals of rationality and functionalism, of a social utopia based on the use of new industrial materials and new modes of production to generate new, efficient, clean-lined forms, were displaced by the imperatives of a capitalist economy, and instead of the decent housing for growing urban populations modernists promised, flagship buildings for corporations were built. No building proved the point more poignantly than the Pan Am. Profoundly disillusioning the public as well as the profession, it marked the shattering of the modernist dream.

NOTES

INTRODUCTION

1 Charles Jencks, *The Language of Post-modern Architecture,* 1976, 9.

2 Charles Jencks, *The Post-modern Reader,* 1992, 24.

3 Mary McLeod, "Introduction," in *Architecture Criticism Ideology,* 1985, 8; Dennis Doordan, *Twentieth Century Architecture,* 2002, 159.

4 On the increasing interest in this aspect of architecture among architectural historians, see Beatriz Colomina, "Collaborations: The Private Life of Modern Architecture," *Journal of the Society of Architectural Historians,* September 1999, 464.

5 Betty Friedan's *The Feminine Mystique,* the point of departure for modern feminism, came out in 1963, same year the Pan Am Building opened. At that time, the number of women in the architecture profession was still small and remained so until the 1970s, when the doors of the profession were finally pried open and their numbers began to rise. Prior to this, the role of women in architecture was relegated mainly to that of the historian or critic. On the rise of women in architecture, see Ellen Perry Berkeley, *Architecture: A Place for Women,* 1989; for a more recent perspective on women and architecture, see Jane Rendell, Barbara Penner, and Iain Borden, *Gender Space Architecture: An Interdisciplinary Introduction,* 2000.

6 The subject grew out of a chapter in my *Pietro Belluschi: Modern American Architect,* 1994. While the Belluschi book was in progress, I delivered a paper on the Pan Am in 1991 at the annual Society of Architectural Historians meeting in Cincinnati, then another in Paris, later published in *Le Revue d'Histoire des Chemins de Fer,* 1994. Since that time, both my thoughts and the topic have expanded. Since then, too, other related books have been published, such as Peter Blake's *No Place like Utopia: Modern Architecture and the Company We Kept,* 1993, confirming my view of the Pan Am as a turning point in attitudes toward modernism, as well as Robert A. M. Stern, Thomas Mellins, and David Fishman, *New York 1960,* 1995, which documents the building on the basis of published sources and underscores the prevalence of anti-Pan Am sentiments (which Stern himself did much to generate). There have also been numerous shorter articles and essays, which I note in the conclusion.

7 On these intellectual upheavals in history, see Arthur Marwick, "All Quiet on the Postmodern Front: The 'Return to Events' in Historical Study," *Times Literary Supplement,* February 23, 2001; Patrick Joyce, "A Quiet Victory: The Growing Role of Postmodernism in History," *Times Literary Supplement,* October 26, 2001. On the changes in architectural history, see Sylvia Lavin, "Theory into History; or, The Will to Anthology," *Journal of the Society of Architectural Historians,* September 1999, 494–499. See also Johannes Albrecht, "Against the Interpretation of Architecture," *Journal of Architectural Education,* February 2002, 194–196.

8 Peter Burke, "History of Events and the Revival of Narrative"; and Giovanni Levi, "On Microhistory,"

in Burke, ed., *New Perspectives on Historical Writing,* 1991; Lynn Hunt, ed., *The New Cultural History,* 1989.

9 Keith Jenkins, "Doing History in the Post-modern World," in *Rethinking History,* 1991, 59–70.

10 Serge Guilbaut, *How New York Stole the Idea of Modern Art: Abstract Expressionism, Freedom, and the Cold War,* 1983, 4–5.

11 Daniel Bell, "Modernism Mummified," in Daniel Joseph Singal, *Modernist Culture in America,* 1991, 166–167.

12 On the balance of public and private interests addressed by Louis Sullivan early on in the City Beautiful Movement, see Manfredo Tafuri, "The Disenchanted Mountain," in Giorgio Ciucci, Francesco Dal Co, Mario Manieri-Elia, and Manfredo Tafuri, *The American City From the Civil War to the New Deal,* 1979, 419.

13 J. P. Bonta, *Architecture and Its Interpretation,* 1979, 138.

CHAPTER 1   GRAND CENTRAL CITY

1 Frederick J. Woodbridge, "Beauty and the Urban Beast," *Royal Architectural Institute of Canada,* July 1953, 206–207.

2 Paul Rudolph, "The Changing Philosophy of Architecture," *Architectural Forum,* July 1954, 120–121.

3 There are numerous of histories of the railroad in New York. My account draws mainly on Carl W. Condit, *The Port of New York: A History of the Rail and Terminal System from the Beginnings to Pennsylvania Station,* 1980; James Marston Fitch and Diana S. Waite, *Grand Central Terminal & Rockefeller Center: A Historic-Critical Estimate of Their Significance,* 1974; newspaper articles; and notes in the Douglas Haskell Papers (Avery Library, Coumbia University), box 96.4. Specific dates tend to differ slightly among the various historians, as well as the names of lines, which frequently changed as railroads merged or changed owners.

4 Edwin G. Burrows and Mike Wallace, *Gotham: A History of New York City to 1890s,* 1999, 432, 583.

5 "Central's History Began in 1831," *New York Times,* January 13, 1962.

6 "Fifteen Killed in Rear End Collision," *New York Times,* January 9, 1902, 1.

7 Douglas Haskell, "The Lost New York of the Pan American Airways Building," *Architectural Forum,* November 1963, 107–111; unpublished notes, Haskell Papers, box 9.4. Appearing at this point, almost a decade and a half before the Museum of Modern Art staged its exhibition on the architecture of the Ecole des Beaux-Arts, at a time when historic preservation in the United States was still embryonic and classical Beaux-Arts buildings such as the Grand Central still largely denigrated by the architectural profession, Haskell's comments were especially astute. It was not until years later that the merit of the Grand Central was generally recognized and its contribution to the Futurist Movement acknowledged in academic scholarship.

8 Haskell, "Lost New York of the Pan American Airways Building," 108; Ester da Costa Meyer, *The Work of Antonio Sant'Elia: Retreat into the Future,* 1995, 129. Among the numerous publications internationally regarding the new terminal were [Grand Central Station], *L'Illustrazione italiana,* February 1, 1913; and "Grand Central Terminal Station, New York," *Town Planning Review* (London), April 1911, 54ff. (copy of last in Haskell Papers, box 96.5).

9 David Marshall, *Grand Central Station,* 1946, 238.

10 One of the first substantive histories of the Grand Central, upon which Haskell (according to his notes) relied on for much of his factual information, was Marshall's *Grand Central Station,* an informal but informative account written by a former writer for the *New York Sun.* A more scholarly account was that provided by the Yale architectural historian Carroll L. V. Meeks, who wrote an article on the Grand Central, apparently at Haskell's bidding, in the *Architectural Forum* of November 1954 ("Today's Grand Central Concourse Is a Victory over 'Complexities Continuous'"); this was later incorporated into Meeks's *The Railroad Station,* 1956. A decade later and reflecting the growing influence of the Historic Preservation Movement in the late 1960s, as well as the mounting interest in Beaux-Arts architecture, which culminated in the 1975–1976 exhibition of the Ecole des Beaux-Arts at the Museum of Modern Art, was Fitch and Waite, *Grand Central Terminal & Rockefeller Center.* Since then, a number of publications have appeared, among them *Grand Central Terminal: City within the City,* edited by Deborah Nevins and published by the Municipal Art Society in 1982 in conjunction with an exhibition marking the 1978 U.S. Supreme Court decision upholding the terminal's landmark status. More recent is John Belle and Maxinne R. Leighton, *Grand Central: Gateway to a Million Lives,* 2000, celebrating the restoration of the terminal by the architectural firm Beyer Blinder Belle, of which Belle is a principal; and still more recent is Kurt C. Schlichting, *Grand Central Terminal: Railroads, Engineering, and Architecture in New York City,* 2001. A comprehensive bibliography of the Grand Central Terminal is on file at the New York City Landmarks Preservation Commission.

11 Marshall, *Grand Central Station,* 258.

12 Meeks, *Railroad Station,* 133–134; Kurt C. Schlichting, "Grand Central Terminal and the City Beautiful in New York," *Journal of Urban History,* March 1996, 332–349.

13 Haskell, "Lost New York of the Pan American Airways Building."

14 Ibid.

15 Meeks, *Railroad Station,* 133.

16 Haskell, "Lost New York of the Pan American Airways Building"; Schlichting, "Grand Central Terminal and the City Beautiful," 332.

17 "Grand Central Area Open for Rebuilding," *New York Times,* March 2, 1955.

18 Erwin S. Wolfson, letter to Robert R. Young, April 22, 1954, cited in "How British Funds Got in Grand Central Deal," *Business Week,* October 31, 1959, 32–33.

19 "A 'Sixth Sense' for Construction," *Engineering News-Record,* May 28, 1959, 56.

20 "World's Loftiest Tower May Rise on Site of Grand Central Terminal," *New York Times,* September 8, 1954.

21 Douglas Haskell, notes on conversation with I. M. Pei re: Grand Central Station, October 19, 1954, Haskell Papers, box 97.8.

22 The actual height of the Grand Central concourse is 150 feet, not 80, as Pei contended. Nevins, *Grand Central Terminal,* 143.

23 Douglas Haskell, letter to Robert R. Young and Patrick B. McGinniss, September 21, 1954, Haskell

Papers, box 97.8; Douglas Haskell, "Can the Grand Central Concourse Be Saved?" *Architectural Forum,* November 1954, 134–139.

24 What in fact "belonged" to whom was an increasingly heated issue at the time. On the question of control of privately owned public space—who controls privately owned public spaces—see Anastasia Loukaitou-Sideris and Trideb Banergee, *Urban Design Downtown: Poetics and Politics of Form,* 1998, 188, and more recently Jerold S. Kayden, *Privately Owned Public Space: The New York City Experience,* 2000. Kayden's book includes only spaces created *after* a 1961 zoning law revision, which changed the rules, hence includes neither the Grand Central Terminal nor the Pan Am Building.

25 Meeks, "Today's Grand Central Concourse Is a Victory over 'Complexities Continuous,'" 139.

26 "Is Grand Central Terminal 'Outmoded'? Owners Consider Replacement Schemes," *Architectural Record,* November 1954, 20.

27 "Central Studies New Terminal Plan," *New York Times,* September 26, 1954. Whether in fact the New York, New Haven and Hartford Railroad had a say in the development of the terminal was a matter of legal dispute that was held up in court for years.

28 "Plan to Update Grand Central Station," *Architectural Forum,* October 1954, 41.

29 "Is Grand Central Terminal 'Outmoded'?" 20; see also Haskell, "Can the Grand Central Concourse Be Saved?" 136–137.

30 "Grand Central Terminal to Become Skyscraper," *Downtown Athletic Club of New York City,* January 1955, 19 (Haskell Papers, box 97.8).

31 Memorandum, Douglas Haskell to Walter McQuade, January 18, 1955, Haskell Papers, box 97.8.

32 "New Plan Studied on Grand Central," *New York Times,* February 8, 1955; "Another Set of Plans Announced for Site of Grand Central Station," *Wall Street Journal,* February 8, 1955, 9; "New Grand Central Plan Would Save Terminal," *New York Herald,* February 8, 1955; "Grand Central's Outdoor Concourse," *Architectural Forum,* February 1955, 116–119.

33 "Grand Central's Outdoor Concourse," 119.

34 Giorgio Cavaglieri, letter to editor, *New York Herald Tribune,* March 9, 1955 (copy in Haskell Papers, box 97.8).

35 "Designers Alter Face of New York," *New York Times,* September 30, 1962.

36 Steven Ruttenbaum, *Mansions in the Clouds,* 1986, 23–30; Tom Shachtman, *Skyscraper Dreams: The Great Real Estate Dynasties of New York,* 1991, 51–52.

37 *New York Times,* December 11, 1992.

38 Dennis Duggan, "The 'Belly' School of Architecture," *New York Herald Tribune,* December 15, 1963, 7–10. Born in Manhattan, Julian attended Columbia University, joined his father's firm in 1921, and became a senior partner in 1938 along with his brother. His specialization was building materials, construction methods, cost estimates, and curtain wall technology. "Julian Roth, 91, dies," *New York Times,* December 11, 1992.

39 Ruttenbaum, *Mansions in the Clouds,* 202.

40 Jane Jacobs, "New York's Office Boom," *Architectural Forum,* March 1957, 105–113.

41 Richard Roth, "High-Rise Down to Earth," *Progressive Architecture,* June 1957, 196–200.

42 Shachtman, *Skyscraper Dreams,* 196–197.

43 Roth, "High-Rise Down to Earth," 196–200.

44 The appeal of the Roth firm, with its reputation for a highly coordinated, efficiently run office, to spec-ulators such as the Urises and Wolfson reflected the tremendous changes that were taking place in architectural practice in the postwar era. According to an article in *Architectural Forum,* the architec-ture profession, a small group of 22,000 regular architects and their employees, was coping with a $40 billion per year building industry. Traditionally architectural practice had consisted of a single cli-ent and a single architect (such as Pope Leo and Michelangelo), with the architect in charge of de-sign and supervision of construction of a single building (such as St. Peter's); moreover, the architect dealt with a small construction crew representing a limited number of crafts. That model prevailed up until the late 1920s, when things began to change. By the postwar era, the client was more likely to be a "hydra-headed corporation"; moreover, the building trades had splintered into specialized fields—foundations, structure, heating, cooling, plumbing, illumination, acoustics, etc.—each with its own set of trained engineers and a separate workforce. In addition to engineers, there were also planning specialists, zoning specialists, code specialists, different kinds of realtors, leasing agents, managers, and labor leaders. Consequently, the architecture profession was having to shift from its traditional focus on the art of individual creation to the art of organization. "The Architect Today," *Architectural Forum,* October 1955, 116–123. On other changes in architectural practice at this time reflected in the Roth firm, see also "Architect's Office," *Architectural Forum,* July 1956, 82, 92. On the Roths' close connections with large-scale Manhattan developers such as Wolfson and the Uris brothers, see Shachtman, *Skyscraper Dreams.*

45 Interview, Murray Shapiro, New York City, May 27, 1994; interview, Richard Roth, Jr., New York City, May 25, 1994; Schachtman, *Skyscraper Dreams,* 196. Shapiro is a structural engineer who joined the Ruderman office in 1950 and was an associate in the office at the time of the Pan Am building. Richard Roth, Jr, is Richard Roth's son, who was fresh out of architecture school at the University of Miami and working in the Roth office by the time these events were taking place.

46 "Modern Office Buildings Planned in the Downtown," *New York Times,* October 16, 1955, 1.

47 On Wolfson, see "A 'Sixth Sense' for Construction"; "Erwin S. Wolfson, Builder of Skylines," *Time,* February 22, 1960, 92; "Intellectual Builder: Erwin Service Wolfson," *New York Times,* September 8, 1960; "Erwin S. Wolfson Is Dead at 60, Leading Builder of Skyscrapers," *New York Times,* June 27, 1962, 35.

48 On Abe Adelson, see "Romance in Lives of City Builders," *New York Times,* February 24, 1929.

49 Interview, Murray Shapiro, May 27, 1994; "A 'Sixth Sense' for Construction."

50 "A 'Sixth Sense' for Construction."

51 Interview, Murray Shapiro, May 27, 1994; "Intellectual Builder: Erwin Service Wolfson"; "Erwin S. Wolfson Is Dead at 60."

52 Ogden Tanner, "Grand Central's Wolfson," *Architectural Forum,* November 1958, 133.

53 "A 'Sixth Sense' for Construction," 55–57.

54 Ibid.

55 Russell Porter, "Grand Central Area Open for Rebuilding," *New York Times,* March 2, 1955, 1, 21. Stevens had sold his interests in the Empire State Building at the same time the Grand Central development was initially proposed. "World's Loftiest Tower May Rise on Site of Grand Central Terminal," *New York Times,* September 8, 1954. Stevens was also the developer of the $75 million Boston Back Bay Center, a commercial complex of hotel, stores, and office tower on twenty-eight acres of an obsolete railroad yard in Boston, in which both Gropius and Belluschi were involved. The project, begun in 1953, was aborted in 1955 by a Supreme Court decision not to allow the tax easement needed to make the center financially viable. Clausen, *Pietro Belluschi,* 251–254.

56 Porter, "Grand Central Area Open for Rebuilding." While not denying the fact that the New York Central held the title to the real estate, the New York, New Haven and Hartford claimed rights to the railroad's real estate holdings based on a century-old lease granted in perpetuity to one of its predecessor companies that provided it with one-half management and operating interest in the real estate as well as in the terminal building. The long, tangled dispute, which eventually involved Wolfson, delaying his plans for the Grand Central, continued well into 1960. "New Haven Road Is Suing Central," *New York Times,* January 13, 1960, 27.

57 Douglas Haskell, letter to I. M. Pei, March 2, 1955, Haskell Papers, box 97.8.

58 Lewis Mumford, "The Sky Line: The Roaring Traffic's Boom—I," *New Yorker,* March 19, 1955, 85ff.; Douglas Haskell, letter to Frederick Woodbridge, March 21, 1955, Haskell Papers, box 97.8. Woodbridge, who was to become president of the New York chapter of the AIA in 1960, played a prominent role in the Grand Central dispute.

59 Haskell, letter to Woodbridge, March 21, 1955.

60 Douglas Haskell, "For All Concerned" [editorial], *Architectural Forum,* April 1955, 172.

61 Nor was it mentioned in either Michael Cannell, *I. M. Pei: Mandarin of Modernism,* 1995, or Carter Wiseman, *I. M. Pei,* 1990. Drawings for the project in the Pei Archives have only recently come to light, published, with a brief description, in Stern, Mellins, and Fishman, *New York 1960.*

62 On Catalano, his work in warped surfaces, and his connections with Belluschi, who was also a close friend of Pei at the time, see Meredith L. Clausen, *Spiritual Space: The Religious Architecture of Pietro Belluschi,* 1992, 128; and *Pietro Belluschi,* passim. Whether it was Belluschi who brought the two men together is unclear, but it seems likely, as he was a mentor to both of them. It was he who brought Catalano to MIT in the early 1950s and he who advised Pei to break his ties with Zeckendorf and start an office of his own.

63 Architects I. M. Pei & Associates, "The Hyperboloid: A Webb & Knapp Project for The Grand Central Terminal," 1956. My thanks to Janet Adams Strong, Director of Communications, and Robert E. Drake of Pei Cobb Freed & Partners, New York, for their assistance in providing this information.

64 According to Pei years later, the project itself was perfectly feasible but did not go ahead because of its significant costs, and Young, who was then caught in internal disputes within the corporation as well as mired in the legal battle with the New York, New Haven and Hartford Railroad, was unwilling to pursue the complex negotiations involved. Telephone interview, I. M. Pei, August 3, 1995; Janet Adams Strong, e-mail to author, February 3, 2000. On the property dispute between the New York Central and New York, New Haven and Hartford Railroads at this time, see "Rail Feud Flares on Park Ave. Plan," *New York Times,* October 3, 1956, in which the New York, New Haven and Hartford, upon learning of another proposed development on Park Avenue, accused the New York Central of suffering an "attack of Zeckendorfitis."

65 "Shuttle May Run Seatless Trains," *New York Times,* January 25, 1956.

66 "How British Funds Got in Grand Central Deal."

67 "Robert Young, Financier, Ends Life in Palm Beach," *New York Times,* January 26, 1958, 1, 78; Russell Porter, "Young Unloaded Stock in Central," *New York Times,* January 26, 1958, 78.

68 "How British Funds Got in Grand Central Deal."

69 This suggests that neither Roth nor Wolfson was displeased with the original 1955 proposal, as Fitch and Waite (1974) maintained, as it seems unlikely they would have submitted it again at this point for the most part unchanged.

70 Glenn Fowler, "Grand Central Plans Building," *New York Times,* May 8, 1958; "New Plan Studied on Grand Central."

71 Fowler, "Grand Central Plans Building." The revised Roth project was also covered in the article, "Grand Central Site for Largest Office Building," *Architectural Forum,* June 1958, 13.

72 "Central Building Sets Rental Plan," *New York Times,* July 6, 1958, vii, 2. My thanks to George Rolfe for his assistance in untangling this and other often highly complicated financial transactions.

73 Walter McQuade, "Architecture—A Scheme for Grand Central City," *Nation,* January 30, 1960.

74 Edgar Kaufmann, Jr. "The Biggest Office Building Yet . . . Worse Luck," *Harper's,* May 1960, 67.

75 James Trager, *Park Avenue: Street of Dreams,* 1990; Christopher Gray, "Is It Time to Redevelop?" *New York Times Magazine,* May 14, 1989, 44–45.

76 "Change Is Cited on Park Avenue," *New York Times,* October 16, 1955.

77 Ibid.

78 "Park Avenue Home Life Gives Way to Business in New Construction."

79 "Central to Lease Site on Park Avenue," *New York Times,* January 13, 1957, 41; "New Skyscrapers Growing Taller," *New York Times,* January 27, 1957, 1; "Sprouting Skyscrapers Are Changing Face of Midtown Manhattan," *New York Times,* February 3, 1957, viii, 1.

80 "A New Park Avenue Comes into Own," *New York Times,* May 19, 1957. The Goelet Estate Company had inherited the landholdings of the Goelet family, which included the Racquet & Tennis Club at 370 Park Avenue; it and the railroad were the two largest property owners in the area.

81 "Businesses Erect Own Skyscrapers," *New York Times,* December 1, 1957, 1; "Park Avenue Building," *New York Times,* December 17, 1957, 63.

82 Ada Louise Huxtable, "The Park Avenue School of Architecture," *New York Times Magazine,* December 15, 1957, 30–31, 54–56. Huxtable was appointed the first full-time architectural critic for the *New York Times* in 1963, remaining in that capacity until she retired in 1982. Suzanne Stephens, "Ada Louise Huxtable in Perspective," *Skyline,* March 1982, 3.

83 Huxtable, "Park Avenue School of Architecture, 30–31, 54–56."

84 In October of the following year, Paul Rudolph was to come out with an article in the *Saturday Review,* later reprinted in the *AIA Journal,* echoing Huxtable's views. He addressed specifically the changes occurring in the city, the losses and the gains, and focused particularly on Park Avenue north of Grand Central as an example of Beaux-Arts urban design whose cohesiveness and unity of aims and ideals had been lost with advent of modernism. Rudolph, "The Changing Face of New York," *Saturday Review,* October 18, 1958, 34, 42; reprinted in the *AIA Journal,* April 1959, 38–39.

85 On the resurgence of architectural criticism and especially the *Architectural Forum*'s role in implementing its new policy of "perceptive criticism" in the architectural press in the late 1950s, see Richard A. Miller, "Disenchantment and Criticism: The State of Modern Architecture, "typed manuscript dated May 1, 1959, in the Haskell Papers, Box 50:1. (Miller was an Associate Editor of the *Forum.*) See also Mitchell Schwarzer, "History and Theory in Architectural Periodicals," *Journal of the Society of Architectural Historians,* September 1999, 342–348, on the general decline in the quality of architectural criticism in trade magazines today.

86 Ada Louise Huxtable, "The Art We Cannot Afford to Ignore (but Do)," *New York Times Magazine,* May 4, 1958, 14–15, 86.

87 On these shifts in cultural values in the postwar era, see Lary May, *Recasting America: Culture and Politics in the Age of Cold War,* 1989.

88 Huxtable, "Art We Cannot Afford to Ignore (but Do), 14–15, 86."

89 Jacobs, "New York's Office Boom."

90 Shachtman, *Skyscraper Dreams,* 196–197.

91 Interview, Richard Roth, Jr., May 25, 1994.

92 According to Richard Roth, Jr., it was he who drew up the list for his father. Wolfson himself was unfamiliar with any of the names mentioned. Ibid.

93 Ibid.

94 Walter Gropius, "Report on Trip to New York, Monday, June 23, 1958," Belluschi Papers, Syracuse University, Syracuse, New York, box 468.

95 Walter Gropius and Pietro Belluschi, letter to Erwin S. Wolfson, Chairman of the Board, Diesel Construction Company, June 25, 1958, Belluschi Papers.

96 On Belluschi's prior experience both in professional practice and as a design consultant, see Clausen, *Pietro Belluschi.*

97 Gropius and Belluschi, letter to Wolfson, June 25, 1958.

98 Grand Central Building, Inc., letter to Walter Gropius, representing The Architects Collaborative, and Pietro Belluschi, July 18, 1958, Belluschi Papers.

99 Ibid.

100 Interview, Richard Roth, Jr., May 25, 1994.

101 J. P. Lohman Organization, press release prepared for Erwin S. Wolfson and his associates, Herbert and Stuart Scheftel and Alfred G. Burger, July 30, 1958, Belluschi Papers.

102 Ibid.

103 "Two Noted Architects to Help Map Center," *New York Times,* July 31, 1958; "Noted Architects to Plan Center," *New York Times,* Sunday, August 24, 1958.

104 "Gropius and Belluschi Advise on Grand Central Tower Design," *Architectural Forum,* September 1958, 47.

105 Tanner, "Grand Central's Wolfson," 132–133, 200.

106 According to Richard Roth, Jr., "it wasn't altruism, I can promise you that," that drove Wolfson to hire Gropius and Belluschi, a rather cynical view that was confirmed in an interview with Belluschi himself, who maintained even more pointedly that Wolfson's bringing in design consultants was "primarily a public relations move." Interview, Richard Roth, Jr., May 25, 1994; Jim Murphy, interview with Pietro Belluschi, *Progressive Architecture,* June 1990, 122–123.

107 On Gropius and his widespread reputation in the 1950s, see James Sloan Allen, *The Romance of Commerce and Culture,* 1983, as well as the article by Cranston Jones on leading "formgivers" in architecture, "Views Compared by Leading Architects," *Architectural Forum,* September 1956, 146ff., a commentary on *Time*'s series of articles on prominent architects at the time.

108 "Harvard Architect Honored," *New York Times,* May 5, 1957.

109 "Showcase for Modern America, Good Neighbor for the Parthenon," *Time,* July 15, 1957, 74. It should be noted here that at the time Belluschi was a member of and spokesman for the five-member advisory board established by the State Department's Office of Foreign Buildings, responsible for drawing up the design guidelines for the design of all State Department buildings abroad, including embassies. Whether he had a hand in Gropius's being awarded the Athens commission is not clear, but given their connections, it is not unlikely. On Belluschi's role in the Foreign Buildings Operation, see Clausen, *Pietro Belluschi,* 219–222.

110 "Biggest Architectural Show," *Life,* November 25, 1957.

111 "University of Baghdad," *Process,* October 1980, 26–29; "University of Baghdad Development," *Process,* May 1985, 90.

112 For an interpretive analysis of Gropius's Chicago Tribune Competition project, its symbolic function, and the "indifference of the skyscraper" in Gropius's thinking, see Tafuri, "The Disenchanted Mountain," 405.

113 Douglas Haskell, "Democracy and Apollo" [editorial], *Architectural Forum,* May 1958, 88.

114 Walter Gropius, "The Curse of Conformity: The Problem of Architecture in the Assembly-line Age," *Saturday Evening Post,* September 6, 1958, 54; excerpted in *Architectural Forum,* May 1959, 209.

115 "Walter Gropius to Get 1959 Architects Award," *New York Times,* March 18, 1959, 41.

116 "The Lawgiver," *Time,* June 29, 1959, 48, 50.

117 "AIA Gold Medal Presentation to Walter Gropius, FAIA," *AIA Journal* 32, August 1959, 80–82.

118 Sam T. Hurst, "Introduction: Twenty Years of TAC," in Walter Gropius et al., *The Architects Collaborative: 1945–1965,* 1966, 8. The organization changed over the years, expanding in size particularly during the late 1950s and early 1960s, when the Pan Am Building was under construction. Originally housed in rented space near the Harvard campus, in 1964, just after the Pan Am was completed, it built its own office building on Brattle Street. It also opened branch offices in other cities, including one in Rome, at this time. It incorporated in 1963, the same year the Pan Am opened.

119 Ibid., 16. This was wholly consistent with the contract Gropius and Belluschi drew up with Wolfson in June 1958, in which Gropius was designated "leader" and final arbiter of the design team. Notice, however, that this was a declaration or principle articulated years *after* the Pan Am project, and

whether it had existed at the founding of TAC or was adopted as a wise procedure as a result of the experience with Belluschi, who had suggested there be but one person in charge when he and Gropius drew up the terms of their collaboration on the Pan Am, is unclear. The impact of the Pan Am project as a whole on the TAC office—its size, organization, direction, and reputation—which, my sense is, was profound, has not been examined.

120 Walter Gropius, "TAC's Objectives," in Walter Gropius et al., *The Architects Collaborative: 1945– 1965,* 1966, 20–21.

121 Walter Gropius, "TAC's Teamwork," in Walter Gropius et al., *The Architects Collaborative: 1945– 1965,* 1966, 24.

122 Sarah P. Harkness, "Collaboration," in Walter Gropius et al., *The Architects Collaborative: 1945–1965,* 1966, 26. On Gropius's concept of collaboration, see Beatriz Colomina, "Collaborations: The Private Life of Modern Architecture," in which Colomina notes that collaboration appeared to be "a '50s thing, a phenomenon of that prosperous postwar decade when teamwork was canonized," citing Gropius and the formation of TAC. As is not uncommon, she also mentions in this context that Gropius "came on board" with the team of Emery Roth & Sons to design the Pan Am Building but makes no mention of Belluschi.

123 On Belluschi, see Clausen, *Pietro Belluschi.*

124 Gropius et al., "Back Bay Center Development/Back Bay Stadtzentrum," *The Architects Collaborative,* 78–83; Clausen, *Pietro Belluschi,* 251–254. The project, which won a *Progressive Architecture* design award in 1954, was also discussed by Sigfried Giedion, who lauded it as an inner-city center for pedestrians only, with parking for six thousand cars underground. Giedion, *Architecture You and Me: the Diary of a Development,* 1958, 128. Its site was that later of the Prudential Center (1960– 1970), by Charles Luckman & Associates.

125 Although in a 1961 interview, while the Pan Am was under construction, Belluschi endorsed the concept of teamwork, in practice he was used to, and typically exercized, unilateral control. See Jonathan Barnett, "Pietro Belluschi Interviewed by Architectural Student Jonathan Barnett," *Architectural Record,* March 1961, 10, 347.

126 Which is what happened on the Pan Am project. According to Richard Roth, Jr., Belluschi "just left" after a couple of months, leaving the bulk of the work to others. This is consistent with what Belluschi himself said about their working relationship on the Pan Am: that Gropius, whose personality was far more assertive than his, simply "took over," hence he bowed out. Clausen, *Pietro Belluschi,* 300.

127 Eero Saarinen, "The Six Broad Currents of Modern Architecture," *Architectural Forum,* July 1953, 110–115; Clausen, *Pietro Belluschi,* 208–209.

128 Joseph Rykwert, review of Isaacs, *Walter Gropius, Times Literary Supplement,* May 1986, 463–464.

129 Belluschi's address on the occasion, "Architecture and Society," was published in the *Journal of the AIA,* February 1951, 85–91.

130 "Architects Hear Educator's Plea," *New York Times,* May 18, 1957; Douglas Haskell to Fred Bassetti, letter of response, December 24, 1957, Haskell Papers, box 89.10.

131 Tearsheet, *Architectural Forum,* Haskell Papers, box 68.1. See also "USA Abroad," *Architectural Forum,* December 1957, 114–115, on Belluschi as member of the State Department's Office of Foreign Buildings three-man advisory board, which was appointed in 1954.

132 "New York's Colossal $175 Million Lincoln Square," *Architectural Forum,* November 1956, 13; "The Dream of Lincoln Center," *New York Times Magazine,* October 18, 1959. This was one of many such articles on the Lincoln Center, which was very much in the news at the time. See also Clausen, *Pietro Belluschi,* 326–333.

133 Belluschi's address, "Architecture and Society," published in the *Journal of the AIA,* was also published in the *Architectural Record,* February 1951, 116–118.

134 Walter Gropius, statement to the press, December 18, 1958, Belluschi Papers; Clausen, *Pietro Belluschi,* 287.

135 Thomas W. Ennis, "Octagonal Office Skyscraper to Rise behind Grand Central," *New York Times,* February 18, 1959.

136 "Design of 'Grand Central City' Accepted," *Progressive Architecture,* March 1959, 157.

137 "Buildings in the News—Gropius-Belluschi-Roth Design for Grand Central City," *Architectural Record,* March 1959, 10.

138 "Perspectives," *Architectural Record,* March 1959, 9.

139 Ray Colcord, Jr., letter to Walter Gropius (with copy to Pietro Belluschi), August 18, 1959, Belluschi Papers.

140 Ibid.

141 Letter, Walter Gropius to Ray Colcord, Jr., August 22, 1959, Belluschi Papers.

142 Walter Gropius, "Design Conception of the Grand Central City Building," August 22, 1959, Belluschi Papers.

143 On the skyscraper as modernist symbol, see Ada Louise Huxtable, "Towering Question: The Skyscraper," *New York Times,* June 12, 1960.

CHAPTER 2   THE PAN AM BUILDING

1 "British Funds Back Grand Central City," *New York Times,* October 22, 1959.

2 "Capital from Abroad: An Analysis of Why British Investment in New York Skyscraper Is First of Its Kind," *New York Times,* October 25, 1959.

3 "How British Funds Got in Grand Central Deal." See also "Britain's Energetic Investor," *Architectural Forum,* January 1960, 14, 16, on the Wolfson/Cotton agreement.

4 "How British Funds Got in Grand Central Deal," 32.

5 "How British Funds Got in Grand Central Deal," 33.

6 "New Haven, New York Central End Dispute on Deal with Wolfson," *New York Times,* January 28, 1960.

7 "Pan Am Builders Obtain Financing," *New York Times,* June 12, 1961.

8 This was later revealed to be the New York State Employees Retirement Fund. "Pan Am Building,

Called a Huge Gamble, Is Opening 91% Rented, 100% Financed," *Wall Street Journal,* March 6, 1963.

9 C. Furnas, Joe McCarthy, and the editors of *Life,* "Skyscrapers, Radomes and Chips," in *The Engineer,* 1966, 100–103; Alden P. Armagnac, "The Most Complicated Building Ever Built," *Popular Science,* Summer 1962.

10 "Erecting Office Building over Complicated Track Layout," *Engineering News-Record* 90, no. 12, March 22, 1923, 532–533; Carl Condit, *American Building Art: The Twentieth Century,* 1961, 14–15.

11 Condit, *American Building Art,* 14–15.

12 Furnas, McCarthy, and the editors of *Life,* "Skyscrapers, Radomes and Chips."

13 Interview, Murray Shapiro, May 27, 1994; Furnas, McCarthy, and the editors of *Life,* "Skyscrapers, Radomes and Chips"; Armagnac, "The Most Complicated Building Ever Built"; and "Sky-High Deal for a Skyscraper," *Fortune,* December 1960, 140ff.

14 Ruderman, James (P.E., Consulting Engineer), "Planning and Construction of the Pan Am Building," *Municipal Engineers Journal* 48, no. 2, 1962, 31–40; Interview, Murray Shapiro, May 27, 1994. According to Shapiro, Ruderman was brought in "before anybody else." On Ruderman, see also "James Ruderman Is Dead; Designer of Largest Buildings," *New York Times,* January 28, 1966.

15 Ruderman, "Planning and Construction of the Pan Am Building," 40.

16 On the Colgate-Palmolive Building, see Ada Louise Huxtable, *Four Walking Tours of Modern Architecture in New York City,* 1961, 18–19; Trager, *Park Avenue,* 1990, 192.

17 Interview, Murray Shapiro, May 27, 1994. According to Shapiro, Wolfson had also considered the Union Carbide site but concluded it was uneconomical because the site, occupied by the old courtyarded Hotel Margarite, lacked a substructure of sufficient strength to support a larger building. As a corporate client, Union Carbide had the financial resources to build on the site, as Wolfson, a speculative builder, did not.

18 Furnas, McCarthy, and the editors of Life, "Skyscrapers, Radomes and Chips"; "Skyscraper Here to Rise Like Vine," *New York Times,* September 20, 1959, vIII, 1.

19 Interview, Murray Shapiro, May 27, 1994.

20 Interview, Murray Shapiro, May 27, 1994. The tallest was still the Empire State Building, completed in 1931, which remained the tallest building in the world until the World Trade Center was completed in 1972. Unlike the Pan Am, both buildings, as well as the RCA Building, were built on solid ground.

21 Ruderman, "Planning and Construction of the Pan Am Building," 32; Kaufmann, "Biggest Office Building Yet . . . Worse Luck," 66.

22 Undated, unidentified four-page typed manuscript, Belluschi Papers.

23 Interview, Murray Shapiro, May 27, 1994. On the wind factor in tall buildings, a matter of growing concern in the late 1950s as buildings increasingly rose in height, see "Air Flow around Buildings," *Architectural Forum,* September 1957, 166ff.

24 Interview with Murray Shapiro, May 27, 1994. The problem with wind encountered with the Pan Am building was mentioned in the *Life/Time* publication on The Engineer, but only in regard to a heliport, which was added later after Pan American World Airways signed on as the building's major tenant, requiring the addition of wind-deflecting aluminum vanes around the edges of the roof. Furnas, McCarthy, and the editors of *Life/Time,* "Skyscrapers, Radomes, and Chips," T*he Engineer,* 1966, 103. On the heliport, see chapters 3 and 6, below.

25 "Skyscraper Here to Rise like Vine," *New York Times,* September 20, 1959, viii, 1.

26 Gropius, "Report on Trip to New York, Monday, June 23, 1958."

27 Walter Gropius, "Notes on the Design of the Grand Central City," July 16, 1958, Belluschi Papers.

28 The use of his name for publicity reasons, however, did not. His name on billboards around Grand Central City as construction on the building began met with objections from the state education department, which requested that his name be removed from the signs and any advertising, as its use for such purposes violated state law. Roth, letter to Erwin S. Wolfson (with copy to Pietro Belluschi), August 18, 1959, Belluschi Papers.

There was also a letter from Ray Colcord chiding Belluschi for missing so many meetings around this time. "Now that the 'wraps' are taken off this project and we are all moving full speed ahead into the working drawing stage," Colcord wrote Belluschi after the Wolfson and Cotton deal had been signed, "it is imperative that you and Gropius *both* be there at meetings," as critical decisions regarding the model, size and type of garage, materials and color of the base building had to be decided. Ray Colcord, Jr., letter to Pietro Belluschi, October 22, 1959, Belluschi Papers; emphasis in original.

29 Norman Fletcher, "Notes, Grand Central City Project, New York Trip, 29–30 July 1958," Belluschi Papers.

30 Walter Gropius, memorandum August 14, 1958, Belluschi Papers.

31 Interview, Norman Fletcher, TAC, Cambridge, Massachusetts, March 28, 1989.

32 "How Local Architects Drew $100 Million Plans," *Boston Globe,* March 1, 1959. By this time, only 25 percent of the building had been rented.

33 Interview, Norman Fletcher, March 28, 1989. See also "Tape-Recorded Interview with Pietro Belluchi, Meredith L. Clausen, interviewer," Archives of American Art, Smithsonian Institution, Northwest Oral History Project, no. 12, 1983, 81ff.

34 "Pirelli Headquarters in Milan," *Architectural Forum,* April 1960, 156.

35 Erwin S. Wolfson, letter to Pietro Belluschi, May 7, 1959, Belluschi Papers.

36 James Ruderman, letter to Richard Roth (with copy to Erwin S. Wolfson), August 28, 1958, Belluschi Papers.

37 Interview, Harry Harmon, Emery Roth & Sons, New York City, July 28, 1995.

38 "How Local Architects Drew $100 Million Plans"; interview, Murray Shapiro, May 27, 1994.

39 Interview, Alex Cvijanovic, Cambridge, Massachusetts, March 30, 1989; Pietro Belluschi, sketches, Belluschi Papers.

40 Interview, Norman Fletcher, March 28, 1989; Walter Gropius and George Santry, president of Structural Concrete Products Corporation, exchange of letters, February–March 1959, regarding Structural Concrete's product Schokbeton, which Gropius considered using in the building, Belluschi Papers.

41 Interview, Norman Fletcher, March 28, 1989; Wolf von Eckardt, "Pan Am's Glass House," *New*

Republic, August 13, 1962, 25. An article in *Architectural Forum* in 1957, a year before Gropius and Belluschi signed on to the Pan Am project, focused on the development of a new lightweight concrete that promised to trim building weight by as much as a third; this spurred the new direction in building design, which the *Forum* predicted was just beginning. "Concrete Battles Its Weight," *Architectural Forum,* September 1957, 162ff.

42   "Textured Masonry Sheathes New Office Buildings," *New York Times,* October 29, 1961.

43   Pietro Belluschi drawing, Belluschi Papers. Gropius had objected to pushing the tower northward on the grounds that it would counter his aim of maintaining adequate distance from the New York Central Building, which he felt was important, but was evidently overruled. Gropius memorandum of telephone call from Richard Roth, September 4, 1958, copy of in Belluschi Papers.

44   "How Local Architects Drew $100 Million Plans."

45   Notes in Pietro Belluschi's hand on phone conversation with Roth, September 4, 1958, Belluschi Papers; Gropius memorandum of telephone call from Richard Roth, September 4, 1958, copy of in Belluschi Papers.

46   Gropius, statement to the press, December 18, 1958.

47   Walter Gropius, letter to Richard Roth, December 23, 1958, Belluschi Papers.

48   Interview, Richard Roth, Jr., May 25, 1994. Belluschi's gradual withdrawal was confirmed in interviews with Norman Fletcher (March 28, 1989) and Alex Cvijanovic (March 30, 1989), as well as with Belluschi himself. Belluschi drawings in the Belluschi Papers are dated August 1958, suggesting his involvement was heaviest at this time.

49   Interview, Alex Cvijanovic, March 30, 1989; interview, Norman Fletcher, March 28, 1989; interview, Richard Roth Jr. and Fred Halden, Emery Roth & Sons, New York City, May 25, 1994; "Tape-Recorded Interview with Pietro Belluschi, Meredith L. Clausen, interviewer," 83ff.

50   Interview, Alex Cvijanovic, March 30, 1989. On Belluschi's work at this time and his modus operandi as a design consultant, see Clausen, *Pietro Belluschi,* 198ff.

51   The Architects Collaborative, letter to Richard Roth, January 13, 1959, Belluschi Papers.

52   Walter Gropius, letter to Ray Colcord, Jr., Vice President, Grand Central Building, Inc., August 14, 1959, Belluschi Papers.

53   Emerson Cohen, Precast Building Sections, Inc., letter to Carl A. Morse, September 11, 1959; Walter Gropius, letter to Erwin S. Wolfson, September 11, 1959; minutes, meeting in Emery Roth & Sons office, October 20, 1959. Although Belluschi prepared some sketches of the precast units, he was not at this point attending meetings, prompting Colcord to express his regret over his absence. Colcord, letter to Belluschi, October 22, 1959, Belluschi Papers.

54   Undated, unidentified four-page manuscript, Belluschi Papers.

55   "Model of Grand Central City Shown," *New York Times,* November 3, 1959, 35.

56   Irving Gershon, Emery Roth & Sons, letter to Walter Gropius, November 20, 1959, Belluschi Papers.

57   Walter Gropius, minutes of meeting in New York with Richard Roth, Belluschi, Irving & Gershon, (of Emery Roth & Sons), Alex Cvijanovic (TAC), November 30, 1959, Belluschi Papers.

58   Harold Schiff, letter to Roth, June 14, 1960, Belluschi Papers; Roth, letter to Walter Gropius, June 16, 1960, Belluschi Papers.

59 Memorandum, "Traffic, Grand Central Terminal," January 6, 1960, Belluschi Papers.

60 Roth, letter to Walter Gropius, February 9, 1960, Belluschi Papers.

61 Ray Colcord, Jr., letter to Walter Gropius, April 28, 1960, Belluschi Papers.

62 Walter Gropius, letter to Roth, April 12, 1960, Belluschi Papers.

63 Minutes, Grand Central City construction meetings, March 24 and April 12, 1960, Belluschi Papers.

64 Gropius, letter to Roth, April 12, 1960; Walter Gropius, letter to Erwin S. Wolfson, April 19, 1960, Belluschi Papers.

65 Minutes, general construction meeting, May 5, 1960, Belluschi Papers; minutes, general construction meeting, May 19, 1960, Belluschi Papers.

66 Minutes, Grand Central City construction meetings, Spring–Summer 1960, Belluschi Papers.

67 Ray Colcord, Jr., letter to Walter Gropius, May 13, 1960, Belluschi Papers.

68 Walter Gropius, letter to Ray Colcord, Jr., October 31, 1960, Belluschi Papers.

69 Walter Gropius, letter to Ray Colcord, Jr., December 9, 1960, Belluschi Papers.

70 Walter Gropius, letters to Roth, December 13, 1960, and December 14, 1960, Belluschi Papers.

71 Carl A. Morse, letter to Roth, January 23, 1961, Belluschi Papers; Roth, letter to Erwin S. Wolfson, January 24, 1961, Belluschi Papers; Walter S. Gropius, letter to Ray Colcord, Jr. (with copies to Roth and Pietro Belluschi), February 28, 1961, Belluschi Papers.

72 Walter Gropius, letter to Roth, February 7, 1961, Belluschi Papers.

73 "Architect for Business in a City of Towers," *Business Week,* September 1, 1962, 55–56.

74 Interview, Murray Shapiro, May 27, 1994.

75 Furnas, McCarthy, and the editors of *Life/Time,* "Skyscrapers, Radomes and Chips."

76 "Company Realigns Executives," *New York Times,* January 4, 1957.

77 "Company Realigns Executives"; "Contractor Makes Consulting Business," *Engineering News-Record,* February 1, 1962. On Carl Morse, see also "Building Skylines Is His Business: Carl Morse of New York's Diesel Construction," *Business Week,* July 11, 1964, 33–34. Glenn Fowler, "Carl Morse, a Builder, Dies at 83; Helped Shape New York's Skyline," *New York Times,* November 16, 1989.

78 Interview, Irwin Miller, New York City, May 27, 1994. Miller, who retired as head of the Tishman Company in 1994, was formerly the president of Diesel Construction, which by the time of the Pan Am Building had become a division of Carl A. Morse, Inc., of which Schiff was president. The company later became Morse Diesel, then Morse Diesel International, which by the time Morse died in 1989 was one of the largest building construction companies in the world. Fowler, "Carl Morse, a Builder, Dies"; interview, Irwin Miller, May 17, 1994; interview, Harold Schiff, by telephone, April 2, 2001.

79 "Carl Morse: Orchestrator of Buildings for 54 Years," *New York Times,* September 23, 1979; "Carl Morse, a Builder, Dies."

80 "Carl Morse, a Builder, Dies"; interview, Murray Shapiro, May 27, 1994. According to Shapiro, "a lot of the people who built America cut their eyeteeth working with Morse on the Pan Am." Among them was Schiff, the last person personally trained by Morse, who joined Diesel Construction in 1958 at the onset of the Pan Am. As project manager, it was his responsibility to establish the construction budget, attend all architectural development meetings, coordinate schedules, and propose items or strategies to keep costs within budget. Working under Morse's supervision, Schiff prepared the contracts, handled the negotiations, and monitored the building site on a daily basis. He later co-founded Schal Associates, a Chicago-based international construction management firm with over three hundred employees, later sold to Bovis, Inc., a subsidiary of the Peninsular & Orient Steam Navigation Company. There was also Peter Lehrer, of Lehrer-McGovern-Bolgan, later to become one of the biggest companies in the field, who began his career with his work on the Pan Am. Irwin Miller, former head of Tishman, also worked for Diesel, learning from Morse. John Cavanaugh, current head of the Diesel Company in New York, was yet another.

81 Interview, Irwin Miller, May 27, 1994; Harold Schiff, correspondence with author, March 14, 2003.

82 Interview, Murray Shapiro, May 27, 1994.

83 "The Contractor," *Architectural Forum,* February 1956, 114–119.

84 "Huge Steel Award Let for New Building Here," *New York Times,* May 13, 1959. A $4 million contract for the wiring of the building, awarded to electrical contractors Fischback and Moore, Inc., in March 1961, also made news. "Four Million, Pam Am Job Let," *New York Times,* March 11, 1961.

85 "Skyscraper Here to Rise like Vine."

86 "Building Plan Filed," *New York Times,* November 25, 1959; "Skyscraper Is Begun," *New York Times,* November 27, 1959.

87 "Big Soundproof Job Awarded," *New York Times,* February 16, 1960.

88 "Westinghouse Lifts Records," *New York Times,* February 24, 1960.

89 "Building Will Get Single Phone Unit," *New York Times,* August 14, 1960.

90 "Wrecking Starts at Grand Central," *New York Times,* June 28, 1960.

91 Another factor for the delay may have been fallout from the 1959 steel strike. On the strike, see Kaufmann, "Biggest Office Building Yet . . . Worse Luck," 68.

92 Erwin S. Wolfson, letter to Pietro Belluschi, July 29, 1960, Belluschi Papers.

93 Erwin S. Wolfson, letter to Richard Roth (with copies to Walter Gropius and Pietro Belluschi), August 26, 1960, Belluschi Papers. On the Fenestra floor panels, see "Bridge Methods Used on Floors," *New York Times,* February 3, 1962.

94 Wolfson, letter to Roth, August 26, 1960. Belluschi Papers.

95 Furnas, McCarthy, and the editors of *Life/Time,* "Skyscrapers, Radomes and Chips," 100–103.

96 Interview, Irwin Miller, May 27, 1994; interview, Murray Shapiro, May 27, 1994.

97 Undated, unidentified four-page manuscript, Belluschi Papers.

98 Interview, Irwin Miller, May 27, 1994. Although it was possible the bankruptcy was due to incompetence, Miller though it more likely was because the company, Dextone, of New Haven, Connecticut, was one of the first companies in the line, and the exceptional size of the Pan Am job might simply have overwhelmed the company's capabilities.

99 "Terminal to Get Bowling Alleys," *New York Times,* August 4, 1960.

100 Robert C. Weinberg, "Station Plan Protested: United Opposition Seen in Bowling Alley in Grand Central" [letter to editor], *New York Times,* August 16, 1960.

101 S. T. Keiley, Manager, Grand Central Terminal, letter to the editor, *New York Times,* August 24, 1960.

102 Douglas Haskell, form letter [to *Architectural Forum* readers], August 1960, Haskell Papers, box 96.6.

103 Douglas Haskell, "Visionless Enterprise," *Architectural Forum,* October 1960, 87.

104 Douglas Haskell, typed manuscript, "Down in the Alleys," Haskell Papers, box 96.6. A note accompanying the manuscript suggests it was destined to be published in the *Oculus,* the bimonthly publication of the New York chapter of the AIA.

105 Haskell letter to Wolfson, January 26, 1961; Wolfson letter to Haskell, February 2, 1961, Haskell Papers, box 97.

106 Victor Gruen, "Plan for Grand Central Opposed," *New York Times,* November 26, 1960, 20.

107 "Architects Hit Plans for Grand Central Bowling," *Architectural Forum,* January 1961, 9, 11.

108 "Bowling Plan Hit in Grand Central," *New York Times,* December 4, 1960.

109 "Of Parks and Terminals" [editorial], *New York Times,* December 6, 1960.

110 Norman Cousins, "Notes on a Changing America" [editorial], *Saturday Review* 17, December 1960, 26, 33.

111 "Group Hits Bowling at Grand Central," *New York Times,* January 5, 1961; "Councilman Fights Bowling Alley Plan for Grand Central," *New York Times,* January 7, 1961; "Bowling over Grand Central" [editorial], *New York Times,* January 10, 1961.

112 James O. Boisi, Vice President of Real Estate, New York Central Railroad, statement at Board of Standards and Appeals hearing on bowling alleys in Grand Central, January 10, 1961, Haskell Papers, box 97.3.

113 "Bowling Barred at Grand Central," *New York Times,* January 11, 1961.

114 "Architects to Keep Their Guardian Eye on Grand Central," *New York Times,* January 24, 1961.

115 "$115 Million Lease Sets a Mark Here," *New York Times,* September 28, 1960, 1; on Trippe's secretive manner, see Marylin Bender and Selig Altshul, *The Chosen Instrument: Pan Am, Juan Trippe, The Rise and Fall of an American Entrepreneur,* 1982, 486–487.

116 "Idlewild: Gateway to the World," *Cosmopolitan,* May 1960, 44ff.

117 For example, "Airports for Tomorrow," *Architectural Forum,* January 1958 123–125; "TWA's Graceful New Terminal," *Architectural Forum,* January 1958, 78–80; "Idlewild, New Aerial Gateway to America," *Architectural Forum,* February 1958, 79–86; "Pan American's New Terminal in New York," *Architectural Forum,* July 1960, 5.

118 "Idlewild: Gateway to the World"; "Pan American World Airways: 1927–1991," *Newsweek,* July 22, 1991, 36. On Pan Am at its peak in the 1960s, see Wayne Biddle, *Barons of the Sky: From Early Flight to Strategic Warfare; The Story of the American Aerospace Industry,* 1991, 208; "With Sky-High Hopes, Pan Am Starts Small," *New York Daily News,* September 26, 1996, 39.

119 John Crudele, "Deregulation and Pan Am's Pancake Landing," *Seattle Post-Intelligencer,* June 14, 1990.

120 On Trippe, see "Pan American World Airways," *Newsweek,* July 22, 1991, 36; "With Sky-High Hopes, Pan Am Starts Small," *New York Daily News,* September 26, 1996; "Juan Trippe, 81, Dies; U.S. Aviation Pioneer," *New York Times,* April 4, 1981; Bender and Altshul, *Chosen Instrument.*

121 Bender and Altshul, *Chosen Instrument,* 182.

122 Ibid., 477.

123 "Juan Trippe, 81, Dies; U.S. Aviation Pioneer," *New York Times,* April 4, 1981.

124 "With Sky-High Hopes, Pan Am Starts Small."

125 Until the late 1970s, according to Barbara Sturken Peterson and James Glab, four of the five largest airlines in the country were housed within a few blocks of each other in the mid-Manhattan area, with Eastern headquartered at Rockefeller Center at Fifth Avenue and 49th Street; Pan Am was in the Chrysler Building before it moved to its namesake building on Park and 45th Street; American and TWA were across the street from each other at Third Avenue and 40th Street. Peterson and Glab, *Rapid Descent: Deregulation and Shakeout in the Airlines,* 1994, 53, 82.

126 Thomas W. Ennis, "Leases Play Vital Role," *New York Times,* October 2, 1960; "Sky High Deal for Skyscraper"; Bender and Altshul, *Chosen Instrument,* 487. It is unclear what Trippe specifically found appealing about the proposed building, whether it was its striking form or that it was designed by two famous architects. My hunch is—and it is only that—that it was the size and location of the building primarily, and its prominent architects, whose names would serve the same public relations role that Lindbergh's did for Pan Am in the 1930s, rather than the design of the building itself.

127 "$115 Million Lease Sets a Mark Here."

128 Ennis, "Leases Play Vital Role."

129 "Sky-High Deal for a Skyscraper."

130 Walter Gropius, letter to Erwin S. Wolfson (with copies to Ray Colcord, Jr., Emery Roth & Sons, and Pietro Belluschi), August 25, 1960, on their discussions with Charles Forberg and Ivan Chermayeff from the Edward Larabee Barnes office, Belluschi Papers; "Sky-High Deal for a Skyscraper."

131 "Tenant Can Pick Building's Name," *New York Times,* January 4, 1959.

132 On the long, difficult, highly secret negotiations between Wolfson and Trippe, see "Sky-High Deal for a Skyscraper"; on Trippe more specifically and his tough negotiating style, see Bender and Altshul, *Chosen Instrument.* Whether Trippe also got Wolfson to agree to a heliport at this time, as Bender and Altshul suggest, is unclear. See "Heliport," chapter 6, below.

133 Walter Gropius, letter to Richard Roth, August 24, 1960, Belluschi Papers; Gropius, letter to Wolfson, August 25, 1960. Barnes, Forberg, and Chermayeff, who were hired by Pan American Airways to work on design issues, were all involved; their presence at meetings concerning interior lighting is mentioned in the August 24 letter from Gropius to Roth. See also "Pan American Ticket Office," below. My thanks to John Zukowsky for his unflagging support and assistance here and elsewhere throughout my Pan Am study.

134 Willis G. Lipscomb, Office of the Vice President, Traffic and Sales, Pan American World Airways, letter to Ray Colcord, Jr., May 3, 1961, Belluschi Papers.

135 Walter Gropius, letter to Erwin S. Wolfson (with copies to Pietro Belluschi, Richard Roth, and Ray Colcord Jr.), October 13, 1961, Belluschi Papers.

136 "Pan Am Ticket Office: An Airy Sweep of Sculptured Space," *Architectural Forum,* August 1963, 98–101; "Pan Am's Ticket Office in the Pan Am Building," *Interiors* 124, November 1964, 90–93. On Forberg and Barnes, see John Zukowsky, ed., *Building for Air Travel: Architecture and Design for Commercial Aviation,* 1996, 24.

137 Gropius, "Curse of Conformity"; Gropius "TAC's Objectives," Gropius et al., eds., *The Architects Collaborative,* 1966, 20.

138 Daniel Bell, "Modernism Mummified," 171, note 5. See also Russell Lynes's essays in *Harper's* on "taste," especially "Highbrow, Lowbrow, Middlebrow," *Harper's,* February 1949, 19–28; and "The Age of Taste," *Harper's,* October 1950, 60–73.

139 Glenn Fowler, "Drab Murals That Once Prevailed Are Avoided," *New York Times,* August 17, 1958.

140 Ada Louise Huxtable, "Art with Architecture: New Terms of an Old Alliance," *New York Times,* September 13, 1959, 20.

141 On the futuristic aspect of Pan Am's imagery, including its appearance in "2001: A Space Odyssey," see John Zukowsky, ed., *2001: Building for Space Travel,* 2001.

142 Harris K. Prior, letter to Pietro Belluschi, June 4, 1960, Belluschi Papers; Pietro Belluschi, letter to Ray Colcord, Jr., June 8, 1960, Belluschi Papers.

143 Ray Colcord, Jr., letter to Pietro Belluschi, August 1, 1960, Belluschi Papers.

144 Walter S. Gropius, letter to Ray Colcord, Jr., December 5, 1960, Belluschi Papers.

145 On Belluschi's churches, see Clausen, *Spiritual Space.*

146 Interview, Alex Cvijanovic, March 30, 1989.

147 Richard Lippold, statement on sculpture for the Pan American Airways (Vanderbilt) Lobby, January 1961, Belluschi Papers.

148 Walter Gropius, letter to René d'Harnoncourt, February 16, 1961, Belluschi Papers.

149 "Talk of the Town: Symbol," *New Yorker,* April 8, 1961, 47–49.

150 "Talk of the Town: Symbol," 47–49."

151 "Pan Am Building to Have Sculpture," *New York Times,* September 3, 1961, vii, 1.

152 Richard Lippold, "Projects for Pan Am and Philharmonic," *Art in America,* Summer 1962, 50–55.

153 "Music World: No Sound at All; Muzak versus John Cage Ends in Silence at Pan Am," *New York Times,* August 12, 1962, ii, 9.

154 "Sculptor Becomes a High-Wire Artist in Pan Am Lobby," *New York Times,* April 25, 1963, 1.

155 "Pan Am Lobby Gets Look of Art Gallery," *New York Times,* July 7, 1963.

156 Gropius evidently had no hand in the Berks sculpture, as there is no mention of it in any of his or Belluschi's documents. The Albers mural was featured in a *New York Times* article the following year on the occasion of its being washed. "Mural in Pan Am Building Gets Face Washed," *New York Times,* December 8, 1963. The work, called "Manhattan," was mentioned but not illustrated in a book on Albers edited by Getulio Alviani (*Josef Albers,* 1988); the work was again mentioned but not illustrated in *Josef Albers: Glass, Color, and Light,* a catalog of Albers's work produced on the occasion of an exhibition of his work at the Guggenheim in 1994–1995. The author, Fred Licht, describes "City" as a small, eleven- by twenty-one-inch work of 1928 (number 27 in the catalog) in which Albers was exploring rhythmic relations of color and light, figure and ground, which Albers abandoned; meanwhile the Bauhaus closed and Albers moved to the United States. In 1963, according to Licht, Albers expanded "City" into the "gigantic Formica screen" he called "Manhattan," which was installed in the Pan Am.

157 [Lippold sculpture], *Architectural Forum,* August 1963, 17. The article in *Architectural Record,* "'Flight' Is Firmly in Place in Pan Am Lobby," August 1963, 24, was, like that in the *Times,* simply descriptive.

CHAPTER 3   THE CLAMOR OF CRITICISM

1 "Crossroads in the City's Heart" [editorial], *New York Times,* June 5, 1958.
2 Robert C. Weinberg, letter to Pietro Belluschi, August 11, 1958, Belluschi Papers; "Can Civic Beauty Be Legislated?" *Architectural Forum,* August 1958, 92.
3 Pietro Belluschi, letter to Robert C. Weinberg, August 14, 1958, Belluschi Papers.
4 Robert C. Weinberg, letter to Pietro Belluschi, August 29, 1958, Belluschi Papers.
5 Richard J. Wengraf, Program Chairman, New York Regional Chapter, American Institute of Planners, letter to Pietro Belluschi, December 7, 1958. Belluschi Papers.
6 Walter C. Reis, letter to the editor, *Architectural Forum,* January 1959, 57–58.
7 Richard Edes Harrison, letter to the editor, *New York Times,* February 23, 1959.
8 Sibyl Moholy-Nagy, letter to the editor, *Progressive Architecture,* May 1959, 59, 61–62.
9 Natalie Parry, letter to Pietro Belluschi, May 21, 1959, Belluschi Papers; Pietro Belluschi, letter to Natalie Parry, May 26, 1959, Belluschi Papers; Walter Gropius, letter to Natalie Parry with copy to Belluschi, May 28, 1959, Belluschi Papers; Natalie Parry, letters to Walter Gropius and Pietro Belluschi, June 12, 1959, Belluschi Papers.
10 Natalie Parry, "In Defense of Grand Central City Building Design," *Progressive Architecture,* August 1959, 49. The argument of inevitability was to be made again with a proposal for another tower by Marcel Breuer twenty years later.
11 "What Is Good Design and Planning in New York?" New School for Social Research, January 1960.
12 Walter McQuade, "Architecture" [on the New School forum, "What Is Good Design and Planning in New York?"] *Nation,* January 30, 1960, 104–105.
13 "Perspectives" [report on New School forum, "What Is Good Design and Planning in New York?"], *Architectural Record,* February 1960, 9.
14 Ada Louise Huxtable, "Marvel or Monster?" *New York Times,* January 24, 1960, x13.
15 Ibid, x13
16 Theodore P. Ferris, Rector, Trinity Church, Boston, sermon, January 17, 1960 (copy in Belluschi Papers).
17 "Erwin S. Wolfson, Builder of Skylines," 92.
18 Paul Liffman, letter to the editor, *New York Times,* May 24, 1960.
19 Kaufmann, "Biggest Office Building Yet . . . Worse Luck," 64–70. Kaufmann had met with Wolfson as well as Gropius, Belluschi, and presumably Richard Roth the previous summer to discuss their aims as well as to get information in preparation for the *Harper's* article. He later sent Gropius an advance copy of the article, which Gropius found "mean" but decided, after discussing it with Belluschi, not to respond to directly. Walter Gropius, letters to Edgar Kaufmann, Jr. (with copies to Pietro

Belluschi), July 13, 1959, and July 21, 1959, Belluschi Papers; Walter Gropius, letter to Erwin S. Wolfson, April 29, 1960, Belluschi Papers.

20 Kaufmann received much of his information about the project from Wolfson himself, who more likely than not stressed the aesthetic rather than economic motivations for his revising the plan. It seems clear that Kaufmann, however, rightly sensed other, more pragmatic factors at play.

21 Kaufmann added here that business experts recommended 2.4 million square feet as the building's optimum size, suggesting that a larger building might have been difficult to fill—again, an economic rather than aesthetic factor.

22 Kaufmann, "Biggest Office Building Yet . . . Worse Luck," 64–70.

23 "Sky-High Deal for a Skyscraper." Gropius and Belluschi had both been contacted about the article over a year earlier and asked to review a preliminary draft (which was substantially different from the final version) for corrections and suggestions. Why the article's publication was postponed is unclear, but it is likely that the onslaught of criticism, which began appearing in force with Moholy-Nagy's letter and the *Harper's* article, held up its publication. Jane Alyea, *Fortune,* letter to Pietro Belluschi, December 8, 1959, with working draft manuscript, "Grand Central City," attached, Belluschi Papers.

24 *Fortune* implied that Pan American World Airways signed on because of the building's design. It seems clear, however, that Trippe was more interested in the site of the building, and the star stature of its prestigious architects, than in a distinctive form, the design of which he showed no interest in. See chapter 2, above.

25 "Sky-High Deal for a Skyscraper," 271.

26 This of course was Jane Jacobs's point, in *Death and Life of Great American Cities,* which also appeared early in the year, about this same time.

27 Bertrand Goldberg, "Two-Shift City," *Architectural Forum,* February 1961, 173.

28 Wayne Andrews, "Something Less than Chartres" [review of Condit, *American Building Art*], *Reporter,* July 6, 1961, 49.

29 Condit, *American Building Art,* 15–16.

30 Emmett Davis, letter to the editor, *New York Times,* August 24, 1961, 28.

31 Huxtable, *Four Walking Tours of Modern Architecture in New York City,* 17.

32 "Gropius Declares 'Anti-Uglies' Could Help City Battle Chaos," *New York Times,* January 5, 1962.

33 "Anti-Uglies," *Architectural Forum,* February 1962, 11. Scully's talk, "Death of the Street," was published the following year in *Perspecta* 8, 1963.

34 Emerson Goble, "New City Image Needed," *Architectural Record,* January 1962, 9.

35 "Conference on Ugliness" [editorial], *New York Times,* April 7, 1962. Douglas Haskell was one of the sponsors of the conference and participated in the planning. Douglas Haskell, memorandum to Joe Hazen (with copy to Peter Blake), March 21, 1962, Haskell Papers, box 61.3; Douglas Haskell, letter to Richard W. Snibbe, Chairman, Design Committee, Aesthetic Responsibility Conference, Haskell Papers, box 61.3.

36 Ada Louise Huxtable, "Our New Buildings: Hits and Misses," *New York Times Magazine,* April 29, 1962, vi, 16–17, 105–106.

37 "Flags Mark Topping-out of Pan Am Building's Steel," *New York Times,* May 10, 1962.

38 Peter Blake, "The Building Boom: Architecture in Decline," *Architectural Forum,* June 1962, 128–129.

39 Ibid.

40 Von Eckardt, "Pan Am's Glass House," 24–26.

41 Ibid. Von Eckardt's article "The Bauhaus" appeared in *Horizon,* November 1961, 58–75.

42 "The Controversial Giant," *Dun's Review and Modern Industries,* September 1962, part 2, p. S138; "Architect for Business in a City of Towers," 54–56; "Doing over the Town," *Time,* September 28, 1962, 56–69.

43 "Architect for Business in a City of Towers."

44 "Doing over the Town."

45 Interview, Murray Shapiro, May 27, 1994; interview, Harold Schiff (Chicago), by telephone, April 9, 2001.

46 "New Skyscrapers Are Designed to Ease Pedestrian Movement," *New York Times,* June 26, 1960.

47 Emerson Goble, "Unity in Diversity," *Architectural Record,* April 1961, 9.

48 Walter Gropius, "True Architectural Goals Yet to Be Realized," *Architectural Record,* June 1961, 147–152. Gropius's article was also published in *Arts & Architecture* 78, May 1961, 14–15, 28–30; and in *Zodiac* 8, 1961, 34–41, with a preface on Gropius by Gillo Dorfles.

49 Emerson Goble, "In Defense of the Pan Am Building: Pan Am Makes a Point; A Plea for the Vertical City as a Planning Principle; A Three-Dimensional City Planned for Pedestrians instead of Autos," *Architectural Record,* May 1962, 195ff. Gropius suggested to Wolfson, in a letter dated March 14, 1961 (Belluschi Papers), that he ask Paul Zucker of the New School to write an article on their behalf, which he was sure *Architectural Record* would publish, adding that he and Belluschi "would prepare some arguments for his use." In his letter to Belluschi of October 2 of that year (Belluschi Papers), Goble thanked Belluschi for sending him material that would "be useful when they get going on the Pan Am story." Goble's article was summarized in a short, inconspicuous article by Edmond J. Barnett, "Architect Lands A Vertical City" *New York Times,* June 9, 1962, 21, which evidently was sent to the *New York Times* in the hopes it would rerun it.

50 Goble, "In Defense of the Pan Am Building."

51 Charles Abrams, "Pan Am Building Defended," *Architectural Record,* May 1962, 197. The article consisted of an excerpt from Abram's speech to the Lower East Side Neighborhood Association, May 13, 1961, a copy of which Belluschi had sent to both Gropius and Mildred Schmertz of *Architectural Record.* In a letter to Gropius (September 22, 1961, Belluschi Papers), Belluschi called Abrams "perhaps one of the most respected of our practical planners" and mentioned Abrams's speech on urban renewal to the association, a paragraph of which he was sending to Schmertz, as he thought it "had direct bearing on the Grand Central and could be used as excellent ammunition."

The argument in defense of congestion was picked up several years later, after the Pan Am Building opened, by William F. R. Ballard, who was sworn in as chairman of the City Planning Commission by Mayor Robert F. Wagner in October 1963. Acknowledging that he was at odds with other members of the commission on a number of "the most controversial subjects of the city's future," including the automobile in midtown Manhattan (which he was all in favor of), he thought the Pan Am Building was "great." "I can't think of a better place to have a big building. It's at the focus of all midtown commutation and transportation, the best place for it. I don't think concentration as such is an evil," he explained. "It is the essence of cities." This was, of course, Belluschi's argument exactly. On Ballard, see Ada Louise Huxtable, "Planner Defends Cars in Midtown," *New York Times,* October 16, 1963, 47, 50.

52 Walter Gropius, "Gropius and Garroway," *Architectural Forum,* April 1960, 177, 179.

53 Among these: "Address by Dr. Walter Gropius, upon Receiving the Honorary Degree of Doctor of Humane Letters from Columbia University," *Arts & Architecture* 78, May 1961, 14–15, 28–30 (a reprint of his speech in toto); "True Architectural Goals Yet to Be Realized," 147–152; "Gropius at Twenty-Six" [memorandum written by Gropius when he was twenty-six years old], *Architectural Review* 130, July 1961, 49–51.

54 Walter Gropius, letter to Paul Zucker, March 24, 1961, Belluschi Papers.

55 Pietro Belluschi, letter to Paul Zucker, March 27, 1961 (with copy to Gropius), Belluschi Papers.

56 Barnett, "Pietro Belluschi Interviewed by Architectural Student Jonathan Barnett," 347, 351.

57 Paul Barrett, "Heliports," in Kenneth T. Jackson, ed., *Encyclopedia of New York,* 1995, 537–538.

58 Bender and Altshul, *Chosen Instrument,* 487.

59 Paul J. C. Friedlander, "Midtown Launch Pad Opens Tuesday," *New York Times,* December 19, 1965.

60 Interview, Murray Shapiro, May 27, 1994.

61 Interviews, Alex Cvijanovic, March 30, 1989, Murray Shapiro, May 27, 1994; Furnas, McCarthy, and the editors of *Life,* "Skyscrapers, Radomes and Chips," 100–103.

62 This feature, according to Richard Roth, Jr., was an aspect of Gropius's design with which those in the Roth office were never happy. But as Roth put it, "when you hire a big name. . . ." Interview, Richard Roth, Jr., May 25, 1994.

63 Walter Gropius, letter to Ray Colcord, Jr., February 15, 1961, Belluschi Papers.

64 Richard Witkin, "Heliport Slated atop Skyscraper," *New York Times,* March 24, 1961, 33.

65 Richard Witkin, "Heliport Takes Shape on Roof of Pan Am Building, *New York Times,* September 21, 1962, 31.

66 Irwin B. Margiloff, "Noise from Helicopter Feared" [letter to the editor], *New York Times,* September 29, 1962.

67 Glenn Fowler, "Framing Begins for Skyscraper," *New York Times,* March 12, 1961, 8:1; "Pan Am Squeezes into New York Skyline," *Business Week,* November 11, 1961, 34–35.

68 "Answer Machine at Pan Am Site Helps Sidewalk Supervisors," *New York Times,* September 10, 1961.

69 "Pan Am Builders Obtain Financing."

70 "Textured Masonry Sheathes New Office Building"; "Concrete Curtain," *Architectural Forum,* February 1962, 10.

71 "Manhattan's Skyline . . . Gets Another Big One," *Newsweek,* December 25, 1961, 66–67. On the other hand, there were several construction site accidents, one of them fatal. Interviews, Ruderman office, 1994; Harold Schiff, e-mail, June 3, 2004.

72 "Bridge Methods Used on Floors."

73 "Escalators Coming to Grand Central," *New York Times,* February 25, 1962.

74 "Complex Equipment Installed in Pan Am's New Skyscraper," *New York Times,* March 17, 1962. As it was described in the *Times,* the $25.4 million system required extraordinary construction to accommodate the complex, sensitive machinery. The system, with its main computer installed in a 5,500-square-foot space on the fourth floor, promised to link 114 cities on six continents, with continuous twenty-four-hour operations throughout the year. A dual air-conditioning system geared to the needs of both the machine and personnel operating it, was also to be installed, circulating a complete change of air every minute.

75 "Umpire Rebuffs Two Unions Here; Neither Gets Jurisdiction in Pan Am Building Dispute," *New York Times,* April 5, 1962, 21.

76 "Flags Mark Topping-out of Pan Am Building's Steel."

77 "Build We Must: New York's Construction Boom, Still Going Strong," *Business Week,* May 19, 1962, 31–33.

78 "Erwin S. Wolfson Is Dead at 60"; "A One-Man Operation in an Organized World," *Business Week,* September 10, 1960, 110–114, 121–124; "The King Is Dead," *Architectural Forum,* August 1962, 13; Lawrence G. O'Donnell, "Pan Am Building, Called a Huge Gamble, Is Opening 91% Rented, 100% Financed," *Wall Street Journal,* March 6, 1963, 16.

79 "A Developing Feature of the City Scene: The Pan Am Building, 59 Stories Tall, Is to Be Completed at the End of the Year," *New York Times,* August 14, 1962, 25.

80 Armagnac, "The Most Complicated Building Ever Built," 70–72; "Up Goes Manhattan! Splendor in the Skies," *Life,* November 9, 1962. See also "New York Nears Completion—Almost," *Architectural Forum,* October 1962, 16.

81 "Pan Am Building Dedicated in New York," *New York Times,* March 8, 1963, 11.

CHAPTER 4   THE BUILDING'S IMPACT

1 Laurence G. O'Donnell, "Pan Am Building, Called a Huge Gamble, Is Opening 91% Rented, 100% Financed," 16.

2 Average rent for office space in midtown Manhattan was $5.25 to $6 per square foot, whereas the average rate per square foot in the Pan Am was $6.75. Ibid.

3 Ibid.

4 "World's Largest Executive Suite," *Business Week,* July 20, 1963.

5 Gay Talese, "Expert Eye," *New York Times Magazine,* May 7, 1961, 38.

6 On the Universal Pictures Building, later called the MCA Building, see Trager, *Park Avenue,* 189; Huxtable, *Four Walking Tours of Modern Architecture in New York City,* 13. Kahn & Jacobs were architects.

7 "Office Building Boom Is Going Nationwide," *Architectural Forum,* May 1963, 14ff.

8 Scully, "Death of the Street," 91–96.

9 Richard Roth, "The Forces that Shaped Park Avenue," *Perspecta* 8, 1963, 97–102.

10 "The Largest Office Building" [editorial], *New York Times,* March 11, 1963, 8.

11 "Extra Grand Central," *Time,* March 15, 1963, 71.

12 "Pan Am Building, Center of a Storm of Controversy, Nears Completion," *New York Times,* April 7, 1963.

13 Ada Louise Huxtable, "Architecture Stumbles On," *New York Times,* April 14, 1963.

14 Ada Louise Huxtable, "The Attainment of Quality," *AIA Journal* 40, July 1963, 89–99.

15 Ada Louise Huxtable, "Something Awry," *New York Times,* December 22, 1963, x15.

16 James T. Burns, Jr. "The Pan Am Building: A Behemoth Is Born," *Progressive Architecture* 44, April 1963, 61–62.

17 Edmund Bacon, letter to the editor, *Progressive Architecture,* June 1963, 174; Edmund N. Bacon, letter to James T. Burns, Jr. (with copy to Pietro Belluschi), April 18, 1963, Belluschi Papers.

18 Albert Bush-Brown, letter to the editor, *Progressive Architecture,* June 1963, 174.

19 Earl P. Carlin, letter to the editor, *Progressive Architecture,* June 1963, 174.

20 Paul Hayden Kirk, letter to the editor, *Progressive Architecture,* June 1963, 174.

21 Edgar A. Tafel, letter to the editor, *Progressive Architecture,* June 1963, 174.

22 Herb Greene, letter to the editor, *Progressive Architecture,* June 1963, 174, 176.

23 C. J. Wisniewski, letter to the editor, *Progressive Architecture,* June 1963, 176.

24 Thomas Stauffer, President, Chicago Heritage Committee, letter to the editor, *Progressive Architecture,* June 1963, 176.

25 Isadore Rosenfield, letter to the editor, *Progressive Architecture,* June 1963, 176.

26 Gunnar Birkerts, letter to the editor, *Progressive Architecture,* July 1963, 156.

27 Raniero Corbelletti, Professor of Architecture, Pratt Institute, letter to the editor, *Progressive Architecture,* July 1963, 156.

28 Leonard K. Eaton, Associate Professor of Architecture, University of Michigan, letter to the editor, *Progressive Architecture,* July 1963, 156.

29 Jim Lamantia, letter to the editor, *Progressive Architecture,* July 1963, 156.

30 Meyer Katzman, letter to the editor, *Progressive Architecture,* July 1963, 156, 158.

31 Carl A. Bystrom, letter to the editor, *Progressive Architecture,* August 1963, 150.

32 Pietro Belluschi, "Eloquent Simplicity in Architecture," *Architectural Record,* July 1963, 131–135; "Gropius' 80th Birthday Marked by Old Friends and Students," *Architectural Record,* July 1963, 10.

33 Mildred Schmertz, "The Problem of Pan Am," *Architectural Record,* May 1963, 151–158 (copy in Haskell Papers, box 36.6).

34 Schmertz, "The Problem of Pan Am."

35 Clarence M. Baker, letter to the editor, *Progressive Architecture,* September 1963, 6.

36 Morton Rader, letter to the editor, *Progressive Architecture,* September 1963, 6.

37 August Heckscher, "Pan Am Building Praised," letter to the editor, *New York Times,* August 31, 1964. It should be noted that Heckscher, for all his praise of the Pan Am's "enchanting" spaces at this point, cites neither it nor Park Avenue in *Open Spaces: The Life of American Cities,* 1977. William H. Whyte, however, does, in his book on open space, *The Social Life of Small Urban Spaces,* 1982, 27, where he points out the Pan Am's utter lack of it. My thanks to Paul Davis for calling the reference in Whyte to my attention.

38 Haskell, "Lost New York of the Pan American Airways Building," 106ff. Haskell was evidently not happy with the article's title and in earlier drafts had thought of calling it "Pan Am: Death of Great Ideas" or "Pan Am: Loss of a City." Typed manuscript, Haskell Papers, box 36.6.

39 Among documents in the Haskell Papers is a boilerplate letter Haskell sent to "Friends" (*Architectural Forum*'s readership), dated September 4, 1958, asking them to list the eleven architectural firms, big or small, that in their opinion led in architectural quality, for a forthcoming *Forum* article on quality in architecture. The letters in response cited Belluschi frequently; none mentioned Gropius. Haskell Papers, box 55.10. On Haskell and Belluschi, see "Letters—Belluschi," Haskell Papers, box 2.1.

40 Douglas Haskell, letters to Walter Gropius, March 22, 1961, March 2, 1962, and December 20, 1963, Haskell Papers, box 2.1.

41 Douglas Haskell, letter to Walter Gropius, January 5, 1960, Haskell Papers, box 2.1; letter to Fitch, January 13, 1960, Haskell Papers, box 2.1. On Fitch's book, part of the Braziller series on great masters, published later that year, see text below.

42 Haskell assumed editorship of the *Forum* in 1949, leaving *Architectural Record,* on whose editorial staff he had served since 1943. Robert Benson, "Douglas Putnam Haskell (1899–1979): The Early Critical Writings," Ph.D. dissertation, University of Michigan, 1987, 427.

43 Typed manuscript, speech, Michigan Society of Architects, 1959, 2, Haskell Papers, box 89.12.

44 Douglas Haskell, letter to Joseph Watterson, Editor, *AIAJ,* July 5, 1961, Haskell Papers, box 90.3.

45 Haskell, "Lost New York of the Pan American Airways Building."

46 Pan Am rates were in fact above average, as *Business Week* pointed out. The main reason why the building attracted tenants willing to pay these higher rents, according to real estate professionals, was its ideal location.

47 This "realty butcher" was of course Boisi, vice president in charge of real estate for the New York Central.

48 William F. R. Ballard, letter to Douglas Haskell, March 16, 1964, Haskell Papers, box 41.6. The symposium, "The Future by Design: A Symposium on the Considerations Underlying Comprehensive Planning for New York City," was aimed at stimulating interest in developing a comprehensive plan for New York. Its major speaker was to address "the values to be sought in New York's future." The theme for panel discussion, "The Forces Shaping New York's Future," which was "to take up the fundamental question of what the shaping forces are that must be reckoned with in comprehensive planning," was straight out of Haskell's "Lost New York" article. Among suggested panelists were Patrick Moynihan, Nathaniel Glazer, Oscar Handlin, Kenneth Clark, Daniel Bell, Hannah Arendt, Thurgood Marshall, Robert C. Wood, Paul Goodman, Herbert J. Gans, Vincent Scully, August Heckscher, Harold Rosenberg, Robert Oppenheimer, Charles Abrams, Constantin Doxiadis, David Riesman, and of course Douglas Haskell. Tentative program, symposium, "The Future by Design," May 28, 1964, Haskell Papers, box 41.6. On Ballard's defense of congestion in the Grand Central area, see Huxtable, "Planner Defends Cars in Midtown"; on the *Forum* article on transportation, which had received an enormous response, with numerous requests for reprints, see "Transportation and the City" *Architectural Forum,* October 1963, 61–83.

49 [Jack Cotton], *Architectural Forum,* May 1964, 11.

50 Ibid.; George Cooper Rudolph, letter to the editor, *Architectural Forum,* June 1964, 60 ("There is crowding," Rudolph wrote, "but it is not as bad as expected.").

51 Fitch and Waite, *Grand Central Terminal & Rockefeller Center,* 7. On Haskell's involvement in this publication, see chapter 6 below.

52 Richard J. Whalen, "A City Destroying Itself," *Fortune,* September 1964, 122.

53 Peter Blake, *God's Own Junkyard: The Planned Deterioration of America's Landscape,* 1964, excerpted in *Architectural Forum,* January 1964, 94–95. Blake's book was reviewed in the *New York Times Book Review* by Huxtable, who clearly sympathized with Blake's thesis. Its message, she wrote, was simple and explicit: Man can ruin anything and often does. Blake's story was told largely by illustrations, among which were pictures of Park Avenue, pre- and post-Pan Am, "a searing indictment," she said, "of a brutal destruction of scale." Unfortunately, the public eye was insensitive to such abuses. "This is the real tragedy of the American Dream, the irony of peace and plenty—that we have settled for the poor, the mean and the ugly in our inescapably physical environment." Ada Louise Huxtable, "America the Beautiful, Defaced, Mutilated" [review of Blake, *God's Own Junkyard*], *New York Times Book Review,* January 12, 1964, vii, 7.

54 Bacon's letter had appeared in *Progressive Architecture,* June 1963, 174; Ballard's was in the *New York Times,* October 16, 1963.

55 Walter Gropius, letter to Peter Blake (with copy to Pietro Belluschi), February 17, 1964, Belluschi Papers; emphasis in original.

56 Peter Blake, letter to Walter Gropius, March 23, 1964, Belluschi Papers.

57 Daniel M. Friedenberg, "Who Owns New York?" *New York Herald Tribune,* February 16, 1964, 7–8; February 17, 1964, 1, 4; February 18, 1964, 6; February 19, 1964, 6. (copies in Haskell papers, box 35.5).

58 Editorial, ["New York is an Architectural Disaster"], *Architectural Forum,* March 1964, 69.

59 Walter Gropius, "Education and Architecture," letter to the editor, *Architectural Forum,* March 1964, 62.

60 "Mailer vs. Scully," *Architectural Forum,* April 1964, 96–97. Norman Mailer, "The Big Bite," *Esquire,* August 1963, 16, 18, 21, 24.

61 "Down with the Savoy Plaza" [editorial], *New York Times,* August 24, 1964, 26. The editorial prompted two letters defending the Pan Am. One said there might be some justification in preserving the urbanity of the 59th Street and 5th Avenue area but asked why editors downgraded the prestige the Pan Am had brought to the Grand Central area, as the letter's author felt it was "a breathtaking architectural masterpiece" that had elevated an area "that was rapidly taking on an air of mediocrity into a prominent and world acclaimed location." M. A. Speller, letter to the editor, *New York Times,* August 27, 1964. The other was from Heckscher, "Pan Am Building Praised" (see discussion earlier in this chapter).

62 Douglas Haskell, "Architecture in Transition," *Architectural Forum,* August-September 1964, 71–80. On the *Forum,* which was revived in 1965 and continued until 1974, see Cervin Robinson, "Obituary. *Brickbuilder—Architectural Forum*: 1892–1974," *Architectural Review* (London), July 1974, 64–65.

63 This was of course the same Henry R. Luce, Trippe's Yale crony, who was to play an influential role in the rise and fall of Pan American World Airways. On Luce and Trippe, whose relationship dated back to the 1920s, see Bender and Altshul, *Chosen Instrument.*

64 Particularly on the West Coast. It was at this time, largely via the *Forum,* that the work of Belluschi, among others, became nationally, then internationally, known.

65 Saarinen, "Six Broad Currents of Modern Architecture," 110–115.

66 "Tributes to Forum" [letters to the editor], *Architectural Forum,* August–September 1964, 21ff.

67 "Blow to Better Building" [editorial], *New York Times,* June 8, 1964, 28.

68 Whalen, "City Destroying Itself," 115–122, 232, 234, 236, 241, 242, 244.

69 This was of course Wolfson's public statement. In fact, as Richard Roth pointed out, the real motivation for a smaller building was economic pragmatism, not public spirit.

70 Whalen, "City Destroying Itself," 122, 242, 244.

71 "Design for a City" [editorial], *New York Times,* October 11, 1967, 46.

72 Glenn Fowler, "Architects Tip Toe in Roiled Urban Water," *New York Times,* June 30, 1968, viii, 1, 9.

73 Christopher Tunnard, *The Modern American City,* 1968. These views of Park Avenue at this time bear comparison to those he expressed over a decade earlier in Christopher Tunnard and Henry Hope Reed, *The American Skyline,* 1956, 160–161, where the authors spoke warmly of the Park Avenue development of the 1920s, and Warren and Wetmore's New York Central Building successful closing the vista at the foot of the avenue.

74 Vincent Scully, *American Architecture and Urbanism,* 1969, 144, 180.

75 William Jordy, American Builders and Their Architects, v. 4, 1976, 8–10.

76 Ada Louise Huxtable, "Architecture by Entrapment," *New York Times,* July 7, 1968, 18D.

77 "Un nuovo grattacielo a New York," *Domus,* no. 358, September 1959, 1–3.

78 Martin Pinchis, "Gropius probabilmente erra a New York" [lettere al direttore], *L'Architettura Cronache—Storia,* October 1959, 435.

79 "Zum Hochhausprojekt von Walter Gropius in New York," *Werk* (Zurich) 46, November 1959, 229–230.

80 "Grand Central City in New York, Ein Vorsclag von Martin Pinchis, Bukarest;" "Einkert in der Vielfalt—ein Paradox der Kultur," *Bauen + Wohnen* 12, December 1959, 18, 20, 409–417.

81 "Der Wolkenkratzer wird an der Stelle gebaut, wo die Grand Central Station in New York die Park Avenue in zwei Teile trennt. Wie beim Leverhaus wird die Basis des Bauwerks von einem niedrigeren Gebäude gebildet. Der Wolkenkratzer selbst ist aber von diesem Gebäude nicht deutlich abgehoben und der Übergang von der horizontalen zur vertikalen Bewegung verunklärt. Zudem steht der Bau eingezwängt im Dickicht anderer Bauten; er hat zu wenig Luft um sich. Der hohe Bau wird zudem eine weitere Verdictung des Verkehrs verursachen, die, wie uns scheint, auf ein unerträgliches Mass gesteigert wird." Ibid., 409.

82 "A propos du 'Grand Central City,'" *L'Architecture d'Aujourd'hui* 31, February/March 1960.

83 "Une mise au point de Walter Gropius," *L'Architecture d'Aujourd'hui* 31, July 1960, xix.

84 Sibyl Moholy-Nagy, "L'architecture américaine prend une nouvelle direction," *L'Architecture d'Aujourd'hui,* 34, April 1964, 82–83.

85 Walter Gropius, "Tradition et continuité de l'architecture," *L'Architecture d'Aujourd'hui,* no. 34, April 1964, 72–77.

86 Ely Jacques Kahn, "Tall Buildings in New York," *Royal Institute of British Architects Journal* 67, October 1960, 451–455.

87 Michel Santiago, "Outrage: Counter Junk," *Architectural Review* (London) 135, May 1964, 372, 374.

88 Bruno Zevi, "Gropius on Park Avenue" [reprinted in translation from *L'Expresso* (Rome)], *Atlas: The Magazine of the World Press* 6, November 1963, 302–303.

89 Walter Gropius, "Correspondence: Gropius on the Pan Am Building," *Atlas: The Magazine of the World Press* 7, March 1964, 191–192.

90 Gropius cited here his *The New Architecture and the Bauhaus,* undated, 108. The reference, however, appears to be incorrect, unless he was citing a different edition from the Faber & Faber edition published around 1936 with a preface by Hudnut, which has only eighty pages. Moreover, the book says little about business districts, other than that he believed restrictions on height were ridiculous; overcrowding, he wrote here, was far more effectively combated by reducing maximum floor area or cubic volume. It appears clear that at this point, anyway, Gropius's vision called for tall towers surrounded by ample space. It also seems odd that he would mention this book in the context of Zevi's attacks, given that several of his statements seem particularly ironic in light of his involvement in the Pan Am: "The demand for more spacious, and above all greener and sunnier, cities has now become insistent" (68); on skyscraper districts in New York and Chicago, which he bemoaned as "planless chaos": "That the skyscraper districts of New York and Chicago are a planless chaos is no argument *per se* against the expediency of multistoried office buildings. The problem is one that can only be solved by control of building density in relation to transport facilities, and by curbing the crying evil of speculation in land values: elementary precautions of which have been signally neglected in the U.S." (76).

91 Bruno Zevi, Facoltà di Architettura, Università di Roma, letter to the editor, *Atlas: Magazine of the World Press* 7, March 1964, 192.

92 Bruno Zevi, "La protesta di Gropius," *L'Architettura* 9, no. 102, April 1964, 866–867.

CHAPTER 5   THE ARCHITECTS

1 "Architect for Business in a City of Towers," 54–56.

2 Duggan, "The 'Belly' School of Architecture," 7–10.

3 "The Skyline Factory," *Newsweek,* September 18, 1967, 98. A second article in the *New York Times* emphasized the same point about the Roths' success: Builders loved them, architects did not. "Tower Evolution Traced by Designer," *New York Times,* December 3, 1967.

4 James D. Landauer, President, Grand Central Building, Inc., letter to Pietro Belluschi, March 4, 1963, Belluschi Papers; Pietro Belluschi, letter to James C. Landauer, March 12, 1963, Belluschi Papers.

5 Pietro Belluschi, letter to Richard C. Sullivan, World Trade Department, Port of New York Authority, June 12, 1962, Belluschi Papers.

6 These included commissions to design the Boston Company and Keystone Buildings in Boston; the Equitable Center in Portland, Oregon; the Sea-First National Bank Building in Seattle; the One Maine Savings Bank Building in Portland, Maine; and the Wellesley Office Park in Wellesley, Massachusetts. There were many, many more. For a complete list of Belluschi's buildings and projects, see Clausen, *Pietro Belluschi*, 412–424.

7 It is unclear whether Belluschi, who was then sixty-five, retired at this time because by law he had to, or because he opted to in light of the growing dissension among his colleagues at MIT over the scale of his independent practice. On the number of deans retiring from major U.S. schools of architecture at this time, among them MIT, see [Retiring Deans: Schools of Architecture] [editorial], *Architectural Forum*, January 1964, 63.

8 Barnett, "Pietro Belluschi Interviewed by Architectural Student Jonathan Barnett," 10, 347, 351.

9 Emerson Goble, "In Defense of the Pan Am Building," 195–200; Mildred Schmertz, "The Problem of Pan Am," *Architectural Record*, May 1963, 151–158.

10 Belluschi, "Eloquent Simplicity in Architecture," 131–135.

11 "Architects' Medal," *New York Times*, January 30, 1972, 8:8. On how he was nominated for the award and by whom, see Clausen, *Pietro Belluschi*, 344–346.

12 Walter Gordon, letter to author, September 12, 1994.

13 Jim Murphy, interview with Pietro Belluschi, *Progressive Architecture*, June 1990, 122–123.

14 Douglas Haskell, "Gropius' Influence in America," *Architecture d'Aujourd'hui* 20, February 1950, 45–48. For a more recent perspective on Gropius in America, see Margret Kentgens-Craig, *The Bauhaus and America: First Contacts 1919–1936*, 2001, and Anthony Alofsin, *The Struggle for Modernism: Architecture, Landscape Architecture, and City Planning at Harvard*, 2002. See also Alofsin, "The Arrival of Walter Gropius In America," on Gropius at Harvard and Joseph Hudnut's role in bringing him there.

15 The reference to Gropius's modesty was one Haskell might well have reconsidered the following year, when Gropius chided him for slighting him by making only a brief mention in *Architectural Forum* of his RIBA Gold Medal and accused him of ethnic bias: "I thought I deserved better from your paper than the mention of my being awarded the RIBA Gold Medal only in a little garbled statement. A friend showed me the full-page announcement that the *Forum* accorded Frank Lloyd Wright, when he received the Gold Medal in 1941. The difference in treatment is startling, maybe because I was not born in this country." Walter Gropius, letter to Douglas Haskell, February 10, 1956, Haskell Papers, box 2.1.

16 Haskell, "Gropius' Influence in America," 45–48. Among those who studied with Gropius at Harvard, many of whom were to emerge as some of the most distinguished architects of their generation, were Pei, Rudolph, Jean Carl Warnecke, Barnes, Ulrich Franzen, Harry Weese, Eliot Noyes, John Johansen, Victor Lundy, and Wilhelm von Molke. [Gropius obituary], *Progressive Architecture*, September 1969, 116–120. On Gropius's students, see also Klaus Herdeg, *The Decorated Diagram: Harvard Architecture and the Failure of the Bauhaus Legacy*, 1983; on the Gropius years at Harvard, see Alofsin, *Struggle for Modernism*.

17 Walter Gropius, "The Necessity of the Artist in a Democratic Society," *Arts & Architecture,* December 1955, 16–17.

18 "The Lawgiver," 48, 50.

19 James Marston Fitch, *Walter Gropius,* 1960; and Fitch, "Three Levers of Walter Gropius," *Architectural Forum,* May 1960, 128ff. Fitch, who had been trained in architecture at Tulane but turned to architectural journalism during the Depression, had served as an Air Force meteorologist in World War II, during which time he traced the effects of climate on people; this no doubt had a formative influence on his views of how buildings are shaped by their environment. "James Marston Fitch, 90, Architect and Preservationist," *New York Times,* April 12, 2000, 26. Gropius was included in Fitch's *Architecture and the Esthetics of Plenty,* 1961, on American architecture and the forces that shaped it; the Pan Am Building, however, was not mentioned.

20 Fitch, *Walter Gropius,* 7–8; "Three Levers of Walter Gropius," 128–133.

21 Allan Temko, "Five Men Who Built on a Lofty Plain," *New York Times Book Review,* January 1, 1961, 7:14.

22 Gillo Dorfles, "Walter Gropius Today," *Zodiac* (Milan) 8, 1961, 34–41.

23 It might be pointed out that not only were there at this point people like Scully, Johnson, and Venturi endorsing the concept of the architect as artist and the architectural star system, but there were also architects such as Frank Gehry on the West Coast, who after getting his architecture degree from University of Southern California went to Harvard to work with Gropius on an advanced degree in urban design and planning. Unhappy with the rigorously doctrinaire Bauhaus training he was subjected to there, Gehry left after less than a year, returning to Los Angeles, where he found much more creative freedom. Gehry, like Michael Graves, under the influence of publicists like Scully, Johnson, and later Charles Jencks, was to emerge as a major figure in the architectural stardom. On the concept of architect as hero/genius in the modern era, see Andrew Saint, *Image of the Architect,* 1983.

24 Cranston Jones, *Architecture Today and Tomorrow,* 1961, 57.

25 "Gropius Declares Anti-Uglies Could Help City Battle Chaos," *New York Times,* January 5, 1962, 14; "Deluded Materialists?" *Newsweek,* January 15, 1962, 20.

26 "Deluded Materialists?"

27 "Gropius' 80th Birthday Marked by Old Friends and Students," 10.

28 "Walter Gropius on the Occasion of his 80th Birthday Celebration," *Arts & Architecture,* July 1963, 18–19.

29 This was of course Thomas Creighton, editor of *Progressive Architecture,* and the comment was one with which Wolfson, in an oft-repeated statement, it should be remembered, agreed. "Wouldn't it be nice?" Wolfson said in effect. "But who would pay for it?" On Gropius's "apologia per vita panamericanus," see Jim Lamantia, letter to the editor, *Progressive Architecture,* July 1963, 156.

30 "Gropius Deplores Mechanical Age," *New York Times,* September 23, 1963; "Gropius Addresses Convocation at Williams," *Architectural Record* 134, November 1963, 10.

31 According to William Pierson, then a young faculty member at Williams, it was "a typical Gropius lecture, filled with broad, philosophical statements, nothing specific. We all just gathered around the great man." Interview, William Pierson, by telephone, December 27, 2000.

32 "Gropius Addresses Convocation at Williams," *Architectural Record,* 10.

33 Walter Gropius, "Tradition and Continuity in Architecture," *Architectural Record,* May–July 1964. Gropius's address was also translated and published in *L'Architecture d'Aujourd'hui,* April 1964, 72–77, and later published in Gropius's *Apollo in the Democracy,* 1968, a collection of his essays.

34 Gropius's remarks on historic building, clearly prompted by his work on the Pan Am, were quoted by Daniel Bluestone as an example of his and other modernists' antipreservationist attitudes in "Academics in Tennis Shoes: Historic Preservation and the Academy," *Journal of the Society of Architectural Historians,* September 1999, 300–307.

35 "Architectural Details 5: Walter Gropius," *Architectural Record,* February 1965, 133–148.

36 Walter Gropius, "L'architetto e la società," *Casabella,* October 1965, 18–21.

37 "A Conversation with Walter Gropius," *Connection,* Summer 1967, 53–63.

38 Colin Rowe, "Waiting for Utopia" [review of Venturi, *Complexity and Contradiction in Architecture*], *New York Times,* September 10, 1967, 18.

39 "A New Tribute to Walter Gropius," *Architectural Record,* May 1968, 10.

40 "Grope Throws His Hat," *AIA Journal,* July 1968, 50–51.

41 Peter Blake, "Old Master of Design," *Life,* June 7, 1968, 49.

42 Gropius, *Apollo in the Democracy.* Among the essays in the collection were "Apollo in the Democracy" (1956), "The Inner Compass" (1958), "Role of the Architect in Modern Society" (1961), "A New Pact with Life" (1963), "The Curse of Conformity" (1958), "The Tree of Life versus Sales Spiral" (1961), and "Tradition and Continuity in Architecture" (1964).

43 Peter Collins, review of Gropius, *Apollo in the Democracy, Progressive Architecture,* April 1969, 156.

44 Among them Forrest Wilson, *Progressive Architecture,* August 1969, 70–71 (which simply excerpted from Gropius's *Scope of Total Architecture,* 1955, maintaining that his remarks made over the course of forty years "could be no more fitting tribute to the man, the teacher, and the architect"); "Tribute to Gropius," *AIA Journal,* August 1969, 16 (which mentions the University of Baghdad and the Gropiusstadt but not the Pan Am); Mildred F. Schmertz, "Walter Gropius, 1883–1969," *Architectural Record,* August 1969, 9–10 (which mentions "the highly controversial Pan Am Building" only in passing).

45 "Gropius, the Shaper of Modern Design, Dies in Boston at 86," *New York Times,* July 6, 1969.

46 David L. Shirey, "Testament of Joy," *Newsweek,* July 21, 1969, 67; emphasis in original.

47 "Walter Gropius" [editorial], *Design* (Bombay), July 1969, 11–12.

48 James R. Mellow, "The Bauhaus Is Alive and Well in Soup Plates and Skyscrapers," *New York Times Magazine,* September 14, 1969, vi, 34–53.

49 "Gropius and the Thread of History" [editorial], *Casabella,* July 1969, 2.

50 Ada Louise Huxtable, "He Was Not Irrelevant," *New York Times,* July 20, 1969.

51 Wolfgang Pehnt, "Gropius the Romantic," *Art Bulletin,* September 1971, 379–392.

52 Marcel Franciscono, *Walter Gropius and the Creation of the Bauhaus in Weimar,* 1971; reviewed by Ise Gropius, Gropius's widow, in *Architectural Forum,* January/February 1972, 21, 24, 28.

53 *Walter Gropius: Buildings, Plans, Projects 1906–1969,* undated (c. 1972), introduction by James Marston Fitch; catalog by Ise Gropius, with technical information provided by TAC. Exhibition catalog circulated by the International Exhibitions Foundation, 1972–1974, with copyright held by Ise Gropius, 1972. The exhibition was sponsored by the Columbia School of Architecture and Bauhaus Archive of Berlin.

54 Ada Louise Huxtable, "Megalopolis Show: Artists and the Urban Scene," *New York Times,* October 31, 1972, 54.

55 Hélène Lipstadt, "Groping for Gropius," *Progressive Architecture,* July 1983, 23–24. Ise Gropius, who was the archivist of her husband's work and guiding force behind the Gropefest tradition, died June 7, several weeks after the celebration. In the fall of 1983, while this was going on in Boston, a conference devoted to a Gropius reassessment was being held at the Goethe Institute in Rome. See Anthony Alofsin, "The Arrival of Walter Gropius in America: Transformations of a Radical Architect," *Walter Gropius e l'habitat del novecento,* 1987.

56 Vittorio Gregotti, "Loos e Gropius," *Casabella,* October 1983, 12.

57 Winfried Nerdinger, *Walter Gropius,* 1985, 288.

58 Jane Holtz Kay, "Harvard's Salute (?) to Walter Gropius," *Progressive Architecture,* November 1985, 25.

59 Marcel Franciscono, review of Isaacs, *Walter Gropius, Journal of the Society of Architectural Historians,* December 1987, 432–433.

60 Reginald R. Isaacs, *Gropius: An Illustrated Biography of the Creator of the Bauhaus,* 1984/1991.

61 Ibid., 283–284.

62 John C. Harkness, ed., *The Walter Gropius Archive,* vol. 4: *1945–1969. The Work of The Architects Collaborative,* 1991, with introduction by James Marston Fitch.

63 Jonathan Hale, "The Failure and Success of Walter Gropius," *Progressive Architecture,* February 1992, 108, 141. On Gropius's increasing conservatism in the United States, see Alofsin, *Struggle for Modernism,* 182.

64 John Peter, *The Oral History of Modern Architecture: Interviews with the Greatest Architects of the Twentieth Century,* 1994.

65 "TAC's Demise," *Architecture,* December 1995, 117.

CHAPTER 6   AFTERMATH

1 "Pan Am Neighbors Attack Heliport: Roof Landing Field Scored as Unsafe and Noisy," *New York Times,* May 22, 1963; "Building Owners Fight Rooftop Heliport," *Aviation Week,* May 27, 1963, 36–37.

2 "By Air to the Airports" [editorial], *New York Times,* July 9, 1963.

3 Samuel D. Leidesdorf, Irwin S. Chanin, and Sol Goldman, "Pan Am Heliport Opposed: Realtors Question Safety of High Facility in Congested Area" [letter to the editor], *New York Times,* July 16, 1963. Goldman was head of the organization that owned the Chrysler Building; Chanin was owner of the Chanin Building.

4 "Renewal Is Voted in City Hall Area," *New York Times,* March 12, 1964, 37.

5 "The Heliport Question" [editorial], *New York Times,* April 24, 1964.

6 Samuel D. Leisdesdorf, "Spread of Heliports Feared . . . if Zoning Change Is Approved" [letter to the editor], *New York Times,* May 2, 1964.

7 Lee S. Kreindler, "Against Pan Am Heliport" [letter to the editor], *New York Times,* June 19, 1964.

8 "Planners Ratify Pan Am Heliport," *New York Times,* November 26, 1964, 1.

9 "O'Connor Assails Pan Am Heliport," *New York Times,* December 21, 1964.

10 Richard Witkin, "Pan Am Heliport Is Voted by City," *New York Times,* January 15, 1965, 1, 18.

11 "Final Tests at Pan Am Heliport," *New York Times,* March 4, 1965, 33.

12 "Helicopter Line Here Is Hopeful," *New York Times,* January 27, 1965, 70; "State's Senators Urge Copter Help,"*New York Times,* March 11, 1965,65; David J. Levy, letter to the editor, *New York Times,* March 23, 1965, 38; Walter Strickland, letter to the editor, *New York Times,* March 29, 1965; "Assembly Gets Bill to Block Use of Pan Am Building's Heliport," *New York Times,* March 24, 1965, 31.

13 "New Midtown Spectacular: A View from a Helicopter," *New York Times,* May 1, 1965, 33.

14 Edward Robinson, letter to the editor, *New York Times,* May 5, 1965, 46.

15 Friedlander, "Midtown Launch Pad Opens Tuesday."

16 Ibid. It was Cummings, it should be remembered, who back in September 1960, upon reading of the plans for the Pan Am Building above the Grand Central Terminal, initially suggested the heliport to Trippe.

17 "Heliport Opened atop Skyscraper," *New York Times,* December 22, 1965, 26.

18 Lee S. Kreindler, letter to the editor, *New York Times,* January 12, 1966, 20.

19 F. Dale Saunders, letter to the editor, *New York Times,* January 24, 1966.

20 "City Study Backs Pan Am Heliport," *New York Times,* March 26, 1966.

21 "Pan Am Heliport Backed by Mayor: Operation, Now Curtailed, Called 'Sound and Safe,'" *New York Times,* July 22, 1966, 36.

22 George B. Litchford, letter to the editor, *New York Times,* November 8, 1966, 38.

23 Grace W. Canfield, letter to the editor, *New York Times,* November 21, 1966, 44.

24 "City Approves Use of Pan Am Heliport for Another Year," *New York Times,* December 1, 1966.

25 "Manhattan's Heliports," *New York Times,* January 3, 1968, 36.

26 "Service at Heliport Facing Suspension," *Aviation Week & Space Technology,* January 19, 1968; "Heliport Service from Roof of Pan Am Building Suspended," *New York Times,* February 16, 1968.

27 Thomas Orchard, letter to the editor, *New York Times,* February 24, 1968, 28.

28 "City Asked to Delay Heliport Reopening on Pan Am Building," *New York Times,* June 3, 1968, 89; Lee S. Kreindler, "Pan Am Heliport Opposed" [letter to the editor], *New York Times,* June 7, 1968.

29 "Heliport Offers Hops to Airports," *New York Times,* February 18, 1969.

30 "Copter Service May Be Resumed from atop the Pan Am Building," *New York Times,* August 29, 1969, 59.

31 "Helicopters in Midtown?" *New York Times,* September 1, 1969, 16.

32 "Plan Commission Approves 34th Street Heliport," *New York Times,* March 18, 1971, 78.

33 "Test Flight," *New York Times,* January 26, 1977, 3.

34 Lee S. Kreindler, letter to the editor, *New York Times,* January 29, 1977, 18.

35 "Mayor's Eye View," *New York Times,* February 1, 1977, 33; "Flights Resume," *New York Times,* February 2, 1977, 2.

36 John Train, "Revived Heliport: This Maddening Irritation" [letter to the editor], *New York Times,* February 26, 1977, 18.

37 Robert Alex Baron, Citizens for a Quieter City, Inc., "Copters in Midtown" [letter to the editor], *New York Times,* April 17, 1977, 7.

38 Ralph Thompson, letter to the editor, *New York Times,* April 30, 1977, 24.

39 "Five Killed as Copter on Pan Am Building Throws Rotor Blade," *New York Times,* May 17, 1977, 1; "A Chopper Turns Deadly," *Newsweek,* May 30, 1977, 27.

40 "Crash of Copter in '77 on Pan Am Building Was the Area's Worst," *New York Times,* April 19, 1979; "New York Airways Acts to File for Bankruptcy," *New York Times,* May 16, 1979.

41 Douglas Haskell, "The Value of Used Architecture," *Architectural Forum,* April 1957, 107–108.

42 Huxtable, "Park Avenue School of Architecture," 30ff. See also her *Four Walking Tours of Modern Architecture in New York City.*

43 "Philip Johnson Fights to Save Omaha Post Office," *Architectural Forum,* January 1959, 11.

44 "Will Rebuilding Save This Landmark?" *Architectural Forum,* July 1961, 116.

45 "New Madison Sq. Garden To Rise Atop Penn Station," *New York Times,* July 25, 1961, 1,55.

46 "With Progress Aforethought: New York's Penn Station, Present and Future," *Architectural Forum,* September 1961, 8.

47 "Kill Him but Save the Scalp" [editorial], *New York Times,* March 21, 1962, 38.

48 "City Acts to Save Historic Sites," *New York Times,* April 22, 1962.

49 "Save Our City," *New York Times,* August 2, 1962, 14; "Agbany vs. Apathy at Penn Station," *Architectural Forum,* September 1962, 5; "Architects Fight Penn Station Plan," *New York Times,* August 3, 1962, 1; "Saving Fine Architecture" [editorial], *New York Times,* August 11, 1962, 16.

50 "Saving Fine Architecture," *New York Times,* August 11, 1962, 16. "Anti-Uglies" alluded to Gropius's plea for an Anti-Uglies group, like that in Britain, in New York, which had appeared in the *Times* earlier in the year. "Gropius Declares 'Anti-Uglies' Could Help City Battle Chaos."

51 Douglas Haskell, "Save Grand Central, Save Robie!" *Architectural Forum,* November 1962, 138.

52 "Pennsylvania Station's Last Stand," *Architectural Forum,* February 1963, 11.

53 "Instinct for Preservation" [editorial], *Architectural Forum,* March 1963, 75.

54 Walter Gropius, letter to Peter Blake [on *God's Own Junkyard*] (with copy to Pietro Belluschi), February 17, 1964, Belluschi Papers; and Gropius, "Tradition and Continuity in Architecture," *Architectural Record,* July 1964, 152. On Belluschi's views of historic preservation, see Clausen, *Pietro Belluschi,* 339. "I'm not a great advocate of keeping and preserving," Belluschi was quoted as saying. "I'm much more interested in keeping the city alive and building." "Pietro Belluschi: Understanding Human Motivations," *Metropolis* (Portland, Oregon), January 1972, 6. On Belluschi's views on Grand Central Station, see "Interview: Pietro Belluschi," *Progressive Architecture,* June 1990, 123.

55 Ada Louise Huxtable, "He Adds Elegance to Modern Architecture," *New York Times,* May 24, 1964.

56 "On the Responsibility of the Architect," *Perspecta,* no. 2, 1953, 45–57. On the debate, see Clausen, *Pietro Belluschi,* 216.

57 Douglas Haskell, letter to Philip Johnson [alerting him to and enlisting his help in blocking the bowl-ing alley proposal for the Grand Central waiting room], January 25, 1961, Haskell Papers, box 97.3.

58 Johnson's talk, "The International Style—Death or Metamorphosis," delivered at the Metropolitan Museum of Art on March 30, 1961, was excerpted in *Architectural Forum,* June 1961, 87; it was also reproduced in *Philip Johnson, Writings,* 1979, 118–122, with introductory remarks by Robert Stern.

59 Robert Stern, introductory remarks, "International Style—Death or Metamorphosis," in *Philip John-son, Writings,* 118.

60 Philip Johnson, *Philip Johnson, Writings,* 120.

61 Philip Johnson, letter to Jürgen Joedicke, December 6, 1961, published in John M. Jacobus, *Philip Johnson,* 1962, and reproduced in *Philip Johnson, Writings,* 124–125.

62 Johnson's comments are quoted in an essay by Irving Kaufman, "The Contexts of Teaching Art," in George Pappas, *Concepts in Art and Education,* 1970, 260. My thanks to Daniel Ediger for calling this reference to my attention.

63 Ada Louise Huxtable, "To Keep the Best of New York," *New York Times Magazine,* September 10, 1961, 44–52.

64 Douglas Haskell, draft of talk on historic preservation, October 1961, Haskell Papers, box 69.2–4.

65 [Threat to Reliance Building, Chicago], *Architectural Forum,* August 1963, 8; [Dodge House's Uncer-tain Future], *Architectural Forum,* October 1963, 8. The Dodge House was demolished in 1970.

66 "Landmarks Legislation" [editorial], *New York Times,* October 22, 1963.

67 Report of the Committee on Codification in favor of adapting a Local Law to Amend the Administra-tion Code of the City of New York, April 6, 1965, Landmarks Preservation file no. 2, Landmarks Preservation Commission, New York City.

68 Statement by the Landmarks Preservation Commission, January 1967 (copy in Haskell Papers, box 97).

69 "Breuer to Design Terminal Tower," *New York Times,* February 24, 1968, 30. On the New York Cen-tral and Pennsylvania merger, see Rush Loving Jr., "The Penn Central Bankruptcy Express," *Fortune,* August 1970, 104.

70 One of the best sources I have found is the report by Nancy Goeschel, Research Department, Land-marks Preservation Commission, September 23, 1980 (in Landmarks Preservation file no. 2, Land-marks Preservation Commission). The report is accompanied by a long, thorough bibliography, including extensive research and a lengthy thesis on the Grand Central Terminal by Landmarks schol-ars. A more recent account is that provided in Nevins, *Grand Central Terminal,* which accompanied an exhibition sponsored by the Municipal Art Society of New York. Charles M. Haar and Jerold S. Kay-den, *Landmark Justice: The Influence of William J. Brennan on America's Communities,* 1989, also includes the Grand Central Terminal case. There is also a chapter on historic preservation and the Grand Central Terminal case in Stern, Mellins, and Fishman, *New York 1960.*

71 "The Historic and Aesthetic Justification for Preserving Grand Central Terminal as a Landmark of the City of New York," undated seven-page manuscript, Landmarks Preservation Commission, file no. 2. It wasn't until close to a decade later that the Museum of Modern Art staged its highly significant exhibition of Beaux-Arts architecture, which included the Grand Central. Arthur Drexler, ed., *The*

Architecture of the Ecole des Beaux-Arts, 1977. This coincided with the publication of Charles Jencks's *Language of Post-modern Architecture,* one of the earliest accounts of the new postmodernist trend that was then beginning to gain momentum.

72 "The Historic and Aesthetic Justification for Preserving Grand Central Terminal as a Landmark of the City of New York."

73 This seems an appropriate place to quote a comment from one of the anonymous reviewers of the manuscript of this book regarding a ceremony he attended in which John Lindsay, former mayor of New York, received an award for his contributions to urban design. The first words of Lindsay's acceptance speech, according to the reviewer, were "If I had been mayor at the time, the Pan Am Building would never have been built." It seemed to the reviewer a reminder, "if one was necessary, of the scars left by this building."

74 On Haskell, see Robert Benson, "Douglas Haskell and the Modern Movement in Architecture," *Journal of Architectural Education,* Summer 1983, 2–9; Benson, "Douglas Putnam Haskell (1899–1979): The Early Critical Writings." Haskell received the AIA Gold Medal in 1979, just months before he died.

75 Douglas Haskell, entries in *Encyclopedia Britannica Yearbook,* Haskell Papers, boxes 61.2 and 68; Haskell memorandum on his course "Architecture and the Entrepreneur," October 4, 1960, Haskell Papers, box 68.4; file, "Architecture and the Entrepreneur," Haskell Papers, box 50.

76 Douglas Haskell, letter to August Heckscher, March 25, 1962, Haskell Papers, box 30.15.

77 On Haskell and the contacts he and other American journalists had with the Bauhaus in the late 1920s, see Margret Kentgens-Craig, *The Bauhaus and America.*

78 Benson, "Douglas Putnam Haskell (1899–1979) The Early Critical Writings," 49.

79 Haskell, "Half a Revolution," introduction to panel discussion, "New Dimensions of Architectural Knowledge," AIA annual convention, Dallas, May 1962.

80 Douglas Haskell, letter to James Landauer, July 16, 1962, Haskell Papers, box 8.4.

81 Frank Williams, "Grand Central City," *Architectural Forum,* February 1968, 48–54.

82 Douglas Haskell, letter to the editors of *Architectural Forum,* February 27, 1968, Haskell Papers, box 97.

83 Douglas Haskell, letter to James Marston Fitch, March 4, 1969. The material Haskell sent presumably served as the point of departure for Fitch and Waite, *Grand Central Terminal & Rockefeller Center.*

84 Douglas Haskell, letter to James Nespole, Attorney-at-Law, Corporate Counsel, Municipal Building, undated [but evidently sometime early in 1972], Haskell Papers, box 96.

85 Douglas Haskell, draft of testimony on Grand Central preservation, May 1, 1972, Haskell Papers, box 97.1. In May, Harmon H. Goldstone, chairman of the Landmarks Preservation Commission, wrote Haskell informing him of their counsel's advice against Haskell's testifying on the grounds that the issues seemed to be all financial and constitutional and that additional testimony on cultural and historic values would probably be ruled irrelevant. Harmon H. Goldstone, letter to Douglas Haskell, May 25, 1972, Haskell Papers, box 97.1.

86 Douglas Haskell, draft of testimony on Grand Central preservation, May 16, 1972, Haskell Papers, box 97.1.

87 Douglas Haskell, letter to Richard Pommer (who chaired the College Art Association session), February 3, 1973, Haskell Papers, box 96.2; Haskell, "The Concentrated Meaning of Grand Central Station in New York" [draft], typed fifteen-page manuscript, dated March 1, 1974, Haskell Papers, box 97.4. The article that grew out of the manuscript, retitled "Futurism with Its Covers On," was published in the *Architectural Review* (London), May 1975, 300–304.

88 "Political Activism New Hippie Thing," *New York Times,* March 24, 1968, 1.

89 Ginsberg, "Howl," 1956, final version 1986, Barry Miles, ed., 6.

90 Graham Hughes, James P. Carse, James B. Harrison, Melvin Hausner, Kai E. Nielsen, Irving Sarnoff (members of various faculties of New York University), "Police Charged with Illegal Violence" [letter to the editor], *New York Times,* May 7, 1968, 46.

91 Ada Louise Huxtable, "Grand Central: Its Heart Belongs to Dada," *New York Times,* June 23, 1968, 10 (copy in Haskell Papers, box 97.5).

92 Sibyl Moholy-Nagy, "Hitler's Revenge: The Grand Central Tower Project Has Dramatized the Horrors Inflicted on Our Cities in the Name of Bauhaus Design," *Art in America,* September–October 1968, 42–43.

93 Arthur C. Holden, "Some Lessons from the Threat to Grand Central Station," developed from his testimony in public hearing before the Landmark Preservation Commission, City of New York, April 10, 1969; reprinted in 1975, 1. Landmarks Preservation Commission, file no. 2.

94 Eric Pace, "Metropolitan Life Plans to Acquire Pan Am Building for $400 Million," *New York Times,* July 29, 1980.

95 Carter Horsley, "Pan Am Weighs Sale of Its Building," *New York Times,* February 13, 1980.

96 "Pennsy Will Sell 23 Valuable Sites in Mid-Manhattan," *New York Times,* June 3, 1971.

97 Pace, "Metropolitan Life Plans to Acquire Pan Am Building for $400 Million."

98 Horsley, "Pan Am Weighs Sale of Its Building."

99 "Big Deals Are Transforming the Industry," *Business Week,* May 12, 1980, 128–129.

100 Pace, "Metropolitan Life Plans to Acquire Pan Am Building for $400 Million."

101 Ibid.

102 "Pan Am Selling Headquarters Building," *Aviation Week,* August 4, 1980, 30.

103 "Manhattan Towers for Sale: The Pan Am Building. Goes for a Stunning $400 Million," *Time,* August 11, 1980, 50.

104 "Why Pan Am Sold the Pan Am Building," *Business Week,* August 11, 1980, 25–27; Carol E. Curtis, "Swallowing a Big Canary," *Forbes,* August 18, 1980, 92.

105 Robert M. Thomas, Jr., "John White, Real Estate Agent Expert in Big Sales, Dies at 75," *New York Times,* April 2, 1995.

106 Anthony DePalma, "Pan Am Lobby Is Upgraded in Effort to Raise Rents," *New York Times,* February 27, 1985.

107 Jerry Cooper, "Pan Am Building Lobby," *Interior Design,* September 1987, 260.

108 Cooper, "Pan Am Building Lobby," 256–263, 317. Platner was also responsible for the design of the Windows on the World restaurant on top of the World Trade Center.

109 Interview, John Belle, Beyer Blinder Belle Architects, New York City, by telephone, June 22, 2000.

110 "Pan American and TWA Approve Plan for Merger," *New York Times,* December 21, 1962.

111 Peterson and Glab, *Rapid Descent,* 29. On Trippe's aim of holding a monopoly on international flights, see "Juan Trippe, 81, Dies"; and Bender and Altshul, *Chosen Instrument.*

112 Peterson and Glab, *Rapid Descent,* 52–53.

113 Bender and Altshul, *Chosen Instrument,* 507.

114 John Crudele, "Pan Am's Descent: Bad Management, Lots of Bad Luck," *Seattle Post-Intelligencer,* June 7, 1990.

115 Peterson and Glab, *Rapid Descent,* 33–34.

116 Crudele, "Pan Am's Descent"; Peterson and Glab, *Rapid Descent,* 90–92.

117 Peterson and Glab, *Rapid Descent,* 90–92.

118 Ibid., 92.

119 Ibid., 145–146.

120 Ibid., 282.

121 Ibid., 255–256.

122 Ibid., 294.

123 Ibid., 297.

124 John Schwartz, "Pan American World Airways: 1927–1991," *Newsweek,* July 22, 1991, 36.

125 Ibid., 36.

126 Agis Salpukas, "Pan Am, Its Cash Depleted, Shuts," *New York Times,* December 5, 1991.

127 "Pan Am: The Last Clipper," *Miami Herald,* December 20, 1991; Peterson and Glab, *Rapid Descent,* 299. On why the Pan Am failed, see Peterson and Glab, whose account of the airline, together with the book by Bender and Altschul and the articles by Crudele, I have relied upon heavily.

Pan Am was in fact not dead yet. In 1996, a slimmed-down version was revived, with airline executives believing that the Pan Am name had not lost its luster throughout the world, despite the airline's financial problems and Flight 103. "We have a very powerful brand name that gives us instant market recognition," one of the airline's executives was quoted as saying in the *New York Daily News.* "With Sky-High Hopes, Pan Am Starts Small," B39. Despite his optimism, two years later Pan Am filed for bankruptcy protection again, and in May 1998, a U.S. bankruptcy judge approved a plan by Guilford Transportation Industries to buy the company. As of 1999, the chairman of Pan American Airways was still exploring ways of returning to operation. "Shutdown Planned of Pan Am Units," *Atlanta Journal and Constitution,* February 27, 1998; "Icahn to Buy Pan American Airways for $43 Million," *Daily Telegraph,* March 14, 1998; "Pan Am Corp," *Wall Street Journal,* May 7, 1998, B20; "Pan Am Looks at Gebaur: Airline Strategy Doesn't Fit City's Plan," *Kansas City Star,* July 24, 1999.

128 Lauren Ramsby, "Will Pan Am Building's Logo Go Way of Airline? More Eyesore Than a Landmark, But One New Yorkers Now Like," *New York Observer,* January 13, 1992, 17.

129 Ramsby, "Will Pan Am Building's Logo Go Way of Airline?" 1, 17.

130 Christopher McLaughlin, First Office DC-10, letter to the Landmarks Preservation Commission, January 18, 1992, Landmarks Preservation file: Pan Am, Landmarks Preservation Commission.

131 Ibid.

132 David W. Dunlap, "Final Pan Am Departure: Sign Change a Sign of Changing Fortune," *New York Times,* September 4, 1992, 3.

133 Ibid., 3.

134 Coleman Lollar, "The Sovereign of the Skies," *Travel & Leisure,* February 1993, 39–40.

135 Gray, "Is It Time to Redevelop?" 46.

136 Interview, Robert Stern, by telephone, July 21, 1995.

CHAPTER 7   CONCLUSION

1 Don Cool, "Landmark on the Seine: Is It Ugly? Is It Sublime?" *Saturday Evening Post,* August 11–18, 1962, 26ff. It was in this general-audience magazine that Gropius's "Curse of Conformity" had appeared four years earlier.

2 "Monuments: Gold Mine in the Sky," *Newsweek,* June 18, 1962, 69–70.

3 Paul Goldberger, "Design Notebook: #230 Park Has Emerged Gleaming," *New York Times,* November 30, 1978, C10.

4 Paul Goldberger, *The City Observed: New York; Guide to the Architecture of Manhattan,* 1979, 127.

5 John Tauranac, *Essential New York: A Guide to the History and Architecture of Manhattan's Important Buildings, Parks, and Bridges,* 1979, 158–159.

6 "Architectural Design Citation: Simon Ungers and Laszlo Kiss," *Progressive Architecture,* January 1983, 116–118.

7 The designs submitted to the 1922 Chicago Tribune Competition might well have been known to Ungers and Kiss, as they were published in Stanley Tigerman, ed., *Chicago Tribune Tower Competition and Late Entries,* 1981, the year before the Unger and Kiss Pan Am rooftop project. On these and other Chicago Tribune Competition designs, see Tafuri, "The Disenchanted Mountain: The Skyscraper and the City."

8 Richard David Story, "The Buildings New Yorkers Love to Hate," *New York,* June 15, 1987, 30–34.

9 "By Any Other Name," *Progressive Architecture,* September 1993, 112.

10 Paul Goldberger, "New York, Lost and Found," *New York Times,* April 9, 1995, 3.

11 Judith Dupré, *Skyscrapers: A History of the World's Most Famous and Important Skyscrapers,* 1996, 56–57.

12 David W. Dunlap, "Preserving the Legacy of Modernist Architecture in New York City," *New York Times,* April 7, 1996, 15.

13 Janet L. Rumble, "Control Tower," *Wallpaper,* September/October 1998, 179–180. My thanks to Gail Fenske and Kathleen Randall for calling this article to my attention.

14 "Talk of the Town," *New Yorker,* June 7, 1999, 29–30.

15 "What Will Our Skylines Look Like?" *Time,* February 21, 2000, 80–82.

16 Carter B. Horsley, "The MetLife Building," <www.thecityreview.com/panam.html>, accessed January 1, 2001.

17 Christopher Gray, "So, Is the Pan Am Building Still as Bad as It was in 1963?" e-mail to Society of Architectural Historians (SAH) Listserve, September 29, 2001. It is an account sent to Gray (Office of Metropolitan History) of what a stonemason and his crew working on the Pan Am Building on the morning of September 11 saw and their reactions; Gray forwarded it to SAH members with its original spelling and informal language intact. The author of the essay himself wished to remain anonymous.

18 Christopher Gray, "Critics Once Called It Ugly; Now They're Not Sure," *New York Times,* October 7, 2001, 9.

19 Steve Cuozzo. "The Wrong Stuff—Keep World Architects Away from Ground Zero," *New York Post,* May 28, 2002. Special thanks to Delphine Daniels, Kathleen Randall, and Russ Craig, former students and now faithful sleuths, for keeping me abreast of news in the Big Apple.

20 Peter Blake, *No Place like Utopia,* xiii–xiv.

21 Paolo Portoghesi, *After Modern Architecture,* 1982, 33.

WORKS CITED

"A propos du 'Grand Central City.'" *L'Architecture d'Aujourd'hui* 31, no. 88 (February/March 1960): xix.

Abrams, Charles. "Pan Am Building Defended." *Architectural Record* 131 (May 1962): 195–200.

"Agbany vs. Apathy at Penn Station." *Architectural Forum* 117 (September 1962): 5.

"AIA Gold Medal Presentation to Walter Gropius, FAIA." *AIA Journal* 32 (August 1959): 80–82.

"Air Flow around Buildings." *Architectural Forum* 107 (September 1957): 166–168.

"Airports for Tomorrow." *Architectural Forum* 108 (January 1958): 123–125.

Albrecht, Johannes. "Against the Interpretation of Architecture." *Journal of Architectural Education* 55 (February 2002): 194–196.

Allen, James Sloan. *The Romance of Commerce and Culture.* Chicago: University of Chicago Press, 1983.

Alofsin, Anthony. "The Arrival of Walter Gropius in America: Transformations of a Radical Architect." In *Walter Gropius e l'habitat del novecento,* 48–66. Atti del Convegno Internazionale Roma, Goethe Institute, 29–30 November 1983. Rome: Effelle Edetrice, 1987.

Alofsin, Anthony. *The Struggle for Modernism: Architecture, Landscape Architecture, and City Planning at Harvard.* New York: Norton, 2002.

Alviani, Getulio. *Josef Albers.* Milan: Arcaedizioni, 1988.

Andrews, Wayne. "Something Less than Chartres" [review of Carl Condit, *American Building Art*], *Reporter,* July 6, 1961, 49–50.

"Anti-Uglies." *Architectural Forum* 116 (February 1962): 11.

"Another Set of Plans Announced for Site of GCS." *Wall Street Journal,* February 8, 1955, 9.

"Answer Machine at Pan Am Site Helps Sidewalk Supervisors." *New York Times,* September 10, 1961, 1.

"The Architect Today." *Architectural Forum* 103 (October 1955): 116–123.

"Architect for Business in a City of Towers." *Business Week,* September 1, 1962, 54–56.

"Architects Fight Penn Station Plan." *New York Times,* August 3, 1962, 1.

"Architects Hear Educator's Plea." *New York Times,* May 18, 1957.

"Architects hit Plans for Grand Central Bowling. "*Architectural Forum* 114 (January 1961): 9, 11.

"Architects' Medal." *New York Times,* January 30, 1972, 8:8.

"Architect's Office." *Architectural Forum* 105 (July 1956): 82, 92.

"Architects to Keep Their Guardian Eye on Grand Central." *New York Times,* January 24, 1961, 31.

"Architectural Design Citation: Simon Ungers and Laszlo Kiss." *Progressive Architecture* 64 (January 1983): 116–118.

"Architectural Details 5: Walter Gropius." *Architectural Record,* 137 (February 1965): 133–148.

Armagnac, Alden P. "The Most Complicated Building Ever Built." *Popular Science,* 181 (Summer 1962) 67–72, 216.

"Assembly Gets Bill to Block Use of Pan Am Building's Heliport." *New York Times,* March 24, 1965, 31.

Bacon, Edmund. Letter to the editor. *Progressive Architecture* 44 (June 1963): 174.

Baker, Clarence M. Letter to the editor. *Progressive Architecture* 44 (September 1963): 6.

Barnett, Edmond J. "Architect Lands a 'Vertical City.'" *New York Times,* June 9, 1962, 21.

Barnett, Jonathan. "Pietro Belluschi Interviewed by Architectural Student Jonathan Barnett." *Architectural Record* 109 (March 1961): 10, 347, 351.

Baron, Robert Alex. "Copters in Midtown" [letter to the editor]. *New York Times,* April 17, 1977, 7.

Barnett, Jonathon. "Architect Lands a 'Vertical City,'" *New York Times,* June 9, 1962, 21.

Barrett, Paul. "Heliports." In *Encyclopedia of New York,* ed. Kenneth T. Jackson, 537–538. New Haven: Yale University Press, 1995.

Bell, Daniel. "Modernism Mummified." In Daniel Joseph Singal, ed., *Modernist Culture in America,* 158–173. Belmont, Calif.: Wadsworth, 1991.

Belle, John, and Maxinne R. Leighton. *Grand Central: Gateway to a Million Lives.* New York: Norton, 2000.

Belluschi, Pietro. "Architecture and Society" [excerpts from address]. *Journal of the AIA* 15 (February 1951): 85–91. "Architecture and Society" [full text of address], *Architectural Record* 109 (February 1951) 116–118.

Belluschi, Pietro. "Eloquent Simplicity in Architecture." *Architectural Record* 134 (July 1963): 131–135.

Bender, Marylin, and Selig Altshul. *The Chosen Instrument: Pan Am, Juan Trippe, The Rise and Fall of an American Entrepreneur.* New York: Simon and Schuster, 1982.

Benson, Robert A. "Douglas Haskell and the Modern Movement in Architecture." *Journal of Architectural Education,* 36 (Summer 1983): 2–9.

Benson, Robert A. "Douglas Putnam Haskell (1899–1979): The Early Critical Writings." Ph.D. diss., University of Michigan, Ann Arbor, 1987.

Berkeley, Ellen Perry. *Architecture: A Place for Women.* Washington, D.C.: Smithsonian Institution, 1989.

Biddle, Wayne. *Barons of the Sky: From Early Flight to Strategic Warfare; The Story of the American Aerospace Industry.* New York: Simon and Schuster, 1991.

"Big Deals Are Transforming the Industry." *Business Week,* May 12, 1980, 128–129.

"Big Soundproof Job Awarded." *New York Times,* February 16, 1960, 61.

"Biggest Architectural Show." *Life,* November 25, 1957, 61, 69–70.

Birkerts, Gunnar. Letter to the editor. *Progressive Architecture* 44 (July 1963): 156.

Blake, Peter. "The Building Boom: Architecture in Decline." *Architectural Forum* 116 (June 1962): 128–129.

Blake, Peter. *Form Follows Fiasco: Why Modern Architecture Hasn't Worked.* Boston/Toronto: Little, Brown and Company, 1974.

Blake, Peter. *God's Own Junkyard: The Planned Deterioration of America's Landscape.* New York: Holt, Rinehart and Winston, 1964.

Blake, Peter. *No Place like Utopia: Modern Architecture and the Company We Kept.* New York: Knopf, 1993.

Blake, Peter. "Old Master of Design." *Life,* June 7, 1968, 49.

"Blow to Better Building" [editorial]. *New York Times.* June 8, 1964, 28.

Bluestone, Daniel. "Academics in Tennis Shoes. Historic Preservation and the Academy." *Journal of the Society of Architectural Historians* 58 (September 1999): 300–307.

Bonta, J. P. *Architecture and Its Interpretation*. New York: Rizzoli, 1979.

"Bowling Barred at Grand Central." *New York Times,* January 11, 1961, 25.

"Bowling over Grand Central" [editorial]. *New York Times,* January 10, 1961, 46.

"Bowling Plan Hit in Grand Central." *New York Times,* December 4, 1960, 1, 6.

"Breuer to Design Terminal Tower." *New York Times,* February 24, 1968, 30.

"Bridge Methods Used on Floors." *New York Times,* February 3, 1962, 33.

"Britain's Energetic Investor." *Architectural Forum* 112 (January 1960): 14, 16.

"British Funds Back Grand Central City." *New York Times,* October 22, 1959, 1.

Brolin, Brent. *The Failure of Modern Architecture*. New York: Van Nostrand Reinhold Company, 1976.

"Build We Must: New York's Construction Boom, Still Going Strong." *Business Week,* May 19, 1962, 31–33.

"Building Owners Fight Rooftop Heliport." *Aviation Week,* May 27, 1963, 36–37.

"Building Plan Filed." *New York Times,* November 25, 1959, 47.

"Building Skylines Is His Business: Carl Morse of New York's Diesel Construction." *Business Week,* July 11, 1964, 33–34.

"Building Will Get Single Phone Unit." *New York Times,* August 14, 1960, 8:7.

"Buildings in the News—Gropius-Belluschi-Roth Design for Grand Central City." *Architectural Record* 125 (March 1959): 10.

Burchard, Marshall. "Will Rebuilding Save This Landmark?" *Architectural Forum* 115 (July 1961): 116–118.

Burke, Peter. "History of Events and the Revival of Narrative." In *New Perspectives on Historical Writing,* ed. Peter Burke. University Park: Pennsylvania State University Press, 1994, 233–246.

Burke, Peter, ed. *New Perspectives on Historical Writing*. University Park: Pennsylvania State University Press, 1991.

Burns, James T., Jr. "The Pan Am Building: A Behemoth Is Born." *Progressive Architecture* 44 (April 1963): 61–62.

Burrows, Edwin G., and Mike Wallace. *A History of New York City to 1898*. New York: Oxford University Press, 1999.

Bush-Brown, Albert. Letter to the editor. *Progressive Architecture* 44 (June 1963): 174.

"Businesses Erect Own Skyscrapers." *New York Times,* December 1, 1957, 1.

"By Air to the Airports" [editorial]. *New York Times,* July 9, 1963, 30.

"By Any Other Name." *Progressive Architecture* 74 (September 1993): 112.

Bystrom, Carl A. Letter to the editor. *Progressive Architecture* 44 (August 1963): 150.

"Can Civic Beauty Be Legislated?" *Architectural Forum* 108 (August 1958): 92–93, 162, 164.

Canfield, Grace W. Letter to the editor, *New York Times*, November 21, 1966, 44.

Cannell, Michael. *I. M. Pei: Mandarin of Modernism*. New York: Southern, 1995.

"Capital from Abroad: An Analysis of Why British Investment in New York Skyscraper Is First of Its Kind." *New York Times,* October 25, 1959, 8:1.

"Carl Morse: Orchestrator of Buildings for 54 Years." *New York Times,* September 23, 1979, 67.

Carlin, Earl P. Letter to the editor. *Progressive Architecture* 44 (June 1963): 174.

Cavaglieri, Giorgio. Letter to the editor. *New York Herald Tribune,* March 9, 1955.

"Central Building Sets Rental Plan." *New York Times,* July 6, 1958, 7:2.

"Central Studies New Terminal Plan." *New York Times,* September 26, 1954, 31.

"Central to Lease Site on Park Ave." *New York Times,* January 13, 1957, 41.

"Central's History Began in 1831." *New York Times,* January 13, 1962, 9.

"Change Is Cited on Park Avenue." *New York Times,* October 16, 1955, 1, 9.

"A Chopper Turns Deadly." *Newsweek,* May 30, 1977, 27.

"City Acts to Save Historic Sites." *New York Times,* April 22, 1962, 1.

"City Approves Use of Pan Am Heliport for Another Year." *New York Times,* December 1, 1966, 63.

"City Asked to Delay Heliport Reopening on Pan Am Building." *New York Times,* June 3, 1968, 89.

"City Study Backs Pan Am Heliport." *New York Times,* March 26, 1966, 27.

Clausen, Meredith. "New York—De Grand Central Station à Grand Central City." *Revue D'Histoire des Chemins de Fer* 10–11 (printemps–automne 1994): 285–295.

Clausen, Meredith L. *Pietro Belluschi: Modern American Architect.* Cambridge, Mass.: MIT Press, 1994.

Clausen, Meredith L. *Spiritual Space: The Religious Architecture of Pietro Belluschi.* Seattle: University of Washington Press, 1992.

Collins, Peter. "Bauhaus Basic Is Best." Review of Gropius, *Apollo in the Democracy. Progressive Architecture* 50 (April 1969): 156.

Colomina, Beatriz. "Collaborations: The Private Life of Modern Architecture." *Journal of the Society of Architectural Historians* 58 (September 1999): 462–471.

"Company Realigns Executives." *New York Times,* January 4, 1957, 34.

"Complex Equipment Installed in Pan Am's New Skyscraper." *New York Times,* March 17, 1962, 39.

"Concrete Battles Its Weight." *Architectural Forum* 107 (September 1957): 162–165.

"Concrete Curtain." *Architectural Forum* 116 (February 1962): 10.

Condit, Carl W. *American Building Art: The Twentieth Century.* New York: Oxford University Press, 1961.

Condit, Carl W. *The Port of New York: A History of the Rail and Terminal System from the Beginnings to Pennsylvania Station.* Chicago: University of Chicago Press, 1980.

"Conference on Ugliness" [editorial]. *New York Times,* April 7, 1962, 24.

"The Contractor." *Architectural Forum* 105 (February 1956): 114–119.

"Contractor Makes Consulting Business." *Engineering News-Record,* February 1, 1962, 40–42.

"The Controversial Giant." *Dun's Review and Modern Industries* 80 (September 1962): pt. 2, S138.

"A Conversation with Walter Gropius." *Connection* 4, no. 4 (Summer 1967): 53–63.

Cool, Don. "Landmark on the Seine: Is It Ugly? Is It Sublime?" *Saturday Evening Post,* August 11–18, 1962, 26–29.

Cooper, Jerry. "Pan Am Building Lobby." *Interior Design* 58, no. 1 (September 1987): 256–263, 317.

"Copter Service May Be Resumed from atop the Pan Am Building." *New York Times,* August 19, 1969, 59.

Corbelletti, Raniero. Letter to the editor. *Progressive Architecture* 44 (July 1963): 156.

"Councilman Fights Bowling Alley Plan for Grand Central." *New York Times,* January 7, 1961, 21.

Cousins, Norman. "Notes on a Changing America" [editorial]. *Saturday Review* 17 (December 1960): 26, 33.

"Crash of Copter in '77 on Pan Am Building Was the Area's Worst." *New York Times,* April 19, 1979, B6.

"Crossroads in the City's Heart" [editorial]. *New York Times,* June 5, 1958, 30.

Crudele, John. "Deregulation and Pan Am's Pancake Landing." *Seattle Post-Intelligencer,* June 14, 1990, B5.

Crudele, John. "Pan Am's Descent: Bad Management, Lots of Bad Luck." *Seattle Post-Intelligencer,* June 7, 1990, B7.

Cuozzo, Steve. "The Wrong Stuff—Keep World Architects Away from Ground Zero." *New York Post,* May 28, 2002, 27.

Curtis, Carol E. "Swallowing a Big Canary." *Forbes,* August 18, 1980, 92.

Davis, Emmett. Letter to the editor. *New York Times,* August 24, 1961, 28.

"Deluded Materialists?" *Newsweek,* January 15, 1962, 20.

DePalma, Anthony. "Pan Am Lobby Is Upgraded in Effort to Raise Rents." *New York Times,* February 27, 1985, 1, 20.

"Design for a City" [editorial]. *New York Times,* October 11, 1967, 46.

"Design of 'Grand Central City' Accepted." *Progressive Architecture* 40 (March 1959): 157.

"A Developing Feature of the City Scene: The Pan Am Building, 59-Stories Tall, Is to Be Completed at the End of the Year." *New York Times,* August 14, 1962, 25.

[Dodge House's Uncertain Future]. *Architectural Forum* 119 (October 1963): 8.

"Doing over the Town." *Time,* September 28, 1962, 56–69.

Doordan, Dennis. *Twentieth Century Architecture.* New York: Abrams, 2002.

Dorfles, Gillo. "Walter Gropius Today." *Zodiac* (Milan) 8 (1961): 34–37.

"Down with the Savoy Plaza" [editorial]. *New York Times,* August 24, 1964, 26.

"The Dream of Lincoln Center." *New York Times Magazine,* October 18, 1959, 18–19.

Drexler, Arthur, ed. *The Architecture of the Ecole des Beaux-Arts.* New York: Museum of Modern Art, 1977.

Duggan, Dennis. "Architectural 'Give and Take' Altering City." *New York Times,* September 30, 1962, 8:1, 6.

Duggan, Dennis. "The 'Belly' School of Architecture." *New York Herald Tribune,* December 15, 1963, 7–10.

Dunlap, David W. "Final Pan Am Departure: Sign Change a Sign of Changing Fortune." *New York Times,* September 4, 1992, B3.

Dunlap, David W. "Pan Am Building to Get a New Name." *New York Times,* September 4, 1992, 25.

Dunlap, David W. "Preserving the Legacy of Modernist Architecture in New York City." *New York Times,* April 7, 1996, 15.

Dupré, Judith. *Skyscrapers: A History of the World's Most Famous and Important Skyscrapers.* New York: Black Dog & Leventhal, 1996.

Eaton, Leonard K. Letter to the editor. *Progressive Architecture* 44 (July 1963): 156.

Ennis, Thomas W. "Leases Play Vital Role." *New York Times,* October 2, 1960, 8:1.

Ennis, Thomas W. "Octagonal Office Skyscraper to Rise behind Grand Central." *New York Times,* February 18, 1959, 35.

"Erecting Office Building over Complicated Track Layout." *Engineering News-Record* 90, no. 12 (March 22, 1923): 532–533.

"Erwin S. Wolfson, Builder of Skylines." *Time,* February 22, 1960, 92.

"Erwin S. Wolfson Is Dead at 60, Leading Builder of Skyscrapers." *New York Times,* June 27, 1962, 35.

"Escalators Coming to Grand Central." *New York Times,* February 25, 1962, 52.

"Extra Grand Central." *Time,* March 15, 1963, 71.

"Fifteen Killed in Rear End Collision." *New York Times,* January 9, 1902, 1.

"Final Tests at Pan Am Heliport." *New York Times,* March 4, 1965, 33.

Fitch, James Marston. *Architecture and the Esthetics of Plenty.* New York: Columbia University Press, 1961.

Fitch, James Marston. "Three Levers of Walter Gropius." *Architectural Forum* 112 (May 1960): 128–133.

Fitch, James Marston. *Walter Gropius.* New York: Braziller, 1960.

Fitch, James Marston, and Diana S. Waite. *Grand Central Terminal & Rockefeller Center: A Historic-Critical Estimate of Their Significance.* New York: New York State Parks & Recreation, 1974.

"Five Killed As Copter on Pan Am Building Throws Rotor Blade." *New York Times,* May 17, 1977, 1.

"Flags Mark Topping-Out of Pan Am Building's Steel." *New York Times,* May 10, 1962, 28.

"'Flight' Is Firmly in Place in Pan Am Lobby." *Architectural Record* 134 (August 1963): 24.

"Flights Resume." *New York Times,* February 2, 1977, 2.

"Four Million, Pan Am Job Let." *New York Times,* March 11, 1961, 33.

Fowler, Glenn. "Architects Tip Toe in Roiled Urban Water." *New York Times,* June 30, 1968, 8:1, 9.

Fowler, Glenn. "Carl Morse, A Builder, Dies at 83; Helped Shape New York's Skyline." *New York Times,* November 16, 1989, 2:17.

Fowler, Glenn. "Drab Murals That Once Prevailed Are Avoided." *New York Times,* August 17, 1958, 8:1.

Fowler, Glenn. "Framing Begins for Skyscraper." *New York Times,* March 12, 1961, 8:1.

Fowler, Glenn. "Grand Central Plans Building." *New York Times,* May 8, 1958, 1.

Franciscono, Marcel. Review of Isaacs, *Walter Gropius. Journal of the Society of Architectural Historians* 46 (December 1987): 432–433.

Franciscono, Marcel. *Walter Gropius and the Creation of the Bauhaus in Weimar.* Urbana: University of Illinois Press, 1971.

Friedan, Betty. *The Feminine Mystique.* New York: W. W. Norton, 1963.

Friedenberg, Daniel M. "Who Owns New York?" *New York Herald Tribune,* February–March 1964.

Friedlander, Paul J. C. "Midtown Launch Pad Opens Tuesday." *New York Times,* December 19, 1965, 10:1.

Furnas, C., Joe McCarthy, and editors of *Life/Time.* "Skyscrapers, Radomes and Chips." In *The Engineer,* René Bubos, Henry Margenau, C. P. Snow, consulting eds, 100–103. New York: Time Inc., 1966.

Giedion, Sigfried. *Architecture, You and Me.* Cambridge: Harvard University Press, 1958.

Goble, Emerson. "In Defense of the Pan Am Building: Pan Am Makes a Point; A Plea for the Vertical City as a Planning Principle; a Three-Dimensional City Planned for Pedestrians Instead of Autos." *Architectural Record* 131 (May 1962): 195–200.

Goble, Emerson. "New City Image Needed." *Architectural Record* 131 (January 1962): 9.

Goble, Emerson. "Unity in Diversity." *Architectural Record* 129 (April 1961): 9.

Goldberg, Bertrand. "Two-Shift City." *Architectural Forum* 114 (February 1961): 173, 175–176.

Goldberger, Paul. *The City Observed: New York; A Guide to the Architecture of Manhattan.* New York: Random House, 1979.

Goldberger, Paul. "Design Notebook: #230 Park Has Emerged Gleaming." *New York Times,* C10 November 30, 1978.

Goldberger, Paul. "New York, Lost and Found." *New York Times,* April 9, 1995, 4:3.

"Grand Central City in New York, Ein Vorsclag von Martin Pinchis, Bukarest." *Bauen + Wohnen* 12 (November/December 1959): 18, 20.

"Grand Central Site for Largest Office Building." *Architectural Forum* 108 (June 1958): 13.

"Grand Central Spruces Up as It Approaches 75." *New York Times,* February 13, 1986, II, 1.

[Grand Central Station]. *L'Illustrazione Italiana* (February 1, 1913).

"Grand Central Terminal Station, New York." *Town Planning Review* (London) (April 1911): 55–64.

"Grand Central Terminal to Become Skyscraper." *Downtown Athletic Club of New York City* (January 1955): 19.

"Grand Central's Outdoor Concourse." *Architectural Forum* 103 (February 1955): 116–119.

Gray, Christopher. "Critics Once Called It Ugly; Now They're Not Sure." *New York Times,* October 7, 2001, 9.

Gray, Christopher. "Is It Time to Redevelop?" *New York Times Magazine,* May 14, 1989, 44–46.

Greene, Herb. Letter to the editor. *Progressive Architecture* 44 (June 1963): 174–176.

Gregotti, Vittorio. "Loos e Gropius." *Casabella* 495 (October 1983): 12.

"Grope Throws His Hat." *AIA Journal* 50, no. 1 (July 1968): 50–53.

"Gropius Addresses Convocation at Williams." *Architectural Record* 134 (November 1963): 10.

"Gropius and Belluschi Advise on Grand Central Tower Design." *Architectural Forum* 109 (September 1958): 47.

"Gropius and the Thread of History" [editorial]. *Casabella* 33, no. 338 (July 1969): 2.

"Gropius Declares 'Anti-Uglies' Could Help City Battle Chaos." *New York Times,* January 5, 1962, 14.

"Gropius Deplores Mechanical Age." *New York Times,* September 23, 1963, 31.

"Gropius' 80th Birthday Marked by Old Friends and Students." *Architectural Record* 134 (July 1963): 10.

Gropius, Ise. Review of Franciscono, *Walter Gropius and the Creation of the Bauhaus in Weimar. Architectural Forum* 136, no. 1 (January/February 1972): 21, 24, 28.

Gropius, Ise. *Walter Gropius: Buildings, Plans, Projects 1906–1969.* Introduction by James Marston Fitch. [Lincoln, Mass.]: Teufen, Switzerland: A. Niggli, Ltd. 1972.

"Walter Gropius: 1883–1969." *Progressive Architecture* 57 (September 1969): 116–120.

"Gropius, the Shaper of Modern Design, Dies in Boston at 86." *New York Times,* July 6, 1969, 1.

Gropius, Walter. "Address by Dr. Walter Gropius upon Receiving the Honorary Degree of Humane Letters." *Arts & Architecture* 78 (May 1961): 14–15, 28–30.

Gropius, Walter. *Apollo in the Democracy.* New York: McGraw-Hill, 1968.

Gropius, Walter. "Correspondence: Gropius on the Pan Am Building." *Atlas* 7 (March 1964): 191–192.

Gropius, Walter. "The Curse of Conformity: The Problem of Architecture in the Assembly-line Age." *Saturday Evening Post,* September 6, 1958, 18, 51–52, 54; excerpted in *Architectural Forum* (May 1959): 209–210.

Gropius, Walter. "Education and Architecture" [letter to the editor]. *Architectural Forum* 135 (March 1964): 62.

"Gropius and Garroway." *Architectural Forum* 112 (April 1960): 177, 179.

Gropius, Walter. "Gropius at Twenty-Six." *Architectural Review* (London) 130 (July 1961): 49–51.

Gropius, Walter. "L'architetto e la società." *Casabella,* no. 298 (October 1965): 18–21.

Gropius, Walter. "The Necessity of the Artist in a Democratic Society." *Arts & Architecture* 72 (December 1955): 16–17.

Gropius, Walter. *The New Architecture and the Bauhaus*. London: Faber & Faber, n.d. [1936].

Gropius, Walter. *Scope of Total Architecture*. New York: Harper, 1955.

Gropius, Walter. "TAC's Objectives." In Walter Gropius et al., *The Architects Collaborative: 1945–1965,* 20–21. Teufen, Switzerland: A. Niggli, 1966.

Gropius, Walter. "TAC's Teamwork." In Walter Gropius et al., *The Architects Collaborative: 1945–1965,* 24. Teufen, Switzerland: A. Niggli, 1966.

Gropius, Walter. "Tradition and Continuity in Architecture." *Architectural Record* (May–July 1964).

Gropius, Walter. "Tradition and Continuity in Architecture." *Program,* no. 3 (September 1964): 4–25.

Gropius, Walter. "Tradition et continuité de l'architecture." *L'Architecture d'Aujourd'hui,* no. 34 (April 1964): 72–77.

Gropius, Walter. "True Architectural Goals Yet to Be Realized." *Architectural Record* 129 (June 1961): 147–152.

Gropius, Walter, et al. *The Architects Collaborative, 1945–1965*. Teufen, Switzerland: A. Niggli, 1966.

"Group Hits Bowling at Grand Central." *New York Times,* January 5, 1961, 33.

Gruen, Victor. "Plan for Grand Central Opposed." *New York Times,* November 26, 1960, 20.

Guilbaut, Serge. *How New York Stole the Idea of Modern Art: Abstract Expressionism, Freedom, and the Cold War*. Chicago: University of Chicago Press, 1983.

Haar, Charles M., and Jerold S. Kayden. *Landmark Justice: The Influence of William J. Brennan on America's Communities*. Washington, D.C.: Preservation Press, National Trust for Historic Preservation, 1989.

Hale, Jonathan. "The Failure and Success of Walter Gropius." *Progressive Architecture* 73 (February 1992): 108, 141.

Harkness, John C., ed. *The Walter Gropius Archive: The Work of the Architects Collaborative*. Vol. 4, *1945–1969: The Work of the Architects Collaborative*. New York: Garland, 1991.

Harkness, Sarah P. "Collaboration." In Walter Gropius et al., *The Architects Collaborative: 1945–1965*. Teufen, Switzerland: A. Niggli, 1966, 26.

Harrison, Richard Edes. Letter to the editor. *New York Times,* February 27, 1959, 24.

"Harvard Architect Honored." *New York Times,* May 5, 1957, 82.

Haskell, Douglas. "Architecture in Transition." *Architectural Forum* 121 (August–September 1964): 71–80.

Haskell, Douglas. "Can the Grand Central Concourse Be Saved?" *Architectural Forum* 101 (November 1954): 134–139.

Haskell, Douglas. "Democracy and Apollo" [editorial]. *Architectural Forum* 108 (May 1958): 88.

Haskell, Douglas. "Save Grand Central, Save Robie!" Editorial. *Architectural Forum* 117 (November 1962): 138.

Haskell, Douglas. "For All Concerned." *Architectural Forum* 102 (April 1955): 172.

Haskell, Douglas. "Futurism with Its Covers On." *Architectural Review* (London) 157 (May 1975): 300–304.

Haskell, Douglas. "Gropius' Influence in America." *L'Architecture d'Aujourd'hui* 20 (February 1950): 45–48.

Haskell, Douglas. "Half a Revolution." Introduction to panel discussion "New Dimensions of Architectural Knowledge," AIA National Convention, Dallas, May 1962.

Haskell, Douglas. "The Lost New York of the Pan American Airways Building." *Architectural Forum* 119 (November 1963): 106–111.

Haskell, Douglas. "The Value of Used Architecture." *Architectural Forum* 106 (April 1957): 107–108.

Haskell, Douglas. "Visionless Enterprise." *Architectural Forum* 113 (October 1960): 87.

Heckscher, August. *Open Spaces: The Life of American Cities*. New York: Harper & Row, 1977.

Heckscher, August. "Pan Am Building Praised" [letter to the editor]. *New York Times,* August 31, 1964, 24.

"Helicopter Line Here Is Hopeful." *New York Times,* January 7, 1965, 70.

"Helicopters in Midtown?" *New York Times,* September 1, 1969, 16.

"Heliport Offers Hops to Airports." *New York Times,* February 18, 1969, 81.

"Heliport Opened atop Skyscraper." *New York Times,* December 22, 1965, 26.

"The Heliport Question" [editorial]. *New York Times,* April 24, 1964, 32.

"Heliport Service from Roof of Pan Am Building Suspended." *New York Times,* February 16, 1968, 1, 75.

Herdeg, Klaus. *The Decorated Diagram: Harvard Architecture and the Failure of the Bauhaus Legacy.* Cambridge, Mass.: MIT Press, 1983.

Holden, Arthur C. "Some Lessons from the Threat to Grand Central Station." Testimony before Landmark Preservation Commission, April 10, 1969. New York: Holden Yang Raemsch Terjesen, 1969; reprinted 1975. (Landmark Preservation Commission, file no. 2)

Horsley, Carter B. "The MetLife Building." Available at <www.thecityreview.com/panam.html> (accessed January 1, 2001).

Horsley, Carter B. "Pan Am Weighs Sale of Its Building." *New York Times,* February 13, 1980, B1, B4.

"How British Funds Got in Grand Central Deal." *Business Week,* October 31, 1959, 32–33.

"How Local Architects Drew $100 Million Plans." *Boston Globe,* March 1, 1959, 20.

"Huge Steel Award Let for New Building Here." *New York Times,* May 13, 1959, 61.

Hughes, Graham, James P. Carse, James B. Harrison, Melvin Hausner, Kai E. Nielsen, Irving Sarnoff (faculty at New York University). "Police Charged with Illegal Violence" [letter to editor]. *New York Times,* May 7, 1968, 46.

Hunt, Lynn, ed. *The New Cultural History.* Berkeley: University of California Press, 1989.

Hurst, Sam T. "Introduction: Twenty Years of TAC." In Walter Gropius et al., *The Architects Collaborative: 1945–1965.* Teufen, Switzerland: A. Niggli, 1966, 8–9.

Huxtable, Ada Louise. "America the Beautiful, Defaced, Mutilated" [review of Blake, *God's Own Junkyard*]. *New York Times Book Review,* January 12, 1964, 7:7.

Huxtable, Ada Louise. "Architecture by Entrapment." *New York Times,* July 7, 1968, 18D.

Huxtable, Ada Louise. "Architecture Stumbles On." *New York Times,* April 14, 1963, 10:23.

Huxtable, Ada Louise. "The Art We Cannot Afford to Ignore (but Do)." *New York Times Magazine,* May 4, 1958, 14–15, 86.

Huxtable, Ada Louise. "Art with Architecture: New Terms of an Old Alliance." *New York Times,* September 13, 1959, 2:20.

Huxtable, Ada Louise. "The Attainment of Quality." *AIA Journal* 40 (July 1963): 89–94.

Huxtable, Ada Louise. *Four Walking Tours of Modern Architecture in New York City.* New York: Museum of Modern Art, 1961.

Huxtable, Ada Louise. "Grand Central: Its Heart Belongs to Dada." *New York Times,* June 23, 1968, 10.

Huxtable, Ada Louise. "He Adds Elegance to Modern Architecture." *New York Times,* May 24, 1964, 18, 100–101.

Huxtable, Ada Louise. "He Was Not Irrelevant." *New York Times,* July 20, 1969, 2:21.

Huxtable, Ada Louise. "Marvel or Monster? Grand Central City Is Mass Architecture." *New York Times,* January 24, 1960, 10:13.

Huxtable, Ada Louise. "Megalopolis Show: Artists and the Urban Scene." *New York Times,* October 31, 1972, 54.

Huxtable, Ada Louise. "Our New Buildings: Hits and Misses." *New York Times Magazine,* April 29, 1962, 6: 16–17, 105–106.

Huxtable, Ada Louise. "The Park Avenue School of Architecture." *New York Times Magazine,* December 15, 1957, 30–31, 54–56.

Huxtable, Ada Louise. "Planner Defends Cars in Midtown." *New York Times,* October 16, 1963, 47, 50.

Huxtable, Ada Louise. "Something Awry." *New York Times,* December 22, 1963, 10:15.

Huxtable, Ada Louise. "To Keep the Best of New York." *New York Times Magazine,* September 10, 1961, 44–45, 50, 52.

Huxtable, Ada Louise. "Towering Question: The Skyscraper." *New York Times,* June 12, 1960, 6:16, 69–71.

"Icahn to Buy Pan American Airways for $43 Million." *Daily Telegraph* (Telegraph Group Ltd.), March 14, 1998, 30.

"Idlewild: Gateway to the World." *Cosmopolitan* (May 1960): 44–49.

"Idlewild: Jet Capital of the World." *Popular Mechanics* (February 1961), 117–122, 240.

"Idlewild, New Aerial Gateway to America." *Architectural Forum* 108 (February 1958): 79–87.

"Instinct for Preservation" [editorial]. *Architectural Forum* 118 (March 1963): 75.

"Intellectual Builder: Erwin Service Wolfson." *New York Times,* September 8, 1960, 30.

"Interview: Pietro Belluschi." *Progressive Architecture,* 71 June 1990, 122–123.

"Is Grand Central Terminal 'Outmoded'? Owners Consider Replacement Schemes," *Architectural Record* 116 (November 1954): 20.

Isaacs, Reginald R. *Gropius: An Illustrated Biography of the Creator of the Bauhaus.* 1st English ed. Boston: Bulfinch, 1991 (originally published by Mann, Berlin, 1984).

[Jack Cotton]. *Architectural Forum* 120 (May 1964): 11.

Jackson, Kenneth T., ed. *Encyclopedia of New York.* New Haven: Yale University Press, 1995.

Jacobs, Jane. *Death and Life of Great American Cities.* New York: Random House, 1961.

Jacobs, Jane. "New York's Office Boom." *Architectural Forum* 106 (March 1957): 105–113.

Jacobus, John M. *Philip Johnson,* New York: George Braziller, 1962.

"James Marston Fitch, 90, Architect and Preservationist." *New York Times,* April 12, 2000, 26.

"James Ruderman Is Dead; Designer of Largest Buildings." *New York Times,* January 28, 1966, 47.

Jencks, Charles. *The Language of Post-modern Architecture.* New York: Rizzoli, 1977.

Jencks, Charles. *The Post-modern Reader.* London: St Martin's Press, 1992.

Jenkins, Keith. *Rethinking History.* London: Routledge, 1991.

Johnson, Philip. "The International Style—Death or Metamorphosis." Speech delivered at the Metropolitan Museum of Art, March 30, 1961; excerpted in *Architectural Forum* 114 (June 1961): 87; also reproduced, with introductory remarks by Robert Stern, in *Philip Johnson, Writings* (New York: Oxford University Press, 1979), 118–122.

Johnson, Philip. *Writings.* With foreword by Vincent Scully and commentary by Robert Stern. New York: Oxford University Press, 1979.

Jones, Cranston. *Architecture Today and Tomorrow.* New York: McGraw-Hill, 1961.

Jones, Cranston. "Views Compared by Leading Architects." *Architectural Forum* 105 (September 1956): 146–149, 168, 172, 176.

Jordy, William. *American Buildings and Their Architects,* vol. 4. Garden City, N.Y.: Anchor/Doubleday, 1976.

Joyce, Patrick. "A Quiet Victory. The Growing Role of Postmodernism in History." *Times Literary Supplement,* October 26, 2001, 15.

"Juan Trippe, 81, Dies; U.S. Aviation Pioneer." *New York Times,* April 4, 1981, 1, 20.

"Julian Roth, 91, Dies." *New York Times,* December 11, 1992, D19.

Kahn, Ely Jacques. "Tall Buildings in New York." *Royal Institute of British Architects Journal* 67 (October 1960): 451–455.

Katzman, Meyer. Letter to the editor. *Progressive Architecture* 44 (July 1963): 156, 158.

Kaufman, Irving. "The Context of Teaching Art," In George Pappas, *Concepts in Art and Education,* 256–273. New York: Macmillan, 1970, 256–273.

Kaufmann, Edgar, Jr. "The Biggest Office Building Yet . . . Worse Luck." *Harper's* (May 1960): 64–70.

Kay, Jane Holtz. "Harvard's Salute (?) to Walter Gropius." *Progressive Architecture* 46 (November 1985): 25.

Kayden, Jerold S. *Privately Owned Public Space: The New York City Experience.* New York: Wiley, 2000.

Keiley, S. T. Letter to the editor. *New York Times,* August 24, 1960, 28.

Kentgens-Craig, Margret. *The Bauhaus and America: First Contacts 1919–1936.* Cambridge, Mass.: MIT Press, 2001.

"Kill Him but Save the Scalp" [editorial]. *New York Times,* March 21, 1962, 38.

"The King Is Dead." *Architectural Forum* 117 (August 1962): 13.

Kirk, Paul Hayden. Letter to the editor. *Progressive Architecture* 44 (June 1963): 174.

Kreindler, Lee S. "Against Pan Am Heliport" [letter to the editor]. *New York Times,* June 19, 1964, 30.

Kreindler, Lee S. "Pan Am Heliport" [letter to the editor]. *New York Times,* January 12, 1966, 20.

Kreindler, Lee S. "Dangerous Heliport" [letter to the editor]. *New York Times,* January 29, 1977, 18.

Kreindler, Lee S. "Pan Am Heliport Opposed" [letter to the editor]. *New York Times,* June 7, 1968, 38.

Lamantia, Jim. Letter to the editor. *Progressive Architecture* 44 (July 1963): 156.

"Landmarks Legislation" [editorial]. *New York Times,* October 22, 1963, 36.

"Largest Office Building" [editorial]. *New York Times,* March 11, 1963, 8.

"Pan Am, The Last Clipper." *Miami Herald,* December 20, 1991, 31A.

Lavin, Sylvia. "Theory into History, or, The Will to Anthology." *Journal of the Society of Architectural Historians* 58 (September 1999): 494–499.

"The Lawgiver." *Time,* June 29, 1959, 48, 50.

Leidesdorf, Samuel D. "Spread of Heliports Feared . . . if Zoning Change Is Approved" [letter to the editor]. *New York Times,* May 2, 1964, 26.

Leidesdorf, Samuel D., Irwin S. Chanin, and Sol Goldman. "Pan Am Heliport Opposed: Realtors Question Safety of High Facility in Congested Area" [letter to the editor]. *New York Times,* July 16, 1963, 30.

Levi, Giovanni. "On Microhistory." In *New Perspectives on Historical Writing,* ed. Peter Burke. University Park: Pennsylvania State University Press, 1994, 93–113.

Levy, David J. Letter to the editor. *New York Times,* March 23, 1965, 38.

Licht, Fred. *Josef Albers Glass, Color, and Light.* New York: Guggenheim Museum, 3rd ed., 1995.

Liffman, Paul. "Plans for Grand Central" [letter to the editor]. *New York Times,* May 24, 1960, 36.

Lippold, Richard. "Projects for Pan Am and Philharmonic." *Art in America* 50, no. 32 (Summer 1962): 50–55.

[Lippold sculpture], *Architectural Forum* 119 (August 1963): 17.

Lipstadt, Hélène. "Groping for Gropius." *Progressive Architecture* 64 (July 1983): 23–24.

Litchford, George B. "City Heliport Praised" [letter to the editor]. *New York Times,* November 8, 1966, 38.

Lollar, Coleman. "The Sovereign of the Skies." *Travel & Leisure* (February 1993): 39–40.

Loukaitou-Sideris, Anastasia, and Tridib Banergee. *Urban Design Downtown: Poetics and Politics of Form.* Berkeley and Los Angeles: University of California Press, 1998.

Loving, Rush. "The Penn Central Bankruptcy Express." *Fortune* (August 1970), 104.

Lynes, Russell. "The Age of Taste." *Harper's* (October 1950): 60–73.

Lynes, Russell. "Highbrow, Lowbrow, Middlebrow." *Harper's* (February 1949): 19–28.

"Mailer vs. Scully." *Architectural Forum* 120 (April 1964): 96–97.

Mailer, Norman. "The Big Bite." *Esquire* 60 (August 1963): 16, 18, 21, 24.

"Manhattan Towers for Sale: The Pan Am Building Goes for a Stunning $400 Million." *Time,* August 11, 1980, 50.

"Manhattan's Skyline . . . Gets Another Big One." *Newsweek,* December 25, 1961, 66–67.

Margiloff, Irwin B. "Noise From Helicopters Feared" [letter to the editor]. *New York Times,* September 29, 1962, 22.

Marshall, David. *Grand Central Station.* New York: McGraw-Hill, 1946.

Marwick, Arthur. "All Quiet on the Postmodern Front: The 'Return to Events' in Historical Study." *Times Literary Supplement,* February 23, 2001, 13–14.

May, Lary, ed. *Recasting America: Culture and Politics in the Age of Cold War.* Chicago: University of Chicago Press, 1989.

"Mayor's Eye View." *New York Times,* February 1, 1977, 33.

McLeod, Mary. "Introduction." In *Architecture Criticism Ideology,* Joan Ockman, ed, 7–11. 1985.

McQuade, Walter. "Architecture." *Nation,* January 30, 1960, 104–106.

Meeks, Carroll L. V. *The Railroad Station.* New Haven: Yale University Press, 1956.

Meeks, Carroll L. V. "Today's Grand Central Concourse is a Victory over 'Complexities Continuous.'" *Architectural Forum* 101 (November 1954): 139.

Mellow, James R. "The Bauhaus Is Alive and Well in Soup Plates and Skyscrapers." *New York Times Magazine,* September 14, 1969, 6:34–53.

Meyer, Ester da Costa. *The Work of Antonio Sant'Elia: Retreat into the Future.* New Haven: Yale University Press, 1995.

Miller, Richard A. "Disenchantment and Criticism: The State of Modern Architecture." Typed manuscript for article, dated May 1, 1959 (Haskell Papers, Box 50:1).

"Model of Grand Central City Shown." *New York Times,* November 3, 1959, 35.

"Modern Office Buildings Planned in the Downtown." *New York Times,* October 16, 1955, 1.

Moholy-Nagy, Sibyl. "Hitler's Revenge: The Grand Central Tower Project Has Dramatized the Horrors Inflicted on Our Cities in the Name of Bauhaus Design." *Art in America* 56, no. 5 (September–October 1968): 42–43.

Moholy-Nagy, Sibyl. "L'architecture américaine prend une nouvelle direction." *L'Architecture d'Aujourd'hui* 34 (April 1964): 82–83.

Moholy-Nagy, Sibyl. Letter to the editor. *Progressive Architecture* 40 (May 1959): 59, 61–62.

"Monuments: Gold Mine in the Sky." *Newsweek,* June 18, 1962, 69–70.

Mumford, Lewis. "The Sky Line: The Roaring Traffic's Boom—I." *New Yorker,* March 19, 1955, 85, 87–88, 90, 93–94.

"Mural in Pan Am Building Gets Face Washed." *New York Times,* December 8, 1963, D8, 166.

Murphy, Jim. [Interview with Pietro Belluschi]. *Progressive Architecture* 71 (June 1990): 122–123.

"Music World: No Sound At All: Muzak versus John Cage Ends in Silence at Pan Am." *New York Times,* August 12, 1962, 2:9.

Nerdinger, Winfried. *Walter Gropius.* Berlin: Bauhaus-Archiv and Cambridge, Mass.: Busch-Reisinger Museum, 1985.

Nevins, Deborah, ed. *Grand Central Terminal: City within the City.* New York: Municipal Art Society, 1982.

"New Grand Central Plan Would Save Terminal." *New York Herald Tribune,* February 8, 1955.

"New Grand Central Terminal." *Architects' and Builders* 11 (new series) (November 1910): 45–51.

"New Haven, New York Central End Dispute on Deal with Wolfson." *New York Times,* January 28, 1960, 41.

"New Haven Road Is Suing Central." *New York Times,* January 13, 1960, 27. "New Midtown Spectacular: A View from a Helicopter." *New York Times,* May 1, 1965, 33.

"New Madison Sq. Garden to Rise Atop Penn Station." *New York Times,* July 25 1961, 1, 55

"A New Park Avenue Comes into Own." *New York Times,* May 19, 1957, 8:1.

"New Plan Studied on Grand Central." *New York Times,* February 8, 1955, 20.

"New Skyscrapers Are Designed to Ease Pedestrian Movement." *New York Times,* June 26, 1960, 8:1.

"New Skyscrapers Growing Taller." *New York Times,* January 27, 1957, 1.

"A New Tribute to Walter Gropius." *Architectural Record* 143 (May 1968): 10.

"New York Airways Acts to File for Bankruptcy." *New York Times,* May 16, 1979, 4:4.

"New York Nears Completion—Almost." *Architectural Forum* 117 (October 1962): 16.

"Noted Architects to Plan Center." *New York Times,* August 24, 1958, 8:10.

"Noted Architects Study New York Opera-Theater Plans." *Architectural Forum* 105 (November 1956): 13.

"O'Connor Assails Pan Am Heliport." *New York Times,* December 21, 1964, 58.

O'Donnell, Laurence G. "Pan Am Building, Called a Huge Gamble, Is Opening 91% Rented, 100% Financed." *Wall Street Journal,* March 6, 1963, 16.

"Of Parks and Terminals" [editorial]. *New York Times,* December 6, 1960, 40.

"Office Building Boom Is Going Nationwide." *Architectural Forum* 118 (May 1963): 114–130.

"$115 Million Lease Sets a Mark Here." *New York Times,* September 28, 1960, 1.

"A One-Man Operation in an Organized World." *Business Week,* September 10, 1960, 110–114, 121–124.

"On the Responsibility of the Architect." *Perspecta* (Yale Architectural Journal) no. 2 (1953): 45–57.

Orchard, Thomas. "Silence over Pan Am" [letter to the editor], *New York Times,* February 24, 1968, 28.

Pace, Eric. "Metropolitan Life Plans to Acquire Pan Am Building for $400 Million." *New York Times,* July 29, 1980, 1, D4.

"Pan Am Builders Obtain Financing." *New York Times,* June 12, 1961, 49.

"Pan Am Building, Center of a Storm of Controversy, Nears Completion." *New York Times,* April 7, 1963, 8:1, 12.

"Pan Am Building Dedicated in New York." *New York Times,* March 8, 1963, 11.

"Pan Am Building to Have Sculpture." *New York Times,* September 3, 1961, 8:1.

"Pan Am Corp." *Wall Street Journal,* May 7, 1998, B20.

"Pan Am Heliport Backed by Mayor: Operation, Now Curtailed, Called 'Sound and Safe.'" *New York Times,* July 22, 1966, 36.

"Pan Am Lobby Gets Look of Art Gallery." *New York Times,* July 7, 1963, 1, 4.

"Pan Am Looks at Gebaur: Airline Strategy Doesn't Fit City's Plan, Official Says." *Kansas City Star,* July 24, 1999, B1.

"Pan Am Neighbors Attack Heliport: Roof Landing Field Scored as Unsafe and Noisy." *New York Times,* May 22, 1963, 80.

"Pan Am Selling Headquarters Building." *Aviation Week,* August 4, 1980, 30.

"Pan Am Squeezes into New York Skyline." *Business Week,* November 11, 1961, 34–35.

"Pan Am Ticket Office: An Airy Sweep of Sculptured Space." *Architectural Forum* 119 (August 1963): 98–101.

"Pan Am to Sell New York Offices." *Wall Street Journal,* July 29, 1980, 3.

"Pan Am Weighs Sale of Its Building." *New York Times,* February 13, 1980, B1, B4.

"Pan Am's Ticket Office in the Pan Am Building." *Interiors* 124 (November 1964): 90–93.

"Pan American and TWA Approve Plan for Merger." *New York Times,* December 21, 1962, 1, 3.

"Pan American's New Terminal in New York, *Architectural Forum* 113 (July 1960): 5.

"Pan American World Airways: 1927–1991." *Newsweek,* July 22, 1991, 36.

"Park Avenue Building." *New York Times,* December 17, 1957, 63.

"Park Avenue Home Life Gives Way to Business in New Construction." *New York Times,* October 7, 1956, 1, 3.

Parry, Natalie. "In Defense of Grand Central City Building Design." *Progressive Architecture* 40 (August 1959): 49.

Pehnt, Wolfgang. "Gropius the Romantic." *Art Bulletin* 53, no. 3 (September 1971): 379–392.

"Pennsy Will Sell 23 Valuable Sites in Mid-Manhattan." *New York Times,* June 3, 1971, 1, 63.

"Pennsylvania Station's Last Stand." *Architectural Forum* 118 (February 1963): 11.

"Perspectives." *Architectural Record* 125 (March 1959): 9.

"Perspectives" [Report on New School forum, "What Is Good Design and Planning in New York?"]. *Architectural Record* 127 (February 1960): 9.

Peter, John. *The Oral History of Modern Architecture: Interviews with the Greatest Architects of the Twentieth Century.* New York: Abrams, 1994.

Peterson, Barbara Sturken, and James Glab. *Rapid Descent: Deregulation and the Shakeout in the Airlines.* New York: Simon and Schuster, 1994.

"Philip Johnson Fights to Save Omaha Post Office." *Architectural Forum* 110 (January 1959): 11.

"Pietro Belluschi: Understanding Human Motivations." *Metropolis* (Portland, Oregon) (January 1972): 6.

Pinchis, Martin. "Gropius probabilmente erra a New York." *L'Architettura Cronache—Storia* (October 1959): 435.

"Pirelli Headquarters in Milan." *Architectural Forum* 112 (April 1960): 156.

"La più grande stazione del mondo inaugurata a New York." *L'Illustrazione Italiana* (Milan) (February 23, 1913).

"Plan Commission Approves 34th Street Heliport." *New York Times,* March 18, 1971, 78.

"Plan to Update Grand Central Station." *Architectural Forum* 101 (October 1954): 41.

"Planners Ratify Pan Am Heliport." *New York Times,* November 26, 1964, 1.

"Political Activism New Hippie Thing." *New York Times,* March 24, 1968, 1.

Porter, Russell. "Grand Central Area Open for Rebuilding." *New York Times,* March 2, 1955, 1, 21.

Porter, Russell. "Young Unloaded Stock in Central." *New York Times,* January 26, 1958, 78.

Portoghesi, Paolo. *After Modern Architecture.* New York: Rizzoli, 1982.

Rader, Morton. Letter to the editor. *Progressive Architecture* 44 (September 1963): 6.

"Rail Feud Flares on Park Ave. Plan" *New York Times,* October 3, 1956, 3.

Ramsby, Lauren. "Will Pan Am Building's Logo Go Way of Airline? More Eyesore Than a Landmark, but One New Yorkers Now Like." *New York Observer,* January 13, 1992, 1, 17.

Reis, Walter C. Letter to the editor. *Architectural Forum* 110 (January 1959): 57–58.

Rendell, Jane, Barbara Penner, and Iain Borden. *Gender Space Architecture: An Interdisciplinary Introduction.* London: Routledge, 2000.

"Renewal Is Voted in City Hall Area." *New York Times,* March 12, 1964, 37.

[Retiring deans, schools of architecture] [editorial]. *Architectural Forum* 120 (January 1964): 63.

"Robert Young, Financier, Ends Life in Palm Beach." *New York Times,* January 26, 1958, 1, 78.

Robinson, Cervin. "Obituary, *Brickbuilder—Architectural Forum:* 1892–1974." *Architectural Review* (London) 156 (July 1974): 64–65.

Robinson, Edward. Letter to the editor. *New York Times,* May 5, 1965, 46.

"Rockefeller U. Opposes City Heliport." *New York Times,* January 18, 1968, 4.

"Romance in Lives of City Builders." *New York Times,* February 24, 1929, 12:3.

Rosenfield, Isadore. Letter to the editor. *Progressive Architecture* 44 (June 1963): 176.

Roth, Richard. "The Forces That Shaped Park Avenue." *Perspecta* 8 (1963): 97–102.

Roth, Richard. "High Rise Down to Earth." *Progressive Architecture* 38 (June 1957): 196–200.

Rowe, Colin. "Waiting for Utopia" [review of Venturi, *Complexity and Contradiction in Architecture*]. *New York Times,* September 10, 1967, 18, 20, 22.

Ruderman, James. "Planning and Construction of the Pan Am Building." *Municipal Engineers Journal* 48, no. 2 (February 1962): 31–40.

Rudolph, George Cooper. Letter to the editor. *Architectural Forum* 122 (June 1964): 60.

Rudolph, Paul. "The Changing Face of New York." *Saturday Review,* October 18, 1958, 34, 42; reprinted in *AIA Journal* 31 (April 1959): 38–39.

Rudolph, Paul. "The Changing Philosophy of Architecture." *Architectural Forum* 101 (July 1954): 120–121.

Rumble, Janet L. "Control Tower." *Wallpaper* (September/October 1998): 179–180.

Ruttenbaum, Steven. *Mansions in the Clouds.* New York: Balsam, 1986.

Rykwert, Joseph. Review of Isaacs, *Walter Gropius. Times Literary Supplement,* May 2, 1986, 463–464.

Saarinen, Eero. "The Six Broad Currents of Modern Architecture." *Architectural Forum* 99 (July 1953): 110–115.

Saint, Andrew. *Image of the Architect.* New Haven: Yale University Press, 1983.

Salpukas, Agis. "Pan Am, Its Cash Depleted, Shuts." *New York Times,* December 5, 1991, C1, C4.

Santiago, Michel. "Outrage: Counter Junk." *Architectural Review* (London) 135–136 (May 1964): 372, 374.

Saunders, F. Dale. "Helicopter Din" [letter to the editor]. *New York Times,* January 24, 1966, 34.

"Save Our City." *New York Times,* August 2, 1962, 14.

"Saving Fine Architecture." *New York Times,* August 11, 1962, 16.

Schlichting, Kurt C. "Grand Central Terminal and the City Beautiful in New York." *Journal of Urban History* 22, no. 3 (March 1996): 332–349.

Schlichting, Kurt C. *Grand Central Terminal: Railroads, Engineering, and Architecture in New York City.* Baltimore: Johns Hopkins University Press, 2001.

Schmertz, Mildred. "The Problem of Pan Am." *Architectural Record* 133 (May 1963): 151–158.

Schmertz, Mildred. "Walter Gropius, 1883–1969." *Architectural Record* 146 (August 1969): 9–10.

Schwartz, John. "Pan American World Airways: 1927–1991." *Newsweek,* July 22, 1991, 36.

Schwarzer, Mitchell. "History and Theory in Architectural Periodicals." *Journal of the Society of Architectural Historians* 58 (September 1999): 342–348.

Scully, Vincent. *American Architecture and Urbanism.* New York: Praeger, 1969.

Scully, Vincent. "Death of the Street." *Perspecta* 8 (1963): 91–96.

"Sculptor Becomes a High-Wire Artist in Pan Am Lobby." *New York Times,* April 25, 1963, 1.

"Seatless, I.R.T. Shuttle Trains Proposed by Transit Board Head." *New York Times,* January 25, 1956, 1, 25.

"Service at Heliport Facing Suspension." *Aviation Week & Space Technology,* January 19, 1968, 27.

Shachtman, Tom. *Skyscraper Dreams: The Great Real Estate Dynasties of New York.* Boston: Little, Brown, 1991.

Shirey, David L. "Testament of Joy." *Newsweek,* July 21, 1969, 67.

"Showcase for Modern America, Good Neighbor for the Parthenon." *Time,* July 15, 1957, 74.

"Shutdown Planned of Pan Am Units." *Atlanta Journal and Constitution,* February 27, 1998, 03F.

Singal, Daniel Joseph, ed. *Modernist Culture in America.* Belmont, Calif.: Wadsworth, 1991.

"A 'Sixth Sense' for Construction." *Engineering News-Record,* May 28, 1959, 55–57.

"Sky-High Deal for Skyscraper." *Fortune* (December 1960): 140–143, 266–267, 271.

"The Skyline Factory." *Newsweek,* September 18, 1967, 98.

"Skyscraper Here to Rise like Vine." *New York Times,* September 20, 1959, 8:1.

"Skyscraper Is Begun." *New York Times,* November 27, 1959, 50.

[Slated demolition of post office in Omaha]. *Architectural Forum* 110 (January 1959): 11.

Speller, M. A. Letter to the editor. *New York Times,* August 27, 1964.

"Sprouting Skyscrapers Are Changing Face of Midtown Manhattan." *New York Times,* February 3, 1957, 8:1.

"State's Senators Urge Copter Help." *New York Times,* March 11, 1965, 65.

Stauffer, Thomas. Letter to the editor. *Progressive Architecture* 44 (June 1963): 176.

Stephens, Suzanne. "Ada Louise Huxtable in Perspective." *Skyline* (March 1982): 3.

Stern, Robert A. M. *New Directions in American Architecture.* New York: G. Braziller, 1969.

Stern, Robert A. M., Thomas Mellins, and David Fishman. *New York 1960.* New York: Monacelli, 1995.

Story, Richard David. "The Buildings New Yorkers Love to Hate." *New York Times,* June 15, 1987, 30–34.

Strickland, Walter. "No Heliport" [letter to the editor], *New York Times,* March 29, 1965, 32.

"TAC's Demise." *Architecture* 84 (December 1995): 117–119.

Tafel, Edgar A. Letter to the editor. *Progressive Architecture* 44 (June 1963): 174.

Tafuri, Manfredo. "The Disenchanted Mountain: The Skyscraper and the City." In *The American City: From the Civil War to the New Deal,* ed. Giorgio Ciucci, Francesco Dal Co, Mario Manien-Elia, and Manfredo Tafuri, 389–503 (trans. Barbara Luigia LaPenta). Cambridge, MA: The MIT Press.

Talese, Gay. "Expert Eye." *New York Times Magazine,* May 7, 1961, 38.

"Talk of the Town." *New Yorker,* June 7, 1999, 29–30.

"Talk of the Town: Symbol." *New Yorker,* April 8, 1961, 47–49.

Tanner, Ogden. "Grand Central's Wolfson." *Architectural Forum* 109 (November 1958): 132–133, 200.

Tauranac, John. *Essential New York: A Guide to the History and Architecture of Manhattan's Important Buildings, Parks, and Bridges.* New York: Holt, Rinehart and Winston, 1979.

Temko, Allan. "Five Men Who Built on a Lofty Plain." *New York Times Book Review,* January 1, 1961, 7:14.

"Tenant Can Pick Building's Name." *New York Times,* January 4, 1959, 1, 2.

"Terminal to Get Bowling Alleys." *New York Times,* August 4, 1960, 27.

"Test Flight." *New York Times,* January 26, 1977, 3.

"Textured Masonry Sheaths New Office Buildings." *New York Times,* October 29, 1961, 5:1, 6.

Thomas, Robert M., Jr. "John White, Real Estate Agent Expert in Big Sales, Dies at 75." *New York Times,* April 2, 1995, 46.

Thompson, Ralph. Letter to the editor. *New York Times,* April 30, 1977, 24.

[Threat to Reliance Building, Chicago]. *Architectural Forum* 119 (August 1963): 8.

Tigerman, Stanley, ed. *Chicago Tribune Tower Competition and Late Entries.* New York: Rizzoli, 1981.

"Tower Evolution Traced by Designer." *New York Times,* December 3, 1967.

Trager, James. *Park Avenue: Street of Dreams.* New York: Atheneum, 1990.

Train, John. "Revived Heliport: This Maddening Irritation" [letter to the editor]. *New York Times,* February 26, 1977, 18.

"Transportation and the City." *Architectural Forum* 119 (October 1963): 61–83.

"Tribute to Gropius." *AIA Journal* 152, no. 2 (August 1969): 16.

"Tributes to Forum" [letters to the editor]. *Architectural Forum* 121 (August–September 1964): 21–23, 28, 36, 45.

Tunnard, Christopher. *The Modern American City.* Princeton, N.J.: Van Nostrand, 1968.

Tunnard, Christopher, and Henry Hope Reed. *The American Skyline.* Boston: Houghton Mifflin, 1956.

"TWA's Graceful New Terminal. *Architectural Forum* 108 (January 1958): 78–80.

"Two Noted Architects to Help Map Center." *New York Times,* July 31, 1958, 14.

"Umpire Rebuffs Two Unions Here: Neither Gets Jurisdiction in Pan Am Building Dispute." *New York Times,* April 5, 1962, 21.

"Un nuovo grattacielo a New York." *Domus,* no. 358 (September 1959): 1–3.

"Une mise au point de Walter Gropius,'" *L'Architecture d'Aujourd'hui* 31, no. 90 (July 1960): n.p.

"University of Baghdad." *Process* 19 (October 1980): 26–29.

"University of Baghdad Development." *Process* 58 (May 1985): 90.

"Up Goes Manhattan! Splendor in the Skies." *Life,* November 9, 1962, 74–84.

"USA Abroad." *Architectural Forum* 107 (December 1957): 114–115.

Venturi, Robert. *Complexity and Contradiction in Architecture.* New York: Museum of Modern Art, 1966.

von Eckardt, Wolf. "The Bauhaus." *Horizon* IV (November 1961): 58–75.

von Eckardt, Wolf. "Pan Am's Glass House." *New Republic,* August 13, 1962, 24–26.

"Walter Gropius" [editorial]. *Design* (Bombay) 13, no. 7 (July 1969): 11–12.

"Walter Gropius on the Occasion of his 80th Birthday Celebration at Harvard." *Arts & Architecture* 80 (July 1963): 18–19.

"Walter Gropius to Get 1959 Architects Award." *New York Times,* March 18, 1959, 41.

Weinberg, Robert C. "Station Plan Protested: United Opposition Seen in Bowling Alley in Grand Central." *New York Times,* August 16, 1960, 28.

"Westinghouse Lifts Record." *New York Times,* February 24, 1960, 52.

Whalen, Richard J. "A City Destroying Itself." *Fortune* (September 1964): 115–122, 232–236, 241–244.

"What Is Good Design and Planning in New York?" [publicity brochure]. New School for Social Research, New York, January 1960.

"What Will Our Skylines Look Like?" *Time,* February 21, 2000, 80–82.

"Why Pan Am Sold the Pan Am Building." *Business Week,* August 11, 1980, 25–26.

Whyte, William H. *The Social Life of Small Urban Spaces.* Washington, D.C.: Conservation Foundation, 1982.

Williams, Frank. "Grand Central City." *Architectural Forum* 128 (February 1968): 48–54.

Wilson, Forrest. [Gropius obituary]. *Progressive Architecture* 50 (August 1969): 70–71.

Wiseman, Carter. *I. M. Pei.* New York: Abrams, 1990.

Wisniewski, C. J. Letter to the editor. *Progressive Architecture* 44 (June 1963); 176.

"With Progress Aforethought: New York, Penn Station, Present and Future." *Architectural Forum* 115 (September 1961): 8.

"With Sky-High Hopes, Pan Am Starts Small." *New York Daily News,* September 26, 1996, 39.

Witkin, Richard. "Heliport Slated atop Skyscraper." *New York Times,* March 24, 1961, 33.

Witkin, Richard. "Heliport Takes Shape on Roof of Pan Am Building." *New York Times,* September 21, 1963, 31.

Witkin, Richard. "Pan Am Heliport Is Voted by City." *New York Times,* January 15, 1965, 1, 18.

Woodbridge, Frederick J. "Beauty and the Urban Beast." *Royal Architectural Institute of Canada* 30 (July 1953), 206–207.

"World's Largest Executive Suite." *Business Week,* July 20, 1963, 70–72.

"World's Loftiest Tower May Rise on Site of Grand Central Terminal." *New York Times,* September 8, 1954, 1, 22.

"Wrecking Starts at Grand Central." *New York Times,* June 28, 1960.

Zevi, Bruno. "Gropius on Park Avenue" [reprinted, in translation, from *L'Expresso,* Rome]. *Atlas: The Magazine of the World Press* 6, (November 1963): 302–303.

Zevi, Bruno. "La protesta di Gropius." *Architettura* 9, no. 102 (April 1964): 866–867.

Zevi, Bruno. Letter to the editor. *Atlas: The Magazine of the World Press* 7, (March 1964): 192.

Zukowsky, John, ed. *Building for Air Travel: Architecture and Design for Commercial Aviation.* Munich and New York: Art Institute of Chicago and Prestel-Verlag, 1996.

Zukowsky, John, ed. *2001: Building for Space Travel.* New York: Abrams, in association with the Art Institute of Chicago, 2001.

"Zum Hochhausprojekt von Walter Gropius in New York." *Werk* 46 (November 1959): 229–230.

ILLUSTRATION CREDITS

Frontispiece   Skyviews Survey

CHAPTER 1

Figure   1.1   Augustus Mitchell, *Mitchell's New General Atlas,* Philadelphia, 1869.

Figure   1.2   New York Public Library.

Figure   1.3   Image donated by Corbis-Bettmann.

Figure   1.4   New York Transit Museum.

Figure   1.5   New York Public Library.

Figure   1.6   Collection of the New-York Historical Society.

Figure   1.7   New York Transit Museum.

Figure   1.8   New York Public Library.

Figure   1.9   Musei Civici, Como.

Figure 1.10   Neg. #58064, collection of the New-York Historical Society.

Figure 1.11   William J. Wilgus Papers, New York Public Library.

Figure 1.12   New York Transit Museum.

Figure 1.13   New York Public Library.

Figure 1.14   New York Transit Museum.

Figure 1.15   Drawing by Shuishan Yu.

Figure 1.16   *Architectural Forum,* October 1954.

Figure 1.17   *Downtown Athletic Club,* January 1955; copy in The Haskell Collection, Avery Architectural and Fine Arts Library, Columbia University in the City of New York.

Figure 1.18   Image donated by Corbis-Bettmann.

Figure 1.19   Photograph by Steven Ruttenbaum, from his book *Mansions in the Clouds: The Skyscraper Palazzi of Emery Roth* (Balsam Press, Inc., 1986).

Figure 1.20   Photograph by Steven Ruttenbaum, from his book *Mansions in the Clouds: The Skyscraper Palazzi of Emery Roth* (Balsam Press, Inc., 1986).

Figure 1.21   Photograph by Steven Ruttenbaum, from his book *Mansions in the Clouds: The Skyscraper Palazzi of Emery Roth* (Balsam Press, Inc., 1986).

Figure 1.22   Jane Jacobs, *Architectural Forum,* March 1957.

Figure 1.23   *Business Week,* September 1, 1962.

Figure 1.24   *Business Week,* October 31, 1959.

Figure 1.25   Pei Cobb Freed & Partners, Architects.

Figure 1.26   *New York Times Magazine,* December 15, 1957.

Figure 1.27   Image donated by Corbis-Bettmann.

Figure 1.28   *Tribune Tower Competition,* Chicago: Tribune Company, 1923.

Figure 1.29   Office of James Ruderman.

Figure 1.30   Photograph by author.

Figure 1.31   Walter Gropius et al., *The Architects Collaborative Inc., 1945–1965.*

Figure 1.32   Author's collection.

Figure 1.33   Author's collection.

CHAPTER 2

Figure 2.1   *Business Week,* October 31, 1959.

Figure 2.2   Image donated by Corbis-Bettmann.

Figure 2.3   Office of James Ruderman.

Figure 2.4   Walter Gropius et al., *The Architects Collaborative Inc.,* 1945–1965.

Figure 2.5   *Architectural Forum,* April 1960.

Figure 2.6   Ezra Stoller © ESTO. All rights reserved.

Figure 2.7   Author's collection.

Figure 2.8   Author's collection.

Figure 2.9   Mo-Sai panels, detail, 1991 (Photograph by author)

Figure 2.10   *New York Times,* November 3, 1959.

Figure 2.11   Archives and Special Collections Department, Otto G. Richter Library, University of Miami, Coral Gables, Florida.

Figure 2.12   *Architectural Forum,* January 1961.

Figure 2.13   Archives and Special Collections Department, Otto G. Richter Library, University of Miami, Coral Gables, Florida.

Figure 2.14   Archives and Special Collections Department, Otto G. Richter Library, University of Miami, Coral Gables, Florida.

Figure 2.15   Archives and Special Collections Department, Otto G. Richter Library, University of Miami, Coral Gables, Florida.

Figure 2.16   Pan American World Airways.

Figure 2.17   Archives and Special Collections Department, Otto G. Richter Library, University of Miami, Coral Gables, Florida.

Figure 2.18   Pan American World Airways.

Figure 2.19   Archives and Special Collections Department, Otto G. Richter Library, University of Miami, Coral Gables, Florida.

Figure 2.20   Archives and Special Collections Department, Otto G. Richter Library, University of Miami, Coral Gables, Florida.

Figure 2.21   Courtesy of Charles Forberg.

Figure 2.22   Photograph by author.

Figure 2.23   Photograph by Joseph Molitor, The Haskell Collection, Avery Architectural and Fine Arts Library, Columbia University in the City of New York.

Figure 2.24   Photograph by author.

CHAPTER 3

Figure 3.1   *New York Times,* January 24, 1960.

Figure 3.2   *Fortune,* December 1960.

Figure 3.3   *Business Week,* September 1, 1962.

Figure 3.4   *Architectural Record,* May 1962.

Figure 3.5   The Cosmopolis of the Future," *King's Dream of New York,* 1908.

Figure 3.6   *Business Week,* November 11, 1961.

Figure 3.7   *Architectural Forum,* September 1962.

Figure 3.8   American Bridge Company.

Figure 3.9   Associated Press/Wide World Photos.

Figure 3.10   American Bridge Company.

Figure 3.11   American Bridge Company.

Figure 3.12   American Bridge Company.

Figure 3.13   Image donated by Corbis-Bettmann.

Figure 3.14   Photograph by Ernie Sisto, *New York Times,* May 10, 1962.

Figure 3.15   *Popular Science,* September 1962.

Figure 3.16   *Popular Science,* September 1962.

Figure 3.17   Archives and Special Collections Department, Otto G. Richter Library, University of Miami, Coral Gables, Florida.

CHAPTER 4

Figures 4.1 a   Vincent Scully, *American Architecture and Urbanism* (New York: Praeger, 1969);
and 4.1 b   Editors of *Look,* in collaboration with Frederick Lewis Allen; *Look at America: New York City* (Boston: Houghton Mifflin, 1948).

Figure 4.2   *AIA Journal,* July 1963.

Figure 4.3   Photograph by author.

Figure 4.4   *Architectural Record,* May 1963.

Figure 4.5   *Architectural Forum,* November 1963.

Figure 4.6   From Peter Blake, *God's Own Junkyard,* 1964 (original source: General Electric Company).

Figure 4.7   Jordy, *American Buildings and Their Architects,* 1976, volume 4.

Figure 4.8   *L'Architettura Cronache-Storia,* October 1959.

CHAPTER 5

Figure   5.1   Photograph by author.

CHAPTER 6

Figure   6.1   Image donated by Corbis-Bettmann.

Figure   6.2   Archives and Special Collections Department, Otto G. Richter Library, University of Miami, Coral Gables, Florida.

Figure   6.3   Archives and Special Collections Department, Otto G. Richter Library, University of Miami, Coral Gables, Florida.

Figure   6.4   Archives and Special Collections Department, Otto G. Richter Library, University of Miami, Coral Gables, Florida.

Figure   6.5   Photograph by Jack Manning, *New York Times,* December 22, 1965.

Figure   6.6   Photograph by Neil Boenzi, *New York Times,* March 27, 1977.

Figure   6.7   Photograph by Larry Morris, *New York Times,* May 17, 1977.

Figure   6.8   *Architectural Forum,* July 1968.

Figure   6.9   The Haskell Collection, Avery Architectural and Fine Arts Library, Columbia University in the City of New York.

Figure 6.10   Image donated by Corbis-Bettmann.

Figure 6.11   *New York Times,* July 29, 1980.

Figure 6.12   Photograph by author.

Figure 6.13   Archives and Special Collections Department, Otto G. Richter Library, University of Miami, Coral Gables, Florida.

Figure 6.14   Photograph by author.

Figure 6.15   Archives and Special Collections Department, Otto G. Richter Library, University of Miami, Coral Gables, Florida.

Figure 6.16   Photograph by author.

CHAPTER 7

Figure   7.1   Laszlo Kiss, Simon Ungers, and Todd Zwigard.

Figure   7.2   *New York Magazine,* June 15, 1987.

Figure   7.3   Photograph by Joseph Molitor, The Haskell Collection, Avery Architectural and Fine Arts Library, Columbia University in the City of New York.

Figure   7.4   Photograph by author.

Figure   7.5   Claes Oldenburg and Coosje van Bruggen Studio.

INDEX

Page numbers in italics refer to illustrations.

Abenad Corporation, 42

Abrams, Charles, 191

Acker, Ed, 359

Action Group for Better Architecture in New York (AGBANY), 326–327

Airline industry, xiv, 22, 26, 32, 128, 311, 314, 346, 357–360, 361–362, 386

Albers, Josef, 142–143, *153,* 228, 296, 354, 407n156

American Institute of Architects (AIA), 3, 35, 75, 262, 282, 337
  Conference on Ugliness, 178–179
  New York Chapter, 2, 157

American Institute of Planners, 157

Andrews, Wayne, 175–176, 248, 370

"Anti-Uglies," 177, 327

"Apollo in the democracy" (concept), 67–69, 159. *See also* Gropius, Walter

Apollo in the Democracy (book), 294–295. *See also* Gropius, Walter
  Collins review of, 294–295

Architectural criticism, xiv, xvi, 53, 56, 58, 227, 232, 257, 384–385, 396n85. *See also* Huxtable, Ada Louise
  Forum's stance on, 23 (*see also Architectural Forum;* Haskell, Douglas)

Architectural Forum, xvi, 26, 255–259

Architectural League of New York, 177, 181

Architectural practice, changes in, xiv, 116–117, 337–338, 393n44

Architectural Record, xvi, 26, 80, 82, 256, 277

Architectural Review (London), 267

L'Architecture d'Aujourd'hui, 266–267, 279

L'Architettura Cronache—Storia, 263, 271

Bacon, Edmund, 228, 230, 252, 270, 303

Baird, George, 373

Ballard, William F. R., 247, 252, 270

Barnes, Edward Larabee, 139, 144

Barnett, Jonathan, 277

Bauen + Wohnen, 266

Beaux-Arts architecture, xiv, 35, 76, 255, 256, 289, 331, 333, 339, 344, 371. *See also* Grand Central Terminal

Belle, John (Beyer Blinder Belle Architects), 354

Belluschi, Pietro, 70–77, *71,* 80, 223, 237, 328
  AIA Gold Medal, 277, 281
  and the *Architectural Record,* 188, 190, 233, 235, 277
  and art work, Pan Am Building, 141–144
  as co-designer of the Pan Am Building, xiii, 2, 50, 59, 77, 84, 87, 117, 156–157, 159, 160–163, 165, 173, 212, 248, 269, 275, 304, 353, 376 (*see also* Gropius/Belluschi/Roth collaboration)
  on collaboration of art and architecture, 142–143
  collaboration with Gropius, 72, 75, 104, 282, 397n119
  contract with Wolfson, 60–61, 97, 397n119
  criticism of, 158–159, 166–171, 173, 179, 180, 183–184, 228, 230, 232–233, 238, 245, 262, 269, 384
  deanship, MIT, xiv, 72, 104
  decline in reputation, xvi, 173, 276–279, 387
  drawing, "Grand Central City" project, 100, *102*
  Equitable Building, 72, *73,* 277
  and Goble, 190, 191
  and historic preservation, 29, 76, 328, 329, 423n54
  and Philip Johnson, 328
  and Kepes, 143

Belluschi, Pietro (*continued*)
  Lincoln Center, 76, 104, 195, 277, 377, 399n132
  and Lippold, 143
  responses to criticism, 159, 196
  stellar reputation, xiv, xvi, 59–62, 64, 75, 158, 163, 167–168, 275
  and Wolfson, 59–60
Beresford Apartments, 35, *36. See also* Emery Roth & Sons
Birkerts, Gunnar, 231
Blake, Peter, xiv, xvi, 160, 181–182, 248–249, 252, 293–294, 385
  God's Own Junkyard, 248–249, 267, 385, 415n53
Board of Standards and Appeals, 120, 124, 126, 127
Boisi, James O., 126–127, 236, 237, 240, 326. *See also* New York Central Railroad
Boston Back Bay Center project, 72, *74,* 98, 282
Breuer, Marcel, 293, 296, 306, 331, 343–345
  proposed Grand Central tower, 331–333, *332,* 338–344
Brumond, Harry L., Grand Central Terminal proposal, 29, *30*
Bunshaft, Gordon, 187. *See also* Skidmore, Owings & Merrill
Burchard, John Ely, 173
Burger, Alfred G., 32, 50
Burnham, Daniel, 16, 35, 84
Burns, James, 227–228, 235
Bush-Brown, Albert, 230
Bystrom, Carl A., 232–233

Cage, John, 151
Casabella, 291, 297, 300
Catalano, Eduardo, 46
Cavaglieri, Giorgio, 33
Chermayeff, Ivan, 111, 143–144
Chicago Tribune Competition project, 64, *66,* 77, 100, 103, 171, 373. *See also* Gropius, Walter

Chimacoff, Alan, 373
Chrysler Building, 137, 242, 357, 362, 373, 382
City Beautiful Movement, xvi, 22, 51, 243, 255, 289, 386
City Centre Properties, 86
Colcord, Ray, 82, 105, 110, 143, 198
Colgate-Palmolive Building, 51–52, 54, 91, 175
Collins, Peter, 294–295
Condit, Carl, 175–176, 248, 384
Conference on Ugliness, 178–179
Construction Management. *See* Morse, Carl
Cotton, Jack, 86, 216, 248, 304, 346
Cousins, Norman, 125–126
Creighton, Thomas H., 160, 174
Cummings, Robert L., 196–198, 314, 318. *See also* New York Airways
Cvijanovic, Alex, 103, 144, 303–305. *See also* The Architects Collaborative (TAC)

Death and Life of Great American Cities, xiii, xv. *See also* Jacobs, Jane
"Death of the Street," 218, *219. See also* Scully, Vincent
d'Harnoncourt, René, 144
Diesel Construction Company, 42–44, 86–87, 114, 119, 210, 253. *See also* Morse, Carl; Wolfson, Erwin
Diesel Electric Corporation. *See* Diesel Construction Company
Domus, 263
Dorfles, Gillo, 283–284
Drexler, Arthur, 187
Dupré, Judith, 377–378, 380

Eaton, Leonard K., 232
Eiffel Tower, 370, 382
Emery Roth & Sons, 29, 34, 35–42, 50–51, 77, 84, 91, 112, 114, 185, 227–228, 277. *See also* Roth, Richard
  Beresford Apartments, 35, *36*
  buildings in New York City, 35, *36, 37, 38, 39, 40,* 59

buildings on Park Avenue, *37,* 40
as co-designers of the Pan Am Building, 77,
    87, 112, 114, 376 (*see also* Gropius/
    Belluschi/Roth project)
Grand Central Terminal proposal, 29–33, *31,*
    44, 49–50, 161, 168, 196
reputation, 58–60, 97, 253, 274–276
and Ruderman, 112–114
San Remo Apartments, *34,* 35
and Wolfson, 35, 40
Empire State Building, 23, 44, 45, 49, 63, 86,
    196, 216–217, 223, 373, 382–383, 400n19
Equitable Building. *See* Belluschi, Pietro

Fellheimer, Alfred, 26–29. *See also* Fellheimer
    and Wagner; Reed and Stem
Fellheimer and Wagner, 27
    Grand Central Terminal proposal, 26–27, *28,*
        168, 196
Ferris, The Reverend Theodore P., 166
Fitch, James Marston, 239, 248, 281, 299, 303,
    340
Fletcher, Norman, 97. *See also* The Architects
    Collaborative (TAC)
Forberg, Charles, 139
Forum. See Architectural Forum
"Four Great Makers" conference at Columbia
    University, 188
Franciscono, Marcel, 298, 301–302
Friedenberg, Daniel M., 253, 337
Futurists, 10, 242, 255, 339. *See also* Sant'Elia,
    Antonio

Garroway, Dave, 193
Ginsberg, Allen, 341, 343
    "Howl," vii, 2, 58, 343, 387
Glenn, John, 201, *205,* 341
Goble, Emerson, 177–178, 188–191, 259, 277,
    302
Goldberg, Bertrand, 174–175
Goldberger, Paul, 371, 376–377
Gordon, Walter, 80, 277–278

Grand Central Building, Inc., 82, 105, 118, 210
"Grand Central City" (Commodore Vander-
    bilt's), *20,* 51, 341
"Grand Central City" (Wolfson's), xvi, 4, 32, 49–
    51, 62–63, 68, 72, 80, 84, *88,* 114, 172, 341,
    385. *See also* Emery Roth & Sons; Grand
    Central Terminal; Pan Am Building; Wolfson,
    Erwin
    Belluschi drawing of, 100, *102*
    circulation, 338–339
    construction of, *95,* 109, 114–120
    controversy over, 86, 161, 167 (*see also*
        "Grand Central City" [Wolfson's], criticism of)
    criticism of, 121, 156–187
    design of, 94 (*see also* Gropius/Belluschi/Roth
        collaboration)
    design process, 105–111
    exterior lighting, 111
    financing of, 86–89
    Gropius and Belluschi involvement in, 94–
        104, *96,* 117, 156, 185, 278–298, 397n106
    lobbies, 111, *113*
    Mo-Sai panels, 105, *106, 107,* 109, 119
    Pan American World Airways signs on, 111
    Plexiglas model, 105, *108*
    site, 80, 87, 89, 168 (*see also* Grand Central
        Terminal)
    steel framing, 92–94, *95,* 117
    structural engineering of, 63, 89–94
    tenants, 111, 201
    wind factor, 93–94
Grand Central Depot, *6,* 7, 10. *See also* Grand
    Central Terminal
    remodeled and enlarged, 10, *12*
Grand Central Office Building, 49, 118, 333,
    334
Grand Central Terminal, 3–4, 10–22, *20, 334,*
    341, 346, 382
    airspace over, xiii, 14, 346
    the Beaux-Arts building, 3, 10, *13,* 14, *18,* 19,
        20, 22, 278, 324, 331, 333, 338
    circulation system, 16, 19, 333

Grand Central Terminal (*continued*)
  City Beautiful Movement ideals, 10, 16, 22, 51
  concourse, 19, *21,* 25, 236, 339, 341
  controversy over, 33, 44, 47, 345
  Depot, *6,* 7, 10
  depressed tracks of, 7, *8, 9,* 51
  and Futurist connection, 10, 242, 255, 339
    (*see also* Sant'Elia, Antonio)
  plans to demolish, 3–4, 22, 25, 27, 92, 156,
    160, 324
  preservation of, 324, 331 (*see also* Haskell,
    Douglas; Landmarks Preservation Commis-
    sion)
  redevelopment plans for, 2–27, 47, 49–51, 80
  site, 46, 50, 59, 63, 89, 328
  transportation network, 10, 14, 89, 244
  urban design, 3, 10, 14, 16, 19, *20,* 22, 333
Graves, Michael, 353
  Portland Public Services Building, 353
Gray, Christopher (Office of Metropolitan His-
    tory, New York City), 368, 383–384
Greene, Herb, 230
Gregotti, Vittorio, 300
Gropius, Ise, 298, 301
Gropius, Walter, 58, 64–69, *65,* 254, 256, 329,
    336, 343–345, 347, 370. *See also* The Archi-
    tects Collaborative (TAC); *Walter Gropius
    Archive*
  AIA Gold Medal, 68, 281
  and "Anti-Uglies" movement, 177
  "Apollo in the democracy" (concept), 67–69,
    159
  Apollo in the Democracy (book), 294–295
  and architectural history, 3, 329 (*see also* His-
    toric preservation)
  "L'architetto e la socìettà," 291
  and art work, Pan Am Building, 141–151
  and Blake, 249, 252
  Busch-Reisinger exhibition, 300–301
  as chairman of the department of architecture
    at Harvard, xiv, 64, 68
  and Chermayeff, 111

  Chicago Tribune Competition project, 64, *66,*
    77, 100, 103
  on collaboration of art and architecture, 142
  collaboration with Belluschi, 72, 75, 104,
    397n119
  contract with Wolfson, 60–61, 97
  criticism of, 157–159, 166, 167–171, 173,
    177, 179, 180, 183–184, 228, 230–233, 238,
    245–247, 249, 252, 262–263, 266–271, 287,
    293–307, 343–345, 354, 371, 384
  "Curse of Conformity," 67, 141
  death, 295
  decline in reputation, xvi, 173, 279–287, 295–
    298, 301–302, 377, 387
  as designer of the Pan Am Building, xiii, 2, 50,
    58–59, 77, 82–84, 87, 117, 119, 138–139,
    156–157, 159, 160–163, 173, 212, 233, 248,
    269, 275, 304, 353, 376, 382
  early proposal with forecourt, plaza, or park,
    96, 97, 169, 233, *234,* 236, 269, 377
  eightieth birthday party, 285–287
  and Goble, 188–191
  and the heliport, 198
  and historic preservation, 29, 76, 288–289,
    328
  and history, 297 (*see also* Historic preser-
    vation)
  Hochschule für Gestaltung address, 280–281
  and Philip Johnson, 328
  and Kepes, 143
  and lighting (exterior) of the building, 198
  and Lippold, 143–144, 145–148, 149
  lobby, 347, 354, *355*
  and Loos, 300
  1972 retrospective exhibition, 298–299
  office building in Piccadilly Circus, 177
  one-hundredth birthday, 299–300
  responses to criticism, 191–195, 249, 252,
    266–267, 269–271, 284–287, 288–289, 291
  "Scope of Total Architecture," 157, 257, 305
  stellar reputation, xiv, xv, 59–62, 64, 68, 158,
    163, 167–168, 256, 275, 295, 377

teamwork concept, 69–70, 189, 239, 279–280, 283–284, 293–294, 296, 297–298, 302, 306–307, 398n122
"Tradition and Continuity in Architecture," 267, 287–290
"Unity in Diversity," 188–189, 266
vision of Pan Am Building, 84, 370, 385
Walter Gropius Archive, 303–305
Williams College address, 286–287
and Wolfson, 58–61, 97
and Zevi, 268–271
Gropius/Belluschi early proposal with forecourt or plaza, *96, 97,* 169, 233, *234,* 236, 269, 377
Gropius/Belluschi/Roth collaboration, 77, 94–104, *96,* 105, 110, 112, 169, 278. *See also* "Grand Central City"
Gropius/Belluschi/Roth project, 63, 77–82, *79, 81,* 158, 168. *See also* "Grand Central City"
Gruen, Victor. 125, 160–163, 165

Hale, Jonathan, 305–307
Harlem (New York and Harlem) Railroad, 4, 7
Harkness, John, 303. *See also* The Architects Collaborative (TAC)
Harkness, Sarah, 70. *See also* The Architects Collaborative (TAC)
Haskell, Douglas, xiv, xvi, 53, 255–258
  and architectural criticism, 53, 237, 239, 257 (*see also* Architectural criticism, *Forum*'s stance on)
  and Belluschi, 239
  bowling alley proposal, 120–127
  College Art Association talk, 341
  and the Grand Central concourse, 25, 32
  criticism of the Pan Am Building, 238–247, 287
  and the Grand Central Terminal, 7, 19, 23, 25–26, 32–33, 45, 46, 50, 121, 127, 156, 239–247, 324, 326, 327, 329, 335–341 (*see also* Grand Central Terminal, urban design)
  and Grand Central urban design, 14, 19, 29, 32–33

and Gropius, 64, 67, 239, 279–280, 336
historic preservation, 324, 326, 327, 329–330, 335, 339–341
"Lost New York of the Pan American Airways Building," 238–247, *241,* 287, 335, 339
and the Pan Am Building, 335, 338, 341, 384 (*see also* Haskell, Douglas, "Lost New York of the Pan American Airways Building")
and Pei, 23, 25, 45
private versus public interests, 14, 22, 127, 242–245, 340–341
proposed book, 335–338
and the railroads, 7, 26, 46, 112–127, 244–245, 255, 339–341
on the Roth proposal, 32–33
and Wolfson, 125, 240, 338
Heckscher, August, 238, 302–303, 335, 376
Heliport, 304–305, 310–324, 325, *313, 316, 317, 323,* 339, 372
  criticism of, 199, 310–312, 314, 318, 320–322, 324
  in Emery Roth & Sons proposal, 50, 196
  fatal accident, 324, *325*
  in Fellheimer and Wagner proposal, 27, 196
  in Gropius/Belluschi/Roth project, 191, *192*
  proposal for, 196–199
Helmsley Building, 353, 363–364, 372. *See also* New York Central Building; New York General Building
Historic preservation, xiv, 289, 324, 326–341, 345–346, 372
Holden, Arthur C., 345–346
Humphrey, Vice President Hubert, 318
Huxtable, Ada Louise, xiv, xvi, 50, 53–54, 59, 156, 216, *225,* 276, 371, 377, 384
  on alliance between art and architecture, 142
  and architectural criticism, 53, 223
  and architectural history, 53, 55, 179
  criticism of the "Grand Central City" (Pan Am) building, 163–166, *164,* 176–177, 223–224, 263
  on Gropius, 297–298

Huxtable, Ada Louise (*continued*)
  and historic preservation, 55, 326, 329
  "Marvel or Monster?" 163–166, *164,* 329,
    370
  on proposed Breuer tower, 343
  on quality in architecture, 55–58, 179–180,
    224–227
  review of 1972 Gropius retrospective exhibi-
    tion, 299
  and the transformation of Park Avenue, 51–
    58, 180

Idlewild Airport, 128. *See also* Kennedy (JFK)
    Airport
Isaacs, Reginald, 299–300, 302–303
  Gropius biography, 302–303, 305–307

Jacobs, Jane, xiv, 40, 58–59, 191, 260
  Death and Life of Great American Cities,
    xiii, xv
James D. Landauer Associates, Inc., 50, 349.
    See also Landauer, James D.
James Ruderman Office, 91, 188. *See also*
    Ruderman, James
Jencks, Charles, xiii, 299, 385
Johnson, Lyndon B., 312
Johnson, Philip, 54, 276, 290, 326, 328–329,
    351, 384
  AT&T Building, 351, 353, 373
Jones, Cranston, 284
Jordy, William, 262–263, 384–385

Kahn, Ely Jacques, 267
Kaufmann, Edgar, Jr., xvi, 167–171, 194, 235,
    384
Kay, Jane Holtz, 301, 384
Keiley, S. T., 120
Kennedy (JFK) Airport, 310–311, 314. *See also*
    Idlewild Airport
Kepes, Gyorgy, 143–144, *152,* 228, 305, 354
Kirk, Paul, 230
Kyle, Gordon I., 217, 223

Landauer, James D., 210, 216, 276–277, 279,
    338. *See also* James D. Landauer Associ-
    ates, Inc.
Landmarks Preservation Commission, 326–
    327, 330–331, 333, 339, 345, 364, 376, 384
Lautenberg, Saul, 42–44
Le Corbusier, 98, 100, 218, 246, 261–262, 279,
    282, 293, 296–297, 302, 328
Lever House, 2, 50, 52–54, 91, 97, 126, 177,
    180, 218, 242, 266, 371. *See also* Skidmore,
    Owings & Merrill
Lindbergh, Charles, 132, 406n126
Lindsay, John V., 312, 320
Lippold, Richard, 142–151, *150,* 294, 354
Lollar, Coleman, 367–368

McGinnis, Patrick B., 25, 27, 45
McKim, Mead & White, 10, 16, 326. *See also*
    Pennsylvania Railroad Station (Penn Station)
  Grand Central Terminal proposal, *17*
McLaughlin, Christopher, 363–365
McQuade, Walter, 29, 161–163
Mailer, Norman, 254
"Marvel or Monster?" 163–166, *164. See also*
    Huxtable, Ada Louise
Meeks, Carroll, 26, 46
Merchandise Mart, 169, 212
MetLife Building, *366,* 376, 377, 382. *See also*
    Metropolitan Life Insurance Company
    (MetLife)
Metropolitan Life Insurance Company
    (MetLife), 347, 349–351, 363. *See also*
    MetLife Building
Mies van der Rohe, Ludwig, xv, xvi, 54, 174,
    256, 279, 282, 293, 296, 297, 302, 328, 329,
    343–344. *See also* Seagram Building
Modernism
  changing attitudes toward, xiii, xvi, 84, 305,
    329, 345, 371, 385
  demise of, xiv, xv, xvi, 305, 371, 376, 385
  European, xvi, 328–329
  ideals of, xiii, xv, 387

and the Seagram Building, xv, 306
Moholy-Nagy, Sibyl, xiv, 158–160, 173, 191, 194, 267, 271
 "Hitler's Revenge," 343–345
MoMA, 181, 370
Morse, Carl, 44, 109, 114–116, 119, 210, 260. *See also* Diesel Construction Company
Mo-Sai panels, 105, *106, 107,* 109, 119
Moses King (publisher), *Dream of New York,* 196, *197*
Mumford, Lewis, 45
Municipal Art Society, 120, 363, 384
Murphy, Jim, 278–279

Nelson, George, 182
Nerdinger, Winfried, 300–302
Nespole, James, 340
New School for Social Research debate, 160–166, 193, 195, 271, 277, 337, 346
New York Airways, 196, 198, 312, 318, 321–322, 324. *See also* Cummings, Robert L.
New York Central Building, 32, 56–57, 80, 97, 100, 158, 218, 221, 262, 286, 288, 371–372, 377. *See also* Helmsley Building; New York General Building; Warren and Wetmore
New York Central Railroad, 3–4, 7, 22, 44–45, 49–53, 87, 90, 240
 air rights over train tracks, 10, 14, 45
 bowling alleys controversy, 120–127
 dispute with New York, New Haven and Hartford Railroads, 45, 47, 89
 real estate holdings, 22–23, *24,* 25, 44–45, 46–47, 50, 52, 53, 120, 175–176, 244–245, 246, 261, 326, 346
 and Zeckendorf, 44–45, 47
New York City Board of Estimates, 312, 322, 327
New York City Planning Commission, 80, 120, 127, 231, 238, 247, 311, 327
New York General Building, 183, 233, 236, 269–270. *See also* Helmsley Building; New York Central Building

New York, New Haven and Hartford Railroad, 4, 45, 47, 87, 118. *See also* McGinnis, Patrick B.
New York Real Estate Board, 87
New York State Realty and Terminal Company, 50

Oldenburg, Claes, "Proposed Colossal Monument for Park Avenue, New York City: Good Humor Bar," 380, *381*

Pan Am Building, *172, 213, 219, 229, 241, 292, 315, 356, 378, 379. See also* "Grand Central City" (Wolfson's); MetLife Building
 art work, 141–151, 246, 305
 bowling alley proposal, 120–127, *122, 123*
 circulation, 188, 191, 278, 304, 338–339
 concourse, with John Glenn launch into space, 201, *204*
 construction of, *95,* 109, 114–119, 199–209, *200, 202, 203, 205, 206, 207,* 210–212
 controversy over, 2, 151, 156–188, 201, 221, 283, 324, 345, 353 (*see also* Heliport; Historic preservation; Pan Am Building, criticism of)
 criticism of, 216, 218–224, 226–228, 230–233, 238–255, 257–260, 263, 266–271, 324, 329, 333, 338, 343–345, 362–363, 370–380, 384
 cutaway view, *209*
 defense of, 188–196, 223, 228–229, 233–238, 268–269
 design process, 105–111
 as emblematic of modernism gone awry, xvi, 247, 254, 255, 261
 exterior lighting, 111, 112, 171, 212
 financial success of, 216–218, 248, 261
 financing of, 86–89, 181
 futurist connection, 10, 242, 255, 310, 314, 339
 heliport (*see* Heliport)
 landmark status, 368, 380

Pan Am Building (*continued*)
  lobbies, 111–112, *113, 150, 152,* 228, 246, 347, 351–354, *352, 355*
  as mistake to avoid, 255, 261, 333, 338, 368, 380, 382
  Mo-Sai panels, 105, *106, 107,* 109, 119, 202–203, 226
  as most disliked, 373, *375,* 376, 380, 382
  name change, 363–367
  opening, 212, *213*
  Pan American World Airways as major tenant, 111, 128–129, 137–138, 174, 217, 261, 303, 315, 386
  Plexiglas model, 105, *108*
  records set by, 50, 117–118, 137, 141, 171, 201, 210, 212, 223, 347, 386
  rooftop addition, 373, *374*
  sale of, 346–351, *348, 359*
  signage, 111, 138–139, 171
  site, xiv, 187, 194, 216, 221, 245, 263, 304, 310, 337, 353 (*see also* Grand Central Terminal)
  steel framing, 94, 117, 201, *205, 206, 208, 209*
  structural diagrams, *172, 211*
  structural engineering of, 89–94, 171
  as symbol, xvi, 78, 83–84, 223, 233, 246–247, 359, 363, 365, 367, 370, 386
  tenants, 217 (*see also* Pan American World Airways)
  ticket office, 139–141, *140, 315*
  topping out of steel frame, 180, 201, *208*
  as transportation hub, 310 (*see also* Pan Am Building, site)
  as turning point in American culture, xvi, 247, 307, 385–387
  wind factor, 93–94, 400n23
Pan American World Airways, xiv, 111, 119, 128–138, 174, 303, 311, 314, 321–322, 324, 364–365, 382, 386. *See also* Trippe, Juan
  and Boeing, 357–358, 367, 382

Boeing jets, *130, 131,* 350, 357–359, 362, 368, 382–383
Boeing Stratocruiser, 132, *134*
China Clipper, 132, *133,* 362
demise of, 357–362, 386–387
final flight, 362
first jet aircraft christened by First Lady Mamie Eisenhower, 132, *135*
first scheduled passenger flight from Key West to Havana, 132, *133*
Flight 103 over Lockerbie, 357, 360
as Pan Am Building's main tenant, 111, 128, 137–138, 174, 217, 261, 303
and sale of building, 346, 349–351
as symbol, 132, 137, 360–362, 367–368
terminal building, Idlewild (later, JFK) Airport, 128, *130, 131,* 314
Park Avenue, 4, 7, 32, 177–178. *See also* City Beautiful Movement
  development of, in 1920s, 7, *11,* 22
  development over tracks, 14, 90 (*see also* Park-Lexington Building)
  postwar transformation of, xiv, 2, 51–58, 176–178, 220–221, 236, 245, 286
  pre- and post-Pan Am Building, 218, *219,* 249, *250–251*
  role of, in Grand Central urban design, 3, 16, 19
  Roth buildings on, *37,* 185, *186,* 276
  vista, xiii, 2–3, 19, 56, *57,* 100, 173, 176, 183, 218, 222, 230, 254, 261–263, *264,* 267, 278, 290, 303, 331, 333, 363–364, 371, 376–377, *377*
Park-Lexington Building, 90
Parry, Natalie, 159–160, 194, 271
Pehnt, Wolfgang, 298
Pei, I. M., 23, 25–26, 45, 46, 56
  Grand Central Terminal project, 23, 25, 27, 45, 46–47, *48,* 63, 168, 236
Penn Central Railroad, 331, 338, 340, 346–347, 372

Pennsylvania Railroad Station (Penn Station), 10, 16, 168, 242, 245, 262, 289, 290, 324, 326, 327–328, 329, 376, 382. *See also* Historic preservation; McKim, Mead & White
Pentagon, 49, 169, 212
Pepsi-Cola Building, 52, 54, 180
Peters, John, 307
Pinchis, Martin, 263, *265,* 266–267
  proposal, Grand Central City, 263, *265,* 266
Pirelli Headquarters Building, 98, *99*
Platner, Warren, 353–354, *355*
Port of New York Authority, 198
Portoghesi, Paolo, 385
Postmodernism, xiv, xvi, 305, 339, 353–354, 373, 376, 385
Private versus public interests, xiii–xiv, xvi, 3, 7, 14, 125, 127, 242, 249, 255, 260, 311–312, 324, 330, 333, 341, 345–346, 370, 387. *See also* Haskell, Douglas

Railroad industry, 26, 386
  decline of, xiv, 4, 22, 128, 244, 386
  history of, in New York City, 4–10
  real estate holdings, 4, 22 (*see also* New York Central Railroad)
RCA Building, 63, 80, 86, 168, 400n19
Reed, Charles. *See* Reed and Stem
Reed and Stem, 16, 27
  Grand Central Terminal proposal, 16, *17*
Reis, Walter C., 157
Rockefeller, Governor Nelson , 318, *319*
Rockefeller Center, 14, 46, 242, 244, 246, 357
Rossi, Aldo, 290
Roth, Emery, 35. *See also* Emery Roth & Sons
Roth, Julian, 35. *See also* Emery Roth & Sons
Roth, Richard, 32, *41,* 253. *See also* Emery Roth & Sons
  as co-designer of "Grand Central City," 62, 110, 118–119, 158, 160, 163, 165
  criticism of, 184–185, 227, 274–276
  "High-Rise Down to Earth," 40, 56, 393n43

list of possible co-designers, 59, 169
on Park Avenue, 220–221
and Wolfson, 40, 42, 59
"Rothscrapers," 51, 59, 274, 276
Rowe, Colin, 293
Ruderman, James, xiv, 90–94, 98, 100, 109, 110, 168, 386. *See also* James Ruderman Office
and Roths, 92, 112, 114
and Wolfson, 90–92
Rudolph, Paul, 3, 33

Saady, Morris, 331
Sant'Elia, Antonio, 10, 243, 255, 339
  Milan Central Station drawing, 10, *15,* 243, 255
Scheftel, Herbert, 23, 32, 50
Scheftel, Stuart, 23, 32, 49, 50, 87
Schiff, Harold, 109, 188, 403n80
Schmertz, Mildred, 233–237, 259, 277, 380
Scully, Vincent, 177–178, 181, 218–220, 222, 290, 328, 371, 384
  American Architecture and Urbanism, 262, 384
  "Death of the Street," xiv, 218–220, *219*
  debate with Mailer, 254
Seagram Building, 50, 52–54, 126, 142, 175, 177, 180, 218, 220, 237, 242, 306, 349, 371, 385
  as milestone in modernism, xv, 385
Seawell, William T., 347, 349, 358–359
September 11, 2001, xiv, 382–383
Shapiro, Murray, 91. *See also* James Ruderman Office
Sikorsky S-61L (helicopter), 321
Skidmore, Owings & Merrill, 54, 142. *See also* Lever House
Spellman, Cardinal Francis Joseph, 318, *319*
Stein, Clarence, 45
Stem, Allen. *See* Reed and Stem
Stern, Robert, 328–329, 367, 368, 384, 389n6
Stevens, Roger L., 44, 72, 393n55
Stirling, James, 373

Tafel, Edgar A., 230

Tauranac, John, 372

Temko, Allan, 283, 384

The Architects Collaborative (TAC), 60, 64, 68–
70, 177, 266, 269, 271, 283, 284, 293, 298–
299, 301, 303–304, 307, 344, 397n118

Trippe, Juan, xiv, 119, 132, *136*, 137, 318, *319,*
321, 346–347, *356,* 357–358, 362, 367. *See
also* Pan American World Airways
and the art work, Pan Am Building, 142–149
deal with Wolfson, 111, 128, *129,* 137–139,
171
and heliport, 196
signage, Pan Am Building, 138–139, 171
his vision, Pan Am Building, 196, 310, 385–386

Trump, Donald, 347, 350

Tunnard, Christopher, 262, 385

Union Carbide Building, 52–54, 91, 126, 175,
177, 180, 184, 194, 242, 244, 400n17

United Nations Secretariat, 100, *101,* 126

Uris brothers, 40, 51, 91–92, 116, 220, 253, 275

Vanderbilt, Cornelius ("Commodore"), 4–10, 51

Vanderbilt, William K., 10, 16, 46

Venturi, Robert, xv, 279, 290, 293, 307, 339

von Eckardt, Wolf, xiv, xvi, 182–184, 370, 384

Wagner, Mayor Robert F., 212, 318, *319*

Walter Gropius Archive, 303–305

Warren, Whitney, 16, 244. *See also* Warren and
Wetmore
Grand Central Terminal perspective draw-
ing, *18*

Warren and Wetmore, 16–22, 32

Weinberg, Robert C., 120, 156–157

Werk, 263, 266

Wetmore, Charles. *See* Warren and Wetmore

Webb & Knapp, 23. *See also* Pei, I. M.; Zeckendorf, William

Whalen, Richard, 248, 259–261

White, John R., 349–351. *See also* James D.
Landauer Associates, Inc.

Wilgus, William J., 14, 16, 84, 248, 341

Williams, Frank, 338–339

Wolfson, Erwin, 42–44, *43,* 159, 275. *See also*
Diesel Construction Company
and appraisal of the building, 217
and the art work, Pan Am Building, 142–145
and construction of the Pan Am, 116–117
contract with Gropius and Belluschi, 60–61, 97
and Cotton, 86
criticism of, 121, 159–161, 167, 169, 173–
174, 179, 183, 188, 245, 253, 260
death of, 210, 338
decision to engage Gropius and Belluschi,
50–51, 56, 58–60, 62, 63–64, 68, 161, 169,
173, 182, 188, 269, 304
as developer of the Grand Central City/Pan
Am, xiv, 23, 29, 32, 40, 44–45, 49, 56, 63,
77, 87, 90, 110, 118–119, 160–161, 163,
169, 199, 304, 338, 386
estate of, 347
financing of the building, 56, 86–87, 89 (*see
also* "Grand Central City"; Pan Am Building)
and Gropius, 50, 156
and Haskell, 125, 240, 338
lease agreement with New York Central, 89
and Morse, 114
rental plan, 50
and Roth, 40, 42, 59
and Ruderman, 90–92
on the site as park, 216, 260
and Trippe, 128, *129,* 137–139, 346
vision of Pan Am Building, 84, 385
and Young, 23, 45

Wolfson Management Corporation, 44, 210

Woodbridge, Frederick, 2

World Trade Center, xiv, 276–277, 382–383,
400n19

Wright, Frank Lloyd, 27, 256, 274, 279, 281–
282, 293, 296–297

Yamasaki, Minoru, xiii, 46, 276–277
Young, Robert, 3, 22–23, 25, 27, 44–45, 47, 49,
    87, 160, 324. *See also* New York Central
    Railroad

Zeckendorf, William, 23, 27, 42–44, 45, 47, 49,
    56, 63, 87, 116, 217
  Grand Central redevelopment plans, 23, 45,
    194, 236
Zevi, Bruno, 268–271, 291, 301
Zodiac, 283
Zoning laws, 2, 80, 83, 158, 180, 193, 194, 220,
    231, 249, 259, 260, 285, 310, 330, 347
Zucker, Paul, 160, 193–195, 270